HANDSWORTH COLLEGE

T27384

KU-573-229

· THE SCHOOL PROJECT ·
· S·H·P ·
OFFICIAL TEXT

BRITAIN
1783–1851

FROM DISASTER TO TRIUMPH?

Charlotte Evers and Dave Welbourne
Series Editor: Ian Dawson

CITY COLLEGE
LEARNING RESOURCE CENTRE

JOHN MURRAY

In the same series

Communist Russia Under Lenin and Stalin	Chris Corin and Terry Fiehn	ISBN 0 7195 7488 9
The Early Tudors: England 1485–1558	David Rogerson, Samantha Ellsmore and David Hudson	ISBN 0 7195 7484 6
Fascist Italy	John Hite and Chris Hinton	ISBN 0 7195 7341 6
The Reign of Elizabeth: England 1558–1603	Barbara Mervyn	ISBN 0 7195 7486 2
Weimar and Nazi Germany	John Hite and Chris Hinton	ISBN 0 7195 7343 2

The Schools History Project

This project was set up in 1972, with the aim of improving the study of history for students aged 13–16. This involved a reconsideration of the ways in which history contributes to the educational needs of young people. The project devised new objectives, new criteria for planning and developing courses, and the material to support them. New examinations, requiring new methods of assessment, also had to be developed. These have continued to be popular. The advent of GCSE in 1987 led to the expansion of SHP approaches into other syllabuses.

The Schools History Project has been based at Trinity and All Saints' College, Leeds, since 1978, from where it supports teachers through a biennial bulletin, regular INSET, an annual conference and a website (www.tasc.ac.uk/shp).

Since the National Curriculum was drawn up in 1991, the project has continued to expand its publications, bringing its ideas to courses for Key Stage 3 as well as a range of GCSE and A level specifications.

© Charlotte Evers, Dave Welbourne 2003

First published in 2003
By John Murray (Publishers) Ltd, a member of the Hodder Headline Group
338 Euston Road
London NW1 3BH

All rights reserved. No part of this publication may be reproduced in any material form (including photocopying or storing in any medium by electronic means and whether or not transiently or incidentally to some other use of this publication) without the written permission of the Publisher, except in accordance with the provisions of the Copyright, Designs and Patents Act 1988 or under the terms of a licence issued by the Copyright Licensing Agency.

Layouts by Janet McCallum
Artwork by Oxford Designers and Illustrators Ltd
Typeset in 10/12pt Walbaum by Wearset Ltd, Boldon, Tyne and Wear
Printed and bound in Spain by Bookprint S.L., Barcelona

A catalogue entry for this book is available from the British Library

ISBN 0 7195 7482 X

Contents

City College	Order No.
LRS Site: Mal	
Acc. T27384	
Class 941·07	

Acknowledgements

Text credits

Text extracts reproduced by kind permission of:

p.41 Source 2.13 Reproduced by permission © N. Gash, *Aristocracy and the People: Britain 1815–65* (Edward Arnold, 1979); **p.58** Source 3.13 © A. Briggs, *The Age of Improvement*, Longman (1960); **p.62** Source 4.3 © A. Briggs, *The Age of Improvement*, Longman (1960), Source 4.5 J. W. Derry, *Politics in the Age of Fox, Pitt and Liverpool*, Palgrave Macmillan (1990) reproduced with permission of Palgrave Macmillan; **p.63** Source 4.6 J. W. Derry, *Politics in the Age of Fox, Pitt and Liverpool*, Palgrave Macmillan (1990) reproduced with permission of Palgrave Macmillan; **p.73** Source 4.27 J. W. Derry, *Politics in the Age of Fox, Pitt and Liverpool*, Palgrave Macmillan (1990) reproduced with permission of Palgrave Macmillan; **p.74** Source 4.29 J. Plowright, 'Lord Liverpool and the alternatives to repression in Regency England', *History Review*, September 1997, Source 4.30 J. W. Derry, *Politics in the Age of Fox, Pitt and Liverpool*, Palgrave Macmillan (1990) reproduced with permission of Palgrave Macmillan; **p.75** Source 4.31 © A. Wood, *Nineteenth-Century Britain*, Longman (1960), Source 4.32 Reproduced by permission © N. Gash, *Aristocracy and the People: Britain 1815–65* (Edward Arnold, 1979); **p.76** Source 4.33 J. Plowright, 'Lord Liverpool and the alternatives to repression in Regency England', *History Review*, September 1997; **p.88** Source 5.18 M. Brock, *The Great Reform Act*, Nelson Thornes (1973), Source 5.20 A. Wood, *Nineteenth-Century Britain*, Longman (1960), Source 5.21 © A. Briggs, *The Age of Improvement*, Longman (1960); **p.121** Source 8.5 M. Brock, *The Great Reform Act*, Nelson Thornes (1973); **p.122** Source 8.6 Reproduced by permission © R. J. Evans, *The Victorian Age 1815–1914*, (Edward Arnold, 1968); **p.125** Source 8.8 Reproduced by permission © N. Gash, *Aristocracy and the People: Britain 1815–65* (Edward Arnold, 1979); **p.126** Source 8.10 M. Brock, *The Great Reform Act*, Nelson Thornes (1973); **p.203** Source 3 Reproduced by permission © N. Gash, *Aristocracy and the People: Britain 1815–65* (Edward Arnold, 1979); **p.204** Source 4 © A. Briggs, *The Age of Improvement*, Longman (1960); **p.235** Source 13.12 © M. Chamberlain, *Pax Britannica? British Foreign Policy 1789–1914*, Longman (1988); **p.236** Source 13.15 © A. Wood, *Nineteenth-Century Britain*, Longman (1960), Source 13.18 Reproduced by permission © R. J. Evans, *The Victorian Age 1815–1914*, (Edward Arnold, 1968); **p.237** Source 13.19 Reproduced by permission © N. Gash, *Aristocracy and the People: Britain 1815–65* (Edward Arnold, 1979); **p.255** Source 15.1 © M. Chamberlain, *Pax Britannica? British Foreign Policy 1789–1914*, Longman (1988).

Photo credits

The Publishers would like to thank the following for permission to reproduce copyright material:

Cover: *main* Victoria & Albert Museum, London/Bridgeman Art Library, *inset* Mary Evans Picture Library; **p.2** Mary Evans Picture Library; **p.3** Mary Evans Picture Library; **p.4** Musée de la Révolution Française, Vizille, France/Bridgeman Art Library; **p.5** British Museum, London/Bridgeman Art Library; **p.6** Hulton Archive; **p.7** The Royal Archives © Her Majesty Queen Elizabeth II; **p.12** Louvre, Paris, France/Bridgeman Art Library; **p.18** Mary Evans Picture Library; **p.19** Private Collection/Bridgeman Art Library; **p.20** *all* Mary Evans Picture Library; **p.21** *t* Leeds Library and Information Services, *b* The Illustrated London News Picture Library; **p.22** *t* Getty Images/TimeLife Pictures, *b* Hulton Archive; **p.23** *all* Mary Evans Picture Library; **p.24** Mary Evans Picture Library; **p.25** Hulton Archive; **p.27** Hulton Archive; **p.28** Science & Society/National Museum of Photography, Film & Television; **p.29** Mary Evans Picture Library; **p.31** Courtesy of the Trustees of Sir John Soane's Museum, London/Bridgeman Art Library; **p.35** Collections/Roy Westlake; **p.37** © The British Museum; **p.40** *t* Roy Miles Fine Paintings/Bridgeman Art Library, *b* © The British Museum; **p.41** Mary Evans Picture Library; **p.44** *t* Hulton Archive, *bl* Camera Press (photo: Terry Kirk), *br* Adam Butler/PA Photos; **p.48** *t* Louvre, Paris, France/Bridgeman Art Library, *b* Mary Evans Picture Library; **p.50** *t* By courtesy of the National Portrait Gallery, London (NPG 135a), *b* By courtesy of the National Portrait Gallery, London (NPG 743 – detail); **p.51** *l* By courtesy of the National Portrait Gallery, London (NPG 655), *r* By courtesy of the National Portrait Gallery, London (NPG 897 – detail); **p.54** *t* Musée de la Révolution Française, Vizille, France/Bridgeman Art Library, *b* Bibliothèque Nationale, Paris, France/Bridgeman Art Library; **p.61** *l* By courtesy of the National Portrait Gallery, London (NPG 6307 – detail), *r* By courtesy of the National Portrait Gallery, London (NPG 1804 – detail); **p.65** Mary Evans Picture Library; **p.68** Mary Evans Picture Library; **p.70** British Museum, London/Bridgeman Art Library; **p.73** Mary Evans Picture Library; **p.75** Mary Evans Picture Library; **p.83** *t* By courtesy of the National Portrait Gallery, London (NPG 1832), *b* By courtesy of the National Portrait Gallery, London (NPG 21 – detail); **p.84** By courtesy of the National Portrait Gallery, London (NPG 772 – detail); **p.96** *tl* Hulton Archive, *tr, bl & br* Mary Evans Picture Library; **p.97** from E.W. Brayley's *Topographical History of the County of Surrey*, vol. 4, 1850 (photo: John Townson/Creation); **p.104** By courtesy of the National Portrait Gallery, London (NPG 208); **p.107** *l* By courtesy of the National Portrait Gallery, London (NPG 405 – detail), *r* By courtesy of the National Portrait Gallery, London (NPG 772 – detail); **p.109** *t & b* © The British Museum; **p.120** Fotomas Index; **p.123** *from left* By courtesy of the National Portrait Gallery, London (NPG 1318 – detail), By courtesy of the National Portrait Gallery, London (NPG 3953 – detail), Mary Evans Picture Library, Mary Evans Picture Library, By courtesy of the National Portrait Gallery, London (NPG 3136 – detail), By courtesy of the National Portrait Gallery, London (NPG 4875 – detail); **p.140** Mary Evans Picture Library; **p.147** Hulton Archive; **p.151** © The British Museum; **p.152** Mary Evans Picture Library; **p.153** *t* © Punch Ltd., *bl* Hulton Archive, *br* Guildhall Library, Corporation of London/Bridgeman Art Library; **p.158** © Leeds Museums and Galleries (Abbey House); **p.159** St James University Hospital, Leeds, Medical Illustrations Dept.; **p.161** By courtesy of the National Portrait Gallery, London (NPG 772 – detail); **p.168** *t* By courtesy of the National Portrait Gallery, London (NPG 316 – detail), *b* Mary Evans Picture Library; **p.169** *t* Hulton Archive, *b* Mary Evans Picture Library; **p.172** *all* Hulton Archive; **p.173** Mary Evans Picture Library; **p.175** *all* Mary Evans Picture Library; **p.179** © Spectrum Colour Library; **p.185** Mary Evans Picture Library; **p.187** © The British Museum; **p.195** *t* Hulton Archive, *c* Oxfordshire County Council Photographic Archives, *b* The British Library; **p.196** The Royal Archives © Her Majesty Queen Elizabeth II; **p.209** Leger Gallery, London/Bridgeman Art Library; **p.211** Château de Versailles, Paris, France/Bridgeman Art Library; **p.213** © The British Museum; **p.215** *t* Private Collection/Bridgeman Art Library, *b* Hulton Archive; **p.216** *l* Musée Condé, Chantilly, France/Bridgeman Art Library, *r* Royal Naval Museum, Portsmouth/Bridgeman Art Library; **p.217** *t* Collections/Liz Stares, *b* Mary Evans Picture Library; **p.218** Royal Naval Museum; **p.219** Private Collection/Bridgeman Art Library; **p.220** © Andrew C. Jackson; **p.222** Apsley House, The Wellington Museum, London/Bridgeman Art Library; **p.224** © The British Museum; **p.227** *t* By courtesy of the National Portrait Gallery, London (NPG 891 – detail), *b* Mary Evans Picture Library; **p.229** Hulton Archive; **p.230** © The British Museum; **p.239** Mary Evans Picture Library; **p.250** By courtesy of the National Portrait Gallery, London (NPG 751 – detail); **p.259** Mary Evans Picture Library.

t = top, *b* = bottom, *l* = left, *r* = right, *c* = centre

Every effort has been made to contact copyright holders, but if any have been inadvertently overlooked the Publishers will be pleased to make the necessary arrangements at the earliest opportunity.

Using this book

This is an in-depth study of Britain 1783–1851. It contains everything you need for examination success and more. It provides all the content you would expect, as well as many features to help both independent and class-based learners. So, before you wade in, make sure you understand the purpose of each of the features.

Focus routes
On every topic throughout the book, this feature guides you to produce the written material essential for understanding what you read and, later, for revising the topic (e.g. pages 33, 106, 208). These focus routes are particularly useful for you if you are an independent learner working through this material on your own, but they can also be used for class-based learning.

Activities
The activities offer a range of exercises to enhance your understanding of what you read to prepare you for examinations. They vary in style and purpose. There are:

- a variety of essays (e.g. pages 77, 114)
- source investigations (e.g. pages 71, 170)
- examination of historical interpretations, which is now central to A level history (e.g. pages 204, 235)
- decision-making exercises which help you to see events from the viewpoint of people at the time (e.g. pages 123, 206)
- exercises to develop Key Skills such as communication (e.g. pages 149, 177, 179).

These activities help you to analyse and understand what you are reading. They address the content through the key questions that the examiner will be expecting you to have investigated.

Overviews, summaries and key points
In such a large book on such a massive topic, you need to keep referring to the big picture. Each chapter begins with an overview and each chapter ends with a key-points summary of the most important content of the chapter.

Learning trouble spots
Experience shows that time and again some topics cause confusion for students. This feature identifies such topics and helps students to avoid common misunderstandings (e.g. page 14). In particular, this feature addresses some of the general problems encountered when studying history, such as assessing sources (e.g. page 72); analysing the provenance, tone and value of sources (e.g. page 37); and explaining contemporary ideas (e.g. pages 141, 147).

Charts
The charts are our attempts to summarise important information in note or diagrammatic form (e.g. pages 43, 214). There are also several grid charts that present a lot of information in a structured way (e.g. page 193). However, everyone learns differently and the best charts are the ones you draw yourself! Drawing your own charts in your own way to summarise important content can really help understanding (e.g. pages 211, 250), as can completing assessment grids (e.g. page 198).

Glossary
We have tried to write in an accessible way but occasionally we have used advanced vocabulary. These words are often explained in brackets in the text but sometimes you may need to use a dictionary. We have also used many general historical terms as well as some that are specific to the study of Britain 1783–1851. You won't find all of these in a dictionary, but they are defined in glossary boxes close to the text in which they appear. The first time a glossary word appears in the text it is in SMALL CAPITALS like this.

Talking points
These are asides from the normal pattern of written exercises. They are discussion questions that invite you to be more reflective and to consider the relevance of this history to your own life. They might ask you to voice your personal judgement (e.g. pages 76, 224, 244); to make links between the past and present (e.g. pages 166, 229); or to highlight aspects of the process of studying history (e.g. pages 28, 259).

Nineteenth-century British history is one of the most popular A level history topics. The content is deeply relevant to the modern world. But the actual process of studying history is equally relevant to the modern world. Throughout this book you will be problem solving, working with others, and trying to improve your own performance as you engage with deep and complex historical issues. Our hope is that by using this book you will become actively involved in your study of history and that you will see history as a challenging set of skills and ideas to be mastered rather than as an inert body of factual material to be learned.

CITY COLLEGE LEARNING RESOURCE SERVICE

Introduction
Britain 1783–1851: from disaster to triumph?

▏1783

The hallmarks of Britain in 1783 were disaster, doubt and loss of empire

In 1783 Britain was in decline, or so many British people thought. The American colonies, so vital to Britain's wealth, had won their independence. Britain's dominance in world trade was falling. Exports had fallen by as much as twenty per cent between 1772 and 1780. It seemed unlikely that Britain would be able to cling onto the rest of its empire, given the huge costs of defending territory as far away as India. Thus it is scarcely surprising that readers of Edward Gibbon's book *The History of the Decline and Fall of the Roman Empire*, published in 1776, believed that Britain was following in the faltering footsteps of Rome.

In parts of Britain, unrest and discontent among working people were evident in the years around 1783. This was usually linked to food shortages or high food prices. In 1764 and 1788 there were food riots in Nottingham. In 1783 a crowd from weaving villages around Halifax besieged the corn merchants and forced them to sell their grain at reduced prices.

Among political writers and philosophers of the late eighteenth century, reform of the constitution was a key idea, and one which could be traced back to the constitutional conflicts of the civil war in the 1640s. Inevitably, such ideas were a challenge to the existing order.

SOURCE I The signing of the American Declaration of Independence, 1776 – the beginning of the American colonies' struggle for freedom

How did Britain make the journey from disaster in the 1780s to triumph in the 1850s? Was it the story of a steady, calm progression to world dominance? Or was it a far more turbulent, problematic story? These are the main themes of this book.

TALKING POINTS

What do you already know about this period?

1 Brainstorm the names, events and discoveries that might explain the changes in Britain between 1783 and 1851.
2 How did political power change in this period? For example, how powerful was the monarchy? What say did ordinary people have in government?
3 How comfortable were people's lives?

1851

The hallmarks of Britain in 1851 were triumph, confidence and the largest empire the world has ever known

Visitors to the Great Exhibition of the Works of Industry of All Nations could have been in no doubt about which was the most powerful country in the world. The Great Exhibition showed off Britain's industrial leadership, power and prosperity. It also showed a country at peace as factories closed so workers could travel by rail to see the exhibition. Whole villages clubbed together to pay for special excursion trains. There were over 6 million visitors in the 140 days the exhibition was held. Despite fears of mobs, drunkenness and a tide of crime there were just 25 arrests for pickpocketing and petty theft.

SOURCE 2 Massive crowds at the Great Exhibition, 1851

How close did Britain come to revolution 1783–1851?

ACTIVITY

1 How would the event shown in Source 1 influence:
   a) British attitudes to revolution
   b) British fears of revolution?
2 What do Sources 2–5 suggest about how close Britain came to revolution?
3 What questions do you need to ask and investigate to decide how close Britain came to revolution?

SOURCE 1 The execution of Louis XVI in 1793, at the height of the French Revolution, sent shock waves through governments around Europe. The revolution dominated European politics, and led to war with Britain that lasted from 1793 to 1815. Even when the French monarchy was restored in 1815, the legacy of fear of revolution continued to dominate European minds. The French Revolution had not simply claimed the lives of the King, Queen and nobles but 17,000 ordinary people had been sent to the guillotine for opposing the revolution (as well as some who supported the revolution).

SOURCE 2 The attack on protesters at St Peter's Field, Manchester, 1819, portrayed in a cartoon called 'Manchester Heroes'. In 1819 protesters held a meeting at St Peter's Field, Manchester, to demand the vote. Men, women and children from all over the region marched in orderly groups from the surrounding mill towns and rural villages. They were suffering from extremely high unemployment and steep increases in the cost of bread. They hoped that having a vote in elections would lead to reforms that would improve their lives. The local magistrates panicked at the sight of so many people at a peaceful meeting and sent in the local yeomanry to arrest the speakers. Eleven people were killed in what became known as the Peterloo Massacre, an ironic comment on the great victory at Waterloo only four years earlier when the British army, led by the Duke of Wellington, finally defeated Napoleon Bonaparte's French forces

Drawn on Stone by L. Haghe.

CHARGE of the 3ʳᵈ DRAGOON GUARDS.

SOURCE 3   An artist's impression of the Bristol riots, October 1831. In 1831 the House of Lords rejected the government's plans to increase the number of men who could vote – from just one man in ten to one in five. Wellington, the great hero of Waterloo, was one of the leaders of the House of Lords. He believed that giving more people the vote would result in a profusion of reforms that would ruin the country, cause civil war and lead to national disaster. His views made him deeply unpopular: crowds stoned his London house and chanted 'Bonaparte for ever'. A mob even threatened to drag him off his horse until soldiers provided an escort. Riots flared in Nottingham and Bristol and were put down by soldiers: twelve men were killed and over 100 were wounded. There were rumours of a march on London. Soldiers, ordered to stop the march, said that they would not do so. In 1832 Parliament finally passed the Great Reform Act allowing middle-class men the right to vote

SOURCE 4 A mass meeting of Chartists at Kennington Common, 1848. In 1848 the Chartists handed their third great petition to the government, calling for their Charter to be made law. Their main demand was that all men should have the vote. The Chartists claimed that there were 5 million signatures on the petition. As revolutions were engulfing countries all over Europe, the government sent Queen Victoria to the Isle of Wight for safety and placed the Duke of Wellington in command of the defence of London. Wellington placed cannon on London's bridges and recruited over 80,000 special constables to help the army and police

SOURCE 5 The six points which the Charter demanded:

- *Votes for all adult males*
- *Secret ballot*
- *Constituencies to have equal numbers of people*
- *Pay for MPs*
- *No requirement to own property in order to become an MP*
- *Annual elections*

HOW CLOSE DID BRITAIN COME TO REVOLUTION 1783–1851?

A summary of events 1783–1851

Year	Events above	Events below
1783	William Pitt becomes Prime Minister	Britain loses its American colonies
1784		
1785		
1786	*The Times* newspaper founded	
1787		
1788	George III first certified insane	
1789		French Revolution begins
1790	Burke's *Reflections on the French Revolution* published	
1791	Paine's *Rights of Man* published. *Observer* newspaper founded	
1792	Mary Wollstonecraft's *A Vindication of the Rights of Women* published	
1793	Murdoch first uses gas to light a house in Cornwall	Louis XVI and Queen Marie Antoinette of France executed / France declares war on Britain
1794	Habeas Corpus suspended	
1795	Speenhamland system of poor relief begins	
1796	Jenner begins vaccination against smallpox	
1797	Naval mutinies at Nore and Spithead	
1798	Newspaper tax increased. Rebellion in Ireland	
1799	Combination Laws passed. Income tax introduced to help pay for the war	
1800	Ireland becomes part of the United Kingdom	
1801	Pitt resigns, Addington becomes Prime Minister	
1802		
1803		
1804	Pitt returns as Prime Minister	
1805		Battle of Trafalgar: Nelson killed
1806	Pitt dies; Grenville becomes Prime Minister	
1807	Grenville resigns; Portland becomes Prime Minister	
1808		
1809	Spencer Perceval becomes Prime Minister	
1810		
1811	George III declared insane again; Prince of Wales becomes Prince Regent	
1812	Spencer Perceval assassinated; Lord Liverpool becomes Prime Minister / Luddite activity in northern England	Britain at war with America
1813		
1814		
1815	Corn Laws passed	Battle of Waterloo – end of the Napoleonic Wars
1816	Spa Fields riot	

HOW CLOSE DID BRITAIN COME TO REVOLUTION 1783–1851?

1817	March of the Blanketeers. Pentrich Rising. Habeas Corpus suspended
1818	Mary Shelley's *Frankenstein* published
1819	Peterloo Massacre. Six Acts. Factory Act
1820	George III succeeded by George IV. Cato Street Conspiracy
1821	*Manchester Guardian* first published
1822	
1823	Huskisson reduces import duties to make trade freer
1824	Repeal of the Combination Laws. RSPCA formed
1825	Stockton and Darlington railway opened
1826	
1827	Lord Liverpool replaced by Canning, then Goderich
1828	Wellington becomes Prime Minister. Repeal of the Test and Corporation Acts
1829	Catholic Emancipation Act passed. Metropolitan Police formed
1830	George IV succeeded by William IV. Wellington resigns; Grey and the Whigs form government. Liverpool–Manchester railway opened. Riots in the countryside
1831	
1832	The Great Reform Act
1833	First government grant for education
1834	Melbourne becomes Prime Minister. Poor Law Amendment Act. Peel's Tamworth Manifesto
1835	Peel briefly takes over as Prime Minister. Melbourne returns as Prime Minister. Municipal Corporations Act
1836	Compulsory registration of births, marriages and deaths
1837	William IV dies; succeeded by his niece, Victoria
1838	Anti-Corn Law League founded
1839	Chartist activity and the first petition to Parliament
1840	Penny Post set up
1841	Peel becomes Prime Minister
1842	Mines Act. Chartist activity and second petition to Parliament. Anti-Corn Law League begins campaigning vigorously
1843	
1844	Bank Charter Act. Companies Act. Factory Act
1845	Failure of the potato harvest in Ireland
1846	Corn Laws repealed. Peel resigns after defeat in a coercion bill. Russell becomes Prime Minister
1847	
1848	Chartist activity and third petition to Parliament. Public Health Act
1849	
1850	
1851	Great Exhibition at Crystal Palace

Revolutions in Europe (1830)

Revolutions in Europe (1848)

TALKING POINTS

1 What might revolutionaries in Britain have hoped to achieve in the period 1783–1851?
2 What might have led to a revolution breaking out?
3 What conditions or other features would have been needed to give a revolution the chance of success?
4 Why might a revolution have failed?
5 Using the timeline identify the period when there was the greatest threat of revolution.
6 Do you think that there was a consistent threat of revolution, a sporadic threat or, in all likelihood, no threat at all?
7 Does one man's demand for reform equal another man's fear of revolution?

CITY COLLEGE
LEARNING RESOURCE CENTRE

How close did Britain come to revolution?

You will use this page on several occasions as you study critical events. Although you have yet to study the events in detail, look back to pages 5–7. Where would you put the events shown in Sources 2–4 on this scale of revolutionary threat below?

The threat of revolution: a 'revolutionary Richter scale'

1	CHEAPER FOOD LOWER PRICES LOWER PRICES HIGHER WAGES	Minor localised demonstrations over food supplies, prices and wages. Local magistrates deal with the offenders.
2	*Reform club*	Radical groups form clubs where they discuss reforms, including parliamentary reform, and a network of linked groups spreads across the country. The government makes the groups illegal, but many still continue to meet.
3		Reform ideas are spread by pamphlets and newspapers, which are widely read by working people. The government puts taxes on publications to price them beyond the reach of working people.
4	VOTES FOR ALL MEN PETITION SIGN HERE	Organisations demanding the vote for working men are established. Peaceful meetings are held in many parts of the country. They present petitions to Parliament, but the petitions are dismissed.
5		Attacks on mills, factories and farms to try to prevent the use of machines that take away jobs. These are local and dramatic events but they do not spread throughout the country. The leaders are arrested – some are transported, others are executed.

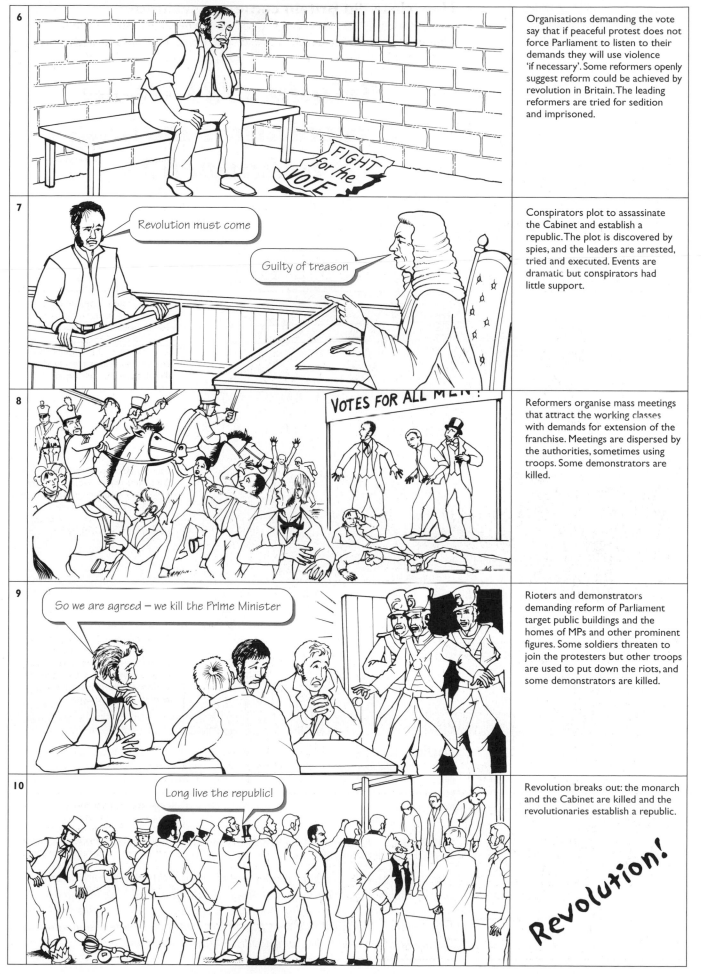

6 Organisations demanding the vote say that if peaceful protest does not force Parliament to listen to their demands they will use violence 'if necessary'. Some reformers openly suggest reform could be achieved by revolution in Britain. The leading reformers are tried for sedition and imprisoned.

7 Conspirators plot to assassinate the Cabinet and establish a republic. The plot is discovered by spies, and the leaders are arrested, tried and executed. Events are dramatic but conspirators had little support.

8 Reformers organise mass meetings that attract the working classes with demands for extension of the franchise. Meetings are dispersed by the authorities, sometimes using troops. Some demonstrators are killed.

9 Rioters and demonstrators demanding reform of Parliament target public buildings and the homes of MPs and other prominent figures. Some soldiers threaten to join the protesters but other troops are used to put down the riots, and some demonstrators are killed.

10 Revolution breaks out: the monarch and the Cabinet are killed and the revolutionaries establish a republic.

1

Britain 1783–1851: a revolution waiting to happen?

CHAPTER OVERVIEW

SOURCE 1.1   The storming of the Bastille, 14 July 1789. The Bastille was a prison in Paris, but was also a royal fortress where weapons were stored. The mob attacked, using five cannon they had captured, and searched for more weapons. After two hours the governor of the Bastille surrendered, and was beheaded. Only about seven prisoners were found and released. The fall of the Bastille was a clear challenge to the King's authority

SOURCE 1.2   A defender of the Bastille gives an eyewitness account of the dreadful events in Paris, 14 July 1789

The streets through which we passed and the houses flanking them (even the rooftops) were filled with masses of people insulting and cursing me. Swords, bayonets and pistols were being continually pressed against me. I did not know how I should die but felt that my last moment had come. Those who had no arms threw stones at me and the women gnashed their teeth at me and threatened me with their fists.

SOURCE 1.3   An extract from *The Illustrated London News*, 1 July 1848

July 1 1848 Civil War in France!
Paris has again become the theatre of one of the most sanguinary struggles that even its blood-stained streets have ever witnessed. Nothing approaching the carnage of the last four days has, it is said, occurred in that capital since the massacre of St Bartholomew. We append the substance of the notes taken by our Artist, of the appearance of the localities which he visited in sketching … [his] illustrations.
Women on the barricade of St Denis:
Although this scene appears too melodramatic to be true, still it is the very drama of reality. To the left waves, in grim terror, the flag inscribed 'Du pain ou la Mort' (Bread or Death), and mounted on the barricade are two women heroically calling upon the insurgents to follow their example of devotedness. The foremost was well known in the Quartier St Denis; she was a fine woman, with black hair, and wore a light blue silk dress; her head and arms were bare. She and her companions were shot whilst in the attitudes [described].

ACTIVITY

1 Why might the events in Sources 1.1–1.3 create fears of revolution in Britain?
2 Who were most likely to fear a revolution?

The period from around 1783 to 1850 was a time of revolution on the continent of Europe. The revolution in France in 1789 led to the overthrow of Louis XVI and the whole monarchical system and to the establishment of a republic. When the Napoleonic Empire was defeated at Waterloo in 1815, France became a monarchy once more until a revolution in 1830 led to the overthrow of Charles X and his replacement by Louis Philippe and a form of constitutional monarchy. 1848 is sometimes called the 'year of revolutions' because there were revolutions in many European countries, including France, where Louis Philippe was overthrown and France again became a republic under Louis Napoleon, later Napoleon III. The whole period was one of instability in Europe. There were many who feared that this instability was present in Britain too, and that revolution was not far beneath the surface.

FOCUS ROUTE

As you work through this chapter complete this chart with summary notes, recording evidence for and against the likelihood of a revolution in Britain.

Evidence for the likelihood of a revolution	Evidence against the likelihood of a revolution

Some historians have argued that there were times when Britain was very close to revolution – between 1815 and 1820, for example, when unemployment and low wages, among other things, led to a series of anti-government protests, or in 1831–32 during the crisis over whether Parliament should be reformed, or in the 1840s when Chartism and strikes in many industrial areas resulted from a trade depression. However, there was no revolution in Britain, in the continental European sense at least, although some reforms and social and industrial changes might be termed 'revolutionary'. The aim of this chapter is to consider whether there was the potential or motive for revolution in Britain during the period 1783–1851.

A   How rapidly was industry expanding between 1783 and 1851? (pp. 14–16)

B   What was the impact of industrial expansion on the people of Britain? (pp. 17–22)

C   Was everyone likely to protest or revolt? Aspects of life 1783–1851 (pp. 23–28)

D   Review: a revolution waiting to happen? (p. 29)

A How rapidly was industry expanding between 1783 and 1851?

The sources on the following pages illustrate some aspects of the industrial expansion that was taking place in Britain at this time. By 1783 the Industrial Revolution had begun, and in some areas, such as iron-making and cotton textiles, the impact was already being felt. But the period from 1783 to 1851 was one of immense industrial change and development. In textiles, coal, iron and engineering, Britain became the greatest industrial nation, so that by 1851, at the time of the Great Exhibition, Britain was known as 'the workshop of the world'. Nevertheless, in 1851, agriculture was still the largest single employer.

FOCUS ROUTE

1 Using the statistics in Sources 1.4–1.15, summarise the changes that took place between 1783 and 1851 in:
   a) textile manufacture
   b) iron and coal production
   c) population size and location
   d) railway transport.
2 Which changes were likely to have had the most impact on the lives of ordinary working people?
3 How might these changes have led to or contributed to revolution?
4 How might these changes have reduced the possibility of revolution?
5 Add evidence to your Focus Route table from page 13.

■ Learning trouble spot

Was everywhere the same?

Many students assume that changes and developments were uniform across the country. It is important to appreciate that some parts of Britain changed relatively little in this period. The figures in Sources 1.4–1.15 show great changes in industrial productivity, the economy and the size and distribution of population. But it is important to remember that in some areas the population actually declined, as people moved away to work in the new industrial areas. Although some people may have been able to earn more in new jobs, those who had relied on home-based industrial production (for example, in the textile industry) to supplement agricultural wages found their potential income dropped as factory-based production gradually took over. Similarly, many skilled workers who had earned relatively high wages, such as handloom weavers, found that as the number of power looms increased, their skills were no longer needed. Such people felt little benefit from increasing industrial output.

SOURCE 1.4 Consumption of raw cotton, 1760–1850

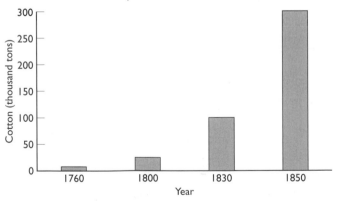

SOURCE 1.5 Export of cotton cloth, 1810–49 (averages for decade)

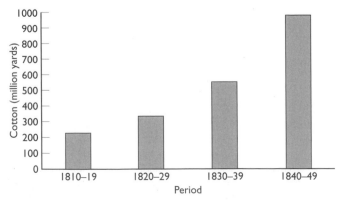

SOURCE 1.6 Iron output, 1800–50

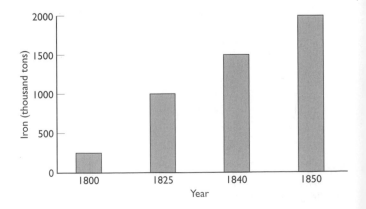

SOURCE 1.7 Coal production, 1770–1846

Coal (million tons) / Year

SOURCE 1.8 Steam power in the textile industry, 1820–50

	1820	1830	1840	1850
Spindles (steam powered spinning)	0.5 m	0.75 m	1.9 m	2.1 m
Handlooms	2.7 m	2.8 m	0.75 m	0.5 m
Power looms (steam powered)	0.2 m	0.5 m	2 m	2.5 m

SOURCE 1.9 Worsted and woollen mills in Bradford, 1834–51

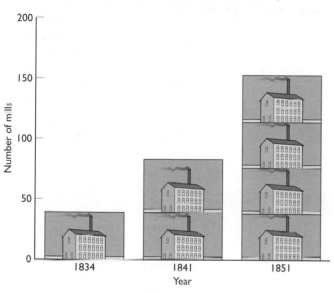

Number of mills / Year

SOURCE 1.10 Power looms in use in the cotton industry, 1813–50

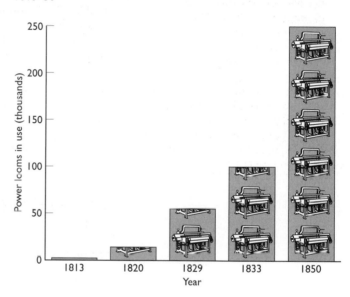

Power looms in use (thousands) / Year

SOURCE 1.11 Percentage of people living in towns and cities

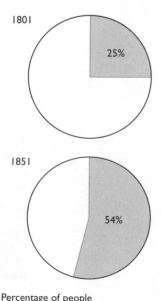

1801 — 25%

1851 — 54%

Key

Percentage of people living in towns and cities

SOURCE 1.12 Birth and death rates per 1000 of the population, 1780–1840

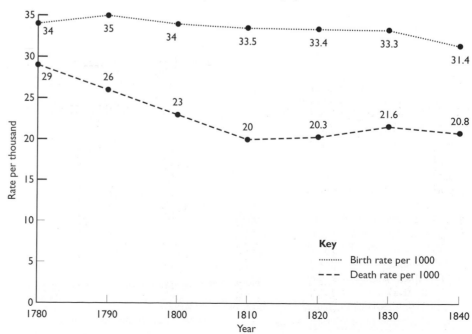

Rate per thousand / Year

Birth rate: 34, 35, 34, 33.5, 33.4, 33.3, 31.4

Death rate: 29, 26, 23, 20, 20.3, 21.6, 20.8

Key

.... Birth rate per 1000

– – – Death rate per 1000

SOURCE 1.13 Population, 1801–51 (approximate figures)

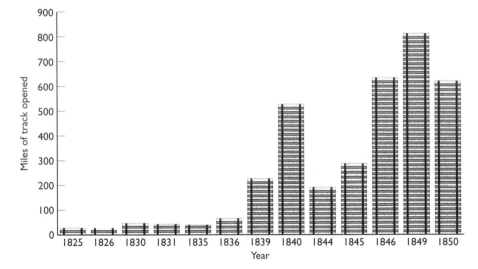

SOURCE 1.14 Railways, 1825–50: miles of track opened each year

SOURCE 1.15 Maps to show changes in population distribution/density, 1801 and 1851

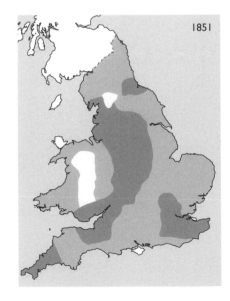

Key

■ Over 120 people per square km

■ 40–120 people per square km

□ Under 40 people per square km

ACTIVITY

1 Explain the links between the information given in Sources 1.4–1.10.
2 Which of the six towns listed in Source 1.13 had the greatest percentage increase in population between 1801 and 1851? Explain why this town should have experienced such growth.
3 Which of the six towns in Source 1.13 had the lowest percentage increase? Explain why this town should have had relatively little increase in population.
4 Study Source 1.15. Where were the areas of highest population density in 1801 and in 1851? Explain the difference.
5 How might the regional differences in industrial development and population expansion have affected the likelihood of revolution?

B What was the impact of industrial expansion on the people of Britain?

The sources in this section cover the growth and changing nature of employment, the development of the railway network, and the expansion of towns.

CITY COLLEGE
LEARNING RESOURCE CENTRE

ACTIVITY

1 Using all the sources in Section B, write the text for a chapter of a school textbook for pupils in Year 9 who are studying nineteenth-century Britain. Your brief is as follows.
  a) The chapter title is 'How did the Industrial Revolution affect the lives of the people of Britain?'
  b) You must not write more than 600 words.
  c) You must include the following topics
    – work and working conditions
    – the effects of railway development
    – the growth of towns and housing conditions.
2 How might these changes have led to or contributed to revolution?
3 Why might these changes have reduced the possibility of revolution?

ACTIVITY

What do Sources 1.16–1.23 suggest were the effects of industrial development between 1783 and 1851?

SOURCE 1.16   National employment, 1801–51

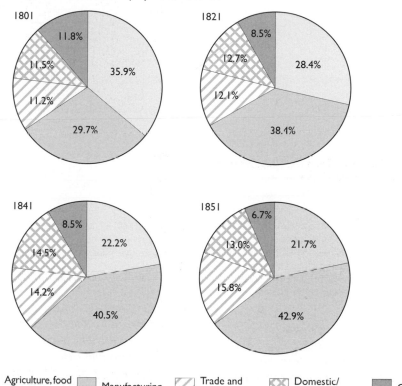

Key

Agriculture, food and fisheries   Manufacturing   Trade and transport   Domestic/personal servants   Other

SOURCE 1.17   Jobs in Bradford, 1851

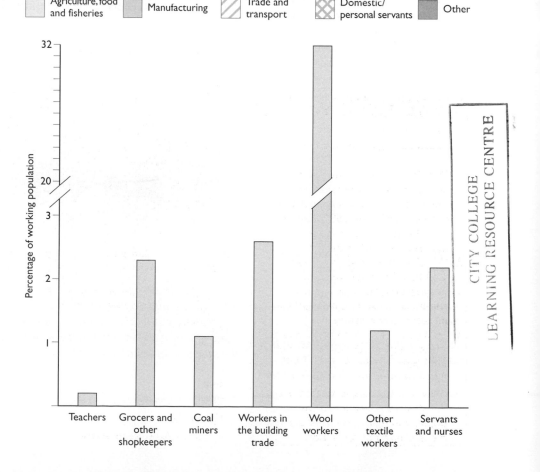

SOURCE 1.18 The effect of depressions in trade and industry on prices and wages, 1800–50

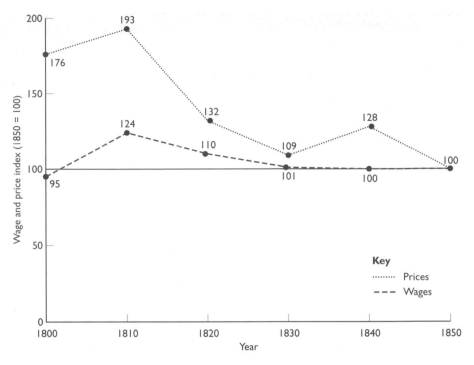

SOURCE 1.19 Extract from the Report of the Children's Employment Commissioners: Mines and Collieries, 1842. A trapper opened and closed the doors, which were there to prevent the spread of fire in mines, in order to let coal wagons through

The little trapper of eight years of age lies quiet in bed; between two and three in the morning his mother shakes him. He fills his tin bottle with coffee, and takes a loaf of bread, and sets out for the pit. All his work is to open the door and then allow the door to shut of itself. He sits alone and has no-one to talk to. He has no light. His hours are passed in total darkness. He knows nothing of the sun.

SOURCE 1.20 The evidence of Margaret Hipps, aged seventeen, who worked with two younger girls pulling coal in a Scottish mine, in the Report of the Children's Employment Commissioners: Mines and Collieries, 1842

At the wall-face where the miner cuts the coal, I fill a bagie [tub on runners like a sledge] with 1½ to 3 cwt. [1cwt. = one hundred weight = about 50 kg] of coal. I then hook it on to my chain and drag it through the seam, which is 26 to 28 inches high, till I get to the main road – a good distance, 200 to 400 yards. There I fill it into a cart. The pavement I drag it over is wet, and I have at all times to crawl on hands and feet.

SOURCE 1.21 A female coal drawer, 1840

SOURCE 1.22 From *The Medical Times* 1843: the effects of some trades on the workers' health and life expectancy. This extract compares the death rate in the fork-grinding industry with the death rate in England and Wales generally

Between 20 and 40 years of age, in this trade, 885 perish out of every 1000, while in England and Wales, only 196.

SOURCE 1.23 Extract from the Second Report of the Children's Employment Commissioners, about working conditions in a lace-making factory near Nottingham

One of her children, four years of age, works for twelve hours a day with only an interval of a quarter of an hour for each meal at breakfast, dinner and tea, and never going out to play; and two more of her children, one six and the other eight years of age, work in summer from 6a.m. until dusk, and in winter from seven in the morning til ten at night, fifteen hours.

ACTIVITY

Using Sources 1.24–1.30:

• identify the benefits brought about by railway development
• explain whether railway development appears to have brought any disadvantages.

SOURCE 1.24 The effects of railway growth, 1847–50. Railway investment reached nearly seven per cent of national income in 1847

Year	Miles open	Employed in building railways	Employed in running railways	Income from railways (£m)
1847	3,500	257,000	47,000	8.5
1848	4,250	188,000	53,000	9.9
1849	5,450	104,000	56,000	11.2
1850	6,300	59,000	60,000	13.2

SOURCE 1.25 The construction of a cutting at Park Village, Camden Town, on the London–Birmingham railway, 1836

SHILLINGS AND PENCE
Throughout this book 's' refers to shillings and 'd' to pence. There were 12d in 1s and 20s in £1.

SOURCE 1.26 Average weekly earnings of those building the railways, 1843–51

	1843	1846	1851
Bricklayers	21s	30s	21s
Navvies (pick men)	16s 6d	24s	15s
Navvies (shovellers)	15s	22s 6d	14s

SOURCE 1.27 Railway travellers in 1847 – first, second and third class passengers, from drawings in *The Illustrated London News*, 1847

SOURCE 1.28 A description of Crewe, a key station on one of the first main lines, written in 1849, quoted in F. B. Head, *Stokers and Pokers*, 1849

The number of workmen [employed by the railway] is 1600. About a hundred yards [from the workshops] there stands a plain, neat building, erected by the company, containing baths, hot and cold, and showers, for the workmen as well as their wives and daughters. To a medical man was given a house and surgery, in addition to which he receives from every unmarried workman 1d per week, if married with a family, 2d a week, for which he undertakes to give attendance and medicine to whoever may require them.

A clergyman with an adequate salary from the company superintends three large day schools. There is also a library and a mechanics institute [and] a vocal and instrumental class.

The town of Crewe contains 514 houses, one church, three schools and one Town Hall, all belonging to the Company.

SOURCE 1.29 An extract from S. Smiles, *The Lives of George and Robert Stephenson*, 1857, describing what became known as 'railway mania' in the 1840s

A reckless spirit of gambling set in, which completely changed the character and objects of railway enterprise ... many persons utterly ignorant of railways ... but ... thirsting after premiums, rushed into the vortex ... and subscribed for shares in lines, of the engineering character and probable traffic of which they knew nothing ... The mania affected all ranks ... The sharpers of society were let loose ... They threw out railway schemes as lures to catch the unwary ... They fed the mania with a constant succession of new projects.

SOURCE 1.30 A drawing of the Great Western Royal Hotel, opened in 1852, next to Paddington station, London. The growth of the railway network led to a huge increase in employment prospects. Although there were fewer jobs for ostlers (who looked after the horses for stagecoaches), the railways created new jobs such as porters, booking clerks, guards, drivers and signalmen. The new railway hotels needed cooks, chambermaids, waiters, hall porters and clerks

FOCUS ROUTE

Add evidence to your Focus Route table from page 13.

SOURCE 1.31 Two views of Leeds. **A** shows Leeds in 1715 by Francis Place, whilst **B** shows Leeds from Beeston Hill in 1858, and was drawn to celebrate Queen Victoria's visit to Leeds to open the new town hall. It shows the rapidly expanding city – industry, housing, railways and new public buildings

ACTIVITY

Using Sources 1.31–1.35:

- describe the impact the expansion of towns and cities identified in Sources 1.11 and 1.13 had on housing conditions
- state to what extent Sources 1.31–1.35 help to explain the figures in Source 1.12.

A

B

SOURCE 1.32 A courtyard in Glasgow in the early nineteenth century. The camera is looking towards the only entrance to the court; the channel in the middle of the paved area was the drain or sewer, and the water supply came from the pump near the steps to the right of the photo

SOURCE 1.33 A plan of a courtyard and back-to-back housing in Nottingham in the 1840s

SOURCE 1.34 The night-soil men: their job was to remove the sewage from cesspits during the night

SOURCE 1.35 Extract from Edwin Chadwick, *Report on the Sanitary Conditions of the Labouring Classes*, 1842

In Hull I met with a mother about 50 years of age and her son, I should think about 25, sleeping in the same bed and a lodger in the same room. In a cellar in Liverpool, I found a mother and her grown-up daughters sleeping in a bed of chaff [straw] on the ground in the corner of a cellar. In the other corner, three sailors have their bed. I have met with upwards of 40 people sleeping in the same room, married and single, including women, young children and young adults of either sex.

ACTIVITY

As a group debate the motion: 'There was no potential for a revolution resulting from the effects of industrialisation in Britain between 1827 and 1851.'

C Was everyone likely to protest or revolt? Aspects of life 1783–1851

CITY COLLEGE
LEARNING RESOURCE SERVICE

FOCUS ROUTE

As you read through this section note any aspects which:

a) suggest that a large proportion of the population were happy with life and therefore unlikely to support revolution

b) suggest that some might have had a motive for revolution.

ACTIVITY

1 To what extent do Sources 1.36–1.40 suggest that both rich and poor had opportunities to enjoy themselves in the early nineteenth century?

2 What aspects of what he saw did the writer in Source 1.40 particularly disapprove of?

In examining a period as long as 70 years and a society as diverse as that of Britain, it is always difficult to make generalised statements about how people felt and what actions they took and why. Society changed rapidly between 1783 and 1851. Britain became an industrialised nation, towns and cities expanded, new jobs came into existence, and new forms of transport and communication developed. For some people it was a time of growing wealth, comfort and increasing expectations. For others the changes led to a greater likelihood of poverty, appalling living conditions and entry to the hated workhouse in old age where husbands and wives were separated, made to wear workhouse clothes, and toiled at tedious tasks that made them feel like criminals.

The issue of whether the standard of living was improving during this period is one which historians have argued over for many years. As a nation, Britain was becoming wealthier. Some groups were becoming wealthier but other once well-off workers descended into poverty. Other groups remained as poor as they had always been. The key question is, which, if any, of the groups was likely to look to revolution as a means of improving their way of life?

This section gives you some information about some aspects of life in the early nineteenth century. The sources cover four areas of people's lives that would have been important in the years 1783–1851 – their leisure time, their safety from crime, their education and their religion.

Leisure time

SOURCE 1.36 A day at the Ascot races, 1844

SOURCE 1.37 An excursion on the River Thames, Easter Monday 1847

SOURCE 1.38 In 1841 Thomas Cook organised the first railway excursion – to a temperance meeting! Within just a few years many thousands were taking railway outings to the seaside, the races, concerts and even public hangings. The railways opened up new opportunities for seaside towns and for rural areas as trippers flooded in from the towns

SOURCE 1.39 The theatre was not always too serious: audiences at a pantomime, c.1850, in the gallery (top) and boxes (bottom)

SOURCE 1.40 Extracts from a parliamentary report by J. C. Symons, written in 1843 after a Saturday night tour of some of the pubs in Leeds

[The pubs were] crowded with lads and girls – a motley assemblage of thieves and youths of both sexes from the factories ... I am confident that of the 600 persons I saw in these places, not above a quarter were turned of 25 years of age, and at least two-thirds were under age. In the beer houses, there were several more children. In almost all there was a sprinkling of professed prostitutes ... A boy of 14 was sitting ... by the side of his father ... this was at half past ten at night, and yet his father seemed to be wholly unaware that there was anything wrong in bringing his child to a beer house ... in some of these places we found a fiddle or some other instrument being played ... in another dancing was going on ... not one of these dancers was above 20 or 21 years of age, and most of them 16 or 17. The prostitutes were easily distinguishable ... by their tawdry finery and the bareness of their necks.

PARISH
The smallest division of local and church government.

THE GALLERY.

THE BOXES.

Law and order

One of the major problems in the rapidly growing towns was the lack of an effective system of policing. The existing system for keeping law and order dated from the Middle Ages. Unpaid magistrates were responsible for law enforcement. Most PARISHES had an unpaid parish constable, whose job was to help the magistrate in catching criminals, keeping an eye on the locality and maintaining order. In some towns, watchmen were appointed to help the constables; they were often elderly men who made little impact. When law and order broke down, often the only way to regain control was for the magistrates to call on the military. As London and the industrial cities of the north and Midlands grew, the system of magistrates, parish constables and watchmen could not cope. Parts of Bradford, for example, were virtually no-go areas for the parish constables in the early nineteenth century. In other cities the policing was in the hands of so few men that it was unlikely they could have been successful in keeping law and order. Although Robert Peel set up the Metropolitan Police in London in 1829, it was the mid-1850s before every part of the country had its own police force – this was because local people were unwilling to be taxed to pay police wages and other costs. If riots broke out, the government had to use soldiers to restore order or, from the 1830s, send police from London on the railways. Not until 1856 did the government pass a law requiring all local councils to set up police forces.

ACTIVITY

1 From Sources 1.41–1.44 what would you identify as the main problem in keeping law and order in the early 1800s?
2 What is the opinion of the writer of Source 1.45 about the use of education to solve the juvenile crime problem in London in the 1840s?

SOURCE 1.41   The policing of Leeds in the 1820s, where the population was over 50,000, from E. Baines, *History, Directory and Gazeteer of the County of York*, 1822

A nightly Watch and Patrol has been established, which are very vigilant in protecting the persons and property of the inhabitants [of Leeds].

In 1826–27 the ten unpaid part-time constables for Leeds consisted of a bricklayer, two joiners, two maltsters, a butcher, a baker, a tailor, a shoemaker and an auctioneer.

SOURCE 1.42   Extract from the *Leeds Intelligencer*, 14 July 1825

We did not complain of the watchmen patrolling the streets ... but for giving way to their gregarious tendencies and becoming stationary in groups of three or four for hours in one street ... Lately four or five of these peripatetic guardians were found sitting in the middle of the night on the steps of a single house.

SOURCE 1.43   Juvenile crime in London, 1839–48

Year	Number of persons under 20 taken into custody	Ratio of juvenile offenders to total population under 20
1839	13,587	1:53
1840	14,031	1:52
1841	17,425	1:42
1842	16,987	1:44
1843	16,316	1:46
1844	13,600	1:56
1845	15,128	1:51
1846	15,552	1:50
1847	15,698	1:50
1848	16,917	1:47

(The population of London rose by 100,000 between 1844 and 1848.)

SOURCE 1.45   A letter to the *Morning Chronicle*, 1848. Ragged schools had been set up for the very poorest children, who were often rejected by the Sunday schools and day schools. A guinea = £1 1s (£1.05)

It appears that the increase in the number of Ragged Schools throughout London since 1844 has been 62; of Ragged School teachers 953; of Ragged School pupils 15,249 and of Ragged School funds, upwards of £4,000. And yet in spite of all this ... the number of offenders under 20 years of age has increased ... by no less than 3,317 – or very nearly one for each guinea that has been given in the hope of reducing juvenile crime.

SOURCE 1.44   A ragged school, 1846 – a means of keeping potential young criminals off the street

CITY COLLEGE
LEARNING RESOURCE CENTRE

Education

Until the 1830s there was no involvement by the state in education. Schools were run by charities or private individuals or groups. Education was not compulsory for children of any social class. Boys from wealthy families, and increasingly from the more affluent middle-class families, attended the public schools. Some were unlucky enough to attend schools such as those exposed by Dickens in his description of Dotheboys Hall in *Nicholas Nickleby*. Girls from affluent families were usually educated at home, where they could learn from a governess the attributes a genteel lady needed. There were schools for girls from middle-class backgrounds. Some provided a sound education, others, like the one attended by Charlotte Brontë and her sisters, and described in her novel *Jane Eyre*, were harsh and often cruel in their treatment of pupils (see Source 1.46).

For working-class children, school was available only in church or charity schools, usually at a fee of a few pence a week. Many very young children attended what were called 'dame schools', which frequently provided nothing more than very poor quality childminding. Because most children, whether in town or country, worked from a young age, most did not attend school regularly.

■ 1A Timeline of developments in education before 1851

1811	National Society founded to support the building of Church of England schools
1814	British and Foreign Society founded to support the building of nonconformist schools
1833	Factory Act requires children working in factories to have two hours schooling a day
	First government grant to education: £20,000 given to the two church societies
1834	Poor Law Act requires all children in workhouses to receive some schooling
	The government grant increased to £30,000
1839	Committee of the Privy Council on education set up to oversee the spending of the grant
	A system of school inspection set up to check that money given to schools was not being wasted
1840	First teacher-training college opened
1846	Government grant increased to £100,000 a year
	Twenty-three teacher training colleges set up, and a system to train the very best pupils to become teachers by working in schools as pupil-teachers before going to training college

ACTIVITY

1 Why was there no government involvement in education before the 1830s?
2 The grant of £20,000 in 1833 (see chart 1A) was, supposedly, less than was spent on the royal stables. Why, then, might it be seen to be a significant payment?
3 What might the growth of libraries, such as those in mechanics institutes, suggest about literacy amongst the working classes? Why might this have concerned or comforted governments in fear of revolution?

SOURCE 1.46 Extract from *Jane Eyre* by Charlotte Brontë, describing a scene at a school run by a charity for orphan girls. The description was based on Brontë's own life at a school for daughters of the clergy in the 1830s

... But Burns immediately left the class, and going into the small inner room where the books were kept, returned in half a minute, carrying in her hand a bundle of twigs tied together at one end. This ominous tool she presented to Miss Scatcherd with a respectful curtsey; then she quietly, and without being told, unloosed her pinafore, and the teacher instantly inflicted on her neck a dozen strokes with the bunch of twigs. Not a tear rose to Burns' eye ... not a feature of her pensive face altered its ordinary expression.

'Hardened girl!' exclaimed Miss Scatcherd; 'nothing can correct you of your slatternly habits: carry the rod away.'

SOURCE 1.47 The monitorial system in use in an East London school in 1839: the older pupils were used to teach the younger ones

The first public libraries, free to use, were opened after the 1850 Public Libraries Act, which allowed boroughs with a population of over 10,000 to build libraries using money from the rates. However, there had been libraries in a small number of towns before 1850, and there were a large number of 'hidden' libraries, that is, collections of books which people could read, but which were not called 'libraries'. Religious societies and Sunday schools often had small book collections. In 1768 a library accessible to anyone who paid a subscription was opened in Leeds. Many of the London coffee houses had libraries that could be used by the customers. Subscription libraries and those in coffee houses were not likely to be available to working people, but there were libraries that were. The mechanics institutes, built to provide education for working men, had libraries. In 1845 the Museums Act allowed collections of books to be made available to the public as 'specimens' and some towns took advantage of this. In 1847 and 1848 libraries were set up under this Act in Canterbury and Warrington.

Religion and the Church

One view of the Victorians is that they were very religious, and went to church at least once every Sunday. Whilst this may have been true of some Victorians, it is equally clear that it was not true of a great many, especially the workers in the new industrial cities. Church attendance in a small community such as a village, where most adults worked for the squire or local landowner, was part of what it was to belong to village society. If someone did not attend the local church, it would be noticed. However, in the growing industrial cities there were no churches in many areas until the 1840s or 1850s, and even if there was a church to go to, it was highly unlikely that an employer would know whether or not one of his possibly hundreds of workers was attending church. In any case, attending church on their one day off a week from the factory was not a priority for many. Moreover, in busy times the factories worked seven days a week, so many workers did not have Sunday off.

The Anglican Church was initially very slow to provide places of worship in many cities, and in these areas the NONCONFORMISTS held sway. For example, in Leeds between 1821 and 1841, as the population rose from 84,000 to 152,000, the Church of England built just eight new churches. In 1838 the *Leeds Mercury* estimated that out of 60,000 working-class people in Leeds, 40,000 never went to church or chapel. The picture was likely to be very different, however, among the middle classes, where it would have been very unlikely that a leading businessman or politician did not attend a place of worship. It was, of course, not always religious reasons that motivated church attendance. Just as a business deal may be done on a golf course today, so in the nineteenth century church or chapel provided good networking opportunities for businessmen.

By 1859 Leeds had 36 Anglican churches in the city and suburbs. Despite all the building, however, by Anglicans, Catholics and nonconformists, in 1851 in Leeds there were only 47,000 seats in places of worship for a population of 173,000. On the Sunday of the census taken in 1851 only 18,933 people attended the morning services and 20,604 the evening services.

NONCONFORMIST
A member of a Protestant Church that did not conform (agree) with many of the teachings of the Church of England (e.g. Methodists, Presbyterians).

SOURCE 1.48 Extracts from the 1851 census of religious worship taken on Sunday 30 March 1851: this shows the number of people attending services in the different churches as a percentage of the population of the town/area. For example, in Bradford a total of 42.7 per cent of the population attended service on the Sunday surveyed in the census. Of these 9.8 per cent of the population went to Church of England churches, 16.9 per cent of the population went to Methodist churches, 5.6 per cent of the population went to Independent churches, 4.9 per cent went to Baptist churches and 3.9 per cent went to Roman Catholic churches. (A small number went to other places of worship.) Note that these figures do not differentiate between those who attended once or twice on the Sunday in question

Attendance as a percentage of the population in each place						
Place	Total	Church of England	Methodists	Independents	Baptists	Roman Catholics
Bath	79.1	48.7	11.1	4.9	3.6	2.6
Bradford	42.7	9.8	16.9	5.6	4.9	3.9
Colchester	89.5	43.5	8.2	22.7	10.5	0.7
Leeds	47.4	16.4	19.8	3.5	2.7	2.9
Liverpool	45.2	18.4	6.0	1.9	1.1	14.7
Oldham	31.7	11.7	8.4	6.5	2.1	1.5
Preston	25.5	5.2	6.4	2.6	1.0	9.1
Cornwall	68.0	19.2	43.8	2.8	1.3	0.3
Durham	42.6	14.4	19.6	2.1	1.4	3.0
Lancashire	44.1	18.8	9.9	4.2	1.8	7.2
South Wales	83.4	15.6	23.9	23.7	17.7	0.6

SOURCE 1.49 The Holy Trinity Church, Paddington, London (built 1844–46). New churches were provided for the growing cities

ACTIVITY

1 What can be said about church attendance in 1851 from the extracts from the religious census (Source 1.48)?
2 Account for the percentage of Roman Catholics in Liverpool.
3 What do the figures suggest about the response of the population to the church building of the 1840s?

TALKING POINTS

1 This section began (on page 23) with a warning about generalisations. Why are generalisations both useful and dangerous for historians?
2 This section has only explored a sample of aspects of British society. What other topics could you investigate to find evidence for the likelihood of revolution?

D Review: a revolution waiting to happen?

TALKING POINT

The guiding principle for governments in this period was *laissez-faire*, which means 'leave alone'. Governments did not think it was their role to interfere in the economic affairs of individuals or in society as a whole. How might this principle of *laissez-faire* affect the likelihood of revolution?

In 1851 Queen Victoria opened the Great Exhibition of the Works of Industry of All Nations. Over the next few months, 6 million visitors attended the Exhibition. Factories closed so workers could travel to London. Entire villages travelled together on railway excursions. The whole event was a celebration of Britain's wealth and suggested a stable, peaceful country. Yet only three years earlier the government had sent Queen Victoria to the Isle of Wight for safety in fear that the Chartists' demand for the vote for all men would lead to revolution. Which scene gives a more accurate impression of Britain in the period 1783–1851 – the crowds queuing for the Exhibition in 1851 or the government placing cannon on London's bridges in 1848?

This chapter has provided information about changes that affected life and society in Britain between 1783 and 1851. The key question raised at the beginning of the chapter was whether there was the potential or motive for revolution during this period. In discussing this question it is important to bear in mind how a revolution becomes possible. For example, do revolutions occur when the masses are completely downtrodden, or is that when revolution is least likely because they do not have the opportunity or means to revolt? Perhaps revolution is more likely when people's hopes of improvement are first raised, then dashed, and when they have the means and leadership for revolt.

Another key element to explore in discussing the potential for revolution is whether people were able to express their views or influence governments peacefully. For example, in the twenty-first century virtually everyone has the chance to vote to support or remove the government. Was that the case in the early 1800s? Chapter 2 continues to explore whether there was the potential for revolution by investigating what say people had in government.

FOCUS ROUTE

Using the information collected in your Focus Route table (page 13) as evidence, decide whether there was the potential or motive for revolution in the years between 1783 and 1851.

ACTIVITY

If television had existed in 1851 it is likely that the Prime Minister, Lord John Russell, would have made a political broadcast in which he summed up, firstly, the state of the nation on the eve of the Great Exhibition and, secondly, the progress made by the country since the beginning of the century.

a) Write the script for his broadcast, giving as positive a picture as possible, whilst not missing out any areas of concern.
b) Write a newspaper review of the programme by a political commentator who does not agree with Russell's views.

SOURCE 1.50 The Crystal Palace, which was designed and built to house the Great Exhibition of 1851

KEY POINTS FROM CHAPTER 1   Britain 1783–1851: a revolution waiting to happen?

1   Revolutions in 1789, 1830 and 1848 in Europe created fear of similar events in Britain.

2   British industry was expanding rapidly. This created work for many, but also led to some workers losing their jobs or seeing their incomes fall as their skills were replaced by machinery.

3   The population of Britain was rising rapidly and towns and cities were growing fast.

4   Working and living conditions for a large proportion of the population were poor.

5   There was no effective police force in most cities before the 1840s.

6   The growth of the railways made communication and travel easier.

7   More working people were receiving a small amount of education, enabling them to read.

8   The influence of the Church, especially on the working classes in cities, was loosening.

9   Although for some groups the period was one of increasing wealth and an improving lifestyle, for others life became more difficult.

2

Why did reformers want to change the political system?

CHAPTER OVERVIEW

Corrupt!

Biased!

Two words people might use to describe elections in the early 1800s. In this chapter you will find out why some people were so angry about the electoral system and why others defended it.

A The Yorkshire election of 1807: a case study of the electoral system (pp. 31–32)

B Who could vote? (pp. 33–34)

C How up to date was the political system? (p. 35)

D Could the rich influence elections? (pp. 36–37)

E Why did politicians defend the electoral system? (p. 38)

F How powerful was the monarchy? (pp. 39–41)

G Review: why did reformers want to change the political system? (pp. 42–43)

A The Yorkshire election of 1807: a case study of the electoral system

SOURCE 2.1 William Hogarth (1697–1764) was a painter and engraver who excelled as a pictorial satirist, depicting both tragic and humorous scenes. He highlighted social issues in his pictures 'Beer Street' and 'Gin Lane', and the corrupt political system in 'The Election III, The Polling' (right)

ACTIVITY

1 What can you learn from Source 2.1 about eighteenth-century elections?

2 Read the account of the 1807 election in Yorkshire on page 32. To what extent does this show that Hogarth's illustration in Source 2.1 was an accurate picture of elections?

3 Make a list of the changes that you think a radical reformer in 1800 would want to make to the electoral system.

POLITICAL PARTIES

In the late eighteenth century, political parties were not as dominant, nor were they organised, as they are today. 'Party politics' is more a distinguishing feature of the period from the 1830s onwards. Before that there were smaller, looser groups in Parliament. Many MPs switched political allegiance, or were Independent, voting on specific issues according to their consciences or interests.

TORIES

The Tories originated around 1680. 'Tory' was a derogatory term for people who supported the King and the Church of England. The word is Irish in origin, meaning Catholic outlaws who lived in the middle, 'bog', counties of Ireland. The literal meaning is 'bog-trotter'.

WHIGS

The Whigs also originated around 1680. They were responsible for ousting James II from the throne in 1688. They were supporters of religious liberty and Parliament. The word is a term of abuse and refers to Scottish brigands called the Whiggamores, who roamed the Western Lowlands.

RADICALS

The word 'radical' comes from 'radix', the Latin word for 'root'. Radicals believed in making major reforms that would get right to the roots of society's problems rather than making minor changes. They therefore wanted big changes to the system of electing MPs to Parliament.

The candidates

Two MPs were to be elected for Yorkshire.

- William Wilberforce (Tory) – highly respected by supporters of both parties for his opposition to slavery; there was little doubt he would be elected.
- Lord Milton (Whig) – a member of a wealthy landowning family in Yorkshire.
- Lord Lascelles (Tory) – a member of a wealthy landowning family in Yorkshire.

The events

- Songs and pamphlets were written attacking the candidates. For example, Milton was attacked because of his youth (he was 21) and his Catholic sympathies. Lascelles, from Harewood House near Leeds, was accused of having links with slavery because his family owned sugar plantations in Barbados.
- Supporters of each candidate threatened one another. A riot broke out in Leeds after the Mayor boxed a young boy's ears for calling out 'Milton forever'.
- Dragoons (mounted soldiers) charged through the streets and raided people's houses on suspicion that they were Whig supporters.
- Milton and Lascelles tried to buy votes by providing free food and ale. Voters were transported to the poll in York in carts, carriages and barges at the candidates' expense. The 221 voters of West Gilling were conveyed to York and back at the cost to Milton of £1900. Milton booked 30 inns along the route and 100 houses in York, providing free accommodation for voters. Parties were held throughout the fifteen days of the election. One cost Lascelles £2630. At the Cross Keys in York, 60 gallons of free beer were drunk at his expense.

The result

- Wilberforce and Milton were elected MPs for Yorkshire.
- Milton was carried through the streets of York amidst post-election brawling. Tories tried to overturn his sedan chair but he was rescued by his supporters. An angry Tory threw a brick, which just missed Milton's head. At an inn outside York, the victorious Milton supporters ran up a bill of £2300.

The cost

- Wilberforce spent £28,200.
- Lascelles and Milton spent over £100,000 each.

CITY COLLEGE
LEARNING RESOURCE SERVICE

FOCUS ROUTE

Make detailed notes in answer to these questions:

1 What proportion and kinds of people could vote around 1800?
2 How fair was the electoral system in the counties?
3 How fair was the electoral system in the boroughs?

FREEHOLDER
Someone who owns land or property outright and forever.

B Who could vote?

In the period between 1780 and 1831, only about eleven per cent of adult men had the right to vote. The electoral system excluded all women and everyone under the age of 21 but also the vast majority of working-class men and even many middle-class men, such as shopkeepers, merchants and tradesmen. Roman Catholics and Dissenters (sometimes known as nonconformists), who belonged to a church other than the Church of England (such as Quakers, Methodists, Baptists), were not allowed to vote or become MPs. MPs also came from a very small group of men. Until 1858 MPs had to be property owners. There was also no salary for MPs (until 1911), which restricted the type of person who could afford to stand for Parliament.

This small number of voters, less than half a million in total, was not distributed evenly around the constituencies. Instead there were great variations in who could vote. There were two kinds of constituency – counties and boroughs. Counties were the shires, such as Yorkshire or Somerset. They each returned two MPs to Parliament, irrespective of their geographical size and population. For example, Rutland was much smaller in size than Yorkshire, but they still both returned two MPs.

In counties the electorate was restricted to '40 shilling FREEHOLDERS' – men who owned land or property worth 40 shillings (£2) a year in rent. This actually meant that quite a large number of men could vote in the counties because this figure of 40 shillings had been fixed in 1430 when it had been more than a year's pay for a well-paid craftsman such as a carpenter. Inflation over the centuries meant that the voters could be, in E. J. Evans's words, 'men of very considerable substance or they might own little more than a cabbage patch' (from *The Great Reform Act*, 1983).

In the boroughs (which had been towns in the fifteenth century) there was no uniform voting qualification. Instead the franchise, the right to vote, was varied and complex. In some towns, some working-class men were able to vote and there was a large electorate – for example, over 5000 voters in Liverpool, Bristol and Preston. However, such boroughs were rare. Only 7 out of a total of 202 had more than 5000 voters. In others there were scarcely any voters at all!

RUTLAND

YORKSHIRE

In boroughs the voters might be:

- all freemen – those who had been given the freedom of the town or had gained it through inheritance, marriage, apprenticeship or purchase
- potwallopers – householders who had a fireplace big enough to boil a cooking pot
- burgages – here it was really the houses or land that was important! The men who lived in them had the right to vote but if they moved house they would lose the right
- scot and lot – householders who paid local taxes such as church and poor rates.

SOURCE 2.2 A map to show the types of voters in various boroughs

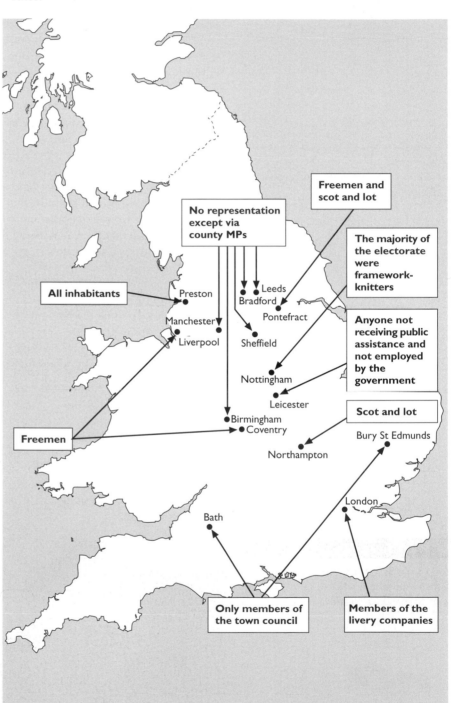

ACTIVITY

Start to compile a list of the reforms that you think a Radical politician in 1800 would want to make to the electoral system. You will continue this list in Sections C and D of this chapter.

FOCUS ROUTE

Make detailed notes in answer to these questions:

1 What were rotten boroughs?
2 How and why was the distribution of MPs out of date?

C How up to date was the political system?

As the electoral system had not changed for centuries, there was a lot that was out of date with the system. The most obvious problem was that of 'rotten boroughs'. These were boroughs that had been sizeable towns in earlier centuries but had shrunk dramatically by the late eighteenth century. However, they still had the right to return MPs.

There were 56 boroughs that had fewer than 50 voters each. For example, Old Sarum in Wiltshire had seven electors; most of Dunwich in Suffolk had fallen into the sea, leaving 38 houses and 14 voters; Gatton in Surrey had six voters; the Cornish towns of Camelford, East Looe and West Looe, Newport, St Germans and St Mawes between them had a population of less than 1000 in 1831, yet sent twelve MPs to Parliament.

SOURCE 2.3   Daniel Defoe, 1726

Old Sarum is an area about one hundred yards in diameter taking in the whole crown of a hill. Near this is one farm house, which is all that remains of any town in or near the place, for the encampment has no resemblance of a town; and yet this is called the borough of Old Sarum, and sends two members to Parliament; who these members can justly say they represent, would be hard for them to answer.

SOURCE 2.4   Sir Philip Francis, on being elected MP for Appleby (Cumbria) in 1802

I was unanimously elected by one elector to represent this ancient borough in Parliament . . . there was no other Candidate, no Opposition, no Poll demanded . . . On Friday, I shall quit this triumphant scene with flying colours, and a noble determination not to see it again in less than seven years.

The impact of the Industrial Revolution was also making the electoral system more out of date every year. In the 1400s northern counties such as Lancashire had small populations and so returned few MPs. However, by 1800 Lancashire towns were growing quickly as people moved to find work in the textile industries. In 1831, 1.3 million people lived in Lancashire but the county had just fourteen MPs (two for the county and twelve from boroughs). In contrast, Cornwall had a population of only 300,000 but had a total of 42 MPs (two for the county and forty for boroughs). Other rapidly growing parts of the north and Midlands had the same problem. Towns such as Manchester, Leeds, Birmingham and Bradford had no MPs of their own (although men from these towns voted in county elections), simply because they had not been important towns 400 years earlier.

ACTIVITY

Add to the list of reforms that you think a Radical politician in 1800 would want to make to the electoral system.

SOURCE 2.5   Old Sarum today

FOCUS ROUTE

Make detailed notes in answer to these questions:

1 What were pocket boroughs?
2 Why were landowners able to influence elections?
3 Why were two-thirds of MPs elected unopposed?

EXAMPLES OF POCKET BOROUGHS

The Cecil family controlled Stamford.
The Montague family controlled Huntingdon.
The Duke of Devonshire controlled Knaresborough.
Lord Harewood controlled Ripon.

D Could the rich influence elections?

The illustration above shows the Duke of Newcastle, one of the wealthiest men in the country, handing out parliamentary seats. Newcastle controlled elections in a number of boroughs and he could simply choose who would be the MP. He owned so much property in these boroughs that the majority of the voters were living or working on his land and so they voted according to his wishes for fear of losing their homes or their jobs. In other words, these constituencies were in Newcastle's pocket and so they were called pocket boroughs. Newcastle wasn't the only nobleman to control pocket boroughs. In 1800 about half of the MPs in Parliament were there because of such patronage.

Landowners who held constituencies in their pockets could check whether electors had voted for their chosen candidate or whether they had voted against their instructions. This was because voting was not by secret ballot, but publicly on the hustings, a platform on which electors had to call out the name of the candidate for whom they were voting. The votes were then recorded in poll books and were available for anyone to look at.

Another problem resulting from pocket boroughs was that many elections were uncontested. General elections were held every seven years or on the death of a monarch. However, in twelve general elections between 1784 and 1831, only 30 per cent of seats were contested on average. The highest percentage of contested elections was 38 per cent in 1818. The major reason why there were so few contests was the system of patronage, which enabled wealthy landowners to choose who would be the MPs for the boroughs in their pockets. For example, once the Duke of Newcastle had made his choice, his political opponents knew there was no point in standing in the election. They could not win.

SOURCE 2.6 An extract from The Report of the Select Committee on Bribery at Elections, Parliamentary Papers, 1835, quoting an interview in which a voter is being questioned by an investigator into bribery at elections

Q. Have you ever known intimidation practised to any extent at a county election?
A. Yes, by landlords over tenants.
Q. In what ways have they exercised that intimidation?
A. By insisting upon their voting as the landlord wished, and it was perfectly understood by them that they would lose their farms if they voted contrary to the wishes and inclinations of their landlords.

Out with 'em! out with their Beds, I kept them in debt on purpose, they'll vote according to conscience will they?!!! I'll let 'em know that they are nothing but his Lordships Slaves — and I am slave driver.

Do not be downcast my lads, there are other House's besides his Lordships, I'll not desert you altho' we have lost the Election!

TREGONY St AUSTLE

Freedom & Purity of Election!!! Showing the Necessity of Reform in the Close Boroughs.

Pub. April 23rd 1820 by G Humphrey 27 St James's St.
23.06. 1820

SOURCE 2.7 This political cartoon by George Cruikshank refers to the election in Tregony, Cornwall, in 1820 when tenants refused to vote for their landlord's candidate

George Cruikshank, 1792–1878
Cruikshank was an artist and caricaturist. He drew for satirical magazines such as the *Scourge* (1811–16), and the *Meteor* (1813–14) and produced etchings for Grimm's *Popular Tales* (1824–26) as well as for Dickens. He became famous for his political cartoons and caricatures, such as those of Napoleon and the Prince Regent (George IV). He used his skill as an artist to focus on moral issues such as alcohol abuse and the use of the death penalty for forging banknotes.

■ **Learning trouble spot**

Using cartoons as historical sources
Students often underestimate the value of cartoons as historical sources simply because they are called cartoons. The word 'cartoon' is misleading because we associate it with *Tom and Jerry* or other TV cartoons. However, cartoons like Cruikshank's drawing recording the Tregony election (Source 2.7) were not intended purely as entertainment. Whilst they did try to amuse, they also made serious points about politics or social issues, just like cartoonists such as Low in the 1930s or Steve Bell today.

We are fortunate that in the eighteenth and nineteenth centuries, there was a prolific number of artists illustrating events, issues and personalities of the time. Their pictures reflect the ideas and attitudes of the artists but also mirror those of sections of society. Some had a powerful influence on raising awareness amongst the public and politicians.

ACTIVITY

1 Describe what happened to the tenants in Source 2.7.
2 How useful do you think a cartoon like this is for historians studying eighteenth-century elections?
3 Re-read Source 2.6. Which of the two sources provides more reliable evidence of corruption at elections?

ACTIVITY

Add to the list of reforms that you think a Radical politician in 1800 would want to make to the electoral system.

FOCUS ROUTE

Make a list of the reasons why opponents of parliamentary reform wished to maintain the 'old constitution'.

E Why did politicians defend the electoral system?

It is sometimes difficult for us to understand why something that we think is wrong or out of date should be defended, often passionately. There are many issues like this in history and in modern politics and society. For example, should Catholics be emancipated; should women have the vote; should Ireland be reunited; should the House of Lords be abolished; should fox hunting be banned? These are often termed controversial or contentious issues. Often behind them is the argument: 'It's tradition. It has been like this for centuries, so why change it?'

It is easy to assume that the people opposing change to the electoral system were simply being selfish by defending their own power. However, there were those who genuinely believed there was no need for change and that the system could not be improved. Despite the strong case for parliamentary reform, there was support for the existing system, the 'old constitution', particularly from landowning Tories. Many of them genuinely believed that no other class was capable of ruling. Land was power, and they had the skills and experience to use this power. After all, the vast majority of the people were uneducated and it was felt dangerous to put power in the hands of 'the ignorant masses'. Therefore supporters of the existing system felt that the ruling classes could represent the interests of all the other sectors of society. Those who could not vote still had the chance to make their views and opinions known to the voters at the hustings or during the election campaigns. The composition of Parliament was also extending beyond the wealthy landowners as overseas merchants, factory owners, doctors, lawyers and ex-military men were taking seats. In short, it could be argued that Parliament was more representative than critics claimed, and that many people were content to leave power in the hands of 'the ruling classes'. After all, in 1800 very few people, even the most radical, envisaged a democratic society in which all adults could vote.

Even the rotten and pocket boroughs were defended. They had enabled politicians of outstanding ability (like Pitt, Liverpool, Canning and Peel) to rise to the top while they were still young. If such men had been obliged to wait until they had fought and won elections against opponents, it might have been much longer before they were able to serve their country in Parliament and in government.

SOURCE 2.8 The Duke of Wellington, then Prime Minister, defending the 'old constitution' in a speech in the House of Lords, 1830

I never read or heard of any measure ... which in any degree satisfies my mind that the state of representation can be improved ... I will go further and say, that the Legislature [Parliament] and the system of representation possesses the full and entire confidence of the country ... Under these circumstances, I am not prepared to bring forward any measure of reform ... I shall always feel it my duty to resist such measures when proposed by others.

ACTIVITY

Write a speech from the point of view of a Tory landowner who wishes to retain the political system as it is. Build into your speech the main demands made by reformers and show why they are not needed.

■ 2A The power of the monarchy and Parliament c.1760

MONARCHS 1760–1901

George III 1760–1820
George IV 1820–30 (also Prince Regent 1811–20)
William IV 1830–37
Victoria 1837–1901

ACTIVITY

The period between 1760 and 1851 was crucial in the changing balance of power of monarch and Parliament. This was partly a result of long-term changes in society and in attitudes to government, and partly due to the accidents of events and personalities.

1 What does each of incidents 1–8 and the Queen Caroline affair tell you about the balance of power between monarch and Parliament?
2 Draw and annotate a new 'balance of power' chart for c.1850.

TALKING POINTS

1 Changes in warfare, religion and the nature of society all helped to reduce the power of the monarchy and increase the power of a government based in Parliament. Suggest why these three factors were important.
2 From the 1790s to the 1820s, Britain experienced a long war with France and also major social change. How well-equipped were George III and George IV to provide leadership in this period, and why was this significant for the long-term power of the monarchy?

Monarchy
- The king chose his own ministers.
- The king made the major decisions on government policy, especially on foreign affairs, although he did so on the advice of his ministers.
- He controlled the election of about 30 MPs and could give titles and important posts in the army and navy to those who supported him. This was a good way of building support for the king's policies and ministers.

Parliament
- The king could not rule without Parliament. He had to call Parliament because Parliament renewed his income each year.
- Parliament could force the king to dismiss a minister. This meant the king had to choose ministers who could work with Parliament.
- There had to be a general election at least every seven years.

By the time George III came to the throne in 1760 the balance of power between monarch and Parliament was roughly equal – they worked in partnership. The monarch was at the centre of government but so too was the Prime Minister. To be successful a Prime Minister needed the support of both monarch and Parliament. Losing the support of either would lead to the Prime Minister losing power and eventually his office.

Incident 1

In the 1770s George III argued that there should be no agreement with the rebellious American colonists, even after the clear defeat of British forces and the Declaration of Independence. In 1780 in Parliament an MP called John Dunning proposed a resolution that 'the influence of the crown has increased, is increasing and ought to be diminished'.

Incident 2

In 1783 George III appointed William Pitt the Younger as Prime Minister at the age of 24. Pitt was not expected to last a week but the King's manipulation of patronage gave Pitt sufficient support to survive long enough to establish himself and prove his worth. George was able to ensure that Charles Fox, whom he disliked, did not become Prime Minister.

Incident 3

In 1801 Pitt resigned as Prime Minister. A major factor in his resignation was his desire to pass an Act granting Catholics political rights, which was opposed by George III who did not want Catholics to have equal rights with members of the Church of England. Pitt returned as Prime Minister shortly afterwards but the question of votes for Catholics was dropped.

Incident 4

In 1820 George IV wanted Parliament to support his wish to divorce his wife, Caroline, but the Prime Minister, Lord Liverpool, refused to do the King's bidding. Two years later, Liverpool appointed George Canning as Foreign Secretary, despite the King's detestation of Canning.

Incident 5

In 1827 Liverpool fell ill and needed to be replaced as Prime Minister. In the past the choice had been the king's but George IV passed the responsibility to the Cabinet.

Incident 6

In 1832 William IV was asked by the Prime Minister, Lord Grey, to be prepared to create a significant number of peers to ensure that a bill reforming the electoral system was passed by the House of Lords. William IV said that 'as a sovereign it was his duty to set his own feelings and prejudices aside'.

Incident 7

In 1839 the Whig Prime Minister, Lord Melbourne, resigned and it was expected that the Tory leader, Robert Peel, would become Prime Minister. However, when Peel requested that Queen Victoria replace the ladies of her bedchamber who had Whig connections with Tory-supporting ladies, the Queen refused and Peel did not take office. Melbourne continued until 1841 when Peel finally became Prime Minister despite Victoria's initial hostility.

Incident 8

During Victoria's reign she had to accept politicians as Prime Minister despite her personal dislike or hostility towards them. Palmerston was Prime Minister from 1855–58 and from 1859–65, and Gladstone was Prime Minister four times despite the Queen's preference for others.

The Queen Caroline affair

George IV's adult life coincided with a series of national crises – long wars with France and riots and threats of revolution at home. A different character might have played a positive role in the politics of the period but George's inadequacies ensured that the responsibility for steering Britain through these years of real crisis lay more and more with elected politicians and with Parliament. When George died in 1830, *The Times* said, 'Never was there a human being less respected than this late king ... what eye weeps for him?'

In 1820, the 'Queen Caroline affair', as it is often known, emerged to pose the government yet another problem.

The Prince of Wales had been forced into a marriage of convenience for financial reasons in 1795. He had no urge to marry because he was contented with his mistress, Lady Jersey, and he had also secretly married a widow, Mrs Fitzherbert, in 1785. However, under the Royal Marriages Act this was an illegal marriage because the Prince had been under 25 years old and had not obtained the King's consent.

Even before her marriage, Caroline was accused of being promiscuous and vulgar. The Prince's words on first meeting Caroline were reported as, 'I feel faint, a glass of brandy if you please'. He is supposed to have spent his wedding night drunk on the floor and his mistress, Lady Jersey, was in attendance throughout. After two or three weeks at most they did not live together as man and wife. However, Caroline had become pregnant, and gave birth to a daughter, Charlotte, in 1795.

Caroline became a social outcast and eventually left England in 1814. She settled in Italy with her lover but in January 1820 George III died, the Prince became King George IV and Caroline returned to England, hoping to be crowned Queen. Probably to her surprise, she was greeted with great enthusiasm by crowds lining her route to London. Her popularity owed more to dislike of the new King than to support for Caroline. George's drinking (mixing alcohol and laudanum), love affairs and extravagances had made him deeply unpopular. One newspaper described him when he became king as 'over head and heels in debt and disgrace ... a man who has just closed half a century without one single claim on the gratitude of his country'.

George was desperate to stop Caroline being crowned Queen. He insisted that the government introduce a bill into Parliament depriving her of her rank and dissolving the marriage, but the bill did not win enough support and had to be withdrawn. This gave Caroline the chance to play the role of a wronged woman, and she became identified with the principles of justice and freedom. Protest meetings were held in different parts of the country, and petitions of support sent; letters were written to her from groups of workers who identified with her oppression. For a brief moment it appeared that Liverpool's

SOURCE 2.9 George, Prince Regent 1811–20 and King George IV, 1820–30

SOURCE 2.10 A cartoon by George Cruikshank entitled 'The Radical Ladder'. It shows Queen Caroline reaching for the crown with the help of Radical support and agitation

government was in danger, more than at any other time since 1812. The new King was so angry at the failure to pass the bill that he threatened to dismiss Liverpool as Prime Minister.

The affair ended in farce as Caroline tried to force her way into Westminster Abbey in July for the coronation ceremony but was resisted by prize-fighters hired to keep her out. Eyewitnesses claimed she behaved like a deranged woman and her popularity fell away swiftly. She died just a month later. 'The Queen Caroline affair' was a crisis for Lord Liverpool's government, but it rode the storm. As for the monarchy, it had never been held in such great contempt.

SOURCE 2.11 The Annual Register, 1820. The Annual Register was a published list of important events of the year

Political party spirit made the presence of the Queen acceptable to many, who cared nothing about her, except so far as she was a means of annoyance to ministers ... The Radicals naturally became her partisans; because they had no better means of decrying the King, than by the eager defence of her cause.

SOURCE 2.12 L. J. Jennings (ed.) *The correspondence and diaries of John Wilson Croker*, 1884. John Wilson Croker was a Tory MP, a friend of Peel and Secretary to the Admiralty, 1809–30

The King wants the Ministers to pledge themselves to a divorce, which they will not do ... He is furious, and says they have deceived him ... The King has certainly intimated intentions of looking for new and more useful servants.

SOURCE 2.13 N. Gash, *Aristocracy and the People: Britain 1815–1865*, 1979

At the very dawn of recovery, the administration was reduced to its lowest point of unpopularity and political weakness, and even threatened for a time with an end to its existence.

SOURCE 2.14 A caricature of Caroline of Brunswick with her Italian lover, Bergami, published in 1821

ACTIVITY

1 Why would workers write letters of support and thousands pray for the Queen?
2 Using the text and Sources 2.11–2.14, explain why Queen Caroline's behaviour was seen as a potential threat to the government.

CITY COLLEGE LEARNING RESOURCE CENTRE

G Review: why did reformers want to change the political system?

By 1800 Britain was changing rapidly, yet the electoral system was still essentially the same as it had been in the sixteenth century. It simply had not adapted to the immense economic and social changes known as the Industrial Revolution. The late eighteenth and early nineteenth centuries therefore saw many riots – the manifestations of those who had no other way of expressing their grievances or influencing the government. Radicals said that the only solution was a major reform of the out-of-date and unrepresentative parliamentary system. They hoped this would lead to the election of MPs who truly understood the problems of ordinary people and who were committed to social reforms.

Between the late 1760s and the early 1780s various groups petitioned for the reform of Parliament. John Wilkes and then Christopher Wyvill began to organise public opinion and exert extra-parliamentary pressure.

John Wilkes was an MP. He published the *North Briton*, a newspaper in which, in 1763, he openly criticised the King. He was arrested for sedition, but released, and fled to France. When he returned, in 1768, he was elected MP for Middlesex. Parliament, however, declared that his opponent had won. This treatment led to public support for him and a press campaign on his behalf using the slogan 'Wilkes and Liberty'. These events stimulated demands from the Radicals for reform of the electoral system.

Wyvill, on the other hand, was a moderate gentleman and clergyman from Yorkshire, who founded the Yorkshire Association in 1779 to press for reform. He encouraged other gentlemen to support his demands, but after some initial success, his influence was limited to his own county and Middlesex. He was involved in organising extra-parliamentary pressure throughout his life, though after 1784 he hoped that Pitt's reforming ministry might satisfy his demands. It is important to understand that men like Wyvill were seeking reform not revolution. They saw government as a partnership between the monarchy, the aristocracy and the House of Commons. There was no desire to abolish the monarchy, erode aristocratic privileges, or give power to the lower orders of society. They simply wished to extend the franchise to the middle classes as a way of buttressing the existing system.

Even within Parliament there were moves to introduce moderate reform. In 1783 a minority of MPs voted for parliamentary reform, and in 1785 William Pitt had the support of 174 MPs when he proposed to abolish 36 of the smallest parliamentary boroughs, and transfer the seats to London and the counties. He also proposed an extension of the franchise to some COPYHOLDERS and LEASEHOLDERS, which would have expanded the electorate a little. Although it was considered a mild reform, it was rejected by the House of Commons.

Because of failure inside Parliament, pressure for reform continued from outside Parliament. However, reformers had to face vested interests, such as the powerful, rich landowners and the aristocracy, who wished to maintain the system as it was because it suited them and served their needs. They were supported by the 'squirearchy' who adopted a paternalistic approach, believing they were capable of representing the interests of other classes in society and that therefore 'ordinary' people did not need the vote. However, these ideas were becoming dated with the major rise in population and the transition from a predominantly agricultural to an industrial economy. One effect of this was the increasing economic importance of the middle classes as producers of wealth. Many would argue that by the end of the eighteenth century the middle classes were more important than the landowners, but that this importance was not matched by political power.

COPYHOLDER
Someone who owns land or property by right of holding a copy of an ancient document giving them ownership (e.g. a copy of a manor court roll). Tenure was often precarious as many of the original documents, which could date back some two hundred years, were lost. Some copyholders owned fairly large amounts of land and were quite wealthy, but many owned only small amounts of land and were relatively poor.

LEASEHOLDER
Someone who owns land or property on a lease that lasts for a set number of years, after which time they cease to own the property (e.g. a 99-year lease).

To what extent do you think that the electoral system increased the likelihood of revolution in the years before 1832?

■ 2B The main elements of the electoral system before 1832

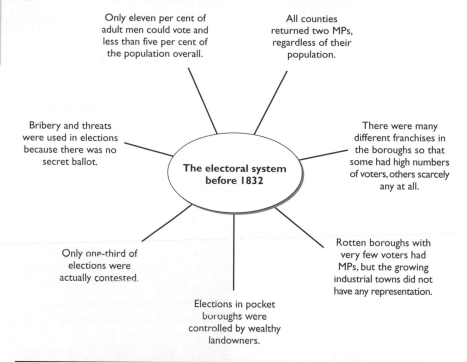

Only eleven per cent of adult men could vote and less than five per cent of the population overall.

All counties returned two MPs, regardless of their population.

Bribery and threats were used in elections because there was no secret ballot.

The electoral system before 1832

There were many different franchises in the boroughs so that some had high numbers of voters, others scarcely any at all.

Only one-third of elections were actually contested.

Rotten boroughs with very few voters had MPs, but the growing industrial towns did not have any representation.

Elections in pocket boroughs were controlled by wealthy landowners.

ACTIVITY

Look at Chart 2B above.
1 Put yourself in the shoes of a Radical politician. Which three of these problems do you think should be reformed first?
2 If you had been a politician concerned about the possibility of revolution, which two aspects of the electoral system would you have been prepared to reform to reduce the possibility of revolution?

KEY POINTS FROM CHAPTER 2

Why did reformers want to change the political system?
1   Until 1832 only eleven per cent of adult men had the right to vote.
2   There were major variations in the franchise, the right to vote, in different parts of the country.
3   The rapidly growing industrial areas and the middle classes were under-represented in Parliament in comparison with the agricultural regions and rural landowners.
4   There were many opportunities for corruption because voting did not take place in secret.
5   There was growing demand for reform of the electoral system but there was also considerable opposition to reform amongst the landed class.
6   The power of the monarchy was in decline as a result of a combination of long-term changes in society and the inadequacy of individual monarchs in the period 1790–1830.

3

How close was Britain to revolution 1783–1815?

CHAPTER OVERVIEW

Why do people protest?

SOURCE 3.1 The Jarrow Crusade of 1936: unemployed men from Jarrow in north-east England walked to London to protest about high levels of unemployment

SOURCE 3.2 Car workers demonstrating against rising prices but no wage increases, 1977

SOURCE 3.3 Environmental protesters campaigning against the proposed Newbury bypass, 1998

ACTIVITY

1 Sources 3.1–3.3 show three protests during the twentieth century.
   a) Why did each of these groups protest?
   b) How did they protest?
   c) What alternative methods do you think they could have used?
2 Sources 3.4–3.5 describe protests in the late eighteenth and early nineteenth centuries. What similarities and differences are there between these protests and those of the twentieth century?
3 Using the information in Sources 3.4–3.5, copy and complete the table below by placing each protest under the appropriate heading. Some may match more than one heading. Two examples have been done for you.

Reasons for protest in the late eighteenth and early nineteenth centuries

Reasons for protest	Example
Political	
Economic	theatre prices
Social	
Religious	anti-Jewish

4 Does the evidence from Sources 3.4 and 3.5 suggest to you that Britain was close to revolution?

SOURCE 3.4 Benjamin Franklin, the American statesman, writer and scientist, writing about Britain in 1760

I have seen, within a year, riots in the country about corn, riots about elections, riots about workhouses, riots of colliers [coal miners], riots of weavers ... riots of Wilkesites [supporters of Wilkes, a political Radical] ... riots of smugglers, in which customs house officers and excisemen [men who tried to prevent smuggling] have been murdered [and] the King's armed vessels and troops fired at.

SOURCE 3.5 I. Gilmour, *Violence in Eighteenth-Century England*, 1992, on the extent of rioting in the late eighteenth century

Englishmen and Englishwomen rioted against turnpikes, enclosures and high food prices, against Roman Catholics, the Irish and Dissenters, against ... Jews, the impeachment of politicians, press gangs ... and the Militia Act, against theatre prices, foreign actors, pimps, bawdy houses, surgeons, French footmen and alehouse keepers, against the gibbets in the Edgeware Road and public whippings, against the imprisonment of London's chief magistrates, against the Excise, against the Cider Tax ... against workhouses and industrial employers, against the rumoured destruction of cathedral spires, even against a change in the calendar.

There were riots at elections and after them, in prisons and outside them, in schools and colleges, at executions, at factories and workplaces, in the law courts at Westminster Hall, outside Parliament and within the palace of Westminster, in theatres, in brothels, in a cathedral close and in Pall Mall at the gates of St James's Palace.

Throughout the period 1783–1815 protests like these made leaders in Britain worried there would be a revolution, just like there had been in America and France. In this chapter you will investigate why they were so worried and decide how close Britain really was to revolution.

A When and why did the protests happen? Was it revolution or 'bread and cheese' that people wanted? (pp. 46–47)

B Did the outbreak of the French Revolution increase the likelihood of revolution? (pp. 48–51)

C How revolutionary were the British reform groups? (pp. 52–53)

D Did the war with France increase the likelihood of revolution? (pp. 54–55)

E How did the government deal with the protests? (pp. 56–57)

F Why was there no revolution in Britain? (pp. 58–59)

When and why did the protests happen? Was it revolution or 'bread and cheese' that people wanted?

FOCUS ROUTE

Using the evidence in this section, summarise as bullet points:

a) the main causes of riots and protests during the period 1780–1815

b) the ways in which people protested.

ACTIVITY

1 Look at the illustrations and accompanying text on these two pages. What evidence is there of the possibility of revolution in the period 1780–1815?

2 What evidence is there that the riots and protests were about social and economic rather than political issues?

3 What are the links between social and economic protest and political protest in these events?

In 1780 the Gordon Riots began in London when a crowd organised by the Protestant Association marched to present a petition to Parliament against toleration for Catholics. MPs refused to debate the petition, so following some fiery anti-Catholic speeches by Lord George Gordon, riots broke out in which houses of Catholics were attacked. The rioting lasted for a week until the army brought order, although they caused most of the 300 deaths resulting from the riots.

In 1783 food riots in Halifax broke out because bread prices were very high. Crowds from nearby weaving villages gathered, led by Thomas Spencer. They besieged the corn merchants and forced them to sell their oats and corn at reduced prices. Spencer and a fellow protester were executed.

In 1791 a mob ran amok in Birmingham for three days. They attacked and burned houses, largely of nonconformists, and released prisoners from the town prison. These events followed a dinner held by middle-class reformers in Birmingham to celebrate the anniversary of the fall of the Bastille in Paris.

In 1792 demonstrations were held in Sheffield to celebrate the victory of revolutionary France against the Austrians at Valmy. A procession of over 5,000 people took place. One banner showed the MP Burke riding on a pig because his book denouncing the French Revolution referred to the 'swinish multitude'. Another banner had a picture of the Home Secretary (Henry Dundas) as half ass, half man.

In 1792 in County Durham, demonstrations were held in Barnard Castle. The words 'No King', 'Liberty' and 'Equality' were written on the market cross.

In 1795 there were food riots across the country, in places such as Nottingham, Gloucester, Newcastle, Carlisle, Cornwall, Cambridge and Burford. These riots were largely due to shortages of grain. People feared famine and high prices, and grain and other food shipments were seized by crowds and sold off at low prices. In Carlisle grain from a warehouse and a ship was taken to the town hall and sold off cheaply.

In 1811–12 there were Luddite riots in Lancashire, Yorkshire, Nottinghamshire and Cheshire. These involved the smashing of new machinery, which was felt to be taking away jobs. In some areas, protesters set fire to mills. In Leeds in January 1812, Oatland Mill was set alight in protest against a newly installed gig mill (a machine for raising and trimming the nap on finished cloth, a job previously done by croppers and requiring much skill).

B Did the outbreak of the French Revolution increase the likelihood of revolution?

France, revolution and war, 1789–1815

FOCUS ROUTE

Using the information in Sections B–D, summarise in note form the evidence that:

a) the French Revolution increased the likelihood of a revolution in Britain

b) there was no increase in the likelihood of a revolution in Britain as a result of the French Revolution.

ACTIVITY

Study Sources 3.6–3.8. What effects do you think news of events like these would have had between 1789 and 1792 on:

a) members of the British Parliament
b) the British royal family
c) campaigners for reform of the constitution in Britain
d) working people in Britain?

SOURCE 3.6 The storming of the Bastille, 14 July 1789. The Bastille was a prison and also a royal fortress where weapons were stored. It was attacked by the mob, and besieged for two hours until the governor surrendered. Its fall was a major blow to the King's authority

SOURCE 3.7 The attack on the Tuileries Palace, 10 August 1792. The initial changes brought by the revolution had not satisfied many and a crowd of about 20,000 attacked the royal palace, setting it on fire and killing 600 of the guards. The royal family escaped

SOURCE 3.8 Reforms introduced by the Constituent Assembly in France, 1790–91

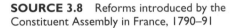

1790
- All noble titles abolished

1791
- New constitution reduced the king's powers so that he could no longer make laws

- Legislative Assembly set up, elected by all men who paid direct taxes equal to two days' pay for a labourer

How was the start of the Revolution viewed in Britain?

ACTIVITY

Look at the reactions to the Revolution shown here.

1 What conclusion do you reach about how people felt about the events in France in 1789?
2 Does there seem to be any evidence that Britain was likely to follow the French example?

ACTIVITY

What evidence of the potential for revolution can you find in the lives and work of the men featured on this page and on page 51?

Some important politicians, writers and philosophers of the early nineteenth century

William Pitt (1759–1806)

Pitt was the younger son of the Earl of Chatham (Pitt the Elder). He was educated at Cambridge, and became a barrister in 1780 and an MP in 1781. In 1782 he became Chancellor of the Exchequer and in 1783 Prime Minister, aged just 24. His government gained a majority in the general election in 1784, and he became the favourite of the King, Parliament and the country. He was in power during the years of the French Revolution and revolutionary wars, but resigned in 1801 due to George III's unwillingness to grant Catholic Emancipation, which would have allowed Catholics to become MPs. In 1800 he introduced the Act of Union, which united Ireland with Britain. He became Prime Minister again in 1804 at a time when Napoleon was threatening to invade Britain.

Charles James Fox (1749–1806)

Fox was educated at Eton and Oxford. He began his political career as a supporter of Lord North, and became an MP for Midhurst when he was only nineteen. In 1774 he fell out with Lord North and joined Rockingham's Whigs in opposition to the government's policy over the American colonies. Fox became a champion of the cause of liberty, freedom of the press, political reform and the reduction of the power of the monarchy (he was very antagonistic towards George III). He was a great wit, and a gambler who was constantly in debt. He became Foreign Secretary for short spells in 1782 and 1783. Fox was Pitt's chief opponent, and he enthusiastically supported the French Revolution. He disapproved of the war with France and withdrew from political life between May 1797 and January 1800. He became Foreign Secretary briefly again in 1806 after Pitt's death.

Richard Price (1723–91)

Price was a Unitarian minister in Hackney, East London. A leading Dissenter, economist and philosopher, he advocated European 'confederacy' as a means to end the war. He was a leading campaigner for parliamentary reform and for nonconformists to have the same civil rights as Anglicans. It was largely due to his sermons praising the French revolutionaries that Edmund Burke wrote his denunciation *Reflections on the Revolution in France*, which was also intended to be an attack on Price and the English Dissenters.

Edmund Burke (1729–97)

Born and educated in Dublin, Burke was a lawyer, political journalist, and a Whig MP. He attacked the power of the crown under George III and defended the American colonists' struggle for independence from Britain. In his *Reflections on the Revolution in France*, published in 1790, he argued that the revolution was an attack on religion, property and society and the traditions of the monarchy and the Church. He predicted the revolution would turn to tyranny and anarchy, and he tried to persuade the British not to follow the French example. Burke was supported by middle- and upper-class people who feared an uprising from the working classes.

Thomas Paine (1737–1809)

Born in Norfolk, Paine became an excise officer, but was dismissed for arguing for a pay-rise for officers as a way of ending corruption in the service. He emigrated to Pennsylvania in 1774, where he wrote *Common Sense* (1776) in which he demanded the American colonies should have complete independence. Returning to Britain in 1788, he joined the opposition to Pitt's government. His *The Rights of Man* was published in 1791 as a reply to Burke. It sold 200,000 copies very quickly. Paine supported the French Revolution and demanded radical political reform in Britain. He advocated the setting up of a republic in Britain, family allowances, old age pensions, compulsory free elementary education, maternity benefits, and a graduated income tax. His ideas led to Pitt's government suppressing his book as dangerous and seditious.

Paine argued that all men were created equal and possessed inalienable rights, including the rights to life, liberty, property and the pursuit of happiness, and that no government could remove those rights. He also argued that to maintain those rights the authority of those in power must be limited and must be subject to the sovereignty of the people. Paine fled to France in 1792, where he became a member of the National Convention. He was arrested for opposing the execution of Louis XVI, and he died in America in 1809.

CONSTITUTIONAL MONARCHY
A form of government in which the monarch's powers are clearly defined, and limited by a parliament.

The impact of the Revolution

The first reaction from the majority of most informed Englishmen to the fall of the Bastille in 1789, as well as to the abolition of the remains of the French feudal system and the establishment of a new CONSTITUTIONAL MONARCHY, was largely friendly. Even George III recognised the justification for the enforced limitation of the power of the French monarchy. Pitt anticipated the establishment of a stable regime in France that would provide the French with the benefits of a constitutional monarchy he believed Britain enjoyed. Amongst those in Parliament the reaction was generally one of modified enthusiasm and there was relatively little fear amongst those in power that Britain would follow France's example. Amongst the radicals outside Parliament the reaction was less restrained, and led to the revival and establishment of reform groups and clubs. The mushrooming of these groups and their success at spreading what were seen as revolutionary ideas changed attitudes towards the events in France, especially after the execution of the King and Queen of France and the beginning of what became known as the Terror. As reform groups emerged and rhetoric grew, fears increased. Whether these reform groups had the potential to start a revolution in Britain on the scale of the one in France is the question you will consider in the next section.

CITY COLLEGE
LEARNING RESOURCE CENTRE

C How revolutionary were the British reform groups?

FOCUS ROUTE

From the information in this section, copy and complete this table to summarise the potential for revolution among the reform societies.

Name of group	Aims	Type of member	Potentially revolutionary? (with reasons)
The Revolution Society			
The Society of the Friends of the People			
Society for Constitutional Information			
London Corresponding Society			
Sheffield Constitutional Society			

ACTIVITY

It is 1792, and the King is concerned about possible revolution in Britain. You have been asked by the Home Secretary to prepare a report for the King on the potential for revolution in Britain. Use the following information about the reform societies, and the map in Source 3.9, to write a report of about 500 words in which you make a judgement about whether revolution is likely and possible.

During the 1790s a number of organisations were formed throughout the country to campaign for parliamentary reform. Following the start of the revolution in France, old reform clubs re-emerged and new groups were formed.

The Revolution Society (1788)
This society first met in 1788 to celebrate the Glorious Revolution of 1688 when Parliament ejected James II and invited William and Mary to become joint monarchs. In 1789 it sent a message of congratulations to the French and urged that 'the two first kingdoms in the world' should unite to promote the cause of freedom.

The Society of the Friends of the People (1792)
A group of younger Whigs, including Charles Grey, later to be Prime Minister, formed this group to press for constitutional reform. It was made up of mainly middle-class Whig supporters. Its annual subscription was a guinea and a half (about £1.50), at a time when a working man might expect to earn about £1 a week. Its members included the playwright Richard Sheridan and the brewer Samuel Whitbread.

Society for Constitutional Information (1780)
This society was founded in 1780 with the aim of distributing free pamphlets on reform. In 1782 at its annual dinner, toasts were proposed to 'the majesty of the people', 'America in arms' and 'despotism at our feet'. One of its leaders, Dr John Jebb, who believed in equal representation, annual parliaments and universal male suffrage, also held that carefully planned public agitation was the way to achieve these aims. In 1791 it re-formed, and appealed to a wider public than groups such as the one to which Grey belonged. Its members included Thomas Paine and the painter George Romney.

London Corresponding Society (1792)
This society was founded by Thomas Hardy, a shoemaker, and chaired by Francis Place, a London tailor, radical thinker and writer, and supporter of Radical MPs in the Commons. It appealed to working people, and its membership was largely from the working classes. It charged only 1d (less than ½p) a week to join, with a 1s (5p) entrance fee. It was divided into branches

CORRESPONDING SOCIETIES

For a very detailed account of the corresponding societies and their activities during the period 1792–99 you should read Chapter 5 of E. P. Thompson, *The Making of the English Working Class*, 1963.

that met weekly, and each branch sent two delegates to a general committee, which met weekly also. It corresponded with other societies in industrial cities such as Sheffield, Manchester and Leeds, as well as those in towns like Rochester and Bath. The membership proclaimed solidarity with the French revolutionaries. In their 'Address to the People' in 1792 they promised 'taxes diminished, the necessaries of life more within the reach of the poor, youth better educated, prisons less crowded ... old age better provided for'. As part of their admission, members had to agree that all adult persons should have the vote in parliamentary elections.

Sheffield Constitutional Society

In 1792 the Deputy Adjutant General, on a trip to the north of England to check on troop dispositions, wrote that he 'found that the seditious doctrines of Paine ... had extended to a degree beyond my conception'. He said that 2500 of the lowest mechanics were enrolled in an association where 'they read the most violent publications, and comment on them, as well as on their own correspondence not only with the dependent societies in the towns and villages in the vicinity, but with those ... in other parts of the kingdom'. In May 1792 it reported nearly 10,000 signatures on a national petition for manhood suffrage.

SOURCE 3.9   A map showing the location of provincial corresponding societies as listed by E. P. Thompson in *The Making of the English Working Class*, 1963

ACTIVITY

Look at the map in Source 3.9.

1 Does this spread of societies provide evidence of the potential for revolution in Britain?
2 It is early 1792, and you are Prime Minister of Britain. A French minister has just made the following promise about British radicals: 'We will fly to their succour. We will make a descent in the island. We will lodge 50,000 caps of liberty. The tyranny of their government will be destroyed.' You have the following choices:
   a) ignore the threats as they are just revolutionary propaganda for French consumption
   b) tighten up security by suppressing political societies in Britain
   c) suggest your government introduce some mild reform of Parliament.
Make your choice and justify it, in a historically correct context, to the rest of your group.

D Did the war with France increase the likelihood of revolution?

In November 1792 the French government offered to aid any peoples in Europe wishing to revolt against their governments. Also in that month the French occupied the Austrian Netherlands and therefore controlled the River Scheldt, a major waterway into Europe. This affected Britain's European trade, and was potentially a serious threat to Britain's economy. Pitt began to see the potential dangers of French 'annexation' in Europe. On 1 February 1793 France declared war on Britain, Spain and the United Provinces.

SOURCE 3.11 The execution of Louis XVI, 21 January 1793

SOURCE 3.10 Marie Antoinette on her way to execution, 16 October 1793

The execution of King Louis XVI in January 1793 shocked people in Britain, even those who had supported the revolution. Asa Briggs, in his book *The Age of Improvement*, puts forward three reasons for a change in attitude in Britain towards the revolution. He suggests, firstly, that the radical groups were very much minority societies and that popular feeling was more often anti-French. Secondly, he argues that the establishment successfully countered the reform groups with their own societies, such as the Association for Preserving Liberty and Property against Republicans and Levellers, which met in the same public house as the Constitutional Society. Groups were organised in the provinces, and anti-reform pamphlets published. His third reason, however, is that majority opinion swung against the French when the revolution turned to terror, dictatorship and aggression. As Briggs says, 'The September massacres and the trial and death of Louis XVI made many young reformers think again.' The Whig Samuel Romilly said, 'One might as well think of establishing a republic of tigers in some forest in Africa as of maintaining a free government among such monsters.'

The change of opinion was evident in a power change in the Commons. Fox and Burke, both Whigs, had opposing views on the revolution, and Fox had been the one with the influence among Whig MPs. In 1791 however, it was Burke who gained influence following the sales of his book, which denounced the French Revolution. In 1794 many leading Whigs joined Pitt's government.

France: revolution and war 1789–1815

Year	Event (above)	Event (below)
1789	Fall of the Bastille	New constitution removes much of the King's power
1791		King and family attempt to escape France – they fail
1792	France declares war on Austria and Prussia	Louis XVI and Marie Antoinette executed. France at war with Britain, Spain and the United Provinces (Belgium and Holland)
1793		The Terror begins, with the aim of enforcing loyalty to the revolution; thousands executed, including many ordinary working people
1794	Terror ended after a *coup d'état*	
1795		Rule of the Directory begins / France successful in war in Spain and Prussia
1796–97	Political instability in France: some royalist uprisings put down	
1797		France takes over northern Italy as result of campaign by General Bonaparte
1799	The Consulate: *coup d'état* brings Bonaparte to power as First Consul	
1801		Austria defeated by the French
1802	Peace Treaty of Amiens between Britain and France / Bonaparte becomes First Consul for life	
1803		War between Britain and France renewed / Coalition between Britain, Russia and Austria, and later Prussia, against France
1804	Napoleon Bonaparte becomes Emperor Napoleon of the French	
1805		Austria defeated
1806	Prussia defeated	
1807		Russia defeated
1808	France at war with Spain (the Peninsular War); Britain supports Spain	
1809		Austria renews the war and is defeated
1812	Napoleon attempts to invade and conquer Russia; defeated and retreats	
1812–13		Britain and Spain defeat the French in Spain
1814	Britain, Russia, Prussia and Austria form a coalition to defeat Napoleon	
1815		Napoleon defeated at Waterloo

HOW CLOSE WAS BRITAIN TO REVOLUTION 1783–1815?

E How did the government deal with the protests?

The war made it even more essential for the government to prevent any possibility of revolution within Britain, and it also increased concerns about potential revolution. The country could not fight a war against France and an internal revolution at the same time. Pitt's government carried out a propaganda war and waged a policy of repression in order to drive the radical movement out of existence. Some reformers had suspended their struggle for reform out of loyalty, but many societies continued to meet even when they were declared illegal. The war also had an adverse impact on trade and industry, leading to many demonstrations, but these were centred more on the unemployment that had resulted from the interruptions to trade than on any revolutionary political aims.

■ 3A Potential for revolution 1795–1812

26 October 1795: a demonstration called by the London Corresponding Society at Copenhagen Fields in London was attended, according to contemporary estimates, by some 100,000 people. A 'remonstrance' was addressed to the King, laying the blame for hunger and distress at the door of parliamentary corruption.

29 October 1795: as the King went to open Parliament, he was booed and stones were thrown at his carriage, breaking a window. There were shouts of 'Down with Pitt', 'No war' and 'No King'. When the King went to the theatre the next day, he was accompanied by over 300 military and 500 constables.

1796: rebellion in Ireland: a French expedition was sent to attempt to start a rebellion in Ireland. It did not land due to a severe storm. However, the knowledge that French help was available led to risings in Ulster, Wexford and Connaught in 1798. Although put down, the rebellions demonstrated the potential danger to Britain.

April and May 1797: a naval mutiny took place at Spithead due to poor pay, bad food and harsh discipline. A second mutiny took place at the Nore. Led by Richard Parker, the sailors demanded a say in the selection of officers. For a critical week the Thames was blockaded, and there was talk among the mutineers of sailing the fleet to France. Among the mutineers were members of the London Corresponding Society. In time of war mutiny posed a serious threat to national security.

1800–01: a number of food riots took place, largely the result of rising food prices and shortages following the blockade imposed by Napoleon during the French Wars. The worst trouble centres were Nottingham, industrial Lancashire and the West Riding of Yorkshire. Some of those involved had political change, not just lower prices, as an aim.

1797–98: a paper was discovered on an Irish priest discussing possible strategies for the French in England following an invasion. The priest was on his way to France when he was arrested.

1811–12: Luddite attacks on machinery and mills throughout the north and north Midlands. The aim was to destroy the machines, which were causing unemployment especially among skilled workers. Supposedly led by Ned Ludd, the Luddites' activities resulted in damage to property and in the injury and murder of some who tried to stop them.

REVOLUTION?

ACTIVITY

1 Study Chart 3A. Which event seems to have the greatest potential for revolution?
2 Use the 'revolutionary Richter scale' on pages 10–11. At what level would you place the events of 1795–1812?
3 Does this list of events suggest revolution was likely?

CITY COLLEGE
LEARNING RESOURCE SERVICE

ACTIVITY

Write the transcript of a television interview held in 1800 between the Prime Minister, William Pitt, and an interviewer (for example, David Frost or John Humphrys), in which Pitt is questioned about the measures taken in the previous six years. Pitt will be expected to explain and justify the measures. Use Chart 3B to help you.

ACTIVITY

1 Explain why the government took each of the actions in Chart 3B.
2 What can you learn from these actions about the extent of the government's anxieties about revolution?

■ 3B What did the government do in response to the revolutionary threat?

1793 The Aliens Act prevented foreigners entering Britain without special permission. It aimed to prevent revolutionaries travelling from France to Britain.

1794 Suspension of Habeas Corpus, which meant political suspects could be held in jail indefinitely.

Corresponding Society leaders arrested; some were transported to Australia.

1795 The Public Meetings Act banned meetings of more than 50 people who planned to petition or demonstrate against King or Parliament.

The Treasonable and Seditious Meetings Act said that anyone found guilty of treason or sedition, either spoken or written, could be classed as a traitor and sentenced to death.

1796 Stamp duties raised to increase the price of newspapers.

Printing presses had to be registered.

More leaders of Corresponding Societies arrested.

Corresponding Societies declared illegal.

1799 The Combination Acts made it illegal for workers to combine (form unions).

1812 Government spies used to identify Luddite activists.

Death penalty introduced for machine breaking.

CITY COLLEGE
LEARNING RESOURCE CENTRE

Why was there no revolution in Britain?

FOCUS ROUTE

Read Sources 3.12–3.14, which present the views of historians about why there was no revolution in Britain. Make a list of all the reasons put forward by the historians as to why there was no revolution.

ACTIVITY

1 Make a list of reasons why there was no revolution under the following headings:
   a) the actions of the radicals
   b) the attitude of the middle class
   c) public opinion
   d) the actions of the government
   e) events in France.
2 Do the historians in Sources 3.12–3.14 agree? If not, why not?
3 As a group, discuss which of the five headings above you think was the most important reason.
4 On your own, answer this essay question: Why was there no revolution similar to that of France in Britain between 1783 and 1812?

Girondins: the first revolutionaries in the French Revolution, who wanted moderate reforms.
Jacobins: the more extreme revolutionaries in France, who were behind the Terror.
Wedgwood, Boulton and Wilkinson: major British manufacturers.
Hardy, Place and Binns: members of the London Corresponding Society, sometimes described as English Jacobins.
Wyvill (the Rev Christopher): a moderate reformer from Yorkshire who published *A defence of Dr Price* (1791) against Burke's views, but at the same time argued against the more extreme views of Paine.

SOURCE 3.12 E. P. Thompson, *The Making of the English Working Class*, 1963

If there was no revolution in England in the 1790s it was not because of Methodism but because the only alliance strong enough to effect it fell apart; after 1792 there were no Girondins to open the doors through which the Jacobins might come. If men like Wedgwood, Boulton and Wilkinson had acted together with men like Hardy, Place and Binns – and if Wyvill's small gentry had acted with them – then Pitt (or Fox) would have been forced to grant a large instalment of reform. But the French Revolution consolidated Old Corruption by uniting landowners and manufacturers in a common panic; and the popular societies were too weak and too inexperienced to effect either revolution or reform on their own . . .

The history of reform agitation between 1792 and 1796 was (in general terms) the story of the simultaneous default of the middle-class reformers and the rapid 'leftwards' movement of the plebian radicals.

SOURCE 3.13 A. Briggs, *The Age of Improvement 1783–1867*, 1960

The regulations and restrictions [reference to the measures taken by the government 1793–99], however, were in harmony with opinion. 'There was not a city, no, not a town', Coleridge wrote, 'in which a man suspected of holding democratic principles could move abroad without receiving some unpleasant proof of the hatred in which his supposed opinions were held by the great majority of the people.' By 1796 Coleridge himself was snapping his 'squeaking trumpet of sedition' . . . and Wordsworth, shocked at French foreign policy, was reading in events 'the doom of France . . . with anger vexed, with disappointment sore'. Even the radical reformer Thelwall, who had been arrested and acquitted in 1794, argued a year later that although he 'adored' the principles on which the Revolution was founded, the 'real object' of the revolutionaries had been lost in six years of 'cutting each others [sic] throats'.

SOURCE 3.14 P. Gregg, *A Social and Economic History of Britain 1760–1965*, 1965

Against such vigorous action [government measures 1793–99] the Reformers had little chance. A black night of repression had fallen. Every little effort of Reform was countered by legislation, by packed juries, unscrupulous judges, and severe sentences. Since there was as yet no police force, the Government had to rely upon the soldiery to keep order. When these were found too ready to sympathise with the people the yeomanry – picked troops of the landowning class – were used instead. Finally it was felt too dangerous to leave the soldiery billeted on the people. And so, for the first time in British history, barracks appeared all over Northern England and in some of the Eastern counties, so that soldiers could be segregated from a discontented populace.

SOURCE 3.15 P. Gregg, *A Social and Economic History of Britain 1760–1965*, 1965

Nowhere and at no time during the Napoleonic Wars was there a revolutionary situation; there was no protest which a moderate reform could not have converted into acclamation for the Government. At every turn it was the legislature which made the revolution out of its own fears, and which magnified the riots of hungry men into incipient French revolution.

ACTIVITY

1 From what you have read in this chapter, find evidence to support and refute P. Gregg's assertion in Source 3.15.
2 Having found the evidence, do you agree with her? Explain your decision.

KEY POINTS FROM CHAPTER 3

How close was Britain to revolution 1783–1815?

1 The period 1783–1815 was one in which there was widespread discontent, and riots and protests over food shortages, high prices and low wages.
2 Reform groups that existed before 1783 were stimulated into renewed activity, and new groups were established, as a result of the start of the French Revolution in 1789.
3 The groups were widespread across the country and varied widely in the type of people who were members as well as in their aims and methods.
4 The outbreak of the war between France and Britain increased anti-French and anti-revolution feeling in Britain.
5 The Terror in France between 1793 and 1794 turned the views of many reformers against the revolution.
6 The war increased the government's fear of possible revolution, especially when there were mutinies in the navy.
7 Between 1793 and 1812 the government introduced a series of measures to suppress revolutionary groups and their ideas.
8 It has been argued that in fact there was no real likelihood of revolution: the government mistook pleas for help with poverty and hunger for potential political revolution.

Why did Lord Liverpool's government choose repression, not reform 1812–22?

CHAPTER OVERVIEW

■ 4A Problems facing Lord Liverpool, 1811–20

1811–13	Protests against new machines in factories
1815	Laws passed to restrict the import of wheat
1816	Income tax abolished
	Riots as a result of food shortages
	Demonstrations in favour of extending the franchise
1817	Prince Regent's coach attacked
	Habeas Corpus Act suspended
	Marches in protest against hunger and unemployment
1819	Mass public meeting demanding the extension of the franchise – dispersed by troops, several people killed
	Acts passed which restricted freedom of the press and freedom to meet and protest
1820	A conspiracy to kill the Cabinet was foiled

ACTIVITY

1 What image of Britain between 1810 and 1820 do the events in chart 4A convey?
2 Do they suggest that revolution was a possibility?

TALKING POINT

If a Prime Minister was assassinated today, what sort of government action would the media demand?

PRIME MINISTER ASSASSINATED

In 1812 the Prime Minister, Spencer Perceval, was assassinated. He had been appointed as Chancellor of the Exchequer in 1807 and Prime Minister in 1809. His period in office was dogged by economic problems, Luddite agitation and the continuing threat from Napoleon. The only British Prime Minister to be assassinated, he was shot in the House of Commons by John Bellingham, a bankrupt who blamed the government for his troubles.

What were the reactions to the news of the Prime Minister's assassination? In Nottingham crowds paraded round the town 'with drums beating and flags flying in triumph'. In Stoke people heard the news from a man 'waving his hat round his head and shouting with frantic joy "Perceval is shot, Hurrah!" ' Cries of 'God bless him' rang out as Bellingham, the assassin, went to the scaffold.

After Perceval's death, Lord Liverpool became Prime Minister. Over the next ten years he had to deal with the war with Napoleon's France and then the economic problems caused by the end of the war. At the same time the impact of the Industrial Revolution was causing unrest and protests, some of which turned to violence and perhaps suggested that a British revolution was at hand. Liverpool, who had witnessed the French Revolution for himself, believed that his most important task was to prevent similar events in Britain. His government took a strong line, repressing protests rather than introducing reforms that addressed the complaints of protesters.

This chapter will investigate the reasons why Lord Liverpool's government used repression rather than reform to deal with the country's problems by exploring these questions:

A How well equipped were Lord Liverpool and his ministers to tackle the country's problems? (pp. 61–63)

B Why was the period 1812–22 a time of distress and discontent? (pp. 64–66)

C How did Liverpool's government react to protests? (pp. 66–74)

D Review: why did Lord Liverpool's government choose repression, not reform 1812–22? (pp. 75–77)

ACTIVITY

1 Look carefully at Sources 4.1 and 4.2. What impression of Liverpool do you get from each of them?
2 Why is it useful to see more than one portrait of a politician such as Liverpool?

A # How well equipped were Lord Liverpool and his ministers to tackle the country's problems?

SOURCE 4.1 Robert Jenkinson, second Earl of Liverpool, painted by Sir Thomas Lawrence in the 1790s. This portrait shows the tall, lanky, young statesman, who was known for his melancholy look, standing next to a plinth bearing a relief (bottom right) of his early hero, the Athenian Demosthenes, who was renowned as a great orator

SOURCE 4.2 Lord Liverpool in later life

TALKING POINT

Many portraits of leading politicians and other people you are studying can be found on the National Portrait Gallery website (www.npg.org.uk). Choose one individual and search for his/her portrait. Before you do so, jot down your image or preconceptions about him or her. Now look at the portrait. What can you learn from it? Does it challenge your preconceptions, and if so, why?

Lord Liverpool (1770–1828; Prime Minister 1812–27)
Robert Banks Jenkinson was educated at Oxford and became a Tory MP in 1790. He inherited his father's title in 1808, to become second Earl of Liverpool (known as Lord Liverpool by contemporaries and historians alike). He served as Foreign Secretary, then Home Secretary and later Secretary for War. He was Prime Minister continuously from 1812 until 1827 when he was paralysed by a stroke. Although he was Prime Minister he did not take part in debates in the House of Commons because he was a lord.

■ **Learning trouble spot**

How do I cope with overload?

Students often complain that in history there seems to be more information to take in than in other subjects. Some claim that it is like doing two A levels. You may find it useful to make manageable lists such as the time chart in Chart 4A, which act as a prompt. Make a set of cards on which you have the main facts. Carry them around so that when you have a free moment you can refer to them. They should jog your memory and help you to associate the details with the events. On the reverse side of the card, jot down opinions held by contemporaries and historians about Liverpool's handling of events, dividing them into for and against categories.

ACTIVITY

Read Sources 4.3–4.6 and Chart 4B.

1 List Liverpool's strengths and then his possible weaknesses as Prime Minister.
2 In what ways was Liverpool's government
   a) well equipped
   b) poorly equipped
   to deal with the country's problems?
3 Look at your answers to questions 1 and 2. Do you think Liverpool's government was more likely to respond to protests and the fear of rebellion with repression or reform? Explain why.

SOURCE 4.3 A. Briggs, *The Age of Improvement*, 1979

In the grasp of principles, mastery of detail, discernment of means and judgement of individuals, he was almost faultless.

SOURCE 4.4 E. J. Evans, *Political Parties in Britain 1783–1867*, 1985

Liverpool's abilities were of the undemonstrative kind ... Liverpool did not have an original mind; he was no innovator; but his talents contributed to his administration's stability. He was a man with whom others could work, a considerate, yet shrewd chairman of a cabinet, a good speaker in the House of Lords and an efficient, conscientious administrator.

SOURCE 4.5 J. W. Derry, *Politics in the Age of Fox, Pitt and Liverpool*, 1990

The resources available to Liverpool were pitiably inadequate, judged by twentieth century criteria. The administrative machine was rudimentary. The Home Secretary and Foreign Secretary composed their own despatches and did much of the routine work which was later the responsibility of officials. The role of government was still limited ... to the handling of public finance, the conduct of foreign relations, the maintenance of public order – though even here the chief responsibility lay with the local magistrates ... When Liverpool and Sidmouth claimed that most of the matters which affected the daily life of the common people lay outside the scope of any government's competence they were recognising elementary truths, as well as giving voice to contemporary assumptions. They believed that the more governments intervened, or sought to intervene, in questions of trade or commerce or manufacture, the less likely it would be that they would do so in a manner which would bring benefits to the people.

TALKING POINT

Would Liverpool's strengths have been obvious to people outside the government? How might this have affected opinions of him?

ACTIVITY

1 Brainstorm the criteria you would use to judge a Prime Minister in the twenty-first century.
2 How would the criteria be different for a Prime Minister in the early 1800s?

SOURCE 4.6 J. W. Derry, *Politics in the Age of Fox, Pitt and Liverpool*, 1990

His fair-mindedness cannot be doubted.

He exercised a considerable degree of authority within the cabinet ... [and] gave colleagues a judicious degree of freedom, [but] he nevertheless determined the overall thrust of government policy.

Liverpool came to the premiership with ample political experience behind him. He had entered politics early ... During the long years of war he had held the most important offices of state.

As a young man he had witnessed the fall of the Bastille. Although it would be foolish to trace all later political responses to that overwhelming experience there is no doubt that he never lost a distrust for popular movements and a hatred for demagogy and violence.

As a young man he had been diffident and shy but [he developed] a quiet confidence and unfussy dependability. He valued the views and opinions of others, but he did not shrink from hard decisions.

He pursued agreed objectives with steady dedication and without false heroics ... he held no grudges and he displayed no malice.

Liverpool recognised that, for much of the time, politicians were reacting to circumstances which they did not control, and dealing with situations which they had neither desired nor created.

TALKING POINT

The Whig leader, Lord Grey, regarded many members of the government as of 'dubious birth and doubtful social status'. Why? Does the information in Chart 4B, about their families, challenge your thoughts about them?

■ 4B Some key members of Liverpool's government

Lord Eldon, Lord Chancellor
His father was a coal merchant in Newcastle. He and Sidmouth have often been branded extreme reactionaries but to many their role in the government was reassuring. They were regarded as capable, competent men who represented the mainstream of opinion.

Lord Liverpool, Prime Minister
His father had been a political adviser to George III.

Lord Sidmouth, Home Secretary
As Henry Addington he had been Prime Minister 1801–04. His father had been a doctor.

Viscount Castlereagh, Foreign Secretary
His family were landowners in Ireland. He was extremely hardworking but heavily criticised because, as the senior minister with a seat in the Commons, he had the task of speaking for the government in the Commons.

Nicholas Vansittart, Chancellor of the Exchequer
He was a Cabinet member who sat in the Commons, and who had the reputation of being a poor speaker. He was made Baron Bexley and moved to the Lords in 1823.

64

WHY DID LORD LIVERPOOL'S GOVERNMENT CHOOSE REPRESSION, NOT REFORM 1812–22?

FOCUS ROUTE

1 Draw a spider diagram to show the reasons why there were protests between 1812 and 1822.
2 Explain why each of the following was likely to increase protests:
   a) the Corn Laws
   b) the abolition of income tax
   c) the Game Laws.

ACTIVITY

Explain the relationship between the situations shown in the top row and those shown in the bottom row in Chart 4C.

B Why was the period 1812–22 a time of distress and discontent?

Although there was a short economic boom at the end of the Napoleonic Wars, Britain was entering a recession by 1816. Industries that had benefited from the war (such as iron, textiles, shipbuilding and armaments) now suffered from falling orders. The demand for British goods in Europe fell as other countries grappled with their own post-war problems. The situation was made worse by the demobilisation of around 300,000 soldiers and sailors, which added to the rising unemployment figures.

For many working people the threat of new machinery in both farming and industry meant the likelihood of unemployment. Steam threshing machines were replacing many farm labourers. Steam-powered spinning machines in cotton mills had virtually replaced home-based spinning by 1800. The power loom, devised by Edmund Cartwright in the 1780s, was threatening the livelihoods of skilled handloom weavers.

■ 4C From handloom to power loom – the decline of the handloom weavers

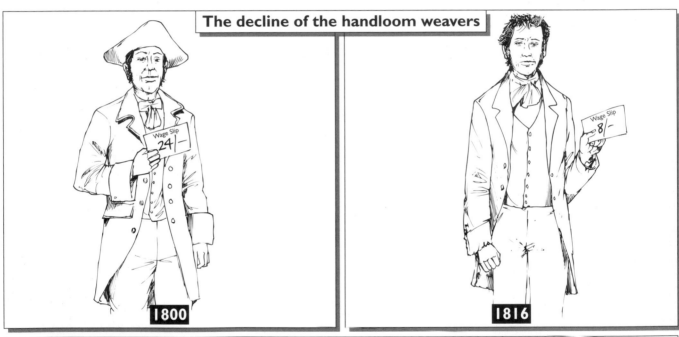

The decline of the handloom weavers

Changes in the production of woven cloth

Throughout 1816 there was unrest. There were disturbances in Norfolk, Suffolk and Essex, where farm labourers demanded fixed prices for corn and meat. Barns were burnt down and threshing machines smashed. Local magistrates used troops to suppress the protests as some rioters were armed with pikes and guns. Five rioters were sentenced to death by hanging. Further north, there were strikes in Newcastle over inadequate wages and the price of bread. Workers in the mines and iron foundries of South Wales and Glasgow also went on strike and there were unemployment marches throughout the Midlands and Lancashire.

The government's introduction of the Corn Laws in 1815 only added to the problems. With the wars at an end, farmers feared a flood of cheap corn from abroad that would ruin landowners and leave labourers at worst unemployed and at best with lower wages. Lord Liverpool saw Britain as a predominantly agricultural society in which those who were earning a living from farming (both landowners and labourers) had to be protected from an influx of cheap foreign corn. As a result the government introduced the Corn Laws, which forbade the import of corn into Britain unless the price that British farmers received for their corn was above 80/- (£4) a quarter (28lb). Critics argued that the government was pandering to the interests of the powerful landowners, whilst those on low incomes, especially in industrial towns, had to pay the penalty of higher bread prices.

ACTIVITY

1 **a)** What is Cruikshank's opinion of the Corn Laws in Source 4.7?
   b) Which details in the cartoon reveal his views?
2 How might each of the following react to the Corn Laws:
   • a factory worker in Bradford
   • a farm labourer in Norfolk
   • a rich landowner in Berkshire?

■ **4D The changing price of wheat per decade, 1780–1829**

	Yearly average price per quarter (28lb)	Peak price	Year of peak price
1780–89	46s 1d (£2.30)	54s 3d (£2.71)	1783
1790–99	57s 7d (£2.88)	78s 7d (£3.93)	1796
1800–09	84s 8d (£4.23)	119s 6d (£5.98)	1801
1810–19	91s 5d (£4.57)	126s 6d (£6.33)	1812
1820–29	59s 10d (£2.99)	68s 6d (£3.43)	1825

SOURCE 4.7 'The Blessing of Peace or the Curse of the Corn Bill' – a cartoon by George Cruikshank drawn in 1815 as an attack on the Corn Laws

SOURCE 4.8 Henry Hunt speaking at Spa Fields, London, 15 November 1816

> Everything that concerns their subsistence or comfort is taxed. Is not their loaf taxed, is not their beer taxed, are not their coats taxed, are not their shirts taxed, is not everything that they eat, drink, wear, and even say, taxed?

TALKING POINT

Use the 'revolutionary Richter scale' on pages 10–11 to assess each protest and to help you fill out column 3 in the Focus Route.

Income tax had been introduced during the French Wars in 1799 as a temporary measure, with the promise that it would be abolished at the end of the war. It had been an invaluable source of revenue for the government and was fairer than many taxes because it was based on income. Liverpool wished to retain the tax after 1815 but there were heated debates inside and outside Parliament, and the bill for abolition was passed by 37 votes. To make up for the government's loss of income, indirect taxes were increased, raising the prices of many foods and other everyday necessities.

For the poor trying to find untaxed food, the Game Laws of 1816 made life even more difficult. In rural areas poaching was considered as a 'legitimate' way of putting food on the table. The Game Laws punished those caught poaching with imprisonment or transportation to Australia for up to seven years. These laws were very unpopular, especially as they came at a time of economic hardship and poor harvests.

C How did Liverpool's government react to protests?

FOCUS ROUTE

Copy and complete this table as you read through Section C. Use a computer spreadsheet to help you to expand the cells as needed.

Protest	Methods of protest	Government reaction	Was this a revolution in the making?
Luddites 1812–15			
Spa Fields 1816			
Blanketeers 1817			
Pentrich 1817			
Peterloo 1819			
Cato Street 1820			

Protest 1: The Luddites, 1812–15

Croppers were highly skilled and well paid textile workers. Their job was to raise the nap on cloth and trim it to finish the cloth with a smooth surface. They had organised themselves into what might be called trade unions and as a result had managed to prevent the introduction of machines that could do their work more cheaply. They were amongst the best paid workers in the cloth industry but in the early 1800s several mill owners installed new machines in their factories. This led to outbreaks of violence – some mills were burned down, machines were smashed, mill owners were attacked and a small number killed. The protesters became known as the Luddites because they left behind them threatening messages signed by a mysterious figure, variously called Ned Ludd, General Ludd or King Ludd.

SOURCE 4.9 General Maitland, in command of 12,000 troops, writing to Lord Sidmouth, the Home Secretary, 10 June 1812

At present the whole of these Revolutionary Movements are limited to the lowest orders of the people generally, to the places where they show themselves, and no concern exists, nor no plan is laid, further than is manifested in the open acts of violence that are daily committed.

67

WHY DID LORD LIVERPOOL'S GOVERNMENT CHOOSE REPRESSION, NOT REFORM 1812–22?

ACTIVITY

Review Sources 4.9–4.11 from Lord Liverpool's point of view.

1 Does it appear that revolution was highly likely, probable, possible or highly unlikely?
2 Could you risk believing that there was no threat of revolution?

SOURCE 4.10 Report of the Secret Committee on the Disturbed State of Several Counties, 1812

It is the opinion of persons both of civil and military status . . . grounded upon various information from various quarters . . . but which for obvious reasons they do not think proper to detail, that the views of some of the persons engaged in these proceedings [Luddite activity] have extended to revolutionary measures of the most dangerous description.

SOURCE 4.11 Samuel Whitbread, a Whig MP, speaking in the House of Commons in 1812

As to the persons who blackened their faces, and disfigured themselves for . . . concealment, and had attended the meeting on Deanmoor, near Manchester, it turned out that ten of them were spies sent out by the magistrates . . . The spies were the very ringleaders of the mischief and incited people to acts which they would not otherwise have thought of.

SOURCE 4.12 F. O. Darvall, *Popular Disturbances and Public Order in Regency England*, 1970

There is no evidence whatever of any political motives on the part of the Luddites. There is not a single instance in which it can be proved that a Luddite attack was directed towards anything deeper than disputes between masters and men, between workmen and their employers . . . while machine breaking, raids for arms, and provision riots were the only overt acts of disorder . . . these aspects of the situation received far less emphasis in the spies' reports than revolutionary plans which never materialised.

Protest 2: Spa Fields, London, 2 December 1816

In December 1816 a public meeting took place at Spa Fields, Islington, London. It was arranged by a group called the SPENCEANS, a small, extremist group whose main aim was the public ownership of all land. Henry Hunt, the famous radical speaker, was asked to address the meeting. However, before Hunt arrived, two Spenceans, Dr James Watson and his son, roused a small section of the crowd into breaking into gunsmiths' shops for weapons and then marching towards the Tower of London. The Watsons and many of their followers had been drinking heavily. Riots broke out, lasting several hours, and there was looting. During the riots the flag of the French Revolution, the tricolour, was raised. Hunt arrived later and spoke to the rest of the crowd who had waited peacefully. In his speech he called for lower taxes and for the reform of Parliament.

> **SPENCEANS**
>
> A group, named after Thomas Spence, that advocated the nationalisation of land to alleviate poverty.

SOURCE 4.13 Radical placards at the Spa Fields meeting, 1816

68

WHY DID LORD LIVERPOOL'S GOVERNMENT CHOOSE REPRESSION, NOT REFORM 1812–22?

SOURCE 4.14 A leaflet that circulated amongst the crowd before the Spa Fields meeting. (The Regent was the future George IV, and Castlereagh was Foreign Secretary and Leader of the House of Commons)

Henry Hunt (1773–1835)

Hunt was a radical politician who became Radical MP for Preston in 1830. He was well known for speaking to large open-air crowds, which earned him the nickname Orator Hunt. His cause was parliamentary reform, but he was too vain, abrasive and erratic to become an effective political leader. He became a folk hero, who wore a white top hat as a symbol of the purity of his cause.

HABEAS CORPUS

Habeas Corpus is a Latin phrase meaning 'you have the body'. The Habeas Corpus Act of 1679 said that anyone arrested had to be brought before a court to be charged with an offence. If the Act was suspended, a person who had committed no offence could be arrested and held for an indefinite period without charges and without trial. Thus the government could imprison those felt to be potential revolutionaries.

TALKING POINT

Do you think the government was justified in suspending Habeas Corpus? (*Warning* – remember hindsight!)

BRITONS TO ARMS!

THE WHOLE COUNTRY WAITS THE SIGNAL FROM LONDON TO FLY TO ARMS! HASTE, BREAK OPEN GUNSMITHS AND OTHER LIKELY PLACES TO FIND ARMS! RUN ALL CONSTABLES WHO TOUCH A MAN OF US; NO RISE OF BREAD; NO REGENT; NO CASTLEREAGH, OFF WITH THEIR HEADS; NO PLACEMEN, TYTHES OR ENCLOSURES; NO TAXES; NO BISHOPS.

SOURCE 4.15 From a report by MPs into the Spa Fields riot

It has been proved ... that some members of these Societies ... conceived the project and endeavoured to prepare the means of raising an Insurrection, so formidable from numbers, as by dint of physical strength to overpower all resistance.

The vast majority of political meetings were peaceful, but the hotheads at Spa Fields had convinced the government that there was a revolutionary situation. Lord Liverpool and his colleagues feared that there was a chance that this was the beginning of a British revolution. 1816 was a particularly dangerous year. Henry Cockburn, an advocate (Scottish barrister) who later became the Whig Solicitor General for Scotland, said, 'I have never known a period at which the people's hatred of the government was so general and so fierce'. Lord Sidmouth wrote to his brother in the summer of 1816, saying 'It is to the autumn and winter that I look with anxiety'. That was when the effects of the poor harvest and economic problems would be felt more severely.

An attack on the Prince Regent (no one was quite sure whether a shot had been fired or a stone thrown) followed closely on the Spa Fields riots. This led to the government suspending the Habeas Corpus Act so that troublemakers or subversives could be imprisoned and taken out of circulation immediately. Despite Sidmouth, the Home Secretary, reassuring the public that they had nothing to fear if they were law-abiding citizens, *The Times* attacked the legislation for taking away 'that great bulwark of our liberties, of our comforts, of our lives'. The suspension of Habeas Corpus was followed by the Seditious Meetings Act in March 1817, which made it unlawful for more than 50 people to assemble together.

Protest 3: The march of the Blanketeers, March 1817

On 10 March 1817, a crowd of around 4000 gathered in St Peter's Field, Manchester. The aim was to organise a protest march to London where the protesters would present a petition to the Prince Regent. Each marcher was to carry a petition wrapped in brown paper tied round his right arm with a bow of white tape. Their demands included parliamentary reform, the abolition of the Corn Laws, and the reinstatement of Habeas Corpus. They also complained about the trade situation, unemployment and the high level of taxation and rents. The majority of protesters were under 30 years old and many were unemployed handloom weavers whose prospects had changed radically in the last fifteen years (see page 64).

SOURCE 4.16 S. Bamford, *Passages in the Life of a Radical*, written in 1839. Samuel Bamford, a Lancashire Radical and weaver, attended the gathering in 1817

I endeavoured to show them that the authorities of Manchester were not likely to permit their leaving the town in a body, with blankets and petitions, as they proposed; that they could not subsist on the road; that the cold and wet would kill numbers of them . . . that any persons might join their ranks who were not reformers but enemies to reform, hired perhaps to bring them and their cause into disgrace . . . Many of the individuals were observed to have blankets, rugs, or large coats, rolled up and tied, knapsack like, on their backs . . . The appearance of these misdirected people was calculated to excite in considerable minds, pity rather than resentment. Some appeared to have strength in their limbs and pleasure in their features, others already with doubt in their looks and hesitation in their steps. A few were decently clothed and well appointed for the journey; many were covered only by rags . . . and were damped by a gentle but chilling rain.

About 300 protesters set out on the long march. It was instilled into them that they must conduct themselves peacefully. This they did, though a magistrate observed that some of the women who cheered them off used violent language and demanded the overthrow of the gentry. On the way they intended to hold meetings in the towns they passed through and, if they could not be accommodated by locals, they would sleep under hedgerows covered by their blankets.

The government was alarmed by such a march, and magistrates ordered the crowd to disperse after reading the Riot Act. The 300 managed to set out but nearly all were turned back by troops at Stockport and Macclesfield. After a brief scuffle, one man was killed and several wounded by the sabres of the yeomanry. Only one made it to London – Abel Couldwell of Stalybridge. He handed the petition to Lord Sidmouth for the Prince Regent, but nothing came of it.

Arrests followed, including that of Samuel Bamford, but after several weeks in prison the protesters were discharged. Home Office sources claimed that the Blanketeers would 'breed commotion in the towns, and by that they will have a heavy body together and try at a revolution'.

Protest 4: The Pentrich Rising, 1817

The government employed spies and *AGENTS PROVOCATEURS* to infiltrate political organisations. Often they did not just report on activities, but even encouraged them. One infamous spy was W. J. Richards, alias 'Oliver'. Oliver informed a group of discontented workers in Pentrich, Derbyshire, that they were part of a massive general uprising and could expect support from Sheffield, Dewsbury, Huddersfield, Leeds, Nottingham, Birmingham and London. The Derbyshire group was led by Jeremiah Brandreth, a 27-year-old skilled worker. On the night of 9 June 1817, as the rain poured down, he set out with about 200 men to march on Nottingham. His associates included stocking-makers, ironworkers and farm labourers. They were armed with pikes, scythes, pitchforks and a few guns.

Brandreth had encouraged his followers with the promise of lots of rum, beef and bread, and 100 guineas each once they had taken Nottingham. Some of his followers thought that when he talked about setting up a provisional government in Nottingham, this meant a government that would provide provisions. En route to Nottingham a farm servant was killed when Brandreth fired a shot through a farmhouse window when its occupants wouldn't let him in. When the men arrived in Nottingham, they were met by troops, not by the thousands of supporters Oliver had led them to expect. Forty-five men were tried for high treason; three were hanged, including Brandreth, and thirty were transported.

SOURCE 4.17 Percy Bysshe Shelley, the poet, in *The Examiner* on 9 November 1817

On the 7th November, Brandreth, Turner and Ludlam ascended the scaffold. We feel for Brandreth the less, because it seems he killed a man. But recollect who instigated him to the proceedings which led to murder. On the word of a dying

CITY COLLEGE
RESOURCE CENTRE

ACTIVITY

1 To whom was Bamford referring in Source 4.16 when he used the phrase 'enemies to reform'?

2 Why were the Blanketeers likely to arouse 'pity rather than resentment'?

3 Why do you think, despite warnings not to go, and the use of government force to stop them, 300 people still set out on the march?

4 Under which legislation were the meeting and the march broken up?

5 Why did the government order the marchers to be dispersed?

AGENTS PROVOCATEURS
Government spies: they infiltrated groups with the aim of encouraging members to take anti-government actions, which would lead to the arrest of members of the group.

70

WHY DID LORD LIVERPOOL'S GOVERNMENT CHOOSE REPRESSION, NOT REFORM 1812–22?

SOURCE 4.18 The moderate Whig, Lord Fitzwilliam, in a letter to Lord Sidmouth

There certainly prevails very generally in the country a strong opinion that most of the events ... are to be attributed to ... Mr. Oliver ... the number of revolutionists is very limited ... and the mass of the people is still sound.

ACTIVITY

Either in writing or discussion put forward arguments for and against the government's handling of the Blanketeers and the Pentrich Rising.

man, Brandreth tells us, that 'Oliver brought him to this', that 'but for Oliver, he would not have been there'. See, too, Ludlam and Turner, with their sons and brothers, and sisters, how they kneel together in this dreadful agony of prayer. With that dreadful penalty before their eyes – with that tremendous sanction for the truth of all he spoke, Turner exclaimed loudly and distinctly, while the executioner was putting the rope round his neck, 'This is all Oliver and the government' ... Troops of horse, with keen and glittering swords, hemmed in the multitudes collected to witness this abominable exhibition. When the stroke of the axe was heard, there was a burst of horror from the crowd. The instant the head was exhibited, there was a tremendous shriek set up, and the multitudes ran violently in all directions, as if under the impulse of sudden frenzy. Those who resumed their stations, groaned and hooted. [The punishment for treason was to be hanged, drawn and quartered. These men were first hanged then cut down and finally their heads were cut off. It seems they were dead when cut down, not alive, as was the usual case.]

Protest 5: The Peterloo Massacre, 1819

Thousands of people were involved in mass meetings throughout the summer of 1819. In Oldham, Manchester and Stockport, there were demands for the reform of Parliament and the repeal of the Corn Laws. Political groups formed in the north, including Hull, York and Newcastle, where reading rooms were established and political discussions held. In Stockport and Blackburn, women formed independent political unions. Radical views were expressed through the independent press such as the *Manchester Observer* and the *Leeds Mercury*. Throughout June there was a series of meetings held across Lancashire, Yorkshire and the Midlands. In July mass meetings in Birmingham, Leeds and London passed without incident. Magistrates were, however, concerned about the one to be held in Manchester on 16 August. Around 60,000 people were expected to converge on St Peter's Field to hear Henry Hunt speak on parliamentary reform.

SOURCE 4.19 'Manchester heroes' – a cartoon by George Cruikshank

ACTIVITY

As you read pages 70–74 about Peterloo, collect evidence either for or against the view that Cruikshank's cartoon (Source 4.19) presents a fair reflection on events.

ACTIVITY

1 How do the writers of Sources 4.20 and 4.21 assess the political situation?
2 What advice did the Home Office (Source 4.22) give to the Manchester magistrates?
3 What evidence is there in the sources that the Manchester magistrates needed to be concerned about 'some alarming insurrection'?

SOURCE 4.20 Five Lancashire magistrates writing to the Home Secretary, Lord Sidmouth, 1 July 1819

We cannot have a doubt that some alarming insurrection is in contemplation ... Urged on by the harangues of a few demagogues, we anticipate at no distant period a general rising, and possessing no power to prevent the meetings which are weekly held, we as magistrates are at a loss how to stem the influence of the dangerous and seditious doctrines which are continually disseminated.

SOURCE 4.21 Mr Norris, the only one of the Manchester magistrates who lived in Manchester, writing to the Home Office on 15 August 1819

The magistrates, the military and the civil authorities of Manchester have been occupied ... in concerting the necessary arrangements for the preservation of the peace tomorrow ... all the accounts tend to show that the worst possible spirit pervades the country ... I hope peace may be preserved, but under all circumstances it is scarcely possible to expect it.

SOURCE 4.22 A letter from the Home Office to the Manchester magistrates before the meeting

Reflection convinces him [Sidmouth] the more strongly of the inexpediency of attempting forcibly to prevent the meeting on Monday. Every discouragement and obstacle should be thrown in its way ... But even if they should utter sedition ... it will be the wisest course to abstain from any endeavour to disperse the mob, unless they should proceed to acts of felony or riot.

SOURCE 4.23 Samuel Bamford, an eyewitness at St Peter's Field, in his *Passages in the Life of a Radical*, written in 1839

We had frequently been taunted by the press with our ragged, dirty appearance at these assemblages; with the confusion of our proceedings, and the mob-like crowds in which our numbers were mustered; and we determined that, for once at least, these reflections should not be deserved ... that we would disarm the bitterness of our political opponents by a display of cleanliness, sobriety, and decorum, such as we had never before exhibited ... At our head were a hundred or two of women, mostly young wives ... A hundred or two of our handsomest ... danced to the music, or sung snatches of popular songs.

SOURCE 4.24 A. Prentice, an eyewitness at St Peter's Field, in *Historical Sketches and Personal Recollections of Manchester: Intended to Illustrate the Progress of Public Opinion from 1792 to 1832*, published in 1851

I saw the main body proceeding towards St. Peter's Fields, and never saw a gayer spectacle ... The 'marching order' of which so much was said afterwards was what we often see now in the procession of Sunday School children ... Our company laughed at the fears of the magistrates and the remark was, that if the men intended mischief they would not have brought their wives, their sisters or their children with them.

The timetable of events
11a.m.
William Hulton (chairman) and other magistrates met at Mr Buxton's house, overlooking St Peter's Field. As the crowd grew in size, they became alarmed.

12 noon
Hulton claimed there were 50,000 in the Field. He decided that 400 special constables would be sent into the crowd to clear a path by forming two lines between the hustings (the platform on which the speeches were to be made) and Mr Buxton's house.

p.m.
The main speakers arrived: Henry Hunt, Richard Carlile, John Knight, Joseph Johnson and Mary Fildes. There were newspaper reporters on the platform, including John Tyas of *The Times*, Edward Baines of the *Leeds Mercury*, John Saxton of the *Manchester Observer*, and John Smith of the *Liverpool Mercury*.

p.m.

The magistrates decided that 'the town was in danger'. Hulton therefore ordered Joseph Nadin, the Deputy Constable of Manchester, to arrest Hunt and other leaders. Nadin insisted that he would need military support. Letters were then sent by Hulton to Major Trafford, commander of the Manchester and Salford Yeomanry, and to Lieutenant Colonel L'Estrange, the commander of the military forces in Manchester. Trafford sent in Captain Hugh Birley, his second-in-command. Eyewitnesses claimed that most of the 60 soldiers were drunk. Birley later defended his men's behaviour by saying they were not drunk; their horses had been scared by the crowd. The Yeomanry made their way through the crowd along the path that had been cleared by the special constables, but as they drew nearer the hustings, the crowd closed ranks to prevent them from arresting Hunt and the other speakers. Others spilled over into the pathway.

Chaos erupted and the Yeomanry began to use their sabres to make a way through the crowd. There was panic and screaming as the crowd tried to flee or protect their families and friends. Birley and his men reached the hustings and arrested Hunt, Knight, Johnson, Moorhouse, Swift, Saxton, Tyas and Wild.

p.m.

Lieutenant Colonel L'Estrange reported to Hulton who told him that the Yeomanry were being attacked by the crowd. L'Estrange sent in Lieutenant Jolliffe and the 15th Hussars to rescue the Manchester and Salford Yeomanry.

2.00 p.m.

Most of the crowd had been cleared by the soldiers, leaving St Peter's Field like the aftermath of a battle: 11 dead and over 400 wounded, including around 100 women.

SOURCE 4.25   Samuel Bamford, an eyewitness, describing the scene at the end of the massacre in his *Passages in the Life of a Radical,* written in 1839

The hustings remained, with a few broken . . . flag-staves erect, and a torn and gashed banner or two drooping; whilst over the whole field were strewn caps, bonnets, shawls, and shoes . . . trampled, torn and bloody . . . Several mounds of human beings still remained where they had fallen, crushed down, and smothered. Some of these [still] groaning; others with staring eyes, were gasping for breath, and others would never breathe more. All was silent, save those low sounds, and the occasional snorting and pawing of steeds.

ACTIVITY

1 Why were the events of 16 August known as 'Peterloo'?

2 Is it justifiable to call the event 'a massacre'?

3 Is there sufficient evidence that the Manchester magistrates needed to be concerned about 'some alarming insurrection' and that their actions were justified?

4 What questions do you need to ask before deciding whether Bamford's account of Peterloo in Sources 4.23 and 4.25 is reliable?

5 In the light of what you have learned on pages 70–72, do you think that Cruikshank's cartoon 'Manchester Heroes' (Source 4.19 on page 70) presents a fair reflection on events?

■ Learning trouble spot

How useful are diaries as an historical source?

Do you keep a diary? Do you always tell the truth? Diaries are a potentially useful source for historians but we must remember that they may have been written for a variety of purposes. They may be made as a record for future reference, such as when a politician writes his or her autobiography. They may be intended solely for the diarist's own use or they may be intended for public consumption, especially after the writer's death. Depending upon their intended purpose, they can be a valuable insight into what one person observed or felt. They can provide personal details that might be unavailable elsewhere. They can supplement more formal records such as Cabinet papers. They can show a continuity or change of attitudes and principles and can be used to support or contradict other contemporary evaluations. Diaries in the nineteenth century were mostly written by the wealthier, educated classes and many politicians, such as Peel, Palmerston, Gladstone and Disraeli, kept diaries. However, we also have memoirs and autobiographies from all classes of society, such as Samuel Bamford's *Passages in the Life of a Radical.*

Whoever the author, all diaries and memoirs must be questioned before accepting their evidence. What was the motive of the diarist? Has he or she exaggerated their own role or minimised the contribution of others? Does their bias influence their judgement? Was he or she really in a position to know exactly what was happening?

SOURCE 4.26 Lord Liverpool, writing to George Canning, a member of the government, shortly after the massacre

When I say that the proceedings of the magistrates ... were justifiable, you will understand me as not by any means deciding that the course which they pursued on that occasion was in all parts prudent ... but, whatever judgement might be formed in this respect, being satisfied that they were substantially right, there remained no alternative but to support them.

How did the government react to Peterloo?

Throughout the week following the massacre, there was an outcry across the whole country. The magistrates were attacked for their handling of the event and the soldiers for their behaviour. *The Times* was the only national newspaper represented on the day and, following the arrest of John Tyas, their reporter, the editor believed that the government was deliberately suppressing news of the incident. Disgust was compounded by Sidmouth sending a letter of congratulations to the Manchester magistrates for their firm action.

SOURCE 4.27 J. W. Derry, *Politics in the Age of Fox, Pitt and Liverpool*, 1990

In private, Liverpool and his ministers were critical of the Manchester magistrates, but they supported them in public. They did so because they knew that without the confidence of the magistracy public order would break down. Its maintenance rested on frail foundations. The resources available to Liverpool for the preservation of law and order were slim. There was no police force ... The regular army was the most efficient and impartial force available for controlling riots, but there was considerable reluctance to use it except as a last resort ... Had the army ... been used ... the casualties at Peterloo would have been less, possibly non-existent.

The government, acting on information from lord lieutenants, magistrates and spies, went on the counter-offensive. They were able to claim that there was a crisis and that revolution was rumbling under the surface. This gave them the justification for repressive legislation. By December 1819, the government had passed the Six Acts to suppress political activity further. The trial of the organisers of the St Peter's Field meeting was held in March 1820. They were charged with 'assembling with unlawful banners at an unlawful meeting for the purpose of exciting discontent'. Hunt was sent to prison for two and a half years. Joseph Johnson, Samuel Bamford and Joseph Healey were sentenced to one year's imprisonment.

SOURCE 4.28 'A Free Born Englishman!' – a cartoon by George Cruikshank, commenting on the passing of the Six Acts in 1819

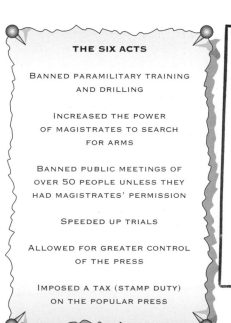

THE SIX ACTS

BANNED PARAMILITARY TRAINING AND DRILLING

INCREASED THE POWER OF MAGISTRATES TO SEARCH FOR ARMS

BANNED PUBLIC MEETINGS OF OVER 50 PEOPLE UNLESS THEY HAD MAGISTRATES' PERMISSION

SPEEDED UP TRIALS

ALLOWED FOR GREATER CONTROL OF THE PRESS

IMPOSED A TAX (STAMP DUTY) ON THE POPULAR PRESS

CITY COLLEGE LEARNING RESOURCE SERVICE

WHY DID LORD LIVERPOOL'S GOVERNMENT CHOOSE REPRESSION, NOT REFORM 1812–22?

74

ACTIVITY

1 Explain the purpose of each of the Six Acts.
2 Make a list of the details in Source 4.28 that reveal Cruikshank's opinion of the Six Acts.
3 How repressive, according to Sources 4.29 and 4.30, were the Six Acts?
4 Why do the historians quoted in Sources 4.29 and 4.30 have a different opinion of the Six Acts from that of Cruikshank?

SOURCE 4.29 J. Plowright, 'Lord Liverpool and the alternatives to "repression" in Regency England', *History Review*, September 1997

The 'Six Acts'... did not on the whole, either in intention or execution, deserve the 'repressive' label which some have tried to apply to them. Three of the Acts merely attempted to plug loopholes in existing laws, a further two were temporary and were not renewed, and the remaining law which banned paramilitary training should not offend even the most ardent defender of civil liberties. 'What is surprising is not their severity but their restraint' (Derry).

SOURCE 4.30 J. W. Derry, *Politics in the Age of Fox, Pitt and Liverpool*, 1990

The famous 'Six Acts'... are now seen as little more than gestures, a response to reassure backbench opinion in the House of Commons and conservative opinion in the country, rather than a prelude to a sustained reign of terror... When defending them in the Commons Castlereagh asserted that there was no intention of indefinitely limiting the traditional rights of assembly or petitioning... Very few actions were taken under the legislation.

Protest 6: The Cato Street Conspiracy, 1820

Arthur Thistlewood was a failed gentleman-farmer, ex-militia man and a Spencean, who had been involved in the Spa Fields riots. Angered by Peterloo and the Six Acts, he challenged Lord Sidmouth to a duel for which he was imprisoned. On release, he determined to take revenge by plotting to assassinate the Cabinet. Thistlewood later said, 'High treason was committed against the people at Manchester. I resolved that the lives of the instigators of massacre should atone for the souls of murdered innocents.'

The plot was organised in a house in Cato Street off the Edgware Road in London. The gang planned to blow up members of the Cabinet while they dined at the Earl of Harrowby's home and then to seize London. But unbeknown to them, George Edwards, a government spy, had infiltrated the gang. There is some suggestion that he played a leading role in the planning and then informed the government before the plot could be carried out. Soldiers arrested the plotters although the Duke of Wellington, by now a member of the government, had suggested that the ministers themselves simply wait for the plotters to break in and then, pistols in hand, arrest them themselves! Thistlewood and four other conspirators were hanged and five others were transported to Australia for life.

ACTIVITY

1 How could such a conspiracy play into the government's hands and help to justify repressive measures?
2 Should we take the Cato Street conspirators seriously or treat them as a 'lunatic fringe'?

FOCUS ROUTE

By now you should have completed the table on page 66. Use it to answer the following questions:

1 What methods were used to express discontent?
2 Were any of the protests successful?
3 What measures did the government take to deal with the protests?
4 What was the principal aim of the government in taking these measures?
5 Did they succeed in their aim?
6 How likely was revolution between 1812 and 1820?

William Cobbett (1763–1835)

William Cobbett was the son of a small farmer and innkeeper. He worked for a law firm in London and for a short time joined the army. He was a strong supporter of parliamentary reform, publishing a cheap weekly newspaper, *The Political Register*, after 1815. He was a good journalist but his ideas were too radical for Liverpool's government. To avoid arrest, he fled to America in 1817. He also waged campaigns over the burden of taxation and the plight of rural labourers. He became MP for Oldham in the first election after the 1832 Reform Act.

75

WHY DID LORD LIVERPOOL'S GOVERNMENT CHOOSE REPRESSION, NOT REFORM 1812–22?

D Review: why did Lord Liverpool's government choose repression, not reform 1812–22?

The Cato Street Conspiracy was the last political disturbance of any note in the troubled post-war period. Trade improved after 1820, and working-class distress diminished. How real had the threat of revolution been during the previous decade?

There was no general desire for revolution, but there was a genuine and forceful demand for reform. William Cobbett's writings were increasingly influential. Cobbett's *Political Register* sold about 200,000 copies in two months during 1816. Hampden Clubs (named after John Hampden, the vociferous opponent of Charles I during the civil war), founded in 1812 by Major John Cartwright and the Radical MP Sir Francis Burdett, were formed throughout the country. They facilitated opportunities to discuss parliamentary reform and spread political ideas amongst the labouring classes. As a result, 700 petitions for the reform of Parliament were presented to the government in 1817 most of them from industrial towns without parliamentary representation. In 1818 the number had risen to over 1500. Union Clubs, often formed by working men, followed the example of the Hampden Clubs, creating the facility for members to hold meetings, sometimes in alehouses, and to read pamphlets and newspapers. Radical publications such as the *Black Dwarf* and the *Black Book* were read eagerly.

The mass of the people was not revolutionary but there were individuals and groups who hoped for some kind of revolution, even if they were unclear exactly how it would come about or how they would take advantage of it. Lord Liverpool's government regarded all such groups and protests as a serious threat. Faced with the Pentrich Rising or any other insurrection, it took measures that have usually been described as 'repressive'.

SOURCE 4.31 A. Wood, *Nineteenth-Century Britain*, 1960

Seldom in English history has a government been so hated by the people. Certainly this was not entirely without justification. If, for example, the taxes on food had been remitted, the situation of the poor might have been relieved a little; instead the income tax, which weighed most heavily on the upper and middle classes, was dropped. Yet the removal of the tax would barely have scraped the surface of the problem. Only a nation-wide system of economic control could have eased the birth-pangs of a new industrial society, and such measures of interference were beyond the power and knowledge of any government of this time.

SOURCE 4.32 N. Gash, *Aristocracy and the People: Britain 1815–65*, 1979

It was understandable that ministers found it difficult to distinguish accurately between causes and effects: Luddism and bread riots, distress and sedition, social protest and political subversion. Disorder presented itself not as a single identifiable problem, but as a succession of regional symptoms, indicating a kind of moral 'distemper' ... of whose real nature and origin they could not be sure ... the Home Office officials were convinced ... of the existence ... of a general wish to start a national revolution. Though the evidence available to the government was fragmentary, there was enough to give colour to this theory and not enough to disprove it. The ignorance and delusion on both sides was compounded by some of the sources on which the authorities relied for their information.

ACTIVITY

Summarise the justifications for the policies of Liverpool's period of office given by the historians in Sources 4.31–4.33.

76

WHY DID LORD LIVERPOOL'S GOVERNMENT CHOOSE REPRESSION, NOT REFORM 1812–22?

SOURCE 4.33 J. Plowright, 'Lord Liverpool and the alternatives to "repression" in Regency England', *History Review*, September 1997

Liverpool's government may be defended [from charges of pursuing unnecessarily repressive policies and of provoking disorder] on three grounds. Firstly, most popular discontent cannot be attributed directly to Liverpool's government but arose as a consequence of the agricultural and industrial revolutions, a massive population increase, the French Revolution, the wars with France and the United States and the transition from wartime to peacetime conditions ...

Secondly, although Liverpool's government may have inadvertently aggravated unrest by mishandling its reaction to these unprecedented problems (such as demobilising too rapidly), in general Liverpool and his ministers strove to minimise hardship. For example, in 1817 the Poor Employment Act made available state loans totalling £750,000 for encouraging the fisheries and public works undertaken by local authorities ...

Thirdly, ... one must remember just how pitifully small Liverpool's resources were for keeping the peace. Lacking either a sizeable standing army or an effective police force, Liverpool's government was obliged to rely on spies and informers ... the government's fears of insurrection were clearly not completely unfounded, however small the numbers of potential revolutionaries and however unrealistic or even farcical their plots may now appear with hindsight.

In evaluating the responses of Liverpool's government it is important to remember that few people believed that it was the government's role to alleviate economic distress. The politicians of the early 1800s saw economic problems such as slumps in trade and the consequent rise in unemployment as 'unavoidable causes', a description used by Sidmouth in 1817. Cyclical trade depressions came and went, and distress would eventually go away. Therefore governments did not interfere in matters such as poverty and unemployment. It was up to the local overseers of the poor to ensure that people did not die of starvation. Schemes to alleviate poverty, such as the Speenhamland system (see Chapter 9), were set up and run on a purely local level, and central government had no hand in them.

To Liverpool and his colleagues, the government's major task was to ensure the peace of the nation, and that meant not only international peace but also peace within the country. Its greatest responsibility therefore was always to maintain law and order, and to protect property. This does much to explain its reaction to the protests and disturbances you have studied in this chapter, especially given how close the politicians were to the French Revolution of 1789. Most adults had real memories of the Terror, and had read accounts of the overthrow of the French government and monarchy, the executions of Louis XVI and Marie Antoinette, and of thousands of others, many of them aristocrats. Some, like Liverpool, had been in Paris at the time. They were not to know whether or not revolution might happen in Britain.

It is easy enough with the benefit of hindsight to look back and say there was never really any threat of revolution or they should have reformed instead of using repression. Liverpool and his ministers believed there was a threat. Could they really have acted any differently?

■ **Learning trouble spot**

The curse of hindsight

Students often cannot understand why an action was taken because they do not see things from the same point of view as the people they are studying. In history, hindsight is a curse. It is easy to say 'surely they should/could have seen that ...' For example, why did most people in Britain not see that Hitler posed a danger to Europe in the mid-1930s? 'Surely they could see that his policies would lead to ...' We, of course, know better because we know what happened from 1938 onwards. They did not. In evaluating people's actions, therefore, it is important to identify what they knew when they took the actions.

How might hindsight make it difficult to understand the actions and thinking of Liverpool and his ministers?

TALKING POINT

The title of this chapter suggests that the government had a choice between repression and reform. Now that you have worked through Chapter 4, do you think they really had such a choice?

77

WHY DID LORD LIVERPOOL'S GOVERNMENT CHOOSE REPRESSION, NOT REFORM 1812–22?

ACTIVITY

1 Discuss and explain why Liverpool's government did not take any of the following actions to eliminate the discontent:
   a) introduce a national unemployment benefit
   b) repeal the Corn Laws
   c) set up a national minimum wage
   d) ban the introduction of new machinery to textile mills
   e) give the vote to all men over the age of 21
   f) reduce indirect taxes on food.
2 Suggest a historically valid (that is, one that was possible at the time) alternative reaction or action that Liverpool's government might have taken towards the protests of 1812–20.
3 Lord Liverpool seemed paranoid about the danger of revolution.
   a) Do you think this was justified?
   b) Do you think he contributed to this danger in any way?

ACTIVITY

Plan one of the following essays:
a) 'Rulers who neither see, nor feel, nor know.' How appropriate is this verdict on Lord Liverpool's administration in the light of his domestic policies between 1812 and 1822?
b) How far was Lord Liverpool's government responsible for the distress and discontent between 1812 and 1822?
c) Why did Lord Liverpool's government choose repression, not reform, between 1812 and 1822?

KEY POINTS FROM CHAPTER 4

Why did Lord Liverpool's government choose repression, not reform, 1812–22?

1 At the end of the Napoleonic Wars, Britain faced serious economic and social problems in a time of rapid industrial change. No politicians had experience of dealing with such a situation.
2 The main reasons for distress and discontent amongst working people were unemployment, low wages, poor living and working conditions, and the fact that they had no right to a vote in elections.
3 Protests occurred at frequent intervals during the period 1812–20, particularly when food prices were high.
4 Politicians did not believe that it was their role to improve social and economic conditions for the population. They saw their main responsibility as being to keep the peace and defend the people from disorder.
5 Liverpool and his government were strongly influenced by the events of the French Revolution and saw potential revolution in every protest.
6 Political protest came largely from radicals who saw political and constitutional reform as the way to solve economic and social problems.
7 The government's principal policies were designed to prevent revolution, using legislation such as the Six Acts and the suspension of Habeas Corpus. These have been described as 'repressive' but were not intended to be permanent.
8 The government had no police force that could deal effectively with protests.
9 Historians have justified Liverpool's policies in that the government faced problems no government had faced before, and that they carried out policies that they deemed were in the best interests of the country as a whole.

CITY COLLEGE
LEARNING RESOURCE CENTRE

5

Can the government of 1822–29 really be described as 'liberal Tory'?

CHAPTER OVERVIEW

Hypothesis 1

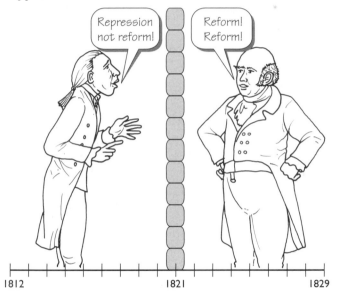

After 1822 the Tory government had a more liberal attitude towards reform. Its reforms show that it was significantly different from the government that had been in power between 1812 and 1821. The term 'liberal Tory' is therefore a valid description of the men in power between 1822 and 1829.

Hypothesis 2

The members of the government of 1822–29 cannot be described as 'liberal Tories'. They did pass some reforms but these built on work begun before 1821. Also, the failure to introduce parliamentary and social reform showed that there was no significant difference between the Tories of 1822–29 and those of 1812–21.

<table>
<tr><td>

ACTIVITY

1 In your own words, summarise the differences between the two hypotheses above.
2 Make a list of questions you want to ask about this period after reading these hypotheses.

</td><td>

The Tory government continued in power between 1822 and 1829. As the economic situation improved and there was less danger of revolution, the government made reforms that have won it the often-used name 'liberal Tory'. In this chapter you will decide whether this title is deserved by testing these two hypotheses against the evidence, and deciding which, if either, is valid. You may decide that neither is valid and suggest a better hypothesis of your own – one which itself can survive the testing process.

A How can you test hypotheses? (pp. 79–81)

B Testing the hypothesis: how much did the Cabinet change after 1822? (pp. 82–84)

C Testing the hypothesis: what kinds of reforms did the government make? (pp. 85–87)

D Review: can the government of 1822–29 really be described as 'liberal Tory'? (pp. 87–90)

</td></tr>
</table>

Testing a hypothesis: a checklist

1   Read the hypothesis through and check that you understand what it is saying.
2   Read or look at each piece of evidence. Does it appear to support or undermine the hypothesis?
3   Analyse each piece of evidence. The questions you need to ask are:
    a) Who wrote it?
    b) When did they write it?
    c) Why did they write it?
    d) For whom did they write it?
    e) Were they involved?
4   Decide, on the basis of your answer to **3**, whether the evidence is reliable or not.
5   Is any of the evidence sufficiently unreliable as to make it unsuitable for supporting or undermining the hypothesis?
6   Having examined the evidence, decide whether any parts of the hypothesis can be undermined, and which hypothesis seems to have the best support.
7   If neither hypothesis seems to be valid, can you suggest a new hypothesis, which the evidence you have examined seems to support?

For many students, testing what a historian says about an event, person or action in the past is a difficult task. You may be presented with two apparently conflicting statements or hypotheses. Which one is correct? How do you know? How can you decide? You may remember work on conflicting views (interpretations) of history earlier in your school life. Was King John a bad king? Was Richard III an evil hunchback who murdered his nephews? Were nineteenth-century factory owners cruel? You probably looked at a few sources giving two different views and tried to decide which view was correct. But if there is evidence that seems to support both sides, how can you decide which view is correct?

You could count up the number of sources supporting each view and conclude that the one with the most sources supporting it must be the correct view. This is what often happens when students first start 'testing hypotheses', but it does have limitations as a technique! Here's an example:

> During a Test match between England and Australia, the England captain appears to get an edge and the ball is caught by first slip, low down near his foot. Eleven Australians claim it is a catch, two English batsmen believe it was not. Does the greater number of Australians mean it must have been a catch?

What else do you need to know, apart from the *amount* of evidence, to check whether evidence is useful? You need to check the *reliability* of the evidence. You will certainly have done some work on this earlier in your study of history. How do you decide whether or not evidence is reliable?

TALKING POINT

Warning: remember that biased evidence is not necessarily unreliable. How can biased evidence be reliable and useful to historians?

80

CAN THE GOVERNMENT OF 1822–29 REALLY BE DESCRIBED AS 'LIBERAL TORY'?

ACTIVITY

1 Decide who was to blame in an accident in which a car driver was killed and a passenger injured. The car swerved to avoid another car coming out of a side road and hit a lamp post. You have several witnesses, but they are giving conflicting versions of what happened. How reliable is their evidence? Complete this table by commenting on whether the evidence is likely to be reliable or not and briefly noting the reason for your decision.

Source of evidence	Number of hours after accident that the interview took place	Reliable or unreliable	Reason or comment on witness
The passenger	3		
Driver of the car behind the one that crashed	4		
Passenger in the car behind the one that crashed	12		
Driver of the car coming out of the side road	10		
Pedestrian near the lamp post who was unhurt but shocked	24		
Pedestrian on other side of the road	24		

ACTIVITY

2 Historians must evaluate the reliability of views or opinions about historical events. Copy and complete this table to evaluate the likely reliability of the six witnesses at Peterloo shown opposite. Re-read pages 70–74 before completing the table.

	Witness 1	Witness 2	Witness 3	Witness 4	Witness 5	Witness 6
Reliable? (yes or no)						
Reasons						

ACTIVITY continued

81

CAN THE GOVERNMENT OF 1822–29 REALLY BE DESCRIBED AS 'LIBERAL TORY'?

Witness 1

Henry Hunt

speaker at
the meeting

Witness 2

Viscount Sidmouth

Home Secretary

Witness 3

Samuel Bamford

a supporter of reform,
present at the meeting

Witness 4

Chairman of
the Manchester
magistrates

Witness 5

Lieutenant Colonel L'Estrange

commander of the
military in Manchester

Witness 6

Robert Mutrie

member of the Yeomanry
in Manchester

3 Which of these six witnesses to the events at Peterloo in August 1819 would have
   been biased? Does that make them unreliable witnesses? Explain your answer.
4 On which of the following written accounts of the events at Peterloo would you
   place most reliance, and why?
   a) An account in the *Manchester Mercury* of 17 August 1819.
   b) An account in the *Manchester Chronicle* of 21 August 1819.
   c) An account by an eyewitness in a book written in 1851.
   d) An account by historian J. W. Hunt in a book published in 1972.
5 Summarise the important points to consider in assessing the reliability and
   usefulness of historical evidence.

82

CAN THE GOVERNMENT OF 1822–29 REALLY BE DESCRIBED AS 'LIBERAL TORY'?

B **Testing the hypothesis: how much did the Cabinet change after 1822?**

FOCUS ROUTE

As you work through Sources 5.1–5.21 on pages 82–88, complete this table to summarise the support for each hypothesis. An example has been given to start you off. Note that some of the evidence may support or contradict both hypotheses.

Source number	Author	Anything known about the author	Date, if known, and context of the source	Reliability of the source	Support for hypothesis 1: yes/no and why?	Support for hypothesis 2: yes/no and why?
5.1						
5.2	Aspinall	Historian	1947; introduction to edition of a Tory MP's diaries	As a historian Aspinall may not be biased and should be reliable	No	Yes, because suggests that changes to personnel not significant
5.3						
5.4						

SOURCE 5.1 The Cabinet before and after 1822

List the changes and continuities to personnel in the Cabinet between 1822 and 1827.

George Canning (1770–1827)

Canning was born in London in 1770. His father, a barrister, died when he was a year old, leaving the family poor. His mother became an actress when widowed, a profession deemed little better than prostitution in the early nineteenth century. Canning's father's brother paid for George to be educated at Eton College and Oxford. A lawyer, he became MP for the rotten borough of Newtown. Canning was Secretary of State for Foreign Affairs from 1796, Paymaster-General in 1800, Treasurer of the Navy in 1801 and Foreign Minister in the Duke of Portland's government in 1806. In 1809 he fought a duel with Castlereagh over Castlereagh's decision to send troops to Holland, which Canning had promised to the Duke of Wellington in Portugal instead. Canning was wounded in the thigh. Canning then left the government and concentrated on writing for publications such as the *Anti-Jacobin Review* and the *Quarterly Review*. He was a supporter of full political and religious rights for Catholics, but a strong opponent of any increase in the franchise. In 1812 he became MP for Liverpool. He was asked to become Foreign Minister but he was unwilling to serve in the same government as Castlereagh. He eventually changed his mind and in 1816 accepted a minor office. When Castlereagh committed suicide in 1822, Canning became Foreign Minister and held the post for the next five years.

William Huskisson (1770–1830)

Born in 1770, Huskisson had a private education before living with his uncle who was physician to the British Embassy. In 1790 he became private secretary to the British Ambassador in France. He returned to England in 1792, at which time Canning asked him to become Secretary to the Admiralty. He was elected as a Tory MP in 1796 and was appointed by Pitt as Secretary to the Treasury, but when Pitt resigned in 1806 he returned to the backbenches. He took a keen interest in financial matters. His publication in 1810 of *Depreciation of the Currency* won him a reputation as one of Britain's leading economists. In 1813 he called for changes in the taxation of imports, and in 1814 joined Liverpool's government and was given responsibility for the proposed Corn Laws. Despite strong opposition to the Corn Laws, he remained convinced that they were needed to protect Britain's farmers.

In 1822 Liverpool appointed him as President of the Board of Trade. In 1823 he became MP for Liverpool and developed a reputation as the leading representative of mercantile interests in Parliament. When Wellington became Prime Minister in 1828, he refused to serve under him and resigned. He became one of the main reformers in the Tory Party, advocating Catholic Emancipation and supporting Russell's calls for MPs for Leeds and Manchester. He also supported the building of railways. In 1830 he was invited to attend the official opening of the Liverpool–Manchester Railway but was knocked down by the *Rocket* as he crossed the line to talk to the Duke of Wellington. He died from his injuries.

What does Source 5.1 suggest about the extent to which the 'new men' – Peel, Canning and Huskisson – were 'new' to the government? What continuities were there? Are they likely to have been significant?

84

CAN THE GOVERNMENT OF 1822–29 REALLY BE DESCRIBED AS 'LIBERAL TORY'?

TALKING POINTS

In assessing whether the Tories were 'liberal' or not, part of the problem is that it all depends what we mean by 'liberal'.

a) As a group brainstorm all the things you think 'liberal' means.

b) How are your ideas coloured by a twenty-first century understanding of the political 'Liberal' with a capital 'L'?

ACTIVITY

Are there any similarities in background, interests and political views evident in the biographies of Peel, Canning and Huskisson?

Robert Peel (1788–1850)
Peel was born in Bury, Lancashire, in 1788. His father, Sir Robert Peel (1750–1830), was a wealthy cotton manufacturer and MP for Tamworth. Educated at Harrow School and Christ Church, Oxford, Peel became a Tory MP in 1809 at the age of 21. When Lord Liverpool became Prime Minister in 1812, he was appointed as Chief Secretary for Ireland. He resigned from the post in 1821 but in 1822 rejoined Lord Liverpool's government as Home Secretary.

SOURCE 5.2 From the introduction to *Henry Hobhouse's Diary*, 1947, by the editor A. Aspinall. Hobhouse was a Tory MP who had been Under Secretary of State at the Home Office under Sidmouth. He assisted Peel in his reforms of the Penal Code

It is too easy to exaggerate the significance of the Cabinet reconstruction of 1822–23. The substitution of Peel for Sidmouth as Home Secretary was unquestionably a change for the better ... Too much, in fact, has been made of the distinction between the pre-1822 Tories, and the progressive Tories under Canning who in that year came to the fore.

SOURCE 5.3 A. Brady, *William Huskisson and liberal reform*, 1928

The infusion of such new blood strengthened and liberalised Liverpool's ministry. It is noteworthy that nearly half of the Cabinet ministers now sat in the House of Commons, while in 1815 more than three-fourths had been peers. The Government had become more representative of the middle and mercantile classes, and from them came the impulse for reform. The reaction against reform ... began to break and although the Chancellor remained on the Woolsack until 1827, he was unable to maintain his hitherto dominant influence. With the entrance of the Canningites to the Liverpool Ministry the first real chapter of English reform in the nineteenth century opened. Peel in the Home Office, Huskisson at the Board of Trade, Robinson under Huskisson's guidance at the Exchequer, struck out boldly on new paths and carried measures that entitle the ministry to rank amongst the great reforming administrations of the century.

SOURCE 5.4 R. Brown and C. Daniels, *Documents & Debates: 19th century Britain*, 1980

The year 1822 did not mark a dramatic volte-face. The policies and schemes adopted between 1822 and 1827 were already in existence and were merely speeded up. Peel, for example, found that the pattern for reform in criminal law had already been set up by the 1819 committee and the work of Romilly, Mackintosh and Buxton. The reforms that occurred in this period were 'concessionary' and did not attempt to alter the fundamental constitutional structure.

ACTIVITY

Can you suggest reasons why the historians in Sources 5.2, 5.3 and 5.4 do not agree on the issue?

Testing the hypothesis: what kinds of reforms did the government make?

85

CAN THE GOVERNMENT OF 1822–29 REALLY BE DESCRIBED AS 'LIBERAL TORY'?

FOCUS ROUTE

Use the sources in this section to write bullet point notes about the reforms of the Tories under these headings:

- trade and the economy
- work, employment and the trade unions
- law and order.

MAGISTRATE
Local justice of the peace who kept law and order and tried minor criminal cases.

ACTIVITY

Read through Chart 5A and Sources 5.5–5.13. In evaluating whether this evidence supports either hypothesis, answer the following questions:

1 Were any of the following problems addressed by the government of 1822–29:
  a) poor housing conditions
  b) lack of education for many children
  c) poverty
  d) adult working hours
  e) the right to vote for all men and women?
2 What long-term, rather than short-term, impact on Britain would the changes described in Chart 5A have had? (To answer this well, you may need to find more detail about some of the reforms.)

■ 5A A summary of the main reforms introduced by the Tories 1822–29

A TRADE

- Reduction of customs duties on imports, many of which were the raw materials used by British industry – for example, cotton, raw silk, raw wool, iron, copper, zinc, tin.
- Removal of restrictions on trade with Britain's colonies, and reduction of duties on goods from the colonies, to encourage trade within the Empire.
- Modification of the Navigation Laws, originally introduced to prevent the Dutch from competing with British trade, but which by the 1820s were restricting British trade with foreign countries.
- Reciprocity of Duties Act 1823, by which the government could make treaties with other countries to set up free trade between them. Between 1823 and 1829, fifteen such agreements were signed.
- Introduction of a sliding scale of duties on imported wheat (1828) as a modification of the Corn Laws of 1815 to allow foreign wheat to enter Britain without any duty once the price for British wheat reached 73s a quarter.

B FINANCE

The Bank Act of 1826 was the beginning of the reform of the banking system. In the 1820s banknotes were simply a way of allowing people to carry money without having to carry coins. A banknote promised that if someone went into a bank and handed the note over they would receive gold in return (£1's worth, £5's worth and so on). The notes in use today still 'promise to pay the bearer on demand the sum of . . .'. However, in the 1820s some banks issued more notes than they had gold stocks, and in 1825 a number of country and London banks had gone out of business following demand for gold from people who held notes. The banks did not have sufficient gold to repay their customers. The Act of 1826 tried both to decrease the number of notes issued and to increase the size of banks, to create greater stability and more confidence. Private banks were no longer allowed to print notes of less than five pounds in value. Greater confidence in the banks led to more investment and helped the expansion of British industry.

C WORK

The Combination Laws, which had made trade unions illegal since 1800, were repealed in 1824. Following a campaign by Francis Place, a parliamentary committee had been set up and Huskisson was persuaded to repeal the laws. After the repeal, hundreds of unions were set up, many coming out into the open, having been organised secretly. In 1825, following a wave of strikes, the law was amended to allow unions to exist, but limiting how they could operate – they were not allowed to 'obstruct' other workers, or try to persuade them to join a union.

D LAW AND ORDER

- The Penal Code was reformed. The death penalty was abolished for over 180 crimes and remained as mandatory only for murder and treason. The jury system was reorganised, and the use of government spies was stopped. However, convicts were still transported to Australia and there were public hangings until the 1860s.
- Before 1800 imprisonment had not been used as a punishment except for debtors and to hold people awaiting trial. The Gaols Act (1823) removed some of the worst abuses, enabling imprisonment to become a major part of the punishment system. Jailers were to be paid instead of relying on getting money from prisoners, women jailers were introduced to look after women prisoners, and all prisoners were to receive some education and visits from doctors and chaplains. Prisons were to be inspected by MAGISTRATES three times a year. However, these reforms only applied to large prisons in London and seventeen main cities.
- The Metropolitan Police Force was set up in 1829, the first official police force in the country. It replaced the Bow Street Runners and nightwatchmen with 1000 paid constables, under the control of a commissioner, with headquarters at Scotland Yard. The police wore a uniform that was deliberately non-military in appearance, and they were armed only with truncheons. Initially, the force operated only in the City of London. The idea spread only slowly to other cities and to rural areas because the notion of a police force was seen as a threat to civil liberties. It was not until the 1850s that every area of the country had a police force.

86

CAN THE GOVERNMENT OF 1822–29 REALLY BE DESCRIBED AS 'LIBERAL TORY'?

Mrs Arbuthnot

Harriet Arbuthnot was a close personal friend of the Duke of Wellington. They corresponded frequently on personal and political matters. In 1824 there were rumours that they were lovers. However, Mrs Arbuthnot's husband, Charles, was also a close friend of the Duke. In her biography of the Duke (*Wellington: Pillar of State*, 1972) Elizabeth Longford described the Duke's reaction to the death of Mrs Arbuthnot in 1834. 'The Duke walked about the room for a few minutes almost weeping aloud before he went to his room. Next morning he left at 8am to be with Charles Arbuthnot.' About a week later the Duke received a letter from Mr Arbuthnot in which he wrote, 'She [Harriet] had no friend in which she was so much attached as she was to you [the Duke] ... I am writing all my thoughts to you, for we were *three*, and you will understand ...'

Mrs Arbuthnot's Diary contains her views of the political events of the early 1800s.

SOURCE 5.5 A. Brady, *William Huskisson and liberal reform*, 1928

The limited nature of Huskisson's tariff reform is apparent. He accepted as wholeheartedly as Peel did later the free trade doctrine, but in its application he was hampered by a number of factors, the most pronounced of which were his party affiliations. He and his associates had to educate both their own party and Parliament. An attempt to effect sweeping changes would merely have stiffened the resistance of the opposition, and perhaps have postponed reform indefinitely.

SOURCE 5.6 F. Bamford and Duke of Wellington (eds), *Mrs Arbuthnot's Diary*, 1950

Herries [Secretary to the Treasury] told me that Huskisson's indecent presumption and haste in altering the trading laws was creating great alarm and dissatisfaction among the merchants of the City.

SOURCE 5.7 Peel speaking in a debate on the Combination Laws, quoted in J. W. Hunt, *Reaction and Reform*, 1972

Men who have no property except their manual strength ought to be allowed to confer together ... for the purpose of determining at what rate they will sell their property.

SOURCE 5.8 Lord Liverpool speaking in the debate about the new Combination Law of 1825, following the strikes that had resulted from the repeal in 1824 of the previous Combination Laws; reported in Hansard

The measure arose almost entirely out of the bill of last session, which had been hastily passed. He had not been aware of its extent, and did not, until it came into operation, know its provisions ... This bill not only prevented the combination of workmen against masters, and of masters against workmen, but prevented the combination of workmen against workmen.

SOURCE 5.9 J. W. Hunt, *Reaction and Reform*, 1972

Three times bills introduced by Romilly to abolish the death penalty for minor offences were passed by the Commons but rejected by the House of Lords. Sir John Mackintosh, the Whig MP who led the campaign after Romilly's death, succeeded in getting a committee of enquiry appointed ... When Peel came into office he accepted most of the findings of this committee, but took the reform process entirely into his own hands ... In 1823 Acts were passed ... to abolish the death penalty for more than a hundred offences, some of which Peel had added to the proposals of the committee.

SOURCE 5.10 A comment on the impact of the Gaols Acts of 1823, 1824 and 1825 in the First Report of the Select Committee of the House of Commons on Prisons, 1835

They have personally inspected the prisons of this metropolis and its neighbourhood, and have examined several of the visiting magistrates, chaplains, and officers of those and other prisons ... and whilst they have the satisfaction of believing that some of our prisons have of late been much improved, yet they cannot refrain from expressing their decided opinion that imprisonment in Newgate, Giltspur St, and the Borough Compter [all London prisons], in their present condition, must have the effect of corrupting the morals of their inmates, and manifestly tend the extension rather than the suppression of crime.

SOURCE 5.11 A report of a speech by Sir Robert Peel on his reforms to the Penal Code, quoted in *The speeches of Sir Robert Peel*, 1853

When he came into office seven years before the present period, the criminal law of Great Britain exceeded in severity the criminal codes of every other part of Europe, and he had then thought it ought to be ameliorated [improved]. He made it, since he had been in office, the great object of his ambition, not to set the example of ameliorating this code [the Penal Code] but to follow the example set by others.

87

CAN THE GOVERNMENT OF 1822–29 REALLY BE DESCRIBED AS 'LIBERAL TORY'?

ACTIVITY

1 What does Source 5.10 suggest about the effect of imprisonment on criminals in the early 1820s?
2 Define, as used in Source 5.12:
   a) opprobrious
   b) sanguinary.
3 Does Source 5.13 suggest that there was any significant change in the criminal law between the early 1820s and the 1830s?
4 What does the introduction of a more effective and efficient police force and criminal code suggest was the *main* aim of the reforms?

SOURCE 5.12   From the London Jurors' petition to Parliament in 1831, on the changes to the Penal Code, quoted in L. Radzinovocz, *A history of English criminal law*, 1948

The recent Acts passed with the professed intention to amend and improve the Criminal laws have not remedied the evil of which an enlightened community have the greatest reason to complain, but have still left those laws a disgrace to our civilisation by retaining the opprobrious distinction of being the most sanguinary of any in Europe.

SOURCE 5.13   Convictions and sentences, 1820 and 1830, from G. R. Porter, *The progress of the nation*, 1836, quoted in D. Beales, 'Peel, Russell and Reform', *Cambridge Historical Journal*, 1974

Year	Number convicted	Sentenced to death	Executed	Executed for murder
1820	9,318	1,238	107	10
1830	12,805	1,397	46	14

D Review: can the government of 1822–29 really be described as 'liberal Tory'?

What have contemporaries and historians said about the idea of 'liberal Tories'? Sources 5.14–5.21 provide you with opinions about their attitudes and their reforms.

SOURCE 5.14   Peel writing to John Croker in 1820, from L. J. Jennings (ed.), *The correspondence and diaries of John Wilson Croker*, 1884

Do you not think that the tone of England – of ... public opinion – is more liberal – to use an odious but intelligible phrase – than the policy of the government? Do you not think there is a feeling, becoming daily more general and confirmed ... in favour of some undefined change in the mode of governing the country?

SOURCE 5.15   A comment on the Tories in 1826 by Mrs Arbuthnot, an opponent of the reformers in the Tory Party, from F. Bamford and Duke of Wellington (eds), *Mrs Arbuthnot's Diary*, 1950

The government, as it is now constituted, has, I think, totally lost ... the confidence of the country. The liberal party, with Mr Canning at their head, court the Opposition and try to shape their measures with a view of catching their votes.

SOURCE 5.16   Comment by a Whig MP in 1826, quoted in A. Mitchell, *The Whigs in Opposition*, 1967

We are certainly, to all intents and purposes, a branch of His Majesty's government. Its proceedings for some time past have proved that though the gentlemen opposite are in office, we are in power, the measures are ours.

ACTIVITY

1 What reason is suggested in Source 5.14 for government reforms?
2 What did Mrs Arbuthnot mean by 'the liberal party' in Source 5.15?
3 What do Sources 5.15 and 5.16 suggest about the nature of Tory government by 1827?

88

CAN THE GOVERNMENT OF 1822–29 REALLY BE DESCRIBED AS 'LIBERAL TORY'?

(see Chapter 4)

ACTIVITY

1 Read Sources 5.17–5.21. How liberal were the Tories according to each writer?

2 What reasons do the historians in Sources 5.17–5.21 give for the development of reforms?

■ **Learning trouble spot**

What was the economic situation between 1820 and 1829?

In the years immediately following the end of the Napoleonic Wars, Britain suffered several periods of economic depression (see Chapter 4). By 1821 the economy had begun to recover, and the early 1820s were a time of relative prosperity for the country as a whole (though not necessarily for all its people). In 1825, however, the 'boom' ended, and in the autumn and winter of 1825 there were bank failures and a stock exchange collapse, which led to many businesses going bankrupt. Some people argued that this was the result of the government's moves towards ending the policy of protecting British manufacturers and farmers from foreign imports. The problems continued into 1826, and in that year a poor harvest added to them. Although there was a recovery, another slump in the economy hit both agriculture and industry in 1829 and 1830.

SOURCE 5.17 D. Beales, *From Castlereagh to Gladstone*, 1969

By comparison with what had gone before, the measures of the Administration between 1822 and 1827 seem notably liberal and reformist. By comparison with what followed they seem merely trivial tinkering … The law could be 'consolidated' but not reformed. Nothing serious could be done about the Church. Slavery could not be abolished.

SOURCE 5.18 W. R. Brock, *Lord Liverpool and liberal Toryism 1820–27*, 1941

With the changes of 1821–23 Liverpool was able to gather round him a group of liberal-minded men ready to take whatever opportunities were offered for economic reform … The next two years were of the greatest importance in the history of economic policy. They saw the application of the principle of free trade, the consolidation of the Customs Laws, the repeal and subsequent re-enactment in a modified form of the Combination Laws, and the launching of a new colonial policy.

SOURCE 5.19 E. J. Evans, *Political Parties in Britain 1783–1867*, 1985

The true difference between the allegedly 'reactionary' and 'liberal' phases of Liverpool's government lies in the state of the economy and the extent of popular unrest to which it gave rise … Huskisson, Robinson and Peel had the good fortune to operate in calmer, more expansionist times, with the solitary exception of the period of financial crisis in 1822–26. Extra-parliamentary agitation ebbed markedly after 1821 and the government could afford to give its attention to economic revival rather than public order … Liverpool's policy of trade liberalisation followed in the footsteps of Pitt's peacetime administration (1783–93).

SOURCE 5.20 A. Wood, *Nineteenth-Century Britain*, 1960

Since the beginning of 1820 Lord Liverpool had been aware that the government needed new blood, and had been hoping to give the Tory Cabinet a more liberal tone. This would win over the moderate reformers and would make a Whig government impossible, since Grey did not feel that he could bring his followers to come to terms with the radicals.

SOURCE 5.21 A. Briggs, *The Age of Improvement*, 1962

Liverpool realised the need for change himself. His replacement of Sidmouth by Peel as Home Secretary in 1822, the change from Castlereagh to Canning at the Foreign Office, the substitution of Robinson for Vansittart, and the entry of Huskisson into the Cabinet, ushered in a period of 'liberal' rule. None of these changes, taken separately, marked a sharp break. When Peel became Home Secretary he found the pattern of reform in criminal law already set; a committee of 1819, the result of the work of Romilly, Sir James Mackintosh and Sir Thomas Fowell Buxton, had laid the foundations for a major revision of criminal law. When Canning replaced Castlereagh, he did not have to formulate a completely new foreign policy; Castlereagh had already been moving unhappily in a direction which Canning followed with enthusiasm. At the Board of Trade, Wallace, the energetic vice-president, had carried out useful work before Huskisson went there and recognised the need for a 'full and complete revision of our commercial system'. He was annoyed indeed at the promotion of Huskisson over his head. The bright new look of the Liverpool government was not an illusion, but neither was it the first move in a political conjuring trick. It was because the times were changing that the government changed. Not only was the country at last in a genuine 'state of peace', but the presence of new elements in society – mercantile and industrial – was increasingly recognised.

89

CAN THE GOVERNMENT OF 1822–29 REALLY BE DESCRIBED AS 'LIBERAL TORY'?

Do the Tories deserve to be known as 'liberal Tories'? Some of the sources you have read suggest that there was a change of attitude on the part of the government. Peel clearly seemed to think in 1820 that there was a change in the political climate of the country and that the government ought to reflect that change (Source 5.14). Mrs Arbuthnot equally felt that the government's approach had changed, although to her mind it was not a change for the better (Source 5.15). Some of the Whigs had begun to feel that the Tory Party had taken over Whig policies (Source 5.16). Brady, in his book about Huskisson and liberal reform, suggests, however, that change came only against stiff opposition (Source 5.5). It would seem that the government's attitude and approach to reform was changing. Some of the men in the Cabinet after 1822 had only been on the edge of government in previous years and were now in more powerful positions, and this meant that their ideas held greater sway.

Did the reforms passed by the government between 1822 and 1829 prevent revolution, or did the lack of unrest and the diminished fear of revolution lead the government to be more willing and able to introduce reforms? It is to some extent a 'chicken and egg' question but it is worth noting that major problems were left virtually untouched. There was no attempt to abolish the much-hated Corn Laws, seen, especially by the working classes, as a means of keeping bread prices higher than they otherwise would have been. Nor was there any intervention to improve the poor living conditions of a large proportion of the population. No action was taken to regulate the working hours of adult males. Nothing was done to provide education for the majority of children. The slave trade in the British Empire had been abolished, but slavery had not. There was determined resistance to any attempt to reform the electoral system. In all these areas the government took no action. Most of the reforms passed by the Tories between 1822 and 1829 would have had little noticeable immediate impact on the person in the field or the street. Raw materials might well have been cheaper, so cutting manufacturers' costs, but this did not translate into wage increases for workers. Modifications to the Corn Laws were not made until 1828 so the issue of artificially high bread prices remained throughout the period. Working people were unlikely to be directly affected by the new banking arrangements after 1826. Despite this lack of action there was no massive uprising or unrest during the period 1822–29. This might suggest that the government felt no need to be seen to be passing measures to prevent the majority from rising up in protest. It may be that it felt no threat of serious social unrest.

One major area of reform, however, which might have had a direct impact, was the changes to the criminal code. The removal of the death penalty for many relatively minor offences, which included stealing a loaf of bread, meant juries were more likely to convict, whereas previously they might have found the accused not guilty, knowing the punishment would be death by hanging. The introduction of an effective police force in London made it more certain that persons committing offences would be caught. This may have contributed to a greater unwillingness to start trouble. However, since the introduction of the Metropolitan Police came only at the very end of the period in 1829, the argument that it may have contributed to the lack of protest and unrest after 1822 is not a strong one.

The other area that would have had some direct impact on many working people was the relaxation of the Combination Laws. Although they placed restrictions on the organisation of strikes and what trade unions could do to put their point across, the new laws did, for the first time, allow working people to combine in unions to negotiate wages and hours of work. Before 1829, however, the growth of unions was not great.

Although, as you have seen, the Tories introduced some far-reaching reforms during the period 1822–29, there were major areas left virtually untouched. In later chapters you will see how successive governments approached issues such as the Corn Laws, the franchise, working-class protest and poverty.

CITY COLLEGE
LEARNING RESOURCE CENTRE

90

CAN THE GOVERNMENT OF 1822–29 REALLY BE DESCRIBED AS 'LIBERAL TORY'?

ACTIVITY

Discuss the view that 'liberal' is an appropriate term to describe the Tory government between 1822 and 1829.

TALKING POINT

Why was there apparently no fear of revolution on the part of the government, and no serious threat of revolution on the part of the people, in the period 1822–29?

ACTIVITY

1 Go back to Section A and reread the checklist for testing hypotheses (page 79).
2 Using the table you completed on page 82:
   a) summarise the support or lack of it for hypothesis 1
   b) summarise the support or lack of it for hypothesis 2
   c) decide which of the two hypotheses you prefer, based on the amount, reliability and validity of the evidence supporting it.
3 There is evidence to contradict both hypotheses. You may feel, therefore, that neither hypothesis 1 nor 2 is acceptable. Devise your own hypothesis about the Tories between 1822 and 1829 and the validity of the use of the term 'liberal Tories'. Your hypothesis must be capable of being tested as you have tested 1 and 2, and must have valid and reliable evidence to support it.

KEY POINTS FROM CHAPTER 5

Can the government of 1822–29 really be described as 'liberal Tory'?

1   In 1822 and 1823 there were changes in the government that introduced younger men to the Cabinet. However, Lord Liverpool remained Prime Minister throughout the period, and many members of the Cabinet after 1822 had been in the pre-1822 administration or had held minor government office.

2   The government introduced some major reforms in the areas of trade, finance, the criminal code, prisons, the police and work, which had important long-term effects.

3   Some of the reforms were continuations of changes already begun before 1822.

4   In several important areas, however, little or nothing was done. There was no attempt to repeal the Corn Laws, to regulate adult working hours, to ameliorate the poor living conditions of many of the population, to abolish slavery, or to reform the electoral system.

5   The term 'liberal' as applied to the Tories of 1822–29 is one which can be defended, but also rebutted. Over the 170 years since that government was in office, its use has been both supported and questioned by historians.

6

Whigs or Tories – who were the reformers?

CHAPTER OVERVIEW

The aim of this chapter is to identify and examine the differences and similarities between the Tories and the Whigs, firstly by looking at some individual MPs, and then by taking an overview of the main reforms between 1827 and 1851.

We shall also consider whether the reforms that they introduced can be considered as 'progress' and decide whether the reforms explain why there was no revolution in Britain between 1827 and 1851.

A Was there such a thing as a 'typical' Whig or Tory MP? (pp. 91–94)

B The similarities and differences: reforming Tories or reforming Whigs? (pp. 95–97)

C Do the reforms explain why there was no revolution in Britain 1827–51? (p. 98)

D Review: Whigs or Tories – who were the reformers? (p. 99)

A Was there such a thing as a 'typical' Whig or Tory MP?

■ 6A Administrations 1827–51

Years	Party in power	Prime Minister	Dates	Elections
1827–30	Tories	Lord Liverpool	to April 1827	
		George Canning	April–August 1827	
		Viscount Goderich	Sept 1827–Jan 1828	
		Duke of Wellington	Jan 1828–Nov 1830	July 1830
1830–34	Whigs	Earl Grey	Nov 1830–July 1834	April 1831 / Dec 1832
		Viscount Melbourne	July 1834–Dec 1834	
1834–35	Tories	Sir Robert Peel	Dec 1834–April 1835	Jan 1835
1835–41	Whigs	Viscount Melbourne	April 1835–Sept 1841	July 1837
1841–46	Tories	Sir Robert Peel	Sept 1841–July 1846	June 1841
1846–52	Whigs/Liberals	Lord John Russell	July 1846–Feb 1852	July 1847

Key

Tories

Whigs

Whigs/Liberals

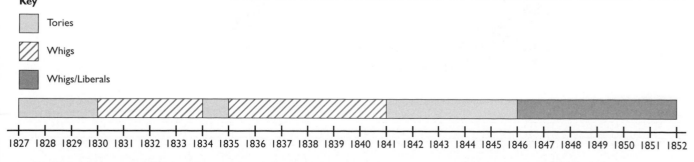

1827	1828	1829	1830	1831	1832	1833	1834	1835	1836	1837	1838	1839	1840	1841	1842	1843	1844	1845	1846	1847	1848	1849	1850	1851	1852

It would appear from Chart 6A that there are clear divisions within the period into Whig and Tory 'eras'. It is also easy to assume that the Tories and Whigs were very different parties, because in the twenty-first century we are used to political parties that have very different beliefs and policies. But how different from each other were the Tories and Whigs in the early nineteenth century?

■ **Learning trouble spot**

Changing parties

1827–51 was a key period in the development of the main political parties. Unfortunately this can be confusing as their names change! By the end of the 1840s the Whigs had become known as Liberals – a mixture of the old Whigs and some Tories who joined the Whigs over the issue of the ending of the Corn Laws (see Chapter 10). The Tories became known as Conservatives in the 1830s and 1840s, the years of Peel's leadership, but more especially during the period after Peel's loss of power in 1846, when the Tories who were left after the Corn Law disputes adopted the name 'Conservative' more formally.

It is also important to remember that, for much of this period, there was no rigid 'party system' and no party organisation as we would recognise it today. Many MPs owed no allegiance to either Whigs or Tories, and sat as independent members. The labels Whig and Tory were not necessarily indicative of an MP's political beliefs. On occasions MPs changed from Whig to Tory or Tory to Whig, but without the outcry with which a change of side in the Commons is received nowadays. It was even known for Whigs to serve in Tory administrations and Tories to serve in Whig administrations, although it did not happen often.

■ 6B The development of the political parties 1780s–1851

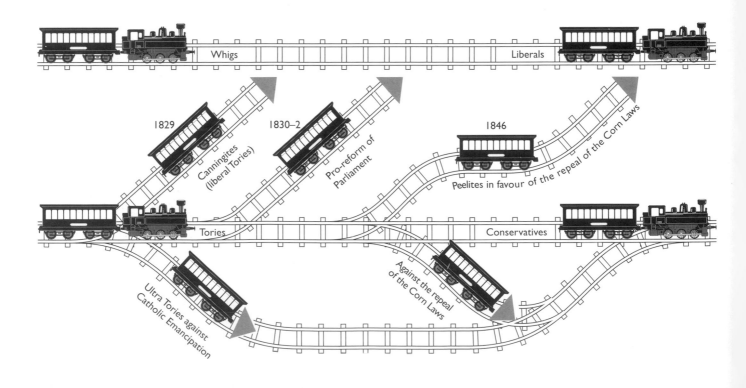

ACTIVITY

Read the biographies (A–N) of fourteen men who were MPs during the period 1827–51 (pages 93–94).

1 Copy and complete columns 1–8 of the table below, using the information in the biographies A–N on pages 93–94. (Note that not all columns can be completed.)
2 When you have completed columns 2–8, fill in column 9. Was the MP a Whig, a Tory or neither (independent)?
3 Research the MPs in the box below, and then match them to the biographies. (You will find the answers on page 261.)

Who were they?

Benjamin Disraeli / John Fielden / Henry Brougham / Earl Grey / Michael Sadler / Joseph Hume / William Gladstone / George Hudson / William Joliffe / Thomas Duncombe / Lord Palmerston / George Howard / Francis Burdett / Lord John Russell

4 Summarise your findings about the type of men who became either Whig or Tory MPs in the first half of the nineteenth century. You could set your notes out under headings such as family background, wealth, education, occupations outside Parliament and political views.
5 Explain whether it is possible to describe the Whigs as reformers and the Tories as reactionaries.
6 Was there such a thing as a typical Whig/Liberal or Tory/Conservative? Explain the reasons for your answer.

MP	Place of birth	Father's occupation	Family background	Family wealth	Education	Occupation	Political views	Whig, Tory or neither?
A								
B								
C								

A Born in Yorkshire. Father owned a small textile business. At the age of ten he was required to work in his family's cotton factory for ten hours a day. Having served his apprenticeship to his father he was made a partner in the business. Father died leaving £200 cash and a business worth about £5000. It expanded rapidly over the years. By 1832 the company was responsible for about one per cent of the total cloth being produced in Yorkshire and Lancashire. Was a Quaker and was concerned about the welfare of the people his company employed. Presented a petition to Parliament for factory legislation to protect child workers. Advocated the introduction of a minimum wage. Believed that adult men should have the vote. Elected to Parliament in 1832. Supported the Chartists' demands. Wanted a national system of state education.

B Father a member of the aristocracy. Educated at Westminster School and Oxford University, then went on a tour of Europe. Returned to England in 1793 and married the daughter of an extremely wealthy banker. On marriage his wife (and therefore 'B' according to the then law) received a dowry of £25,000. In 1797 his father-in-law purchased a rotten borough for £4000. He gave the seat to his son-in-law who became a member of the House of Commons. One of the few members of the House of Commons to support the idea of parliamentary reform. Spent £100,000 during two elections in 1804 and 1806. Was elected for a London constituency where most of the voters were shopkeepers and ARTISANS who had a strong dislike of aristocratic privilege.

C Born in Liverpool. Father an MP and successful businessman. Educated at Eton and Christ Church, Oxford, where he gained a reputation as a fine speaker. At university he denounced the proposals for parliamentary reform. Elected for a pocket borough in 1832. Achieved minor office within two years of entering the Commons, and was involved in early railway legislation. Became a convert to Corn Law repeal in the 1840s.

D Born in Scotland. Father a landowner in Westmoreland. Studied science and mathematics at Edinburgh University at the age of fourteen. Became interested in law. Joined the faculty of advocates (Scottish bar) in 1800. At university developed radical political opinions and wrote articles dealing with the issue of social reform. Worked as a lawyer for three years. In 1803 he moved to London where he became friends with a group of radicals. Developed a reputation as a lawyer with progressive views. Was offered a pocket borough seat in Parliament in 1810 and although he disapproved of this corrupt system he accepted the seat in order to enter the House of Commons.

ARTISAN
A skilled craftsman

CITY COLLEGE
LEARNING RESOURCE SERVICE

E Born in Yorkshire. Father a farmer. Educated at the local school then apprenticed to a draper. Eventually became a partner in the business. Was left £30,000 in a will. Invested successfully in railways and became very wealthy. Was active and influential in local politics. Elected as an MP in 1845. Active in opposing any government regulation of the railways.

F Born in Hampshire. Father a member of the aristocracy. Educated at Harrow School, Edinburgh University, and St John's College, Cambridge. Aged 22 he paid £1500 to become an MP. The legality of the election was challenged but he became MP for a pocket borough the following year. He refused a high Cabinet office at 25 because he felt he was too young. Took up another post, which he held for twenty years before taking up a major Cabinet post. Became a supporter of reform of Parliament.

G Born in London. Father was an author. After a private education 'G' trained as a solicitor. Was also a writer and interested in politics. In the early 1830s stood in several elections and was eventually elected in 1837. Supported triennial parliaments and the secret ballot, and was sympathetic to the demands of the Chartists.

H Born in London. Father a member of the aristocracy who supported parliamentary reform. Spent a short time at Westminster School, and then was educated at home. Father encouraged him to take an interest in politics and he developed a sympathy for the poor. Went to Edinburgh University. Father arranged for him to be elected to a 'family seat'. Took an active part in the campaign for parliamentary reform.

I Born in Derbyshire. Moved to Leeds where he became an importer of Irish linen. In 1829 was elected as an MP. Was active in the campaign for factory reform and was a leader in the campaign to reduce working hours. Lost his seat in the 1832 general election.

J Born in Scotland. Father a shipmaster. Was apprenticed to a local surgeon and worked as a doctor for the EAST INDIA COMPANY. Soon gained a senior position in the company. Returned to Scotland a rich man, and turned his attention to politics. Was elected in 1812. Once in Parliament his political views began to change. Supported universal suffrage and Catholic Emancipation. Also suggested the setting up of savings banks, the abolition of flogging in the army, and an end to imprisonment for debt. By 1830 was seen by many as the leader of the movement for universal suffrage in the House of Commons. In 1839 helped to present the Chartist petition for parliamentary reform.

EAST INDIA COMPANY
A company which set up trading posts in India in the early 1700s. By the 1750s it was effectively governing these areas on behalf of Britain. The India Act of 1784 took these powers from the Company and placed a Governor-General in charge to control political affairs, while the East India Company continued to control trade.

K Born in Yorkshire. Father a large landowner and member of an aristocratic family. Educated at Harrow School then joined a Guards regiment. Retired from the army and began to look for a seat in the House of Commons, and was elected in June 1826. Became a strong supporter of parliamentary reform. His seat disappeared in the 1832 reform and he had to find another. One of the few members of the House of Commons willing to argue the case for universal suffrage. Considered it his responsibility to represent the views of the working people as well as those who had actually voted for him. Argued that the Chartists were reasonable men who deserved the vote.

L Father a vicar. He joined the army and at the age of nineteen took part in the Peterloo Massacre. In 1832 he tried unsuccessfully for Parliament. He was successful in 1833 but was defeated in 1835. He became an MP again in 1837 and held the seat until 1866 when he was granted a baronetcy.

M Father a member of the aristocracy. Educated at Eton and Christ Church, Oxford. In 1826 his father arranged for him to be elected for one of the boroughs under his control. Took a particular interest in removing all religious forms of discrimination, especially those against Catholics and Jews. In 1830 was elected as an MP for Yorkshire. Called the proposed 1832 Reform Act 'a safe, wise, honest, and glorious measure'.

N Father an important military commander and staunch Tory. Educated at Eton and King's College, Cambridge, and then toured Europe. Aged 22 he became an MP. Did not agree with universal suffrage but felt that there was a strong need to improve the parliamentary system in Britain. Joined with a group of pro-reformers to obtain 'a more equal representation of the people in Parliament' and 'to secure to the people a more frequent exercise of their right of electing their representatives'. In 1797 introduced a petition in favour of constitutional reform, which was defeated by 256 to 91 votes. In the 1790s spoke against the suspension of the Habeas Corpus Act and opposed the Seditious Meetings Bill.

B The similarities and differences: reforming Tories or reforming Whigs?

■ **Learning trouble spot**

What changes to the economy happened during this period?
Many students underestimate the importance of financial and fiscal changes in underpinning industrial development during this period. Key factors in the economic development and progress during the period 1830–51 were the changes and improvements in banking and finance, and the freeing of trade between Britain and other countries. Reforms that made banks more reliable led people to have greater confidence in them and to use them more. This, in turn, led to money being available for investment in British industry. The banks also lent money to other countries for projects such as railway building, and the interest on these loans constituted an 'invisible export'. The banks also provided banking facilities for overseas countries, for which they charged fees.

As a result of a series of measures during the period 1823–46, which reduced and eventually virtually abolished import duties, trade became more free, and British manufacturers could buy their raw materials at lower prices. This stimulated industrial production and development. Overseas countries who sold their raw materials to Britain were more likely to buy British goods in return. This freeing of trade, far from leading to the ruin of British industry as some had feared, in fact contributed to its expansion.

ACTIVITY

1 Read through the descriptions of the Acts on pages 96–97. For each one decide whether you think it was passed by the Tories/Conservatives or by the Whigs/Liberals. Try to put a date to the Act, too.
2 Check your answers on page 261 and then make two lists:

   • Whig/Liberal Acts
   • Tory/Conservative Acts.

3 Organise the Acts under the following headings according to the area the Act dealt with (you may wish to put some under more than one heading):

   • political
   • work
   • housing/health
   • social
   • economic
   • religious
   • law and order.

4 Once you have found out the correct dates, put the dates against each Act.
5 From the information you have gained on reforms between 1827 and 1851, decide whether the Whigs/Liberals or Tories/Conservatives were the reformers.
6 Explain your decision in a short presentation. Justify your answer by using specific Acts as evidence for your decision.

Penny Black stamp

A Penny Post – set up a national postage system in which mail was paid for in advance by the sender; payment was indicated by an adhesive stamp.

B Reform Act – extended the right to vote to more men; gave many industrial towns MPs for the first time; removed MPs from places in which only a handful of people had votes.

C Reform of the Penal Code – many minor crimes no longer punishable by death.

D Tithe Commutation Act – replaced the tithe (a tax of one-tenth of annual produce to be paid to the Church) with a cash rent. Non-Anglicans felt it should have been abolished completely.

E Formation of the Metropolitan Police force – the first police force, established in London, to be unarmed, with a uniform deliberately not military in style.

Victorian policemen

F Catholic Emancipation – gave Roman Catholics equal political and civil rights with Anglicans and nonconformists.

G Public Health Act – set up a central Board of Health in London, with three commissioners and a medical officer, but only for five years. Set up local boards of health in towns with a death rate above 23 per 1000, or where ten per cent of the ratepayers petitioned the central board in London. The local board could, if it wished, pave streets, supply water and provide drainage, but it was not compulsory, and many did not. Ratepayers were usually anxious to keep costs down.

H Registration of Births, Marriages and Deaths – made compulsory.

I The repeal of the Test and Corporation Acts – allowed nonconformists (but not Catholics) equal political and civil rights with Anglicans (members of the Church of England).

Bluegate Fields, London

Convicts exercising in Pentonville Prison

J Municipal Corporations Act – abolished the old town corporations, many of which had been corrupt, and set up borough councils in large towns and cities, elected by male ratepayers for a term of three years. Boroughs had to have a paid treasurer, and accounts had to be audited. Boroughs had to establish a police force. Towns that had no council could apply to become boroughs, but the Act's stipulations were not compulsory.

K Prisons Act – set up the prisons inspectorate, followed by the building of several new prisons.

L Factory Act – no children under nine to work in factories; children aged nine to thirteen to work no more than eight hours a day, and to have two hours schooling a day; young people aged fourteen to eighteen to work no more than twelve hours a day.

M Poor Law Amendment Act – set up a system by which help for people in poverty was available only inside a workhouse, where conditions were often very unpleasant.

N Marriage Act – allowed Dissenters and Catholics to be married legally in their own churches provided a civil registrar was present at the service.

O Government grant to education – £20,000 given to two Church Societies to establish new schools.

> ENDOWED SCHOOLS
> Schools whose funds came from money left to them, often in a will.

A church school

P Factory Act – set the maximum working day for young people under eighteen and adult females at ten hours and the working week at 58 hours.

Q Custody of Infants Act – allowed mothers to have custody of children under seven if parents separated.

R Grammar Schools Act – enabled ENDOWED SCHOOLS to amend the curriculum set out in the original endowment and introduce new subjects.

S Railway Gauge Act – set a standard gauge across the country for railway tracks.

T Bank Charter Act – regulated the working of banks. Aimed at producing confidence in the banking system and at stopping the collapse of small banks that did not have sufficient gold reserves to back the issue of notes; limited the issue of new banknotes, including by the Bank of England.

U Repeal of the Corn Laws – abolished the regulations that had helped to keep the prices of wheat, and therefore of bread, higher than they might otherwise have been.

V Companies Act – all companies had to be officially registered, and issue prospectuses and accounts.

From the Mikado's list of punishments, by W.S. Gilbert

W Railways Act – the government would have the power to buy up railway companies after 21 years of existence after 1844. Each company was obliged to run one third-class train per day on its line at a fare which did not exceed 1d per mile, and which stopped at every station. It was intended to provide cheap travel for the working class, but the trains were slow and many companies ran the trains at inconvenient times. They became known as 'parliamentary trains'.

X Abolition of slavery in the British Empire – slaves to be set free within a year; £20 million paid to slave owners in compensation.

Y Mines Act – prohibited boys under ten and all females from working underground in mines.

CITY COLLEGE LEARNING RESOURCE CENTRE

Do the reforms explain why there was no revolution in Britain 1827–51?

ACTIVITY

Choose the three reforms that you think contributed most towards preventing revolution in Britain between 1827 and 1851. Give reasons for your choice.

One view of history, often referred to as the 'Whig' view and largely dating from the late nineteenth and early twentieth centuries, is that history is the story of the steady improvement of mankind. This view therefore sees change as the same thing as progress. Section B of this chapter suggests that there was a vast amount of change in the early nineteenth century. Was all this change progress, improving everyone's lives? And if it was, does this explain why there was no revolution in this period?

Some historians do not see the changes of the early nineteenth century as progress in every way. There are two reasons for this. Firstly, many of the changes meant that people's lives were much more closely controlled than they had been previously. This was seen by many as government interference in people's lives and was not welcomed by those who argued that it was not the government's role to take care of people's welfare. The term 'nanny state' had not been invented in the early 1800s, but it was what people who supported *laissez-faire* feared. For example, the new police force was seen not as a means of protection but as a means of control. The factory and mines Acts were also seen as government interference, not only by the owners, who objected to forced reductions in working hours and the abolition of child labour, but by many workers who objected to these Acts because they potentially cut a family's income. Even the public health Acts were opposed – for example, *The Times* newspaper objected to the government telling people how they should live.

Secondly, historians argue about whether or not the standard of living really did improve during the nineteenth century. It is possible to find a plentiful supply of evidence for both sides of the argument. If you look back over Section B of this chapter you will find evidence for improvements in many people's lives, but there is also evidence that life did not improve for others. Some legislation was permissive, that is it allowed change to happen, but did not enforce it. The early public health Acts are examples of this kind of legislation. Standards of public health and hygiene did not improve in all towns or cities because reform was not compulsory. The middle classes in many towns did not see why they should pay taxes to provide sewers or fresh water for the poor, so these facilities were not introduced. This meant that change did not affect all people in the same way, and while some might have welcomed the right to vote, others might have preferred a clean water supply. While some might have welcomed an efficient banking system, others might have wished for higher wages. Thus while for some, life did get better, for others, there was still plenty to protest about.

ACTIVITY

A report has been commissioned to find out how people feel about their living and working conditions in 1851 and what progress, if any, they feel that the changes of the previous twenty years have made to their lives. The commission has asked each individual to make a statement.

1 Work in pairs or alone. Write a statement in response to the commission for each individual listed below.
   a) Edward Jameson, a Methodist middle-class businessman aged 60.
   b) Beatrice Wilson, a 55-year-old wife of a middle-class businessman.
   c) James O'Leary, a working-class man, Roman Catholic, aged 40, with a wife and seven children.
   d) Sarah Lonsdale, a working-class woman, aged 30, married with four children under twelve.
   e) Tom Wakefield, a working-class boy, works in a mine, aged fifteen.

   f) Annie Cooper, a working-class girl, housemaid, aged fourteen.
   g) George Swift, an unemployed man aged 30, with a wife and three children under six.
2 Explain why some individuals might have felt that change had equalled progress and others might not.
3 Which individuals, if any, might have been supporters of revolution, and why?
4 Which individuals would be most likely to have considered revolution unnecessary, and why?

D Review: Whigs or Tories – who were the reformers?

Which party was the real reforming party? Both Whig and Tory governments passed Acts that improved working and living conditions, albeit in a small way. Both also introduced financial reforms that helped industry and business expand. The work of the Tories between 1841 and 1846 in establishing an efficient and effective banking system can be seen as crucial to Britain's economic development which, in turn, had a major impact on the growth of industry and hence on job opportunities. But both parties also placed restrictions on people's lives that had been unheard of in earlier times. Although the Whigs got rid of some limitations in reforms such as those allowing marriages in non-Anglican churches, they also set up the hated workhouse system in their Poor Law Amendment Act, 1834. This was seen by many as an unnecessarily cruel system.

ACTIVITY

Write plans for the following three essays, and complete the third as a full essay.

a) 'Between 1830 and 1851 considerable progress had been made in improving the quality of life for the majority of people in Britain.' Do you agree with this statement? Give your reasons.
b) Who made the greater contribution to reform between 1827 and 1851 – the Whigs or the Tories?
c) Do the reforms introduced between 1827 and 1851 explain why there was no revolution?

KEY POINTS FROM CHAPTER 6

Whigs or Tories – who were the reformers?

1 Political parties did not exist in the early nineteenth century in the same way as they do in the twenty-first century.
2 The differences between Whigs/Liberals and Tories/Conservatives were often slight and it is not always easy to say who was a typical Whig/Liberal or Tory/Conservative in the early nineteenth century.
3 When in government, both parties passed Acts which suggest they were reformers, and other Acts which suggest they were not.
4 Some of the reforms might have contributed to the lack of revolution in Britain, in contrast to many parts of Europe between 1830 and 1848 – for example, in France, Italy and the Austrian Empire.
5 The early nineteenth century was a time of considerable change, but that did not necessarily mean progress for all members of society.

7

Catholic Emancipation: a revolution in attitudes?

CHAPTER OVERVIEW

In 1829 the Tory government introduced a reform that went against the principles of the vast majority of its supporters both in Parliament and outside. They proposed to give Roman Catholics equal civil and political rights with Anglicans. The reasons why Wellington and Peel pursued a policy of Catholic EMANCIPATION that many regarded as a betrayal of their party are investigated in this chapter.

A Why was there discrimination against Catholics? (pp. 100–102)

B Why was the repeal of the Test and Corporation Acts significant? (pp. 102–103)

C Why was the County Clare election in 1828 so important? (pp. 104–105)

D How did the government respond to the dilemma created by O'Connell? (pp. 106–111)

E What were the implications of Catholic Emancipation? (pp. 112–113)

F Review: Catholic Emancipation: a revolution in attitudes? (p. 114)

EMANCIPATION
Freedom; political emancipation – the freedom to vote.

A Why was there discrimination against Catholics?

■ 7A Religious groups and beliefs in the eighteenth and nineteenth centuries

TALKING POINT

Why was it important in the sixteenth and seventeenth centuries for everyone in the country to be of the same religion? To what extent had this changed by the 1800s?

FOCUS ROUTE

1 Which events suggested to Protestants that Catholics were potential traitors?
2 What evidence is there that anti-Catholic feeling was still strong by the early 1800s?
3 How great was anti-Catholic feeling in Parliament by 1825?

Roman Catholics
Christians who belong to a Church headed by the Pope. Until the sixteenth century it was the only Christian Church in Britain.

Protestants
Originally so-called because they 'protested' against the teachings of the Roman Catholic Church. Therefore they are members of a variety of non-Catholic Churches.

Anglicans
Christians who belong to the Church of England. The head of the Church of England has been the monarch since the time of Henry VIII. The Church of England is often referred to as the 'Established' Church.

Dissenters
Those who 'dissented' from, or disagreed with, the teachings of the Roman Catholic or Anglican Churches. Examples of Protestant Dissenters are Methodists, Presbyterians, Quakers and Baptists.

In Ireland in the early nineteenth century almost 90 per cent of the population was Catholic. However, the majority of landowners (and therefore employers) and all important government officials were Protestant. Many Catholics had the vote in parliamentary elections because they owned enough property to qualify. However, a Catholic could not sit in Parliament as an MP because the oath of allegiance which all MPs took on entering Parliament was one which no Catholic could possibly take. The reasons for this oath lay in the history of the previous 300 years.

1534–53
Henry VIII broke away from Rome and became Head of the Church in England, replacing the Pope. Henry's Church adopted a very moderate form of Protestantism but under Henry's son, Edward VI, the country became radically Protestant. Signs of Catholicism in churches, such as wall paintings and silver candlesticks, were removed and Bibles written in English rather than Latin were introduced.

1553–58
Mary I, a Catholic, re-established Catholicism. Nearly 300 people, including five bishops, who refused to change back to Catholicism, were burned to death. Mary was nicknamed 'Bloody Mary'.

1558–1603
Elizabeth re-established moderate Protestantism. Many people wished to remain Catholic and refused to attend Protestant services, although they could be very heavily fined for this refusal. However, Elizabeth did not pursue these laws severely because she 'did not want to make windows into men's souls'. Elizabeth survived several Catholic plots to replace her with her cousin, Mary, Queen of Scots, and also defeated the Spanish Armada, which was sent with the aim of bringing England back to Catholicism.

1605
The Gunpowder Plot: an attempt to kill King James I and his ministers at the opening of Parliament. According to the government it was a plot by Catholics to kill James whom they intended to replace with a Catholic monarch.

1625–42
Charles I and Archbishop Laud were suspected by the Puritans of trying to return the country to Catholicism. Charles' wife, Henrietta Maria, was a French Catholic. Religious suspicions were a major factor behind the civil war of 1642–46.

Ave Maria

1649–60
In September 1649, during a military campaign in Ireland to put down rebellion against the new republic, Oliver Cromwell's army massacred civilians as well as soldiers at Drogheda.

1661–73
The Corporation Act 1661 barred anyone who would not worship according to the rites of the Anglican Church from holding public office. The Test Act 1673 debarred Catholics from holding any military or civil offices.

Welcome William and Mary!

Thanks for inviting us!

1688
James II was deposed because many nobles and MPs feared that he was about to return the country to Catholicism. James' wife had a son, to be raised as a Catholic. Until the birth, James' daughter, Mary, a Protestant, would have succeeded, but then England was faced with another Catholic monarch. Parliament forced James to abdicate in favour of the Protestant monarchy of James' daughter and her husband William of Orange.

1689
Bill of Rights: in future no Catholic and no one married to a Catholic could sit on, or be in line of succession to, the throne.

1715
James II's son, 'The Old Pretender', attempted to regain the throne, which he regarded as his. His English supporters were defeated at the Battle of Preston.

Bonnie Prince Charlie's Army

DERBY

1745
James II's grandson, 'Bonny Prince Charlie', attempted to regain the throne, which he regarded as rightfully his. With his army he marched south into England and reached Derby before, on the advice of his generals, he turned north again. He was finally defeated at the Battle of Culloden.

1778–80
The Catholic Relief Act 1778 allowed Catholics to acquire property.

ST PATRICK'S CATHOLIC CHURCH

1780
The Gordon Riots: following an anti-Catholic demonstration by the Protestant Association set up by Lord George Gordon, anti-Catholic riots broke out in London in which Catholic churches were destroyed and over 300 people were killed.

1801
In the Act of Union of 1801, Ireland became a part of the United Kingdom. The arrangement was agreed to as long as Catholics were allowed to have full civil and political rights. George III, however, refused to agree to it, arguing that his coronation oath bound him to uphold the Protestant religion, and George IV followed the same line.

To 1828
By 1828 no progress on allowing Catholics the same civil and political rights as Protestants had been made. In 1819 an attempt at emancipation was rejected by the Commons by two votes. In 1821 a bill was passed in the Commons but thrown out by the Lords. In 1822 and 1823 the Lords again rejected bills for partial emancipation, which the Commons had passed. In 1825 Sir Francis Burdett introduced an Act for the emancipation of Catholics into the Commons. It was carried by a majority of seventeen votes but following a speech by the Duke of York (the King's brother, and next in line to the throne) who declared that he would never as King give his assent to equality of status for Catholics, the Lords rejected it by 170 votes to 130.

CATHOLIC EMANCIPATION: A REVOLUTION IN ATTITUDES?

ACTIVITY

What are the two main reasons Liverpool gives in Source 7.1 for opposing any emancipation of Catholics?

SOURCE 7.1 Extracts from a speech made by Lord Liverpool in 1819 against Catholic Emancipation

The principle of the constitution, as established in 1688, was essentially Protestant; the connection of a church and a limited monarchy was absolutely essential to the existence of civil liberty and of constitutional government; and in deciding the question that the King must be Protestant, they had also decided that the government must be Protestant likewise . . .

The Roman Catholics not only brought a qualified allegiance, but differed from other dissenters in this, that they not only questioned the King's supremacy, but acknowledged a foreign one . . . It was not true that the Church of Rome exercised no power except in matters purely ecclesiastical . . . There could be little doubt that if the Catholic hierarchy possessed the power they would use that power in pursuit of further objects, namely the attainment of at least a participation of the property enjoyed by the clergy of the established church . . . instead of producing harmony and peace, the proposed concession would rather serve to give birth to a perpetual contest between the Catholic population and the priesthood on the one hand, and the Protestant proprietors and friends of the Protestant establishment on the other.

■ **Learning trouble spot**

A limited monarchy

The phrase 'limited monarchy' used by Lord Liverpool in Source 7.1 is one which many students find difficult to understand. In the Middle Ages there were few limits on what a monarch could do, providing he had money and an army. There was no regular parliament to ask awkward questions, and even when a parliament was called it was usually restricted in what it could discuss, and was there only to grant taxes and offer advice. Over a long period of time, from the reign of Henry VIII onwards, the powers of Parliament gradually increased and the powers of the monarch became more restricted. The civil war in the 1640s, the execution of Charles I, the abdication of James II and the invitation by Parliament to William and Mary to become monarchs, largely on Parliament's terms, meant that by the mid-1700s the monarchy had limited powers. No monarch could do just as he or she wished (see page 110).

FOCUS ROUTE

1 List the reasons for repealing the Test and Corporation Acts.
2 Explain why the repeal of the Test and Corporation Acts made it more difficult to continue to discriminate against Catholics.

B # Why was the repeal of the Test and Corporation Acts significant?

In 1828 the Test and Corporation Acts were repealed. These Acts, which prevented all but Anglicans from holding public office or sitting in Parliament, had not operated fully for many years. This was because every year Parliament passed an Act to pardon Dissenters who had broken the laws by taking public office or becoming members of Parliament; Dissenters were not perceived to be as threatening as Catholics. However, the pardon did not apply to Catholics, who were still debarred from public office.

SOURCE 7.2 Lord John Russell, a young Whig, sets out his reasons for introducing a bill for the Acts' repeal

The great principle . . . is that every man . . . should be at liberty to worship God according to the dictates of his conscience, without being subjected to any penalty or disqualification whatsoever . . . History will not justify you in maintaining these acts . . . the Dissenters of the present day feel nothing but loyalty to the House of Hanover [the royal family] . . . All ground of necessity fails, the acts having been suspended for more than three-quarters of a century . . . the abrogation of such laws . . . will be more consonant to the tune and spirit of the age.

ACTIVITY

Who was the 'Pretender' mentioned in Source 7.3? (See page 101.)

SOURCE 7.3 The case for repeal of the Test and Corporation Acts as put forward in the Annual Register, Vol 70, 1828

The case for removal of the disabilities was claimed as a matter of right, unless some strong ground of expediency could be established against them, and the existence of any such ground of expediency was denied. They had originally been imposed when everything was to be dreaded from a Catholic prince ... nothing was now to be dreaded, from a royal family, which, by the necessity of the Constitution, must be Protestant. They had been imposed to guard against danger from the Pope and a pretender; now a pretender no longer existed, and the Pope was impotent ... the spirit of popery had changed and been mitigated; and even if they should attempt to persecute, the attempt would be futile in a Protestant country.

Above all it was absolutely necessary to grant the demands of the Catholics; because otherwise the Catholics would not allow Ireland to enjoy a moment's repose, and ... would render that part of the United Kingdom ... the source of alarm, of discord, of expensive compulsory government in peace, and in war, a source of positive weakness.

■ **Learning trouble spot**

The Test and Corporation Acts   type it out

Students often do not understand exactly how and why these Acts existed and what they meant for people who were not members of the Church of England. The 1673 Test Act debarred non-Anglicans from holding any military or civil office. The 'test' was the oath of allegiance, which required Catholics to deny their religious beliefs. Even the heir to the throne, James, Duke of York (later James II), was obliged to give up his post as Lord Admiral in 1673 as a result of this Act. The 1661 Corporation Act was an Act that prevented non-Anglicans from holding any public office – such as being a member of a town corporation.

ACTIVITY

1 Study Source 7.2. Why did Russell feel that the Act should be repealed?
2 Explain the statement in Source 7.3 that 'everything was to be dreaded from a Catholic prince'.
3 What is the main line of argument in Source 7.3?
4 What problem with Ireland is implied in the final phrase of Source 7.3 – '... and in war, a source of positive weakness'?

ACTIVITY

It is 1828. Parliament is debating the repeal of the Test and Corporation Acts. Either:

a) write a speech to be made in the House of Commons by a Methodist MP, supporting the right of Catholics to hold public office and become MPs
b) write a speech to the House by a Methodist MP opposing the extension of rights to Catholics
   Or:
c) As a class set up a debate in which you, as MPs in 1828, debate the motion that 'the repeal of the Test and Corporation Acts should apply to Catholics as well as to Dissenters'.

FOCUS ROUTE

1 What were O'Connell's aims?
2 Why was the Catholic Association so dangerous in the eyes of the government?
3 What qualities did O'Connell have as a leader?
4 What was the central issue in the County Clare election?
5 What problem did the election of O'Connell create for the government?

C Why was the County Clare election in 1828 so important?

The campaign to give Catholics full political rights was led by Daniel O'Connell. His ultimate aim was to repeal the Act of Union and establish an Irish parliament in Ireland to run domestic affairs. In 1823 he was one of the founders of the Catholic Association, to which Catholics, including thousands of poor Irish peasants, paid 1d a month, known as the 'Catholic rent'. Very soon the association had the support of the Catholic Church and the vast income of £1000 a week. O'Connell rejected the use of violence but he warned the British government that if reform did not take place, the Irish masses would start paying attention to more violent leaders. However, when delegates met in Dublin to discuss political matters this seemed too much like an Irish parliament for the government in London, and it banned the Catholic Association in 1825. O'Connell did not find it too difficult to evade the ban and the association backed candidates in Irish elections who would promise to support Catholic Emancipation at Westminster.

Daniel O'Connell (1775–1847)
Daniel O'Connell was born in County Kerry in 1775. His family were members of the Irish Catholic aristocracy. Although the family was fairly wealthy, they were denied status, opportunity and influence because they were Catholics. O'Connell was educated at some of the best Catholic colleges in Europe and became a lawyer. His interest in politics began while he was in London, where he became familiar with the ideas of radicals like Tom Paine and Jeremy Bentham (see pages 51 and 146). He became involved with the United Irishmen, a group inspired by the French Revolution. During the 1798 uprising in Ireland, O'Connell went into hiding, fearing arrest even though he opposed the uprising. He argued that political and religious equality should be obtained through legal methods. O'Connell gradually turned to politics and by 1815 was acknowledged as the leader of the campaign for Catholic Emancipation. His strengths as a leader were his intelligence, tactical ability, great energy and a voice 'you could hear a mile off, as if it were coming through honey'.

■ 7C The Catholic Association's aims

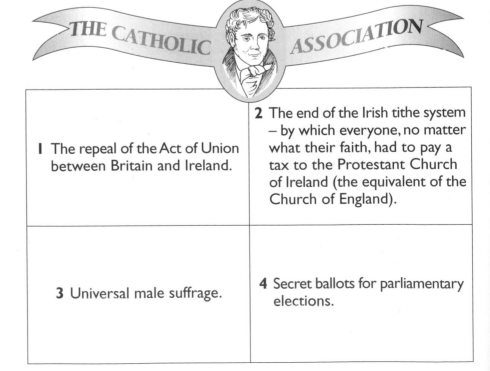

THE CATHOLIC ASSOCIATION

1 The repeal of the Act of Union between Britain and Ireland.	2 The end of the Irish tithe system – by which everyone, no matter what their faith, had to pay a tax to the Protestant Church of Ireland (the equivalent of the Church of England).
3 Universal male suffrage.	4 Secret ballots for parliamentary elections.

SOURCE 7.4 An extract from Daniel O'Connell's election manifesto, June 1828

The oath at present required by law is 'that the sacrifice of the mass, and the invocation of the blessed Virgin Mary, and other saints, as now practised in the Church of Rome, are impious and idolatrous'. I would rather be torn limb from limb than take it.

ACTIVITY

1 What is meant by the words 'invocation', 'impious' and 'idolatrous' in Source 7.4?
2 Why would a Catholic refuse to take that oath?

FREEHOLD
Land or property owned outright.

RETURN
The announcement of the number of votes cast for each candidate in an election.

ACTIVITY

1 What fear is implied in the final sentence of Source 7.6?
2 It is July 1828. You are Robert Peel, the Home Secretary, and you have received Fitzgerald's letter (Source 7.6). Prepare a report for the Prime Minister which:
   a) outlines the key aspects of recent events
   b) identifies the implications for the future and the dilemma facing the government.

In May 1828 the need for a by-election became apparent in County Clare, in Ireland. The MP, Vesey Fitzgerald, had been appointed President of the Board of Trade, and by the existing rules a newly appointed minister had to resign his seat and fight a by-election. Fitzgerald was a popular MP, a Protestant who favoured Catholic Emancipation and, at first, the Catholics could not find a candidate willing to stand against him. Eventually, in June, O'Connell was persuaded to fight the by-election as a way of showing Catholic feeling on the issue of emancipation. The qualification to vote was ownership of land worth £2 a year (the 40s FREEHOLD), and there were enough Catholic voters to ensure O'Connell won. More worrying for those opposed to Catholic Emancipation, a victory for O'Connell created the prospect of Catholics winning large numbers of seats at the next general election. This would give rise to a situation in which a group of Catholics would be elected but would be unable to take their seats in the House of Commons.

SOURCE 7.5 Extracts from O'Connell's address to the electors of County Clare, June 1828, from R. Huish, *Memoirs of Daniel O'Connell*, 1836

You will be told I am not qualified to be elected: the assertion, my friends, is untrue – I am qualified to be elected, and to be your representative. It is true that as a Catholic, I cannot, and of course, never will, take the oaths at present prescribed to Members of Parliament; but the authority which created these oaths [the Parliament] can abrogate them ... Electors of County Clare! Choose between me, who abominates that oath, and Mr Vesey Fitzgerald, who has sworn it full twenty times! Return me to Parliament, and it is probable that such a blasphemous oath will be abolished forever ...

The discussion which the attempt to exclude your representative from the House of Commons must excite will create a sensation all over Europe and produce such a burst of contemptuous indignation against British bigotry, in every enlightened country in the world, that the voice of all the great and good in England, Scotland, and Ireland, being joined to the universal shout of the nations of the earth will ... render it impossible for Peel and Wellington any longer to close the doors of the constitution against the Catholics of Ireland.

SOURCE 7.6 Extracts from a letter from Vesey Fitzgerald to Robert Peel, 5 July 1828, following the election in County Clare. Fitzgerald explains that the polling has gone on for several days but he has given up any hope of winning

My Dear Peel,
The election, thank God, is over ... I have polled all the gentry and all the fifty-pound freeholders – the gentry to a man.

Of others I have polled a few tenants of [illegible] only, my own, and not much besides what adhere to me in that way ...

The Sheriff declared the numbers tonight. To go on would have been idle. I have kept on for five days, and it was a hopeless contest from the first. Everything was against me. Indeed I do not understand how I could not have been beaten by a greater majority.

The Sheriff has made a special RETURN ... it will force Parliament instantly to take it up. It states that I was proposed, being a Protestant, as a fit person to represent the county in Parliament; that Mr O'Connell, a Roman Catholic, was also proposed; that he, O'Connell, had declared before the Sheriff that he was a Roman Catholic and that he intended to continue a Roman Catholic.

It states that a protest was made by the electors against his return; as well as the certificate that he was called to the Bar as a Roman Catholic.

It states the numbers for each candidate – and thus it leaves the return ...

I care not for anything since I have terminated the contest. For the degradation of the county I feel deeply, and the organisation exhibited is so complete and so formidable that no man can contemplate without alarm what is to follow in this wretched country.

CITY COLLEGE LEARNING RESOURCE CENTRE

D How did the government respond to the dilemma created by O'Connell?

ACTIVITY

How would you expect Wellington and Peel to resolve the dilemma created by the County Clare election, given their earlier careers?

Peel

Wellington

WHICH WAY TO TURN?

A civil war

Emancipation

OATH OF ALLEGIANCE FOR MPs

FOCUS ROUTE

1 What alternatives were there for Wellington and Peel in late 1828? Copy and complete this table, explaining why each suggested action may or may not have been possible in late 1828.

2 Does the completed table suggest one course of action as being preferable to the others? Explain your answer.

Course of action	Reasons for taking this action	Reasons against taking this action
A Refuse to allow O'Connell and any future Catholics elected as MPs to take their seats.		
B Persuade Parliament to pass a 'coercion bill' to allow military action in Ireland to keep law and order.		
C Persuade Parliament to raise the qualification to vote in Ireland from 40s (£2) to 200s (£10), thus removing the right to vote from large numbers of Catholics.		
D Ask the King to dissolve Parliament and call an election in the hope of getting a much more 'Protestant' Commons, which would reject any proposals for Catholic Emancipation.		
E Resign and let the Whigs form a government and sort the problem out.		
F Persuade Parliament to pass a bill for Catholic Emancipation.		
G Any other actions.		

The Duke of Wellington, Prime Minister in 1828
Born Arthur Wellesley, son of the Earl of Mornington, in Dublin in 1769, Wellesley was educated at Eton and a military school in France, was commissioned in the army and became aide-de-camp to the Lord-Lieutenant of Ireland. In 1797 he served in India, where he impressed his superior officers and was made administrator of the conquered territory. He returned to England and in 1806 was elected MP for Rye in Sussex. The following year the Duke of Portland appointed Wellesley as his Irish Secretary. Wellesley remained in the army, however. In 1808 he was sent to help the Portuguese fight the French and later took command of the British army in the Peninsular War, forcing the French out of Spain. In 1814 he was made Duke of Wellington for his military services. Wellington was in command of the forces that finally defeated Napoleon at Waterloo in June 1815. He returned to politics in 1818 when he became Master-General of the Ordnance in Liverpool's government. In 1828 he replaced Lord Goderich as Prime Minister.

Robert Peel, Home Secretary in 1828
(See page 84 for Peel's earlier career.)
When Lord Liverpool became Prime Minister in 1812, Peel was appointed as Chief Secretary for Ireland. Although Peel believed that civil discrimination against Catholics was wrong, he was not prepared to countenance the idea of full emancipation, including the right to vote. In 1814 he decided to suppress the Catholic Board, an organisation started by Daniel O'Connell. This was the start of a long conflict between the two men. In 1815 Peel challenged O'Connell to a duel. Peel travelled to Ostend but O'Connell was arrested on the way to fight the duel. In 1818 Robert Peel retired from his post in Ireland. This upset the Irish Protestants in the House of Commons and 57 of them signed a petition urging him not to leave a post that they believed he had 'administered with masterly ability'. Oxford University acknowledged Peel's 'services to Protestantism' by inviting him to become its MP.

In 1822 Peel rejoined Lord Liverpool's government as Home Secretary, but resigned when George Canning became Prime Minister in 1827. Canning was an advocate of Catholic Emancipation and so Peel felt he could not serve under Canning. Peel returned to government as Home Secretary in the government led by Wellington.

For Wellington and Peel, the prospect following O'Connell's election was a bleak one. If they kept the oath of allegiance, thus effectively banning O'Connell from sitting in the Commons, there was a distinct possibility of violence, and even civil war, in Ireland. Both Wellington and Peel had been opponents of Catholic Emancipation for years, fearing that Catholic voters for Catholic MPs might ultimately lead to a call for Irish independence from the union with Britain and the break-up of the United Kingdom.

For both men, however, the prospect of civil war was too great. Wellington knew that the 25,000 soldiers available for deployment in Ireland could not suppress a civil war there, even when Britain was at peace elsewhere. Wellington and Peel knew that they had to act quickly. Civil war in Ireland seemed imminent, and the Catholic Association, which had been banned, was openly reformed. Ominously, so too were rival Protestant ORANGE GROUPS in northern Ireland.

SOURCE 7.7 The Duke of Wellington speaking to another politician, summer 1828

I have probably passed a longer period of my life engaged in war than most men and I must say this: if I could avoid by any sacrifice whatever even one month of civil war, I would sacrifice my life in order to do it.

ORANGE GROUPS
Protestant groups who took the name from William of Orange – the Protestant King invited by Parliament to replace James II, a Catholic, in 1688.

ACTIVITY

1 What do the figures in Source 7.9 tell you about the attitudes to Catholic Emancipation in the Commons between 1812 and 1828?

2 You are a civil servant at the Home Office in August 1828. You have been asked to write a short paper of not more than 500 words, setting out the reasons for, and the reasons against, changing the law to give Catholics equal civil and political rights, following the events in County Clare. You must ensure that the Prime Minister receives a balanced view.

SOURCE 7.9 Results of voting in the Commons on various measures to give Catholics civil and political rights (figures quoted by Peel in his speech introducing the Emancipation bill in 1829)

Date	For	Against
1812	235	106
1812	264	224
1819	243	245
1821	majority 19 for	
1825	majority 21 for	
1826	majority 21 for	
1827	272	276
1828	272	266

ACTIVITY

Summarise, in your own words, the reasons Peel gave to the King for believing the question of emancipation must be discussed by the Cabinet (Source 7.10).

SOURCE 7.8 Extracts from a confidential memorandum from Peel to Wellington, 11 August 1828

I have uniformly opposed what is called Catholic Emancipation, and have rested my opposition upon broad and uncompromising grounds. I wish I could say that my views upon the question were materially changed ... but ... I cannot deny that the state of Ireland under existing circumstances is most unsatisfactory; that it becomes necessary to make your choice between different kinds and different degrees of evil ... and maturely consider whether it may not be better to encounter every risk of concession than to submit to the continuance, or rather perhaps the certain aggravation, of existing evils.

One major problem facing Wellington and Peel lay in persuading King George IV to allow the Cabinet to discuss the issue. The King had banned discussion in the Cabinet of any move to emancipate Catholics and was delaying a response to a request to discuss the matter. The issue was now an urgent one. Peel had decided to resign over the issue, but wrote a memorandum to the King, which he first sent to Wellington. It was accompanied by a note to say he would remain in office if Wellington believed his presence was needed if emancipation were to be passed by the Tories. On 14 January Wellington delivered Peel's memorandum to the King and, following discussions with members of the Cabinet, George IV gave his permission for them to discuss Catholic Emancipation.

SOURCE 7.10 Extracts from Peel's memorandum to George IV, 12 January 1829

I think that the Roman Catholic question can no longer remain what is called an open question, but that some definite course must be taken with respect to it by His Majesty's servants in their collective capacity ...

... The more I consider the subject the more I am satisfied that a government ought to make its choice between two courses of action ... either to offer united and unqualified resistance to the grant of further privileges to the Roman Catholics, or to undertake to consider without further delay the whole state of Ireland, and to attempt to make some satisfactory adjustment on the various points which are involved in what is called the Catholic question ...

... it remains to be considered which of the two is most practicable or most expedient to adopt ...

... no man can ... honestly advise the formation of an exclusive Protestant government ...

... there are ... considerations which incline me to think that the attempt to settle the question should be made ...

First – there is the evil of continued division between two branches of the Legislature on a great constitutional question.

Secondly – the power of the Roman Catholics is unduly increased by the House of Commons repeatedly pronouncing an opinion in their favour.

Thirdly – in the course of last autumn, out of a regular infantry force ... amounting to about 30,000 men, 25,000 were stationed either in Ireland or on the west coast of England with a view to the maintenance of tranquillity in Ireland.

Fourthly – though I have not the slightest apprehension of the result of civil commotion – though I believe it could be put down at once – yet I think the necessity of being constantly prepared for it while the government is divided ... on the Catholic question, is a much worse evil than its actual occurrence ...

Fifthly – the state of political excitement in Ireland will soon render it almost impracticable to administer justice in cases in which political or religious considerations are involved ...

These are practical and growing evils ...

My advice therefore to His Majesty will be, not to grant the Catholic claims, or any part of them, precipitately and unadvisedly, but in the first instance to remove the barrier which prevents the consideration of the Catholic question by the Cabinet ...

The fears and views of the two sides

SOURCE 7.11 'The terrors of Emancipation or A Bugabo for old women and children' – a cartoon by George Cruikshank. This drawing supports the views of Wellington and Peel and suggests that the fears of their opponents were unfounded. The figure holding the anti-Catholic petition is Lord Eldon

SOURCE 7.12 'Funeral of the constitution' – a cartoon by George Cruikshank. Eldon is shown as Hamlet; Peel (removing his waistcoat) and Wellington as gravediggers of the constitution. In the background, O'Connell and his followers take over St Paul's Cathedral, and York Minster is in flames

ACTIVITY

1 In Source 7.11 how does Cruikshank convey the impression that the fears of the people on the right of the picture are ridiculous?
2 In Source 7.12 why does Wellington refer to Peel's waistcoat as 'orange peel'?

George IV, however, still delayed giving his agreement to a bill being introduced into Parliament. Wellington made it clear to the King that he had no choice and on 4 March George IV wrote to Wellington 'as I find the country would be left without an administration, I have decided to yield my opinion to that which is considered by the Cabinet to be for the immediate interest of the country.'

Peel introduced the bill for Catholic Emancipation into the Commons on 6 March 1829 in a speech that lasted four hours. It took a month to get the bill through the Commons. In the end it was passed by 320 to 142. The Whigs voted with the government; the anti-Catholic Tories (the Ultras) against it. In the Lords, Wellington had a more difficult time, and there was a majority of only two votes, assisted by some bishops who did vote for the bill. George IV, however, delayed giving his assent and so the Cabinet resigned. For a day the country was without a government, forcing the King to give in and recall Wellington. For the King the prospect of a Whig government was even worse than that of Catholic Emancipation.

SOURCE 7.13 Extracts from Peel's speech in the Commons, introducing the bill, setting out the reasons for it and the reasons for his apparent change of mind. The 'he' referred to is Peel, as this extract is taken from the records of Parliament

Nearly the most painful circumstance that could be imposed on a public man, in the performance of public duty, must be when, after long acting with a number of individuals . . . he finds himself called upon . . . to separate from them. [However] his Majesty's ministers stood in a situation different from that in which [other MPs] were placed . . . they had . . . contracted an 5
obligation . . . from which they could not relieve themselves by any reference to past declarations . . . from the duty of giving the best advice. He asked . . . whether [MPs] would wish his Majesty's ministers to retain . . . opinions, when they appeared to be incompatible with the great interest which they were called upon to guard? . . . He retained the same opinion which he ever 10
entertained in reference to [Catholic Emancipation] . . . but he had no hesitation in saying, that the pressure of present evils was so great and overwhelming, that he was willing to encounter the risk of those contingent dangers, rather than, in the existing situation of the country, to endure, not only the continuance, but the aggravation of the present system . . . 15
. . . In four . . . out of the five Parliaments [since 1807], the House of Commons had come to resolutions in favour of the concessions [to Catholics]. It was not, however, so with the other House of Parliament . . . it could not be denied that the difference between the Houses of Lords and Commons on this point was an evil . . . It was their intention to effect the removal of civil and 20
political disabilities, subject, however, to those exceptions and regulations which to them appeared necessary . . .
. . . His hon. friend [the MP for Ripon] had taunted [the Duke of Wellington] . . . with having allowed their fears to be excited, and with being intimidated into concessions. In his opinion, no motive could be more justly branded as 25
ignominious, than that which was usually termed cowardice. But there was a temper of mind much more dangerous than this, though it might not be so base – he meant the fear of being thought to be afraid. Base as a coward was, the man who abandoned himself to the fear of being thought a coward, displayed little less fortitude . . . he would tell his hon. friend that the 30
disorganisation and disaffection which existed in Ireland could not be looked upon without fear, and that to affect not to fear it would be to affect insensibility to the welfare of the country . . .
. . . The conclusion to which he, in conjunction with [the Cabinet], had arrived, had not been influenced by the Catholic Association, nor by the 35
difficulties which might present themselves in once more meeting the parliament . . . they were of opinion, that it was not for the king's service, for the dignity of the Crown, nor for the welfare of the country, that hostility to concessions to the Roman Catholics should still be persisted in.

ACTIVITY

What reasons does Peel give for supporting Catholic Emancipation when his personal view was against it?

ACTIVITY

What does the King's letter to Wellington, of 4 March, and the resignation of the Cabinet tell you about royal power in 1829?

The news of the progress of the bill was followed across the country in the newspapers.

SOURCE 7.14 C. Brontë, *Diary of the Year*, 1829. Charlotte Brontë, later a leading novelist, describes how her family in Yorkshire kept in touch with events in London. The Brontë family regularly read the *Leeds Intelligencer* (a Tory newspaper) and the *Leeds Mercury* (a Whig newspaper)

I remember the day when the Intelligencer Extraordinary *came with Mr Peel's speeches in, containing the terms on which the Catholics were to be let in. With what eagerness Papa tore off the cover and how we all gathered round him and with what breathless anxiety we listened as one by one they were disclosed and explained and argued upon so ably and so well, and then, when it was all out, how aunt said that she thought it was excellent and that the Catholics could do no harm, with such good security. I remember also the doubts as to whether it would pass the House of Lords ... and when the paper came which was to decide the question, the anxiety was almost dreadful with which we listened to the whole affair; the opening of the door; the hush; the royal dukes in their robes and the Great Duke in green sash and waistcoat; the rising of all the persons when he rose; the reading of his speech – Papa saying that his words were like precious gold; and lastly the majority ... in favour of the bill.*

ACTIVITY

1 Read Source 7.14. Why should Charlotte Brontë's father have been particularly interested in Catholic Emancipation?
2 Choose three phrases that best illustrate the interest and excitement the Brontës felt about the issue.

The Catholic Emancipation Act, 13 April 1829

1 Declared an end to the Catholic Association.

2 Repealed all the laws that subjected Catholics to civil discrimination and allowed Catholics to sit in both houses of Parliament (although a Catholic could not become Lord Lieutenant of Ireland, or Lord Chancellor, monarch or regent). A new oath required them to deny the Pope had any power to intervene in domestic affairs, to recognise the Protestant succession, and agree never to attempt to overthrow the Established Church.

3 Raised the qualification for a vote in the Irish counties from ownership of freehold property worth £2 to ownership of freehold property worth £10.

FOCUS ROUTE

Explain what the Catholic Emancipation Act said and the purpose of each of the three parts of the Act.

FOCUS ROUTE

1 What was the immediate impact of the Catholic Emancipation Act:
   a) in Ireland
   b) on the Tory Party?
2 What were the long-term effects for the Tory Party?

E What were the implications of Catholic Emancipation?

The result of the County Clare election

O'Connell was obliged by the government to refight the County Clare election. Although the new voting qualification cut out a large number of the previous electors, he won again. Throughout Ireland, the number of voters disenfranchised by the Act was about 80,000. This treatment of O'Connell and the 40s. freeholders lost Peel and Wellington much of the potential goodwill they might have received from Irish Catholics. In addition, they also lost the support of the Protestant landlords in Ireland who could never forgive Peel's and Wellington's 'betrayal'.

The short-term results of the Act for the Tory Party

The Tory centre – followers of Peel and Wellington over Catholic Emancipation

The Tory Ultras – betrayed by their leader

The Canningites – liberal Tories who wanted parliamentary reform

Whigs

The Tory Party was split. The liberal Tories were already opposed to Wellington over electoral reform and now the Ultra Tories felt betrayed by their leader. This latter group felt that the nation was opposed to Catholic Emancipation, and many argued that a Parliament which was more fully representative of the country's wishes would never have passed the Act. As a result, some began to support moves for reform of Parliament. The Tory Party had thus split into three groups. It was only the fact that the Whigs were also split that allowed Wellington's administration to continue through the summer. In the autumn, when the new Parliament met (a general election had been held after the death of George IV), the cracks were too great to be papered over. When Wellington announced that he saw no reason for any reform of Parliament, the Tory Party finally disintegrated. The old Tories were still angry over Catholic Emancipation and the Canningites, who had had enough of compromise with the old Tories, joined with the Whigs.

Other short-term results

- Wellington, Peel and their supporters were vilified in some newspapers and by many of their former followers. The Dowager Duchess of Richmond decorated her drawing room with stuffed rats, which she named after Peel, Wellington and their supporters.

- Wellington challenged the Earl of Winchelsea to a duel over disparaging comments the Earl had made about Wellington's part in passing the Act. Wellington fired first and deliberately wide so the Earl, with relief, fired into the air and apologised.

- The House of Commons was criticised for thwarting the will of the people. Critics argued that the Act had been passed against the Protestant will of the country by those who represented corrupt pocket boroughs. Thus they argued reform of Parliament was needed.

- The campaign by O'Connell and the Catholic Association provided an example of organisation and extra-parliamentary pressure, which was taken up by the Birmingham Political Union and other supporters of the idea of reform of Parliament.

- During the passage of the bill, Peel had resigned his seat for Oxford University, and stood in the by-election there, hoping for a demonstration of support. Instead, the Tory voters vented their rage and threw him out. A door in Christ Church, Oxford, still bears some anti-Peel graffiti from this time. Peel was due to move the resolution preceding the bill on 5 March. An arrangement by which Sir Manasseh Lopes resigned his seat in a pocket borough allowed Peel to be re-elected by 2 March. The circumstances surrounding Peel's election, which was managed by Lopes, his nephew the Mayor of Westbury, and his nephew's brother-in-law, were somewhat unsavoury, even by 1829 standards.

The long-term effects for the Tory Party

The split in the Tory Party meant that for some time it was difficult for the Tory leader to be certain of sufficient support to form a government with any hope of surviving. The Tories were out of office until 1841, except for two very brief interludes. During that time, Peel rebuilt the party as the Conservatives, basing its principles on those expounded in his Tamworth Manifesto of 1834 (see page 161). Many in the party never forgave Wellington and especially Peel for what was seen as a betrayal of one of the most important underlying tenets of the Tory Party – support for the Church of England. Those alive in 1846 were even more disbelieving when Peel again seemed about to betray and destroy the party over the Corn Laws issue (see Chapter 10).

CITY COLLEGE
LEARNING RESOURCE CENTRE

Review: Catholic Emancipation: a revolution in attitudes?

The purpose of this section is to help you to draw together your thoughts about why Catholic Emancipation was passed. Was it the result of a revolution in attitudes? Was it passed for pragmatic reasons? Was it passed because of pressure from outside Parliament? Was it the result of long-term changes and developments? Was it the result of a short-term series of events? In short, why did it happen?

ACTIVITY

Choose one of the following essays:

a) 'It was fear that made Wellington and Peel accept the need for Catholic Emancipation in 1829.' Do you agree? Explain your answer.

b) Were the actions of O'Connell more important than the changing attitudes to Catholics in leading to Catholic Emancipation in 1829?

ACTIVITY

1 From the information in this chapter, list the main reasons why Catholic Emancipation was passed in 1829.
2 Divide the list into long-term and short-term causes.
3 Divide the list into those causes that were outside the government's control and those that were the result of government actions/within the government's control.
4 Decide which factors are the most important in an explanation of why Catholic Emancipation was passed.
5 In what ways did the campaign for Catholic Emancipation, the events leading to emancipation, and the Act itself, alter the situation in Britain as regards:
   a) political parties/groupings
   b) the electorate
   c) the positions of Wellington and Peel in Parliament, and in the country
   d) attitudes towards further reform, including reform of Parliament?

KEY POINTS FROM CHAPTER 7

Catholic Emancipation: a revolution in attitudes?

1 At the beginning of the nineteenth century, Catholics in the United Kingdom did not have equal civil and political rights with Protestants. They could not, for example, become MPs.
2 In the first 25 years of the century, several attempts were made to extend rights to Catholics, but all failed, largely due to opposition in the House of Lords.
3 In 1823 Daniel O'Connell established the Catholic Association to campaign for equal civil and political rights for Catholics.
4 In 1828 the repeal of the Test and Corporation Acts as they applied to Dissenters made continued discrimination against Catholics harder to justify.
5 The election of O'Connell at the 1828 County Clare by-election led to a situation in which the Prime Minister, Wellington, and Home Secretary, Peel, were faced with a choice between the possibility of civil war in Ireland or moving ahead with Catholic Emancipation.
6 Their own personal experiences of war and of Ireland led Wellington and Peel to decide to introduce a bill for Catholic Emancipation against their personal beliefs.
7 The bill became law in April 1829, removing nearly all restrictions on Catholics holding public office.
8 The Act had significant short- and long-term effects for the Tory Party. Within a few months the splits in the party resulting from the emancipation issue led to defeat in the Commons and Wellington's resignation. The Whigs came to power, and except for two very brief periods the Tories remained out of office until 1841.
9 The liberal 'Canningite Tories' finally split with the Tory Party and joined the Whigs.
10 Peel was never forgiven by some members of the Tory Party for his support of emancipation. He was felt to have betrayed the party.
11 The coming to power of the Whigs made reform of Parliament more likely than it would have been under the Tories.

8

Why was the Great Reform Act passed in 1832?

CHAPTER OVERVIEW

George Beck dressed with great care. He chose his smartest trousers, a clean shirt and clean gloves. He knew he had to look his best. The crowd was expecting it – the crowd that was gathering to watch George Beck die.

Later that day, outside the courthouse in Nottingham, Beck and two others were hanged. The crowd, every one a supporter of the three who died, chanted 'Murder! Murder!' as the men used their last words to protest their innocence. Murder it was, official murder, for as the Duke of Rutland had written earlier to Lady Shelley, 'The juries at Nottingham have been summoned, and threatened, so as to mete out justice ... six men will be executed, and eight transported!'

Why did Beck die? He was accused of being a ringleader of the reform riots in Nottingham in 1831, which had led to the burning of Nottingham Castle, home of the Duke of Newcastle. The riots had followed the news that the House of Lords had voted against a bill to give more men the vote. Similar riots had broken out in Bristol, leading the government to fear revolution. Somebody had to be made an example to frighten people away from revolution. That was why Beck had to hang.

Despite its strong stance against the rioters, the government did give way to reform, passing the 1832 Reform Act, often known as the Great Reform Act. This chapter investigates the reasons why the Act was passed by the Whig government in 1832 and three other closely linked questions:

- Was the Reform Act a radical move by the government or was it really a very conservative reform?
- Was the government motivated by fairness or by fear of revolution in finally introducing changes to the electoral system?
- Did this reform of Parliament prevent a revolution either in 1830–32, or in the longer term?

A Calendar of events 1830–32 (pp. 116–117)

B Why did the Whigs come to power in 1830? (pp. 118–121)

C Conservative or radical? What kind of reformers were the Whigs likely to be? (pp. 122–127)

D Why did the Whigs persevere with reform following the rejection of the first two bills? (pp. 128–130)

E Why was the Reform Act passed in 1832 when the bills had been rejected in 1831? (pp. 131–132)

F Does the 1832 Reform Act deserve to be called the Great Reform Act? (pp. 133–135)

G Review: why was the Great Reform Act passed in 1832? (pp. 135–136)

A **Calendar of events 1830–32**

1830

May	June	July	August
	26 June Death of George IV; accession of William IV	24 July General election called July–Aug Voting in election	
September	**October**	**November** New Parliament met – Wellington still PM 15 Nov Wellington's government defeated 16 Nov Wellington resigned; Grey and the Whigs took office	**December**

1831

January	February	March	April
14 Jan Cabinet committee on reform reported 30 Jan Cabinet committee's report sent to King		1 Mar First reform bill introduced to Commons	20 Apr Whigs defeated by 299 votes to 291 23 Apr Parliament dissolved; election called
May	**June**	**July** 24 July Second reform bill introduced to Commons	**August**
	May–June Voting in election		
September 22 Sept Bill passed second reading in Commons by 345 votes to 236	**October** 8 Oct Bill defeated in Lords 8–10 Oct Riots in Derby and Nottingham 29–31 Oct Riots in Bristol	**November**	**December** 6 Dec Parliament reassembled 12 Dec Third reform bill introduced to Commons 18 Dec Bill passed second reading in Commons by 324 votes to 162

1832

January	February	March	April
15 Jan William IV agreed to create new peers to avoid defeat in Lords		22 Mar Bill passed third reading in Commons by 355 votes to 239	14 Apr Bill passed second reading in Lords by 184 votes to 175
May	**June**	**July**	**August**
7 May Government defeated on an amendment to the bill

9 May King refused to create new peers; Cabinet resigned

15 May King recalled Grey as PM

18 May King agreed to create new peers if necessary | 4 June Bill passed third reading in Lords by 106 votes to 22

7 June Bill received royal assent | | |
| **September** | **October** | **November** | **December** |
| | | | |

■ Learning trouble spot

The basic procedure for passing an Act of Parliament

The House of Commons first reading: the bill (a proposal to create a new law or Act) is introduced.
Second reading: the bill is debated in the Commons. A vote is taken.
Committee stage: the bill is discussed in detail by a committee. It may be altered.
Third reading: the bill, possibly altered, is debated in the Commons. A vote is taken.
The House of Lords: The bill goes through the same procedures as in the Commons.
Royal assent: If the bill has passed all these stages, it is then agreed by the monarch and finally becomes law.

TALKING POINT

To what extent are actions by governments the result of deliberate intentions or the unintended outcomes of events beyond their control?

CITY COLLEGE LEARNING RESOURCE CENTRE

■ **Learning trouble spot**

How did economic changes affect the demand for reform?

In explaining the demand for reform of Parliament, students often underestimate the significance of economic factors. The expansion of industry had led to the growth of a relatively wealthy industrial middle class. Many of its members owned businesses, both large and small. They were the producers of wealth for Britain, yet the majority had no say in the government of the country because they had no vote in parliamentary elections. Most were educated and economically and politically aware. They wanted a parliament and a government that were prepared to pass laws that would benefit Britain and British industry, and as a result (and not entirely coincidentally) themselves. They did not want a government that seemed to favour the landowning interests, which dominated Parliament because of the restricted franchise and over-representation of rural areas.

Many workers demanded the vote for other reasons. They saw their only real hope of improving wages and conditions of work was through a parliament that was elected by them, with men from their class as MPs. Many of these men felt that as the country was becoming wealthier, they seemed to be getting poorer.

B Why did the Whigs come to power in 1830?

FOCUS ROUTE

1 Why was there a demand for electoral reform?
2 How did Catholic Emancipation increase the likelihood of electoral reform?
3 What evidence is there that the reform issue dominated the 1830 election?
4 How might the Swing Riots have both strengthened and weakened the cause of reform?
5 How did Wellington's response to the possibility of reform weaken the Tory Party?

In 1830 there was a growing belief among many involved in politics that the system of electing MPs was in need of change due to the following reasons.

- There was no uniform qualification for a vote.
- Many elections were never contested so even those who had a vote had no opportunity to use it.
- Voting was public, and failure to vote for your landlord or employer could lead to eviction.
- Many constituencies were pocket boroughs, controlled by landowners who decided who should stand as a candidate for election.
- Constituencies had, in most cases, been established in medieval times and some towns with MPs had ceased to exist. Many more rotten boroughs consisted of nothing but a few farms where a handful of voters returned an MP to Parliament. In contrast, the rapidly expanding and often politically aware middle classes in the large and growing industrial cities did not have MPs of their own.

The identification of these problems did not mean that a reform bill was certain to be introduced into Parliament in 1830 or 1831. There was still a Tory government, headed by Wellington and others opposed to reform. However, events took over, accelerating the move towards reform.

The impact of the unexpected

Catholic Emancipation was the first of those events. This was a major boost for reformers in four ways. Firstly, it had shown that there were men in Parliament who would support further amendments to the constitution. Secondly, it had demonstrated the effectiveness of peaceful tactics combined with the threat of violence. Thirdly, it had proved that royal opposition was no longer an obstacle to significant reform. Finally, the crisis of Catholic Emancipation had split the Tories, weakening their ability to block electoral reform.

■ 8A The break-up of the Tories after 1828

Split 1, 1828
Wellington became Prime Minister. The liberal Tories – those who had supported Canning (Canningites) and who supported Catholic Emancipation – would not serve under him.

Wellington

Split 2, 1829
The Ultra Tories abandoned any support for Peel and Wellington after what they saw as the 'betrayal' of the party over the issue of Catholic Emancipation.

■ 8B The division of political groups after 1829

RADICALS	WHIGS	LIBERAL TORIES	TORIES	ULTRA TORIES
Leading members Sir Francis Burdett Lord Durham Sir Henry Brougham	**Leading members** Lord Melbourne Earl Grey Lord John Russell Sir James Graham	**Leading members** William Huskisson Viscount Palmerston	**Leading members** Duke of Wellington Sir Robert Peel Henry Goulburn	**Leading members** Duke of Cumberland Duke of Newcastle Lord Eldon

■ 8C The impact of the 1830 election

Wellington's Tory government was weakened by the reduction in the number of his supporters in the Commons.

Reform was seen to be a vote-winning measure.

Whig doubters saw supporting reform as a means of regaining power.

WHY WAS THE GREAT REFORM ACT PASSED IN 1832?

OPERATIVES
People who operated machinery in factories.

The death of George IV in June 1830 provoked the final crisis for the Tories. As usual, a general election was held after the new monarch, William IV, ascended the throne. The voting, in July and August, created an opportunity for widespread protest against the existing electoral system. In many areas voters abandoned their old allegiances to Whigs and Tories. Many candidates who declared themselves against reform, including some longstanding MPs, were defeated. Thomas Gooch, MP for Suffolk since 1806, and E. P. Bastard, whose family had held a Devon seat since 1784, were both beaten. Henry Brougham, a pro-reform supporter of the Whigs, was elected as one of the MPs for Yorkshire, the first non-Yorkshireman to be elected for the county since the Reformation. Wellington remained Prime Minister, and continued to govern until the new Parliament met in November. But he was warned by Lord Wharncliffe that, 'The demonstration in favour of reform at the general election of 1830 satisfied me that the feeling upon it was not ... temporary and likely to die away.'

Another result of the election was the reappearance of political societies. In Birmingham the first meeting of Thomas Attwood's Political Union was attended by approximately 15,000 people. Its aim was the reform of the House of Commons, to be achieved by a 'general political union of the lower and the middle classes of the people'. It was to be strictly law-abiding, thus attracting middle-class members whilst giving the government no reason to suppress it. Similar groups sprang up all over the country in large cities and small towns. Leeds was a hotbed of reform, with the Radical Political Union demanding votes for the working class, the Leeds Political Union part middle class, part OPERATIVES, and the Leeds Association dominated by the Whig élite in Yorkshire. At the other end of the scale, a political union based on the Birmingham model was formed at Stow-on-the-Wold. These enthusiasts for political reform were well aware of events in France, where three days of fighting in Paris at the end of July overthrew the monarchy of Charles X and replaced him with Louis Philippe.

In England the violence came in the form of the Swing Riots – protests in farming districts about low wages, high prices and unemployment, which were attributed to the introduction of new machinery on farms, such as steam threshing machines.

TALKING POINT

Where would you place these events on the 'revolutionary Richter scale' (pages 10–11)?

SOURCE 8.1   Forms of protest in the most active counties, c.1833

	Number of incidents c.1833			
	Machine breaking	**Arson**	**Robbery**	**Wage riots**
Hampshire	52	15	76	14
Wiltshire	97	18	62	–
Berkshire	78	13	47	14
Kent	37	61	–	29
Sussex	11	34	12	47
Norfolk	29	19	–	3
Total for country	**416**	**316**	**219**	**162**

SOURCE 8.2   An example of a letter from Captain Swing's supporters. (Spelling is as in the original)

This is to inform you what you have to undergo gentlemen if providing you don't pull down your meshines and rise the poor mens wages the married men give tow and six pence a day the singel tow shillings or we well burn down your barns and you in them this is the last notis.

ACTIVITY

'It would be surprising if a movement so widespread and which frightened the government so much – for however brief a spell – had been without influence on reform legislation.' E. Hobsbawm and G. Rude, *Captain Swing*, 1969.
Riots and protests had not led to reform between 1815 and 1819, so why might they have more influence in 1830–31?

SOURCE 8.3   A cartoon about the Swing Riots. In the bottom right-hand corner is a reference to the need for parliamentary reform

When Parliament met in November 1830 the Whig leader Lord Grey suggested to Wellington that reform of Parliament was the only way to solve the problems facing the Tory government.

SOURCE 8.4 Wellington's views, as expressed in a speech in the Lords on 2 November 1830. In the second drawing, Wellington is sitting next to Lord Aberdeen, the Foreign Secretary

> I have never heard of any measure which could in any degree satisfy my mind that the state of representation could be improved, or be rendered more satisfactory to the country at large.

> I am fully convinced that the country possesses at the present moment a legislature which answers all the good purposes of legislation, and this to a greater degree than any legislature ever had answered in any country whatever.

> I will go further, and say that the legislature and the system of representation possesses the full and entire confidence of the country.

> Shame! Shame!

> What can I have said which seems to make so great a disturbance?

> You have announced the fall of your government, that is all.

SOURCE 8.5 M. Brock, *The Great Reform Act*, 1973

[Aberdeen's reply] was an understatement. Wellington had announced the fall of the system.

ACTIVITY

Prepare a two-minute broadcast report explaining why the Tory government has fallen and how this is linked to the question of electoral reform.

ACTIVITY

1 Summarise Wellington's views in the extracts from his speech in Source 8.4.
2 What do you think Wellington believed were the 'good purposes of legislation'?
3 How true was Wellington's statement in the third speech bubble?
4 Explain why Aberdeen (lower picture) thought that Wellington's government would fall.
5 In what way is Brock's assessment (in Source 8.5) of what Wellington had said different from Aberdeen's?

Wellington's government was weakened by his speech opposing reform (see Source 8.4). The liberal Tories now allied with the Whigs, in favour of moderate reform. Wellington received little help from the Ultra Tories, who were still looking for revenge after Wellington's support for Catholic Emancipation, and collapse came quickly. After defeat on a financial bill on 15 November, Wellington resigned the next day. Following the splits in the Tories there was no alternative leader who could guarantee enough support to form a government, and so the King invited Lord Grey to form a government. It was, in effect, a coalition of Whigs, some Canningite Tories, such as Palmerston, Huskissonites and even the Ultra Tory Richmond, who became Postmaster-General. It was to take the Whigs another year and a half to achieve reform of Parliament.

CITY COLLEGE LEARNING RESOURCE CENTRE

C Conservative or radical? What kind of reformers were the Whigs likely to be?

TALKING POINT

What kinds of reform would you regard as either conservative or radical in the context of 1830?

FOCUS ROUTE

Copy and complete the table below with evidence from this section.

Evidence that the Whigs would introduce conservative electoral reforms	Evidence that the Whigs would introduce radical electoral reforms

For many people, the change from a Tory to a Whig government might well have passed unnoticed. Its methods of dealing with protest in rural areas, for example, followed closely that of its predecessors.

SOURCE 8.6   R. J. Evans, *The Victorian Age 1815–1914*, 1968

Wellington's government had dealt severely with the outbreaks of lawlessness, and their successors followed the same line. Magistrates ... were everywhere encouraged to take the harshest measures ... There was no police in country districts, so, as usual, troops were employed, and Melbourne [the Home Secretary] appointed Special Commissioners to try the hundreds of labourers and farmhands who had been arrested. Three hundred men were tried at Winchester, of whom two, one a boy of sixteen [for knocking off the hat of a member of an important local family] were executed, ninety-nine transported for life, and only sixty-seven acquitted. In Wiltshire, one hundred and fifty-four were transported ... Altogether in southern England, for riots in which not a single person was killed, the government executed nine, and transported for life over four hundred and fifty men and boys.

Grey's Cabinet

Grey's Cabinet was one of the most aristocratic in the nineteenth century. Only four of its members were not in the House of Lords. Of the four, Viscount Althorp was heir to the Spencer earldom, Palmerston was an Irish peer and so sat in the Commons, and Lord John Russell was the third son of the Duke of Bedford.

The Whigs soon set up a committee to formulate reform plans, consisting of Lord Durham (the chairman), Sir James Graham, Viscount Duncannon and Lord John Russell. Their instructions from the Cabinet were '[to prepare] ... an outline of a measure ... large enough to satisfy public opinion and yet to afford sure ground of resistance to further innovation, yet so based on property, and on existing franchises and territorial divisions, as to run no risk of overthrowing the [existing] form of government'.

Charles, Earl Grey (1764–1845) Educated at Eton and King's College, Cambridge, Grey became MP for Northumberland aged 22. In 1792 he joined a group of pro-reform Whigs whose objective was to obtain 'a more equal representation of the people in Parliament' and 'to secure to the people a more frequent exercise of their right of electing their representatives'. In 1793 he introduced a parliamentary reform bill, arguing that one of the basic principles established by the Glorious Revolution of 1688 was the freedom of elections to the House of Commons. Grey added that 'a man ought not to be governed by laws, in the framing of which he had not a voice, either in person or by his representative, and that he ought not to be made to pay any tax to which he should not have consented in the same way'. The proposal was defeated by 282 votes to 41.

In 1806 he became leader of the Whigs in the Commons, and in 1807 he inherited his father's title and moved to the House of Lords.

You are a member of the Cabinet committee on reform. You have to present your proposals to the Cabinet. You have narrowed the decision down to a series of options.

1 Decide which of the options below you wish to adopt and outline your proposals to the rest of the class, who should act as the Cabinet.
2 Justify your proposals in terms of your instructions.
3 Take a vote on which set of proposals the Cabinet wishes to accept.

Options available for reforming the electoral system

A The redistribution of seats/constituencies throughout the country. Choose one option.

EITHER	OR	OR
Every county to elect two MPs; counties with over 150,000 inhabitants to have two extra MPs; all boroughs with a population over 10,000 to elect one MP; boroughs with under 2000 people to lose their MP if they have one.	Every county to elect three MPs; all boroughs with over 10,000 inhabitants to elect one MP; boroughs with a population over 20,000 to elect two MPs; boroughs with fewer than 1000 people to lose their MP if they have one.	Every county to elect two MPs; all boroughs with over 5000 inhabitants to elect one MP; boroughs with over 10,000 people to elect two MPs; boroughs with fewer than 2000 inhabitants to lose their MP if they have one.

B Who should get a vote:

a) in the boroughs (towns)? Choose two options.

EITHER	OR	OR
All men over the age of 21 who pay rates (local taxes).	All men who are employed in a job or who own a business.	All men who own or occupy property worth £10 a year in rental value.

b) in the counties? Choose two options.

EITHER	OR	OR
All men over the age of 21 who pay rates.	All men who hold land as COPYHOLDERS or LEASEHOLDERS, worth £20 per year.	All FREEHOLDERS who own land or property worth £5 a year in rental value.

C How is voting to be carried out? Choose one option.

EITHER	OR	OR
In public, by telling the returning officer, who will record the vote on paper.	By secret ballot, by writing the name of the candidate on paper.	By secret ballot, by marking a cross against the name of the candidate on a printed paper.

D What is to be the maximum time between elections? Choose one option.

EITHER	OR	OR
One year	Five years	Seven years

COPYHOLDER
Someone who owns land or property by right of holding a copy of an ancient document giving them ownership (e.g. a copy of a manor court roll). Tenure was often precarious as many of the original documents, which could date back some two hundred years, were lost. Some copyholders owned fairly large amounts of land and were quite wealthy, but many owned only small amounts of land and were relatively poor.

LEASEHOLDER
Someone who owns land or property on a lease that lasts for a set number of years, after which time they cease to own the property (e.g. a 99-year lease).

FREEHOLDER
Someone who owns land or property outright and forever.

Lord John Russell (1792–1878)

Russell was the third son of the sixth Duke of Bedford. He was educated at Westminster School for a short time, but mainly at home due to his poor health. At the age of fourteen he wrote in his diary, 'What a pity that he who steals a penny loaf should be hung, whilst he who steals thousands of the public money should be acquitted'. In 1809 he went to Edinburgh University, and in 1813 his father arranged for him to be elected to the family seat of Tavistock. He was granted the courtesy title, Lord John Russell. He supported the Whigs and took an active part in the campaign for parliamentary reform.

In 1820 Russell became MP for Huntingdonshire. For the next twelve years he was the leader of the Whig campaign in the House of Commons for parliamentary reform. In 1828 he proposed a bill to repeal the Test and Corporation Acts and in 1829 he led the successful campaign for the Catholic Relief Bill. In 1832 he introduced the bill for reform of Parliament to the Commons. He was Prime Minister between 1846 and 1852.

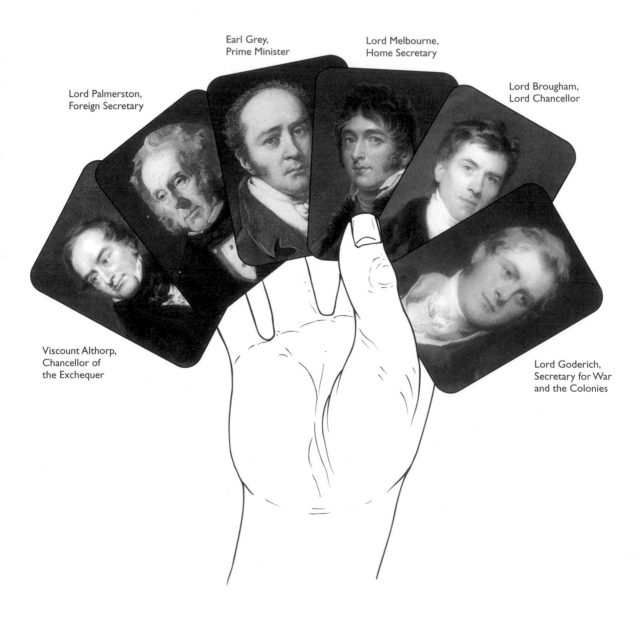

Lord Palmerston,
Foreign Secretary

Earl Grey,
Prime Minister

Lord Melbourne,
Home Secretary

Lord Brougham,
Lord Chancellor

Viscount Althorp,
Chancellor of
the Exchequer

Lord Goderich,
Secretary for War
and the Colonies

CITY COLLEGE
LEARNING RESOURCE SERVICE

ACTIVITY

1 Compare your class proposals (from the Activity on page 123) with those of the actual committee. Explain any differences between the two sets of proposals.
2 What were the intentions of the committee in its proposals about seat redistribution and the franchise?
3 In a plan to reform the franchise in 1820, Russell had proposed a £5 rental franchise. Why do you think the committee set the figure at £20?
4 Why do you think Durham proposed to introduce a secret ballot?
5 Why might those who were concerned about the large amount of corruption at elections have *opposed* the secret ballot?

The Cabinet committee's proposals, January 1831

County seats	• Counties with over 150,000 inhabitants to gain two further MPs and become two constituencies instead of one.
Borough seats	• To lose both MPs if under 2000 inhabitants. • To lose one MP if between 2000 and 4000 inhabitants. • Towns over 10,000 inhabitants with no MP to be given seats.
Voters in counties	• Freeholders of land worth 40s. a year (calculated on its rental value). • Copyholders with land worth £10 a year. • Leaseholders with land worth £50 a year.
Voters in boroughs	• Existing electors to keep the vote if still resident in the borough. • Occupiers renting (or owning) houses worth at least £20 a year (in rental).
Method of voting	• Secret ballot to be introduced.
Maximum length of a parliament	• To be seven instead of five years.

The aims and motives of the Whigs in reforming Parliament

TALKING POINT

What is the difference between an aim and a motive? Identify the five aims and one motive in Source 8.7.

SOURCE 8.7 The instructions given to the Cabinet committee for drawing up the first reform proposals

[To prepare] ... an outline of a measure ... large enough to satisfy public opinion and yet to afford sure ground of resistance to further innovation, yet so based on property, and on existing franchises and territorial divisions, as to run no risk of overthrowing the [existing] form of government.

SOURCE 8.8 N. Gash, *Aristocracy and the People: Britain 1815–65*, 1985

For Grey, however, reform was also an act of statesmanship. The antiquated structure of the English electoral system was defensible only if it produced administrations that both worked and were acceptable to public opinion. Once executive government faltered ... and the system came under hostile or even merely objective scrutiny, its anomalies and abuses were obvious ...

The primary purpose of the Reform Bill introduced by Russell in March 1831 was to rally middle-class support round the aristocratic system ... The political advantage was twofold. It would strengthen the constitution by securing the support of what ... Grey described as the 'real and effective mass of public opinion ... without whom the power of the gentry is nothing'. At the same time it would detach the middle classes from a dangerous alliance with the lower classes, founded on common dissatisfaction with the aristocratic system ...

The object of the ministers was to amend and make acceptable the old system, not to design a new one.

ACTIVITY

Read through Sources 8.8–8.10. List the aims identified by each writer.

1 Is there any agreement between the different writers?
2 Are there any differences?
3 Is there one aim that seems to be more important than others according to the writers?

SOURCE 8.9   E. Evans, *The Great Reform Act of 1832*, 1983

Grey believed ... that moderate reform was the only secure route to political stability. He would not abandon the principle of aristocratic government; rather the Whigs wished to strengthen it by attaching to the existing constitution the new forms of propertied classes ... The Whigs aimed to frustrate democracy by increasing the franchise.

SOURCE 8.10   M. Brock, *The Great Reform Act*, 1973

The cabinet knew ... that they must outbid Peel to succeed. To produce a mild Bill which he could modify and adopt as his own would play into his hands. The only way to check-mate him was to produce one sweeping enough to enlist strong support in the country. Then he ought to recognise that even if he defeated the measure and drove the government out he would be too unpopular to take their place.

But to attribute [the Bill's] scope to motives of party advantage would be a distortion. The underlings may well have thought this way. Grey and Althorp did not ... They wanted, not so much office and official salaries, as social peace and security for property ...

They brought in a sweeping Bill because the events of 1830 had told them that it was now an urgent task to sweep away the electoral system ... Grey and his colleagues were convinced that any attempt to retain the system would provoke an explosion.

ACTIVITY

1 Identify the aims and motives of the Whigs in Sources 8.11–8.16.
2 Compare the aims and motives in these sources with those you have listed from the historians in Sources 8.8–8.10. What differences can you see?
3 How would you explain any differences?
4 Which of Sources 8.11–8.16 are likely to be the most reliable in providing an accurate version of the aims and motives of the Whigs? Justify your choice.
5 Are the views of historians likely to be more or less reliable than the words of the Whigs themselves in identifying the aims and motives of the Whigs? Explain your answer.

SOURCE 8.11   Earl Grey speaking in the House of Lords in 1831

The principle of my reform is to prevent the necessity for revolution ... there is no-one more dedicated against annual parliaments, universal suffrage, and the ballot, than I am.

SOURCE 8.12   Lord John Russell introducing the bill to the Commons in March 1831

I come now to the utmost difficult part of this subject – the explanation of the measure, which, representing the King's ministers, I am about to propose to the house ... [those ministers] have thought that no half measures would be sufficient – that no trifling ... with so great a question should give stability to the Throne – authority to Parliament – or satisfaction to the country ... The chief grievances of which the people complain are: first, the nomination of Members by individuals; second the Elections by CLOSE CORPORATIONS; third, the Expense of Elections.

SOURCE 8.13   Lord Brougham, a leading Whig reformer, discussing who should be enfranchised, 1831

By the people, I mean the middle classes, the wealth and intelligence of the country, the glory of the British name.

SOURCE 8.14   Earl Grey quoted in M. Brock, *The Great Reform Act*, 1973

A great change has taken place in all parts of Europe since the end of the war in the distribution of property, and unless a corresponding change can be made in the legal mode by which that property can act upon the governments, revolutions must necessarily follow. This change requires a greater influence to be yielded to the middle classes, who have made wonderful advances both in prosperity and intelligence.

CLOSE CORPORATIONS
Groups who governed some towns and cities; they were often dominated by a rich patron who ensured that the corporation was made up of his supporters. Normally they were self-electing in that re-election was by the other members of the group.

SOURCE 8.15 Lord Hatherton in a note on a letter from Althorp in January 1831

By an extensive enfranchisement of new places and by a division of counties, the tory [sic] proprietors might be won over, through a disclosure of so many new views of personal interest.

SOURCE 8.16 Lord Palmerston speaking in the Commons on 3 March 1831 in the debate on the first reform bill

Any man who looked at the workings of the present system must see that there were five great and peculiar blemishes, which it was necessary to remove ... The first of these was the system of nomination by the patrons of boroughs; the second, the gross and barefaced corruption which prevailed among the lower classes when their votes become necessary to the higher; the third, the absence of all adequate balances of representation with respect to the great manufacturing and commercial towns; the fourth the great expense of elections; and the fifth the very unequal and unjust distribution of power among the middle and lower classes ... The object the government had in view ... was first to give representatives to the great manufacturing towns; next, to add to the respectability of the electors; and then to increase the number of those who claim to enjoy the right of choosing their representatives ... the Ministers disclaimed any intention to sever the ties which bind together the middle classes and the aristocracy.

■ **Learning trouble spot**

Identifying aims, motives and intentions
When trying to identify the aims, motives and intentions of people in the past, students frequently take at face value what individuals or groups state to be their aims. It is important to understand why this may not be appropriate and why people may not have stated their aims or motives entirely honestly. It may not, for example, have been in the Whigs' best interest to admit that one of their intentions was to prevent any potential co-operation between the middle and working classes in their move towards democracy.

It is also important to appreciate differences between the past and the present. People's actions are influenced by their attitudes, values and beliefs. Because these were often very different from those today, it is important to take these differences into consideration when explaining why people acted as they did. In the early nineteenth century, the idea of one man one vote was not universally assumed to be the ideal, nor was the idea of women being enfranchised a widely supported one, either by men or, indeed, by most women. A further problem that complicates the picture is that aims and motives often change, usually as a result of changing circumstances. This may mean that initial intentions do not survive, and the outcome is different from the one originally intended. Finally, people's actions are not always logical or rational, and are therefore sometimes difficult to explain.

ACTIVITY

Bearing in mind what you know about the state of the country, and the arguments for and against reform in the early 1830s, complete either a) or b).

Write a speech to be given in the Commons debate on the first reform bill in March of 1831 by either:

a) a Whig MP for a county in East Anglia supporting reform of Parliament, or
b) a Tory MP for a constituency in south-west England opposing reform.

TALKING POINT

Why was the Whig reform bill introduced in 1831 unlikely to be a radical reform of the electoral system? If Whig leaders were anxious about the possibility of revolution, why did they not introduce a more radical reform of the electoral system?

FOCUS ROUTE

Identify the reasons why the Whigs persevered with reform despite the defeat of the first two bills.

ACTIVITY

Read Source 8.17. Were Wellington's fears in 1831 entirely selfish?

D Why did the Whigs persevere with reform following the rejection of the first two bills?

The first two reform bills, March and July 1831

On 1 March 1831 the first reform bill was introduced into the Commons by Lord John Russell. It passed the second reading by just one vote but was defeated at the committee stage. Grey had two options. He could resign and ask the King to appoint another Prime Minister, or he could ask the King to dissolve Parliament, in which case a general election would follow. Grey asked for a dissolution because, with the proposals for reform now public knowledge, Grey would get a large majority in an election. William IV arrived at Westminster to announce the dissolution of Parliament in the middle of a debate. An eyewitness said that as he 'looked at the King upon the throne with the crown loose upon his head, and the tall, grim, figure of Earl Grey beside him, with the sword of state in his hand, it was as if the King had got his executioner by his side'.

The election, as normal, was spread over a period of weeks. In some areas, there was violence. A mob attacked Wellington's house and broke about 30 windows before a servant fired two blunderbusses in the air and the crowd ran off.

SOURCE 8.17 The Duke of Wellington in a letter to Mrs Arbuthnot, 1 May 1931

It may be relied upon that we shall have a revolution. I have never doubted the inclination and disposition of the lower orders of the people ... they are rotten to the core. They are not bloodthirsty, but they are desirous of plunder. They will plunder, annihilate, all property in the country. The majority of them will starve; and we shall witness scenes such as have never yet occurred in any part of the world.

The 1831 election

The anti-reformers were heavily defeated, losing two-thirds of the 60 contested borough seats they had held. In the counties only 6 of the 82 MPs who had voted against the bill were re-elected. Three of these six were in constituencies where the other seat was won by a pro-reformer. Only in Shropshire and Buckinghamshire did anti-reformers win both seats.

The government was returned with a majority of 140. However, not all supporters of reform supported the bill the government had introduced. Henry Hetherington MP, editor of *The Poor Man's Guardian*, who supported 'one man one vote', saw that the £10 borough franchise would give the vote to the lower middle class, but would not enfranchise most of the working class. So while others argued that they should support the bill as a first step to further reform, Hetherington argued that this bill would lead to the newly enfranchised lower middle classes preventing any further extension of the franchise.

First reform bill, March 1831

County seats	• Two MPs for each Riding of Yorkshire. • 26 other counties to have two MPs. • Isle of Wight to have one MP.
Borough seats	• 60 boroughs to lose two MPs (under 2000 inhabitants). • 47 boroughs to lose one MP (2000–4000 inhabitants). • 11 boroughs with no MP to gain two MPs. • 21 boroughs with no MP to gain one MP.
Voters in counties	• Freeholders of land worth 40s. a year (calculated on its rental value). • Copyholders with land worth £10 a year (rental value). • Leaseholders with land worth £50 a year with a lease of at least 21 years.
Voters in boroughs	• Existing electors to keep the vote if still resident in the borough. • Occupiers renting (or owning) houses worth at least £10 a year (in rental).
Method of voting	• Voting was to be open not secret.
Maximum length of a parliament	• To remain at seven years.

> **ACTIVITY**
>
> Compare the proposals in the first bill with the proposals made by the Cabinet committee in January 1831 (see page 125).
>
> 1 What changes are there?
> 2 Suggest reasons for these changes.

Second reform bill, July 1831

> This bill differed very little from the first bill. The only significant change was a plan to give the vote in the counties to tenants renting property worth at least £50 a year.

The second bill was introduced in July 1831. It passed through the Commons with a majority of 140 but there was still a large majority against reform in the Lords. On 8 October the Lords rejected the bill by a majority of 41. Parliament was prorogued (discontinued) until November while the government tried to decide what its next step should be.

The Cabinet had not given up hope of passing a reform bill. The anti-reformers in the Lords were not a united group. Some opponents suggested that they might not be so opposed if a compromise bill could be achieved. During October and November these 'waverers' in the Lords began to negotiate a compromise. In November Lord Wharncliffe sent Grey the details of his modifications to the bill. The Cabinet found most of them to be unacceptable. A further attempt at compromise in early December also failed. In any case, the government was not convinced that the 'waverers' could guarantee the passage of the bill in the Lords. They did not, for example, speak for Wellington and his supporters. However, the government learned from the discussions which minor concessions might win it support for a third bill. It began to prepare the new bill to include as many of the concessions as it could without altering its main aims significantly. As these negotiations went on, the news from across the country was dramatic.

> **ACTIVITY**
>
> 1 What was the difference between those likely to get the vote in the counties in the first bill and the second bill?
> 2 What effect would this proposal have had on the type and number of voters in the counties?

CITY COLLEGE
LEARNING RESOURCE CENTRE

ACTIVITY

How could the headlines on the right have been used to support the case of:

a) those who opposed reform
b) those who supported reform
c) organisers of moderate reform movements
d) the Cabinet?

TALKING POINT

Where would you place these events on the 'revolutionary Richter scale' (pages 10–11)?

ACTIVITY

Choose one of the following activities.

1 It is mid-November 1831. You are the chairperson of a *Question Time* type television programme. You have the opportunity to question Lord John Russell for the Whigs and Sir Robert Peel for the Tories on the events since the proroguing of Parliament. Draft your questions to each politician. You are allowed four questions to each. Write the answers to the questions from **one** of the two politicians.

2 Organise the class to act out the programme, with individuals playing the parts of chairperson, politicians and audience.

3 Organise a 'hot-seat' session in which Lord John Russell, Sir Robert Peel, the Duke of Wellington and Lord Wharncliffe have to justify their actions against the background of violence across the country.

October/November 1831 – imminent revolution?

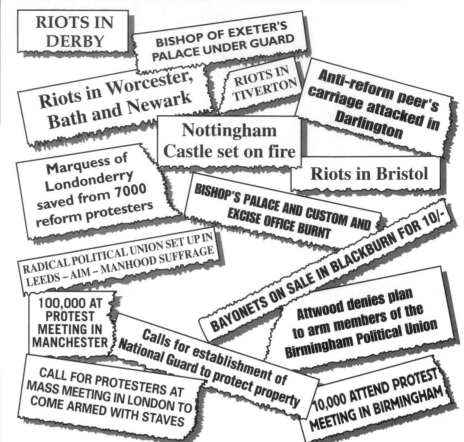

RIOTS IN DERBY

BISHOP OF EXETER'S PALACE UNDER GUARD

Riots in Worcester, Bath and Newark

RIOTS IN TIVERTON

Anti-reform peer's carriage attacked in Darlington

Nottingham Castle set on fire

Riots in Bristol

Marquess of Londonderry saved from 7000 reform protesters

BISHOP'S PALACE AND CUSTOM AND EXCISE OFFICE BURNT

RADICAL POLITICAL UNION SET UP IN LEEDS – AIM – MANHOOD SUFFRAGE

BAYONETS ON SALE IN BLACKBURN FOR 10/-

Attwood denies plan to arm members of the Birmingham Political Union

100,000 AT PROTEST MEETING IN MANCHESTER

Calls for establishment of National Guard to protect property

CALL FOR PROTESTERS AT MASS MEETING IN LONDON TO COME ARMED WITH STAVES

10,000 ATTEND PROTEST MEETING IN BIRMINGHAM

SOURCE 8.18 Reverend J. L. Jackson describing the Bristol riots in a letter, 31 October 1831

During the whole of Saturday Bristol was in a state of considerable ferment from the arrival of Sir C. Wetherall, the Recorder [Judge]. In the evening the multitude assembled before the Mansion House in Queen Square, and smashed the windows by a volley of stones in the front of the building. Yesterday morning when I was going to Bristol to serve the church of a friend, I learnt that the populace had actually broken into the Mansion House, and forced the cellars and were destroying and gutting the house. Three individuals were killed by the soldiers and more wounded. In the afternoon we heard the multitude was assembled in much greater masses, and about four o'clock we saw the new City and County Gaol in flames; afterwards the Bridewell and prison in the Gloucester Road, about a mile from Bristol. In the course of the evening Queen's Square was fired and the Bishop's palace. Of Queen's Square two whole sides have been burnt down, including the Mansion House. Other property to an immense amount is also destroyed. This morning an actual slaughter has taken place; it is supposed, though of course nothing precise can be known at present, that about seventy persons have been killed, besides a large number who have been wounded. The military charged through some of the principal streets, cutting right and left.

ACTIVITY

Is there sufficient evidence to support the view that Britain was 'close to revolution in the autumn of 1831'? Justify your answer.

E Why was the Reform Act passed in 1832 when the bills had been rejected in 1831?

FOCUS ROUTE

1 Using the calendar of events on pages 116–117 as a guide, prepare your own chronology of the political events of December 1831 to June 1832.
2 Why did Grey resign as Prime Minister in May 1832?
3 Why did the Tories eventually abandon opposition to the reform bill?

SOURCE 8.19 Sir Robert Peel, speaking on the third reform bill, December 1831

I will continue my opposition to the last, believing, as I do, that this is the first step, not directly to revolution, but to a series of changes which will affect the property, and totally change the character, of the mixed constitution of this country.

SOURCE 8.20 An extract from Wellington's speech, on the third reading of the reform bill, in Hansard

Notwithstanding the opposition of this house [the Minister] brought in a measure stronger and worse than any one of the measures before introduced, and this measure he wished to force through the House by a large creation of peers ... if this be a legal and constitutional course of conduct ... there is no doubt that the Constitution of this House and of this country is at an end.

ACTIVITY

Write a speech to be made during the third reading in the Commons of the third reform bill by either:

a) a Tory MP from a London constituency arguing against reform
b) a Whig MP from a northern county constituency arguing for reform
c) a Tory MP from south-west England who opposed reform but has now changed his views and supports reform.

The negotiations with the 'waverers' during November and December 1831 led to some modifications to the bill.

- The qualification as a freeman to vote did not now include those who had purchased the position of freeman. A freeman was someone who was honoured by their town or city for service to their town or city.
- Householders had to be ratepayers to qualify for the vote and must not be in arrears with payment of their rates.
- The schedules of boroughs to be disenfranchised was redrawn based on the number of houses rather than the number of voters in the 1821 census, which left slightly fewer seats to be redistributed.

The Cabinet was able to convince reformers that none of these amendments significantly altered the character of the reform bill, although they would result in a slightly reduced electorate.

The third reform bill was introduced into the Commons on 12 December 1831. It passed its second reading on 18 December by 324 votes to 162, although Peel continued to oppose it vehemently.

Despite success in the Commons, getting the bill through the Lords was still a major problem, even with the support of the 'waverers'. The Cabinet had to decide how it would act if, or more likely when, the Lords rejected the bill. The riots seemed to have been quelled relatively easily, with seven men executed, but would the threat of revolution return if the bill was rejected? The Cabinet's solution was to ask the King to make enough peers 'to secure the success of the bill' if all other means of achieving success failed. On 15 January the King agreed to the creation of a small number of new peers – if necessary. However, the actual number that the King might agree to was not clear. The opposition majority was expected to be about twenty, so the King believed he was being asked to create 21 new peers. Grey, however, acknowledged that more might be needed if the creation of new peers resulted in some existing peers abandoning their support for the bill. Rumours were circulating that between 24 and 40 peers might switch sides.

The waverers were, however, convinced that the bill must not be rejected again. If it was, the creation of a large number of new peers who were supporters of reform would make it almost impossible for the Lords to amend bills from a reforming Commons in the future. The waverers aimed to allow the bill to pass the second reading, and then take every opportunity to amend it at the committee stage. On 26 March 1832 the bill went to the Lords. The second reading was passed on 14 April by just nine votes.

Grey was well aware that this small majority could not be guaranteed at the crucial third reading. New Whig peers were likely to be needed. Following amendments in committee, the bill went back to the Lords for its third reading. Wellington argued strongly against both the bill and Grey's plans for forcing the bill through.

On 7 May the Lords rejected the bill with its amendments by 151 votes to 116. Events now moved swiftly and dramatically. Grey asked the King for 50 or 60 new peers but William IV refused to create so many. Grey therefore resigned on 9 May and the King asked Peel to form a government. However, given the demand for reform in the Commons and amongst the public, even Peel would have had to introduce some kind of reform bill. He did not feel able to switch policies and ideals again so soon after pushing through Catholic Emancipation against his party's wishes. Peel therefore refused to take office. Wellington took on the task and for several days attempted to put together a Cabinet.

'The Days of May' – imminent revolution?

TALKING POINTS

1 Where would you place these events on the 'revolutionary Richter scale' (pages 10–11)?
2 Do you think revolution was likely during the 'Days of May'? Why might revolution be more or less likely than at other periods you have studied?

7 May

200,000 AT MEETING OF BIRMINGHAM POLITICAL UNION

9 May

National Political Union meeting – thousands attend

10 May

Common council of London petition for reinstatement of reforming Cabinet

500 NEW MEMBERS FOR BIRMINGHAM POLITICAL UNION

25,000 SIGN PETITION IN MANCHESTER IN SUPPORT OF REFORMERS

13 May

CALL FOR A TRADE BOYCOTT AND A RUN ON THE BANK OF ENGLAND – £1.6m WITHDRAWN IN 10 DAYS

What would happen if the reform issue was not settled quickly? The *Morning Chronicle* of 18 May demanded that Grey be reinstated and added, 'we are otherwise on the eve of the barricades'. The regiment of the Scots Greys was ordered to 'rough sharpen' its sabres and be ready to stop a reform march from Birmingham to London, but the soldiers let it be known that they would not stop a peaceful march. Lord John Russell later said that the 'Days of May' were the only time in his political life when he felt uneasy as to the result of events. However, on 15 May Wellington acknowledged that his implacable opposition to reform made it impossible for him to create a Cabinet, admitting 'The King had better send for Lord Grey at once ... he will have to do it at last; and it is not right to keep the country in agitation during the interval'.

The King summoned Grey to take office again. Wellington promised to abandon active resistance to the bill and to abstain from the vote. The bill went through the Lords in seven days. The third reading was carried by 106 votes to 22 on 4 June. A large number of peers abstained from voting and so the creation of new peers was not needed. The royal assent was given on 7 June. As the clerk of the court pronounced 'Le Roi le veult' (the King wishes it), he was handed a note which read, 'It would surely have been more appropriate if you had said "la canaille le veult" (the mob wishes it)'.

ACTIVITY

1 What fear of Wellington's is implied when he says 'it is not right to keep the country in agitation'?
2 When else have you seen evidence of such a concern influencing Wellington's political decisions?

Third reform bill (the 1832 Reform Act), December 1831–May 1832

County seats	• Two MPs for each Riding of Yorkshire. • 26 other counties to have two MPs. • Isle of Wight to have one MP. • Seven English counties to gain a third MP. • Three Welsh counties to gain a second MP.
Borough seats	• 56 boroughs to lose both MPs. • 31 boroughs to lose one MP. • 22 new boroughs with two MPs to be created. • 19 new boroughs with one MP to be created.
Voters in counties	• 40s freeholders. • £10 copyholders. • £50 leaseholders with lease of at least 20 years. • £10 leaseholders with lease of at least 60 years. • £50 tenants, if occupiers.
Voters in boroughs	• Owners or occupiers of property worth £10 or more a year in rent.
Method of voting	• Voting to be open not secret.
Registration of voters	• Voters had to register by putting their names on the electoral roll, and pay a fee of 1/- (about half a day's wages for a factory worker).
Maximum length of a parliament	• Seven years.

FOCUS ROUTE

1 Using Sources 8.21–8.25, summarise the main changes resulting from the Reform Act in terms of constituencies, the electorate and the make-up of the Commons.
2 The quotation below summarises the Whigs' original aims for a reform bill:
   'A measure ... large enough to satisfy public opinion and yet to afford sure ground of resistance to further innovation, yet so based on property, and on existing franchises and territorial divisions, as to run no risk of overthrowing the [existing] form of government.'
   a) Identify as many elements as you can that demonstrate that their aims were achieved.
   b) Do any parts of the Reform Act conflict with these aims?

ACTIVITY

Peel believed that the reform bill would alter for ever the balance of the constitution by changing the nature of the electorate and the distribution of seats in the Commons. Was he right? Use Sources 8.21–8.25 to help your argument.

CITY COLLEGE LEARNING RESOURCE SERVICE

CITY COLLEGE
RESOURCE CENTRE

SOURCE 8.21 A map showing boroughs that lost both MPs, 1832

1 Callington
2 Camelford
3 Saltash
4 East Grinstead
5 Downton
6 Ludgershall
7 Old Sarum

SOURCE 8.22 A map showing boroughs that gained one or two MPs, 1832

Key to places
▲ Boroughs that gained 2 MPs
■ Boroughs that gained 1 MP

SOURCE 8.23 The size of the electorate in England and Wales, 1831–32

Counties
1831 — 201,899
1832 — 83 per cent increase — 370,379

Boroughs
1831 — 164,391
1832 — 72 per cent increase — 282,398

SOURCE 8.24 The proportion of adult males entitled to vote in England and Wales, 1831 and 1833

1831 — 11%

1833 — 18%

Key
Proportion entitled to vote as percentage of adult male population

SOURCE 8.25 Composition of the House of Commons, 1830 and 1832

1830		
Counties	186
Boroughs	447
Universities	5
Total	658

1832		
Counties	253
Boroughs	399
Universities	6
Total	658

Total number of MPs

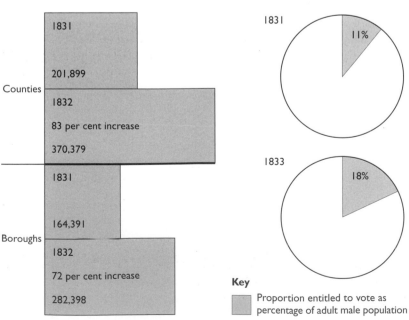

TALKING POINT

The 1832 Reform Act did not include several demands made by radical groups:

- Universal male suffrage (achieved 1918)
- Annual parliaments (never achieved: maximum length reduced to five years in 1911)
- Abolition of property qualification for MPs (achieved 1858)
- Salaries for MPs (achieved 1911)
- Secret ballot (achieved 1872)

Why did reformers want each of these reforms and why were they not made in 1832?

ACTIVITY

1 a) Who did not have political power in 1827 but did in 1832?
  b) Who still had no political power in 1832 and why?
  c) Why was there no secret ballot?
2 a) In what ways did the Reform Act of 1832 differ from the original proposals of the committee in 1831? (See page 125.)
  b) What *kind* of changes were made?
  c) Why might these changes have been made?
3 a) In which part of the country were most of the boroughs which lost MPs?
  b) In which part of the country were most of the boroughs which gained MPs?
  c) One aim of the Act was to create representatives in Parliament of industries and crafts. For which industry or craft would these new boroughs have provided representation after 1832?

- Macclesfield
- Whitehaven
- Stoke-on-Trent
- Whitby
- Sheffield
- Manchester
- Walsall
- Leeds
- Devonport
- Merthyr Tydfil
- Birmingham

ACTIVITY

The Reform Act of 1832 is often called the Great Reform Act. The question of whether or not the Act deserves such a title depends on how 'great' is defined.

1 Discuss what criteria you would use to decide whether or not an Act of Parliament was 'great'.
2 Using these criteria, list the arguments for and against the 1832 Reform Act being 'great'.
3 Did the Whigs intend the Act to be 'great'?
4 Why might historians reach different conclusions from those of contemporaries?
5 Do you think the 1832 Reform Act should be called the Great Reform Act?

G Review: why was the Great Reform Act passed in 1832?

Students studying the 1832 Reform Act often fail to appreciate that reform was the result of a number of factors, some of which can be traced back over a lengthy period of time and, at first glance, have little relationship with reform. Causes may be long term, building up over many years, or short term trigger factors, which create the 'spark' for an event. Drawing together this web of factors is a difficult task and deciding which were the key factors is even more challenging. Now is the time to accept that challenge!

contributory – one cause among others.
significant – a cause that can be identified (with an explanation of why) as more important than the others.
essential – the cause that can be identified as the one without which the event would not have happened because other causes depend on it or are linked to it.

ACTIVITY

1 In pairs or groups, write down the reasons for the passing of the Reform Act individually on slips of paper or card.
2 Arrange your cards under the following three headings:
  a) contributory factors
  b) significant factors
  c) essential factors.
3 Compare your lists with other pairs or groups. Does your list agree with theirs? If not, can you explain why not? Justify your choice to a pair or group whose list is different.
4 Is it possible to point to any factor that was *essential* in bringing about the Reform Act?

ACTIVITY

Write an essay in answer to the following question: To what extent were fear and pragmatism the major factors in the passing of the Great Reform Act?

TALKING POINTS

A key question raised at the beginning of this chapter was whether the reform of Parliament prevented revolution, both in the period 1830–32 and in the longer term up to 1850.

1 Was revolution likely between 1831 and 1832?
2 If so, when exactly was it likely?
3 Did the reform campaign contribute to a revolution not happening?
4 Why might the Reform Act of 1832 have helped to reduce the possibility of future revolution?

KEY POINTS FROM CHAPTER 8

Why was the Great Reform Act passed in 1832?

1 The demand for some changes to the franchise and to the distribution of MPs became a major issue during the early nineteenth century as industrialisation changed the nature of the country and society.
2 The passing of the Catholic Emancipation Act in 1829 indicated that amendments to the constitution were possible.
3 When Wellington's Tory government fell and the Whigs, led by Earl Grey, took power, they proposed some moderate reform. This included plans to enfranchise the middle classes and to provide MPs for many of the new industrial towns and cities, while disenfranchising boroughs which had few or no voters.
4 The first attempt at reform was defeated against a background of increasing discontent and violence, which escalated after the Lords rejected the second bill in October.
5 The third bill was introduced in December 1831 and was again rejected by the Lords. Grey resigned when the King refused to create enough peers to overcome the Lords' opposition. After Wellington unsuccessfully attempted to form a government, and further outbreaks of violence, Grey and the Whigs returned to government.
6 The Reform Act was passed by the Commons in June 1832.
7 The Act enfranchised many middle-class men, and gave representation to towns and cities such as Sheffield, Bradford and Oldham. It removed representation from places such as Dunwich, Fowey and Lostwithiel.
8 The size of the electorate increased by about 75 per cent overall, but still only about 18 per cent of the adult male population was entitled to vote.
9 The secret ballot had not been introduced.
10 While the Great Reform Act disappointed many reformers, it was a major change because it opened the door to further reforms, both political and social. Peel had been correct in predicting that this reform would be only the beginning of change whereas Grey's hopes of using mild reform to put an end to further reform were to be disappointed.

Was the 1834 Poor Law Amendment Act really the New Starvation Law?

CHAPTER OVERVIEW

The workhouse

SOURCE 9.1   Charlie Chaplin describing his first days in the Lambeth workhouse in the 1890s in *My Autobiography*, 1964

Although we were aware of the shame of going into the workhouse, when Mother told us about it both Sydney and I thought it adventurous and a change from living in one stuffy room. But on that doleful day I didn't realise what was happening until we actually entered the workhouse gate . . . for there they made us separate, Mother going in one direction to the women's ward and we in another to the children's. How well I remember the poignant sadness of the first visiting day; the shock of seeing Mother . . . garbed in workhouse clothes. How forlorn and embarrassed she looked! In one week she had aged and grown thin, but her face lit up when she saw us. Sydney and I began to weep, which made Mother weep . . . Eventually she regained her composure . . . She smiled at our cropped heads and stroked them consolingly, telling us we would soon all be together again.

ACTIVITY

1 Why do you think Chaplin's mother was so 'forlorn and embarrassed'?
2 Can you think of a modern equivalent of the fear of the workhouse?

Fear of the workhouse dominated the lives of the poor from the 1830s and lingered well into the twentieth century. Many said they would rather starve than enter one.

Until 1834 the poor had, for the most part, received help in the form of OUTDOOR RELIEF – money and sometimes food, which they received while still living in their homes. This was paid for out of local taxes. However, this system was replaced by The Poor Law Amendment Act. This law introduced a new national system of support for the poor, based on the use of workhouses.

This chapter will investigate why the 1834 Poor Law Amendment Act was introduced and how it affected the poor. Did it help them or should it be more aptly described as the 'New Starvation Law'?

> **OUTDOOR RELIEF**
> Help given in the form of cash 'outside' the workhouse.

A What was poverty in the 1830s and who were 'the poor'? (pp. 138–141)

B What ways of alleviating poverty existed in the early 1800s? (pp. 142–143)

C What problems existed with the provision of help for the poor in 1830? (pp. 144–145)

D What were the plans for a new system of poor relief? (pp. 146–149)

E What impact did the Act of 1834 have and how did people react to it? (pp. 150–156)

F Review: was the 1834 Poor Law Amendment Act really the New Starvation Law? (pp. 157–159)

LEARNING RESOURCE CENTRE ... Y COLLEGE

FOCUS ROUTE

1 List the major causes of poverty in the 1830s.
2 List the main items of expenditure and income for poor families at this time.
3 a) What was meant by the term *laissez-faire*?
   b) Why did many people, both rich and poor, believe in *laissez-faire*?
   c) Why did the government not organise a national system of help for the poor?

ENCLOSURE
Process which took place during the late eighteenth and early nineteenth centuries that led to the open fields of medieval society being replaced by fields enclosed by walls or hedges.

A What was poverty in the 1830s and who were 'the poor'?

A problem facing anyone studying poverty in Britain in the nineteenth century is that 'poverty' may well mean something very different to people in the twenty-first century than it did to people in the 1830s. Is poverty in the twenty-first century not having enough food? Is it not being able to 'eat out' regularly? Is it not having clean clothes? Is it not being able to buy the latest designer clothes? Is it not having a washing machine? Is it not having satellite TV, a computer or TV in the children's bedrooms? Is it not owning at least one car per family? Consider how many of these things would not have even been available in the 1830s. What, then, was 'poverty' in 1830?

Poverty in the first half of the nineteenth century was caused by many factors and it was not restricted to one type of worker in one geographical area. Poverty in rural areas was sometimes due to declining employment opportunities for farm labourers. This was caused by greater efficiency in farming following the enclosure of farm land and the use of machinery for some work (for example, steam threshing). Opportunities for casual farm work were declining, despite the creation of some new jobs resulting from enclosure, such as hedging and ditching. At the same time the population was growing, which meant more mouths to feed and not enough jobs for everyone.

However, poverty was not just the result of unemployment. Many people who did have a job received such low wages that even bare existence was a struggle. Families relied on any money brought into the home by family members, however young or old, but there were fewer opportunities for supplementary income than there had been. Farm workers had once added to their wages by weaving small amounts of woollen cloth, which they had sold locally, but competition from the new factories turning out miles of cloth cheaply had put an end to that source of income. ENCLOSURE usually removed free common grazing land, making it impossible for labourers to supplement their income by keeping a few animals on the common for milk or meat.

In the towns and cities poverty was at least as bad as in the countryside. New jobs in factories did not pay good wages and, as many of them could be done by women who were cheap to employ, men found that there was little work for them. Particularly hard hit were skilled craftsmen such as handloom weavers. In the late eighteenth and early nineteenth centuries they had been relatively prosperous, but the water- and steam-powered looms of the factories were much cheaper to run and could be 'minded' by women. Handloom weavers faced a stark choice – either take low paid work in factories, if it was available, or accept unemployment.

If people were unemployed, they faced poverty, and there might be many reasons why someone had no work. There were those who were too young to work, although children did work in fields and factories to support themselves from very young ages. There were those too old to work, although there was no concept of retirement, and people worked until they could not possibly do so. There were those who were ill or disabled, and there were plenty of the latter following the Napoleonic Wars. There were also those who chose not to work although fit and well.

ACTIVITY

1 a) In groups or pairs decide how to define modern-day poverty. How would you know that someone is poor?
   b) Feed your findings back to the other groups/pairs. Compile a class definition.
2 How do you think poverty would have been defined in the 1830s? How would you have known someone was poor then?
3 Make a list of likely causes of poverty in 1830.

more children

enclosure

low wages

new machines

loss of free grazing land

end of domestic cloth production

Causes of poverty in rural areas

TEXTILE MILL

Women workers wanted – low wages paid

Causes of poverty in urban areas

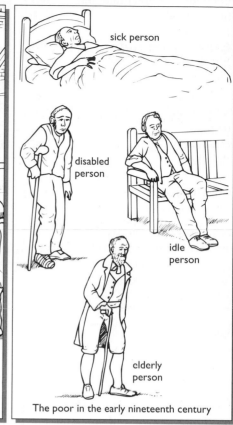

sick person

disabled person

idle person

elderly person

The poor in the early nineteenth century

■ Learning trouble spot

What was the value of money in the 1830s?

It is often difficult for students today to understand what money would have bought in the nineteenth century. Wages of even £10 a week, which would have seemed a fortune to working men in 1835, sound ludicrously low to people in the twenty-first century. In the 1830s, earnings varied considerably across the country and within regions, and according to the job done. In 1800 the weekly wage for a farm labourer would have been around 10s (50p). That would not have kept a family alive, and they relied on other family members, including the children, to earn money. A skilled worker such as a handloom weaver might have earned £2 a week, and in the early 1800s these workers were the 'aristocracy' of the working class. An adult loom-minder in a mill in Manchester earned less than £1 a week. They were often women.

By the mid-nineteenth century a farm labourer might have earned £2 a week, still hardly enough to feed his family. A middle-class man might have earned between £200 a year (as a headteacher in a village school, for example) or perhaps £1000 a year with a small business. Even with an income of £200 a year, the headteacher might have employed a general servant, who would have been paid about £10 to £15 a year. Few people, even among the middle class, bought their own homes; renting was the norm.

At the top of the 'class pyramid' the upper classes – the bankers, barristers and solicitors (men like Soames Forsyte in John Galsworthy's novels) – would have had incomes of several thousand pounds a year. A family with £2000 a year could have afforded to employ a cook, two or three housemaids, a ladies' maid, a nursery maid, a coachman and a footman. Servants' wages were very low, but in a wealthy house around 1825 the butler could expect to earn £55 a year, the housekeeper £25, and the cook (if good, and especially if French) £85. This was in addition to their board, food and uniform. The scullery maid, the lowest form of life in the servants' hall, would be lucky to get £10 a year.

140

WAS THE 1834 POOR LAW AMENDMENT ACT REALLY THE NEW STARVATION LAW?

Prices *c*.1800

56lb flour (for breadmaking)	6/3
10lb oatmeal	1/11
1lb butter	1/-
1lb beef/mutton/pork	5d
1lb bacon	8d
50lb potatoes	1/3
2 pints whole milk	3d
2 pints skimmed milk	1½d
1oz tea	8d
4oz sugar	6d
1lb butter	8d
1 cwt coal	6d
rent of two small rooms per week	2/- to 3/-

***c*.1800 typical weekly wages**

For a working man in mill/factory:
£1 10s–£2 per week
For a clerical worker (e.g. in a factory office): £2–£2 10s per week

Prices *c*.1840

4lb loaf of bread	9d
1lb meat	5d
1lb butter	9d
40lb potatoes	1/4
1 pint beer	2d
1 cwt coal	1/7
rent of two small rooms per week	2/6

ACTIVITY

1 Read Sources 9.2 and 9.4. What problems did these families face?

2 Would you expect to see a daughter's babysitting income included in a family budget today? Why was it included in 1795?

3 What would be the impact for the family when the neighbour no longer needed the babyminder?

4 How could these families have balanced the budgets?

5 How do you know that the children in Source 9.3 are poor?

6 How much reliance would you put on Source 9.3 as evidence of poverty in the mid-nineteenth century?

7 How much reliance would you put on a novel (such as that in Source 9.6) as evidence about poverty in the early/mid-nineteenth century?

8 Is John Fox's evidence (Source 9.5) any more reliable than the drawings and the novel?

SOURCE 9.2 A typical weekly budget of a labourer's family, 1795

Income		
Man (carter)	12s	0d
Wife (cotton rover)	0s	6d
Daughter aged twelve (babyminding for neighbour)	2s	6d
Daughter aged nine (babyminding for neighbour)	2s	0d
Total income	**17s**	**0d**

Expenditure		
Rent	2s	0d
Fuel	0s	7d
Cheese	1s	6d
Oatmeal bread	5s	0d
Meat	1s	6d
Tea and sugar	1s	3d
Potatoes	1s	6d
Milk	1s	2d
Butter	1s	0d
Soap, candles, groceries	1s	0d
Clothes	2s	0d
Total expenditure	**18s**	**6d**

Rent – two small rooms for one year, about £5
1s = 5p; 1d = approx. ½p; 1s 6d (also written 1/6) = approx. 8p

SOURCE 9.3 Poverty in Birmingham, from the *Illustrated London News*, a weekly publication that depicted current events. This picture was first published in May 1842

141

WAS THE 1834 POOR LAW AMENDMENT ACT REALLY THE NEW STARVATION LAW?

SOURCE 9.4 The shopping list of Elizabeth Whiting, a 40-year-old widow with four children, December 1839. She paid 3s a week in rent, but had fallen behind and owed £1.13s. She was a cleaner and brush-maker; she earned nothing this week, last week 3s and the week before 5s 8d. From S. R. Bosanquet, *The rights of the poor and Christian almsgiving vindicated*, 1841

Dec 15th 1839	s	d
Sunday: bought on Sunday night, potatoes 1½d; bacon 2d, candle ½d, tea and sugar 2d, soap 1½d, coals 2d, loaf 8½d	1	6
Monday: tea and sugar 2d, butter 1½d, candle ½d		4
Tuesday: coals		2
Wednesday: tea and sugar 2d, candle ½d, wood ½d, potatoes 1d		4
Thursday: coals		1
Friday and Saturday	–	–
Total expenditure	2	5

SOURCE 9.5 From a report by John Fox, Medical Officer of Cerne Poor Law Union, Dorset 1842

In many of the cottages ... the beds stood on the ground floor, which was damp three parts of the year; scarcely one had a fireplace in the bedroom, and one had a single pane of glass stuck in the mud wall as its only window, with a large heap of wet and dirty potatoes in one corner. Persons living in such cottages are generally ... very dirty, and usually in rags, living almost wholly on bread and potatoes, scarcely ever tasting animal food.

SOURCE 9.6 E. Gaskell, *Mary Barton*, 1848. Mrs Gaskell was married to a Unitarian minister with a parish in Manchester. The underlying themes of many of her novels relate to social, economic and political issues of the mid-nineteenth century. In *North and South* for example she deals with differences between the industrial north and the rural south, and in *Mary Barton* she uses the Chartist movement as the background

You went down one step ... into a cellar in which a family of human beings lived. It was very dark inside. The window panes were many of them broken and stuffed with rags, which was reason enough for the dusky light that pervaded the place even at midday ... They began to penetrate the thick darkness of the place, and to see three or four little children rolling on the damp, nay wet, brick floor, through which the stagnant, filthy moisture of the street oozed up; the fireplace was empty and black; the wife sat on her husband's chair, and cried in the dank loneliness.

TALKING POINT

In *David Copperfield* one of Charles Dickens' most famous characters, Mr Micawber, said, 'Annual income twenty pounds, annual expenditure nineteen and six, result happiness. Annual income twenty pounds, annual expenditure twenty pounds and six, result misery.' How realistic was Micawber's comment?

TALKING POINTS

1 a) List the ways in which poverty is alleviated or prevented in Britain today.
  b) How many of these methods do you think were used before 1850?
2 Who is responsible today for trying to ensure that people do not suffer poverty and its effects?
3 Why would many people have had a different view about who should be responsible in 1830?
4 Explain how supporters of *laissez-faire* would have responded to any suggestion in 1830 that the government should be involved in organising help for the poor.

■ **Learning trouble spot**

Laissez-faire
Students often have difficulty with this concept, because in the twenty-first century it is accepted that the welfare of the people is a concern of government. We often hear the phrase 'the government should do something about it', no matter what 'it' is. However, in the early nineteenth century, *laissez-faire* was the dominant concept. *Laissez-faire* meant that it was not the government's role to 'interfere' in people's lives. The phrase means 'leave alone' – that is let people run their own lives. The government's role was to maintain the peace and security of the country, not to take care of the population.

This attitude is often considered by students as selfishness on the part of those in power. They think that the well-off should have been concerned about those who had problems such as poor housing or long working hours. However, *laissez-faire* was not just supported by the better-off. Many working people also believed that their lives were none of the state's business. For example, many parents saw the government's proposals to limit children's working hours in factories in the mid-nineteenth century as interference in parents' rights over their children. There were similar responses to suggestions later in the century that all children should attend school by law, which would have prevented many children earning money for the family. Taken to its extreme, *laissez-faire* meant that government should play no part in welfare, working or housing conditions, public health, or economic activities. The impact of this concept was very strong in the early nineteenth century, and led to much opposition to proposed reforms, or 'interference' as reforms were seen by supporters of *laissez-faire*.

142

WAS THE 1834 POOR LAW AMENDMENT ACT REALLY THE NEW STARVATION LAW?

B What ways of alleviating poverty existed in the early 1800s?

FOCUS ROUTE

1 What was the role of workhouses at the beginning of the 1800s?
2 What were the main systems of outdoor relief in 1830?
3 What were the advantages and the disadvantages of systems such as the Speenhamland and Roundsman for:
a) workers
b) the unemployed
c) employers
d) those who paid poor rates?

■ 9B Poor relief in the early nineteenth century

The system for helping the poor in the early years of the nineteenth century was not one system but many, all of which had evolved over more than 200 years. The main Acts which made up the Poor Law were:

1601 THE ELIZABETHAN POOR LAW

- Parish authorities were responsible for looking after the poor in the parish.
- A poor rate – a tax used to help the poor – was to be collected.
- An overseer of the poor was to be appointed to decide how much money was needed and how much tax each property owner should pay.
- The IMPOTENT POOR were to have relief.
- The able-bodied poor were to be found work.
- Beggars were to be punished.

IMPOTENT POOR
People who were poor because they were too old or ill to work.

1662 SETTLEMENT ACT

- Set out who was entitled to be a settled labourer. A person without a settlement could be sent away from the parish if he asked for help.
- Workers could get certificates to allow them to go to another parish for work; the certificate said the worker's parish would take him back if he needed help.
- The old and sick were put into ALMSHOUSES or poorhouses to be looked after.

ALMSHOUSES
Accommodation provided by charities for the elderly and/or poor.

1723 WORKHOUSE TEST ACT

- Parishes could provide a workhouse where the able-bodied poor would be given work.
- If an able-bodied person refused to go into the workhouse they would not be entitled to relief from the parish. (By 1776 there were nearly 2000 workhouses in England, each with between 20 and 50 inmates.)

1782 GILBERT'S ACT

- Parishes could group together into 'UNIONS', to build workhouses.
- Workhouses were to be only for the old, sick and orphans.
- The able-bodied poor were to be given 'outdoor relief' – money.

UNIONS
Groups of parishioners who joined together to build a single workhouse to serve the whole group.

ACTIVITY

In groups of four, each take one of the Acts in Chart 9B.

1 Explain to the others in your group the main features of the Act and especially:
   a) the aspects that would help the poor
   b) the aspects that were intended to stop the idle getting help.
2 Identify the main trends in poor relief between 1600 and 1800.

'Outdoor' relief

The ways in which outdoor relief was given were many and varied, but in the early 1800s many parishes, especially in southern England, began to use a system that had first been developed by the magistrates at Speenhamland in Berkshire in 1795. It became known as the Speenhamland system. The idea of this system was that a person's wages would be made up to an amount that the magistrates thought was needed to feed a family, based on the price of a loaf of bread (a 'gallon' loaf, weighing just under 9lb). The amount needed took into consideration whether a man was married and how many children he had.

Another method of outdoor relief was the Roundsman system. There were several variations, but all held to the basic principle that any unemployed workers would go *round* the parish to look for work. If an employer gave a person work, the worker would receive a small amount from the employer – not a full wage – and to this would be added a small amount from the parish funds.

■ 9C The Speenhamland system

When a loaf costs	Income should be for				
	single man	single woman	man and wife	man/wife with one child	man/wife with two children
1s	3s	2s	4s 6d	6s	7s 6d
1s 3d	3s 9d	2s 3d	5s 6d	7s 3d	9s
1s 6d	4s 3d	2s 6d	6s 3d	8s 3d	10s 3d
1s 9d	4s 6d	2s 9d	6s 9d	9s	11s 3d

(The amount increased for each additional child.)

ACTIVITY

1 What help would a man with a wife and two children get who earned 9s a week when a loaf cost 1s 6d?
2 What would happen if this man's employer cut his wages by 2s a week?
3 What would happen if the man decided not to work part of the week and only earned 7s?
4 What would happen if the man lost his job and became unemployed?

C What problems existed with the provision of help for the poor in 1830?

SOURCE 9.7 Poor rates, 1802–32

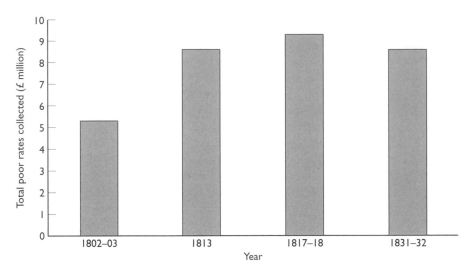

SOURCE 9.8 Spending on poor relief, 1802–33

Year	Expenditure
1802	£4.1m
1812	£6.7m
1815	£5.7m
1818	£7.5m
1821	£6.3m
1824	£5.7m
1827	£6.3m
1830	£6.8m
1833	£6.3m

SOURCE 9.9 A map to show annual expenditure on poor relief, 1834

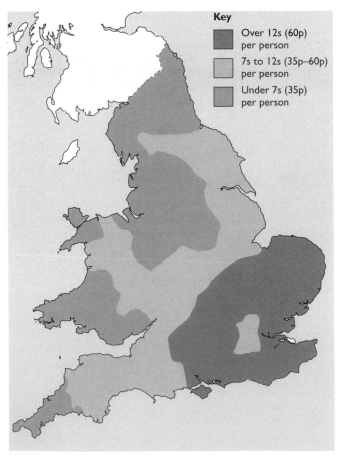

Key

- Over 12s (60p) per person
- 7s to 12s (35p–60p) per person
- Under 7s (35p) per person

SOURCE 9.10 Amount paid out in poor relief in 1831 per head of the population

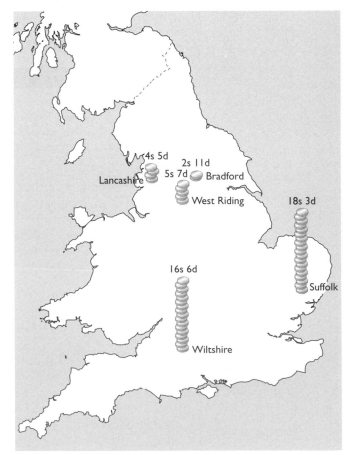

145

WAS THE 1834 POOR LAW AMENDMENT ACT REALLY THE NEW STARVATION LAW?

SOURCE 9.11 Wages of handloom weavers in Bolton, 1800–30

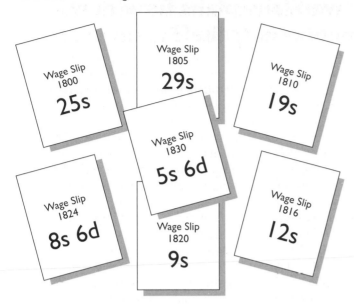

Wage Slip 1800 — **25s**
Wage Slip 1805 — **29s**
Wage Slip 1810 — **19s**
Wage Slip 1830 — **5s 6d**
Wage Slip 1824 — **8s 6d**
Wage Slip 1820 — **9s**
Wage Slip 1816 — **12s**

SOURCE 9.12 The birth rate per thousand, 1780–1830

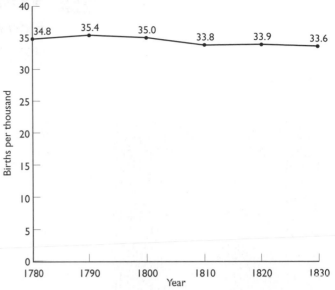

SOURCE 9.13 Population, 1781–1831

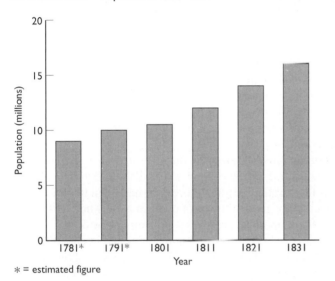

* = estimated figure

SOURCE 9.14 Extract from T. Malthus, *An Essay on the Principle of Population as it affects the future Improvement of Society*, 1798. Revd Thomas Malthus was a writer on economics. He argued that supplies of food do not increase at the same rate as population increases. He said that population increase was controlled by famines and that outdoor relief only encouraged population increase

The labouring poor ... seem always to live from hand to mouth. Their present wants employ their whole attention and they seldom think of the future. Even when they have an opportunity of saving they seldom exercise it, but all that is beyond their present necessities goes, generally speaking, to the ale-house. The poor laws of England may therefore be said to diminish both the power and the will to save among the common people.

ACTIVITY

How would Source 9.14 support the belief in *laissez-faire*?

The pre-1834 system of poor relief

The systems for poor relief that existed before the Act of 1834 were not without their advantages. They were not uniform across the country, and therefore were usually adapted to local circumstances. They were locally administered by people who lived in the area and understood the problems. Whilst the officials may not have always been very sympathetic towards those claiming help, they often knew the claimants personally. Many schemes, such as the Speenhamland system, allowed people who had a job, but whose wages were low, to receive some monetary help. These schemes used the idea of a 'minimum wage' – usually based on the price of bread and the size of the family.

In industrial towns and cities, where unemployment was frequent but often short-term as a result of factories closing for short periods between contracts, locally based schemes that allowed families to be supported on a temporary basis worked reasonably effectively. Such schemes could also cope with the problem of very large numbers of people being unemployed at any one time, for perhaps only a few weeks, before work became available again.

The commission that was asked to investigate the working of the existing poor laws was largely concerned with the costs of the existing schemes, which were felt to be too high, and were rising. It was looking for a system that would be effective, but that would, above all, keep costs down.

ACTIVITY

Read through Sources 9.7–9.14. Work either as individuals or as a group. It is 1833. You are a member of a committee set up by Parliament to consider the provision of poor relief in England. You are asked to:

a) identify the problems
b) suggest what needs to be done to eliminate the problems.

Edwin Chadwick (1800–90)
Chadwick was a barrister by profession, and for a time was Jeremy Bentham's secretary, and a disciple of Benthamism. He was appointed an assistant commissioner in the Poor Law Commission's investigations, and within a year became a commissioner. He made the major contribution to the final report. When the new Poor Law Commission was set up to run the Poor Law in 1834, Chadwick was disappointed to be appointed as Secretary to the Commission, and not commissioner. In later years Chadwick campaigned for improvements to public health, following his major report, *An Enquiry into the Sanitary Conditions of the Labouring Population of Great Britain* published in 1842. In 1848 he was appointed Commissioner of the Board of Health but was forced to retire in 1854 on health grounds. Although renowned for his tremendous vitality and passion for reform, he was also regarded as quarrelsome, self-opinionated, disloyal when he felt he was right, and unshakeable in his view to the point of obstinacy. For many involved in local government in mid-nineteenth-century English towns, he was perhaps their most hated bureaucrat. His work received no official recognition until he was awarded a knighthood aged 89.

D What were the plans for a new system of poor relief?

By 1830 the amount of money spent on supporting the poor was an important issue in the minds of those who paid the poor rates and those whose responsibility it was to use the money. Although the amount spent on poor relief had dropped from its peak in 1818–19, it still remained high. In the towns the wages of many skilled workers were declining rapidly, so that even those with jobs were becoming poorer. In some rural areas the amount spent per head was nearly six times that spent in the industrial areas. In addition, between 1811 and 1831, the population increased by about 30 per cent and the birth rate showed no signs of decreasing significantly. Such rapid population increase meant that there were more and more mouths to be fed.

In February 1832 the government set up a commission to investigate the working of the existing Poor Law, and to suggest changes and improvements that might be made. There were eight commissioners and 26 assistant commissioners, whose task was to obtain evidence from around the country. Among the leading members of the commission were the Bishop of London, the lawyer and writer Edwin Chadwick, and the economist Nassau Senior. Chadwick had been employed for a time as secretary to the philosopher Jeremy Bentham, and had been greatly influenced by Bentham's philosophy of Utilitarianism.

The members of the commission were well aware that there was a widespread belief, particularly amongst those who paid poor rates, that too many paupers were simply too lazy to work. They also believed that the system of local administration of workhouses by individual parishes led to inefficiencies in the spending of the poor rates. The Utilitarian influence on Chadwick meant he saw this as an area ripe for reform. This demand for greater efficiency, which it was expected would lead to a fall in the cost of poor relief, was one of the key factors behind the arguments of those in favour of a centrally administered system.

The assistant commissioners investigated the various methods of helping the poor across the country, collecting evidence from about 3000 parishes, including some where outdoor relief for the able-bodied had been totally abolished, and help was only given, to all types of poor, in a workhouse. These parishes were known as dis-pauperised parishes. One example was at Southwell in Nottinghamshire, where the cost of poor relief had been cut from £1884 for the year 1821–22 to £786 for the year 1823–24 as a result of the work of the overseer of the poor, George Nicholls. The assistant commissioners were especially disapproving of parishes such as one in Kent where they found that the workhouse was full of sturdy labourers, sitting around a stove, with a generally overfed, mutinous and insubordinate appearance. After two years of taking evidence, the 300-page report was published in February 1834.

ACTIVITY

1 Choose one of the following people:
   - a farm worker on a low wage, with a wife and three children aged six months, two years and four years
   - a farm owner in East Yorkshire, employing six labourers
   - a shopkeeper in a small village in Suffolk
   - a single male cotton spinner in a factory in Manchester
   - a widow, with four children aged between ten and fifteen, all living in Cornwall
   - an owner of a worsted factory in Bradford, employing 300 workers
   - a man aged 75, unable to work as a result of arthritis.

   Use what you have learned about help for the poor before 1830 in Section B to prepare a short presentation for the person you have chosen, to be given to a government committee investigating the state of the Poor Law. Explain in which ways the existing system is wrong and how it needs changing.
2 Could the people listed really have made their feelings about the Poor Law known to Parliament?

FOCUS ROUTE

1 Summarise the *key* points in Sources 9.15–9.22 in one or two sentences.
2 Copy and complete this table, adding to the list any aims not listed.

Aims	Evidence from the proposals
To cut the cost of poor relief	
To reduce the poor rates	
To transfer control of poor relief into the hands of the ratepayers	
To transfer responsibility from individual parishes with unpaid overseers to the unions with some central control	

PARISHIONERS
In this context this refers to those who depended on the parish authorities for food, money or shelter.

SOURCE 9.15   Extract from *The Report from His Majesty's Commissioners for Inquiring into the Administration and Practical Operation of the Poor Laws, 1834*

Section A: The progressive character of burdens and evils associated with the existing law

A great part of the expense is incurred, not by the direct payment out of the rates, but by the purchase of unprofitable labour. Where rate-payers are the direct employers of work-people, they often keep down the rates, either by employing more labour than they actually want, or by employing PARISHIONERS, when better labourers could be obtained. The progressive deterioration of the labourers in the pauperised districts, and the increasing anxiety of the principal rate-payers ... to shift [their burden] ... on the inhabitants of neighbouring parishes ... appear to have greatly increased this source of indirect and unrecorded loss.

ACTIVITY

What problem have the commissioners identified in Section A of their report (Source 9.15)?

SOURCE 9.16   Extract from *The Report from His Majesty's Commissioners for Inquiring into the Administration and Practical Operation of the Poor Laws, 1834*

Section B: Principles of a sound system

The most pressing of all the evils which we have described are those connected with the relief of the able-bodied ... In all extensive civilised communities ... the occurrence of extreme necessity is prevented by alms-giving, by public institutions supported by endowments or voluntary contributions ... but in no part of Europe except England has it been thought that the provision ... should be applied to more than the relief of indigence, the state of a person unable, or unable to obtain, in return for his labour, the means of subsistence. It has never been deemed expedient that the provision should extend to the relief of poverty; that is the state of one, who, in order to obtain a mere subsistence, is forced to have recourse to labour.

... The first and most essential of all conditions is that the situation [of the person applying for relief] shall not be made really or apparently as eligible as the situation of the independent labourer of the lowest class ... Every penny bestowed, that tends to render the position of the pauper more eligible than that of the independent labourer, is a bounty on indolence and vice. We have found that as the poor rates are at present administered, they operate as bounties of this description, to the amount of several millions annually.

ACTIVITY

1 Read Source 9.16. What situation do the commissioners feel is worthy of help, and what is not?
2 In your own words explain the meaning of the sentence 'Every penny bestowed, that tends to render the position of the pauper more eligible than that of the independent labourer, is a bounty on indolence and vice'.

■ Learning trouble spot

Benthamism/Utilitarianism
Jeremy Bentham, who had trained as a lawyer, formed a philosophy by which the worth of anything might be assessed by asking 'what use is it?', or in more detail, 'is it useful in promoting the greatest happiness of the greatest number?' Those who followed Bentham's philosophy, which came to be known as Utilitarianism, believed that the lot of mankind could be improved by the application of this principle of 'utility'. Bentham formulated a set of principles for reform which included the acquisition of the facts by a commission of inquiry, the framing of legislation based on its report, and the drafting of regulations which would be enacted by a central administrative authority.

148

WAS THE 1834 POOR LAW AMENDMENT ACT REALLY THE NEW STARVATION LAW?

ACTIVITY

How does withdrawing relief lead to higher wages (see Source 9.17)?

SOURCE 9.17 Extract from *The Report from His Majesty's Commissioners for Inquiring into the Administration and Practical Operation of the Poor Laws*, 1834

Section C: The effect of reform on wages
The withdrawal of relief in aid of wages appears to be succeeded by effects in the following order: First, the labourer becomes more steady and diligent; next, the more efficient labour makes the return to the farmer's capital larger, and the consequent increase of the fund for the employment of labour enables and induces the capitalist to give better wages.

ACTIVITY

What two consequences of dis-pauperisation of parishes are put forward in Section D (Source 9.18)?

SOURCE 9.18 Extract from *The Report from His Majesty's Commissioners for Inquiring into the Administration and Practical Operation of the Poor Laws*, 1834

Section D: Effect of dis-pauperisation on morals and content of labourer
The next class of specific effects which have followed the application of the principle of keeping the condition of the pauper inferior to that of the independent labourer, is, that it has arrested the increase of population, which the evidence shows to be produced by the present state of the law ... In Swallowfield ... the number of improvident marriages is diminished by about one half ... In Bingham, the diminution of improvident marriages was about one half; and yet ... illegitimate births, instead of having been promoted by the diminution ... have been repressed still more effectually ... One characteristic of the dis-pauperised parishes is the comparative absence of crime ... In Bingham ... during the two years preceding 1818, seven men were transported for felonies; now there is scarcely any disorder in the place. In Uley and Southwell parishes crime has similarly ceased.

ACTIVITY

Why would the evidence in Section E (Source 9.19) appeal to middle-class rate-payers and voters in England?

SOURCE 9.19 Extract from *The Report from His Majesty's Commissioners for Inquiring into the Administration and Practical Operation of the Poor Laws*, 1834

Section E: Results of offering work instead of allowance
Wherever the principle [of offering work instead of allowance] ... has been carried into effect ... its introduction has been beneficial to the class for whose benefit the Poor-Laws exist. We have seen that in every instance in which the able-bodied labourers have been rendered independent of partial relief, or of relief otherwise than in a well-regulated workhouse:

1 Their industry has been restored and improved.
2 Frugal habits have been created or strengthened.
3 The permanent demand for labour has increased.
4 And the increase has been such, that their wages ... have in general increased.
5 The number of improvident and wretched marriages has diminished.
6 Their discontent has been abated, and their moral and social condition in every way improved.

ACTIVITY

Explain in your own words what is being proposed in Section F (Source 9.20).

SOURCE 9.20 Extract from *The Report from His Majesty's Commissioners for Inquiring into the Administration and Practical Operation of the Poor Laws*, 1834

Section F: Proposed abolition of outdoor relief to able-bodied
First ... all relief whatever to able-bodied persons or their families, otherwise than in well-regulated workhouses ... shall be declared unlawful, and shall cease ... and that all relief afforded in respect of children under the age of 16 shall be considered as afforded to their parents.

CITY COLLEGE
LEARNING RESOURCE CENTRE

ACTIVITY

Which *key* words and phrases in Section G (Source 9.21) would have appealed to middle-class rate-payers and voters in 1834?

ACTIVITY

Why do you think the proposals in Source 9.22 were included?

APPRENTICING

The method by which some workhouses got rid of child paupers by apprenticing them to businessmen, usually for a fee; the apprentices were usually little more than slaves.

SOURCE 9.21 Extract from *The Report from His Majesty's Commissioners for Inquiring into the Administration and Practical Operation of the Poor Laws*, 1834

Section G: Need of central supervision

We have received no definite plan for the purpose (of administration) and we have prepared none. We trust that immediate measures for the correction of the evils in question may be carried into effect by a comparatively small and cheap agency, which may assist the parochial or district officers, wherever their management is in conformity to the intention of the legislature; and control them wherever their management is at variance with it ... We propose that the management, the collection of rates, and the entire supervision of the expenditure ... shall continue in the officers appointed immediately by the rate-payers ... We recommend therefore a Central Board to control the administration of the Poor Laws ... and that the Commissioners be empowered ... to frame and enforce regulations for the government of workhouses ... and that such regulations shall, as far as may be practicable, be uniform throughout the country.

SOURCE 9.22 Other recommendations from *The Report from His Majesty's Commissioners for Inquiring into the Administration and Practical Operation of the Poor Laws*, 1834

We recommend ... that the Central Board be empowered to make such regulations as they shall think fit respecting the relief to be afforded by APPRENTICING *children ...*

We recommend that the mother of an illegitimate child born after the passing of the Act, be required to support it, and that any relief occasioned by the wants of the child be considered relief afforded to the parent.

ACTIVITY

1 Choose one person from the list below and write a short presentation in which you explain your reactions to the commission's proposals. Deliver your presentation orally to the rest of the group.

- a farm worker on a low wage, with a wife and three children aged six months, two years and four years
- a farm owner in East Yorkshire, employing six labourers
- a shopkeeper in a small village in Suffolk
- a single male cotton spinner in a factory in Manchester
- a widow, with four children aged between ten and fifteen, all living in Cornwall
- an owner of a worsted factory in Bradford, employing 300 workers
- a man aged 75, unable to work as a result of arthritis
- a Member of Parliament, who owned a farm in Sussex, and believed in the principle of Utilitarianism.

2 Summarise, in note form, the reactions of all those on the above list.

150

WAS THE 1834 POOR LAW AMENDMENT ACT REALLY THE NEW STARVATION LAW?

E What impact did the Act of 1834 have and how did people react to it?

The Whig government did not waste any time in putting the recommendations of the commission into practice. The commission's report was published in February 1834. In April a bill to implement its recommendations was introduced into the Commons. By August the Poor Law Amendment Act was law. Within Parliament at least, there was little opposition to the changes being proposed to the way of supporting the poor. The main provisions of the new law are shown below.

POOR LAW AMENDMENT ACT 1834

- Outdoor relief will continue for the old and infirm.

- Outdoor relief will be abolished for the able-bodied. The only relief available to an able-bodied man (and his family) will be in a workhouse. (This was known as the 'workhouse test'.)

- Conditions in the workhouses are to be made 'less eligible' than those of the lowest paid labourers in work (the principle of 'less-eligibility').

- A central Poor Law Commission based at Somerset House in London will administer the new law. Three commissioners will oversee the system and impose uniformity across the country.

- Parishes will be joined together to form Poor Law unions, each with a central workhouse. Each parish will contribute to the funds of the union from a poor rate.

- The workhouses will be run by an elected Board of Guardians, who will employ a full-time master and matron of the workhouse. Rate-payers will elect the Guardians.

- There will be seven 'classes' of pauper, to be kept separate within the workhouse:
  – men infirm due to age or illness
  – able-bodied men and youths over fifteen
  – boys aged seven to fifteen
  – women infirm through age or illness
  – able-bodied women and girls over fifteen
  – girls aged seven to fifteen
  – children under seven.

FOCUS ROUTE

1 Copy and complete the table to show the commission's proposals and whether the 1834 Act fulfilled these proposals.

Changes that needed to be made	Commission's proposals	1834 Poor Law Amendment Act
Outdoor relief for able-bodied paupers		
Outdoor relief for the old and the sick		
Workhouse conditions		
Administration of the system		
Separation of classes of pauper		

2 In what way was the 'workhouse test' a test?
3 What do you think was the main concern of the guardians in running a workhouse, and why?
4 The new Act was intended to deal with the effects of poverty – to alleviate poverty where it occurred. What major problem did it not deal with?

151

WAS THE 1834 POOR LAW AMENDMENT ACT REALLY THE NEW STARVATION LAW?

ACTIVITY

1 Write a television news bulletin for 1 September 1834 in which the new Poor Law is outlined and the chairman of a Board of Guardians is interviewed to give his views about what the Act will achieve.
2 What attitudes towards the change in the law does the cartoonist in Source 9.23 convey?

Once established, the Central Board sent out assistant commissioners to all parts of the country to advise unions on how to set up new workhouses. In a parish or group of parishes where there was no existing workhouse, one was built, usually to plans supplied by London architect Sampson Kempthorne. The commissioners drew up diet sheets for inmates and lists of regulations. The Boards of Guardians had to send to the Central Board in London copies of the minutes of their meetings, details of the number of paupers in the workhouse, and accounts of expenditure. By 1839 most of the 15,000 parishes had been grouped into 600 unions and about 350 new workhouses had been built. The new workhouses were paid for by raising money from the rates.

The effect of the new law on the poor

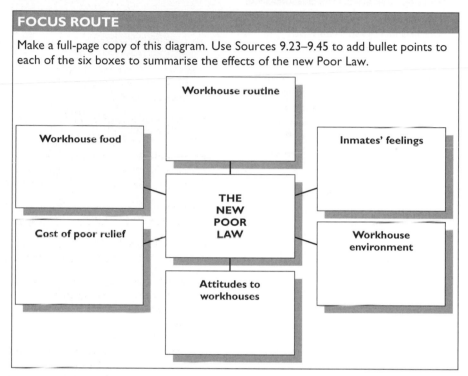

FOCUS ROUTE

Make a full-page copy of this diagram. Use Sources 9.23–9.45 to add bullet points to each of the six boxes to summarise the effects of the new Poor Law.

- Workhouse routine
- Workhouse food
- Inmates' feelings
- THE NEW POOR LAW
- Cost of poor relief
- Workhouse environment
- Attitudes to workhouses

REACTIONS

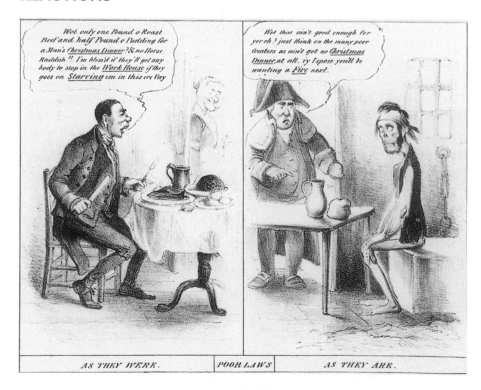

SOURCE 9.23 The old and new Poor Law as seen by a cartoonist in December 1836, not long after the new Poor Law was introduced

SOURCE 9.24 R. Oastler, *The Right of the Poor to Liberty and Life*, 1838. Oastler was a woollen manufacturer in West Yorkshire

What is the principle of the New Poor Law? The condition imposed by Englishmen by that accursed law is that man shall give up his liberty to save his life! That before he shall eat a piece of bread, he shall go to prison.

ACTIVITY

1 The writer of Source 9.24 lived and worked in Yorkshire and had campaigned for a reduction in working hours for factory workers. The events described in Source 9.25 and shown in Source 9.26 happened in the textile-producing areas of Yorkshire and the north-west. Why might opposition to the new Poor Law have been especially violent in the industrial areas of northern England?

2 What attitudes towards the new Poor Law do the poems in Sources 9.27 and 9.28 convey?

3 Are poems such as these a reliable and useful source of evidence for historians?

SOURCE 9.25 J. Holden, *A short history of Todmorden*, 1912, describing events in 1838. John Fielden MP, chief spokesman of the Anti-Poor Law Movement in Parliament and a factory owner from Todmorden in West Yorkshire, had refused to pay the poor rate. Two constables had been sent to seize goods to pay the fine. The period 1837–38 saw considerable opposition in West Yorkshire to the new law

From all sides hundreds of angry men and women hurried to the village. A terrible scene ensued. The horse and cart were thrown violently down, with one of the constables on top. The cart was smashed and burned. The two constables were compelled by the mob to swear never to engage in the like business again.

SOURCE 9.26 An attack on Stockport workhouse in August 1842

SOURCE 9.27 An extract from a broadsheet circulating in Bradford in the mid-1830s

Come you men and women unto me attend
And listen and see what for you I have penned
And if you do buy it and carefully read
T'will make your hearts within you to bleed.

The lions at London, with their cruel paw
You know they have pass'd a Starvation Law
These tigers and wolves should be chained in a den,
Without power to worry poor women and men.

When a man and his wife for sixty long years
Have toiled together through troubles and tears
And brought up a family with prudence and care
To be sent to the Bastile [sic] it's very unfair.

And in the Bastile [sic] each woman and man
Is parted asunder – is this a good plan?
A word of sweet comfort they cannot express
For unto each other they have no access.

SOURCE 9.28 Extracts from a poem in G. W. Fulcher, *The Village Paupers and Other Poems*, 1845. In this poem a man asks the Poor Law Guardians for help as he has been ill, and although now fit has no work

– A friendly feeling, generous and strong
Spread through the Board – they felt it must be wrong
The slender pittance harshly to refuse,
But they, alas! were left no power to choose;
The man was able by his work to live,
And further aid, it was not theirs to give; –
They offer'd him 'The House', 'or they would take
Two of his children, for their Father's sake' ...

... then came the dreaded day,
When they would send a part at least away;
But crowding round, the weeping children hung
Upon his knees, or to his garments clung; –
'Father!' 'dear Father!' 'Oh not me!' 'not me!'
Each wildly shrieked in childish agony ...
... The Mother on her Husband's shoulder leant
Till all her weak resolve again gave way,
She would decide some future day
Which should be left and which be sent away
Unable still to sever love's strong tie,
They would together live, together die ...

PUNCH'S PENCILLINGS. - Nº· LXII.

153

WAS THE 1834 POOR LAW AMENDMENT ACT REALLY THE NEW STARVATION LAW?

THE "MILK" OF POOR-LAW "KINDNESS."

SOURCE 9.29 'The Milk of Poor-Law Kindness'– a cartoon from *Punch* magazine, 1843

FEELINGS

ACTIVITY

1 Using Sources 9.29, 9.30 and 9.1 (page 137), identify the different feelings people had about going into the workhouse.
2 Sources 9.30 and 9.1 (page 137) both date from fifty years after the passing of the Poor Law Amendment Act in 1834.
   a) What does this tell you about attitudes towards poverty and workhouses?
   b) Are these valid sources for a historian studying the Poor Law Amendment Act of 1834?
3 Why is one workhouse in Source 9.31 very plain in appearance and one much more decorative?

SOURCE 9.30 R. Jefferies, *Hodge and his Masters*, 1880

Plain as is the fare, it was better than the old man had existed on for years; but though better it was not his dinner. He was not sitting in his own chair, at his own table, round which his children once gathered ... At home he could lift the latch of the garden gate and go down the road if he wished. Here he could not go outside the boundary – it was against the regulations.

THE ENVIRONMENT

A
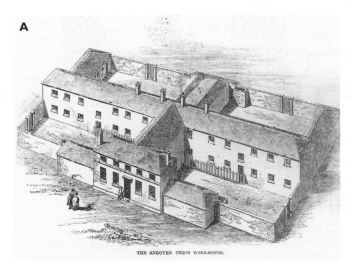
THE ANDOVER UNION WORKHOUSE.

B

SOURCE 9.31 Two mid-nineteenth century workhouses – the workhouse at Andover, Hampshire (**A**) and the City of London Workhouse (**B**). Some local boards were able to raise more money and were willing to spend more on the appearance of the workhouse than others

SOURCE 9.32 A typical daily timetable in a workhouse

6.00a.m.	Get up, wash, dress, roll-call
6.30a.m.	Prayers, breakfast (to be eaten in silence)
7.15a.m.	Exercise in the yards
8.00a.m.	Work
11.00a.m.	Prayers, Bible reading, hymns
12.00p.m.	Lunch (eaten in silence)
12.30p.m.	Exercise in the yards
2.00p.m.	Work for the adults; school for the children
4.00p.m.	Prayers, religious instruction
5.00p.m.	Hymn singing
6.00p.m.	Supper (eaten in silence)
6.30p.m.	Religious service
9.00p.m.	Bed

154

WAS THE 1834 POOR LAW AMENDMENT ACT REALLY THE NEW STARVATION LAW?

SOURCE 9.33   A plan of a typical mid-nineteenth-century workhouse

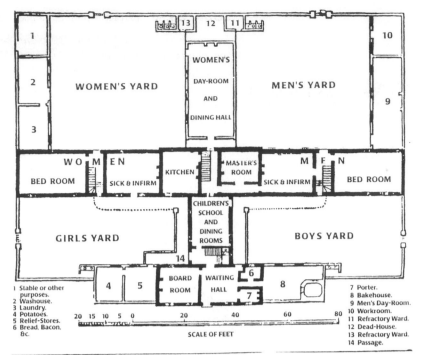

1 Stable or other purposes.
2 Washouse.
3 Laundry.
4 Potatoes.
5 Relief-Stores.
6 Bread, Bacon, &c.

7 Porter.
8 Bakehouse.
9 Men's Day-Room.
10 Workroom.
11 Refractory Ward.
12 Dead-House.
13 Refractory Ward.
14 Passage.

SCALE OF FEET

[K.]   No. 2.   One Pair Plan.

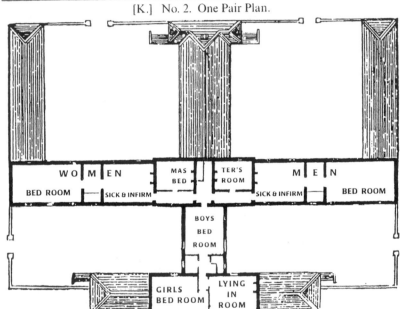

ACTIVITY

What can you deduce from Sources 9.32 and 9.33 about the treatment of adults and children in workhouses?

SOURCE 9.34   Extract from the novel *Paved with Gold* by Augustus Mayhew, 1858. Augustus Mayhew was the brother of Henry Mayhew, who conducted a detailed survey of the poor in London in the 1850s

The ward itself was a long, bare, white-washed apartment, with square post-like pillars supporting the flat-beamed roof, and reminding the visitor of a large unoccupied store-room . . . Along the floor were arranged what appeared at first sight to be endless rows of empty orange chests, packed closely side by side, so that the boards were divided off into some two hundred shallow-tanpit-like compartments, and in these the visitors soon learnt, were berths . . . In each of them lay a black mattress, made of some shiny waterproof material, like tarpaulin stuffed with straw. At the head of every bunk, hanging against the wall, was a leather . . . that looked more like a wine-cooper's apron than a counterpane. These are used as coverlids because they are not only strong and durable, but they do not retain vermin.

SOURCE 9.35   Extract from *Pall Mall Gazette*, 1866. The readership of the *Gazette* was likely to be the middle and upper classes

An adventurous gentleman tested the accommodation provided for the homeless . . . in Lambeth Workhouse . . . There were neither bags of straw nor rugs for the entire number, so that shivering men and boys were huddled together, sometimes four on one bag . . . Imagine a space about 30 feet by 30 feet, a dingy whitewashed wall, the fourth side of the shed boarded in; the remaining space hung with flimsy canvas with a gap at the top. This shed was paved with stone, the flags thickly encrusted with filth. Half through the night there was a tumult of cursing and telling of obscene stories, whilst smoking tobacco. At one o'clock, ten more men came in – great hulking ruffians, and all madly swearing because there was no toke [thick slice of bread] for them.

155

WAS THE 1834 POOR LAW AMENDMENT ACT REALLY THE NEW STARVATION LAW?

ACTIVITY

What reasons are there for the conflicting versions of the treatment of the poor in workhouses given in Sources 9.34–9.36?

SOURCE 9.36 Extract from the *Dumfries and Galloway Courier*, 1837

Having become weary of the abuse and praise alternately lavished on the workhouse system, a friend selected one about ten miles from London ... and without difficulty obtained permission to inspect and overlook everything. For two or three days he became an amateur boarder, and although he slept elsewhere, confined himself strictly to the fare ... of the house. I could myself board permanently in the same house with comfort ... The situation is splendid ... The women and female children have what may well be called landscape gardens of their own. The whole apartments are airy and roomy; everything is kept as clean as a new shilling and wears an air of comfort.

FOOD

SOURCE 9.37 A typical workhouse diet for able-bodied men and women

Sunday/Tuesday/Thursday

	Breakfast	Dinner	Supper
Men	6 oz bread/gruel	5 oz meat/8 oz potatoes	6 oz bread/broth
Women	5 oz bread/gruel	5 oz meat/8 oz potatoes	5 oz bread/broth

Monday/Wednesday/Saturday

	Breakfast	Dinner	Supper
Men	6 oz bread/gruel	1½ pt soup	6 oz bread/2 oz cheese
Women	5 oz bread/gruel	1½ pt soup	5 oz bread/2 oz cheese

Friday

	Breakfast	Dinner	Supper
Men	6 oz bread/gruel	14 oz suet or rice pudding	6 oz bread/2 oz cheese
Women	5 oz bread/gruel	12 oz suet or rice pudding	5 oz bread/2 oz cheese

Old people of 60 years and upwards may be allowed 1 oz of tea, 5 oz of butter, 7 oz sugar per week, instead of gruel for breakfast, if deemed expedient; children over nine to receive the same diet as women.
(1 pint = 0.57 litres; 1 ounce (oz) = 28 grams)

SOURCE 9.38 Extract from the Report of a Parliamentary Select Committee on the Andover Union Workhouse, 1846, in which a workhouse inmate comments on the diet

We looked out for fresh bones ... and then we used to be like a parcel of dogs over them ... sometimes I have had one that was stale and stunk, and I ate it even then ... because I was hungered I suppose. You see we only had bread and gruel for breakfast, and as there was no bread allowed on meat days for dinner, we saved our bread from breakfast, and because a pint and a half of gruel is not much for a man's breakfast. We ate the stale and stinking meat ... I once saw Eaton take up a horse's leg, and take the hair off it, and eat the flesh. The leg was not cooked.

SOURCE 9.39 An extract from Charles Dickens, *Oliver Twist*, 1837, in which Dickens describes Oliver Twist's early life in a workhouse

The evening arrived; the boys took their places ... the gruel was served out ... The gruel disappeared; the boys whispered to each other, and winked at Oliver, while his next neighbours nudged him. Child as he was, he was desperate with hunger, and reckless with misery. He rose from the table, and advancing to the master, basin and spoon in hand, said, somewhat alarmed at his own temerity: 'Please, sir, I want some more.'

SOURCE 9.40 Extract from H. Taine, *Notes on England*, 1867, in which the French historian describes a visit to a workhouse in Manchester

The daily ration of each inmate consists of two pounds of this oatmeal and a pound and a half of potatoes; four times a week the allowance is increased by four ounces of pie or of meat without the bone. The drink is water, except during illness. We were astounded; this place was a palace compared with the kennels in which the poor dwell ... Nevertheless there is not an able-bodied inmate of this workhouse at the moment ... The workhouse is regarded as a prison; the poor consider it a point of honour not to go there.

ACTIVITY

1 To what extent would you accept the extract in Source 9.39 from *Oliver Twist* as reliable evidence about a workhouse?
2 The Bastille was a prison in Paris that was attacked and pulled down at the start of the French Revolution. To what extent does the evidence support the view of many working people that the workhouses were Bastilles?

The effect of the new Poor Law on the cost of poor relief

SOURCE 9.41   Extract from the *Third Annual Report of the Poor Law Commissioners*, 1837

At a meeting of the Board of Guardians held at Highworth, on Wednesday the 11th of January, 1837, the following resolutions were ... carried unanimously: That the financial savings of the ratepayers, since the formation of the Union, as compared with the average expenditure of the three preceding years, is upwards of 54 per cent per annum.

SOURCE 9.42   W. White, *History, Gazetteer and Directory of Suffolk*, 1855

The total average annual expenditure of the 46 parishes for the support of the poor, during the three years preceding the formation of the Union [the Thingoe union in Suffolk] was £13,538. In 1840, the expenditure was only £9026.

SOURCE 9.43   Extract from *Operations of the Poor Law Amendment Act in the County of Sussex*, 1836 – a report on the last quarter of 1835 from Uckfield Union in Sussex, formed in early 1835

In the month of December, 1834, in the corresponding quarter of the last year, upwards of two hundred and fifty labourers were out of employment, and receiving relief in consequence for their families ... In the quarter just past, at the end of a week's frost and when the snow had stopped most of the operations in agriculture, the greatest number of able-bodied men in the workhouse was twenty eight ... The well-regulated system of employment, the irksome confinement, the discipline of the workhouses, and I trust a sincere desire to reform, has induced some who were unmarried to enlist as soldiers.

SOURCE 9.44   Spending on poor relief, 1830–80

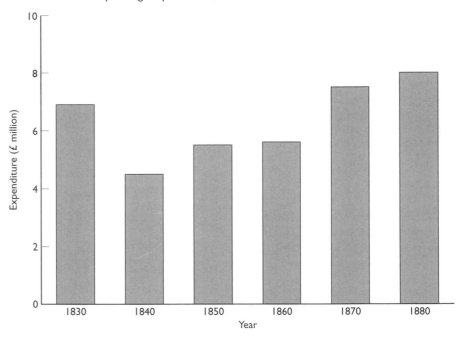

ACTIVITY

'The introduction of the new Poor Law led to a decrease in the cost of poor relief and a decline in the amount of outdoor relief given.'

1 Use the information in Sources 9.41–9.45 to test this hypothesis.
2 Explain the problems in testing the hypothesis from the evidence available.

TALKING POINT

Several sources refer to the separation of different groups of paupers within the workhouse. This separation is usually used to illustrate the cruelty of the system. Was the decision to separate the elderly, the sick and the children in 1834 *necessarily* cruel?

SOURCE 9.45   Number of paupers relieved inside and outside the workhouse, 1839–90

	Outside	Inside
1839	800,000	125,000
1850	900,000	125,000
1860	700,000	100,000
1870	850,000	150,000
1880	600,000	190,000
1890	590,000	200,000

F Review: was the 1834 Poor Law Amendment Act really the New Starvation Law?

...Y COLLEGE
LEAR...NG RESOURCE CENTRE

ACTIVITY

How far did the Act achieve its aims? Use the information in the sources and in the text to examine this question.

ACTIVITY

To give you an overview of this topic prepare two three-minute broadcasts for television news. Address the following questions in your broadcasts:

1 Why was reform of the system of poor relief needed by 1834?
2 To what extent did the Poor Law Amendment Act solve the problems of poverty?

The main aims of the 1834 Poor Law Amendment Act were:

- to cut the cost of poor relief
- to reduce the poor rates
- to transfer control of poor relief into the hands of the ratepayers
- to transfer responsibility from individual parishes with unpaid overseers to the unions with elected Boards of Guardians, and some central control from London.

The 1834 Act was implemented gradually. The first unions were established in the south of England, and not until about 1837 were attempts made to set them up in the north. The 'workhouse test' was never enforced across the whole country. There was a problem in enforcing the system in areas where unemployment was spasmodic and short-term. This was especially true in the textile-manufacturing areas of Yorkshire and Lancashire, where mills often closed for brief periods at times of low demand for cloth, putting several hundred people out of work at once. It was impossible to provide workhouse accommodation for such numbers when they might be unemployed for only perhaps two or three weeks. Thus outdoor relief had to continue and the Act was modified during the 1840s to allow for this. Violent and organised resistance also delayed action.

The principle of 'less eligibility' also proved difficult to enforce. It would have been very difficult to have made conditions in the workhouse worse than those in which many workers lived. In fact, the conditions in the workhouse, however basic, were frequently far better than in the slums and hovels in which many of the poor lived. For many it was not the environment they found hard to bear but the limitations on their independence and the division of their family.

The workhouses were inspected by the assistant commissioners, employed by the Central Commission in London. However, there were so few assistant commissioners that a workhouse was likely to be inspected just twice a year at most. This allowed considerable freedom to the master of the workhouse to run it as he wished. There were great variations in conditions and treatment across the country, and this led to some serious mistreatment, as at Andover in 1845, which led to an investigation in 1846 (see Source 9.38 on page 155). Partly as a result of this, the Poor Law Commission was replaced by the Poor Law Board, the head of which was an MP and therefore directly answerable to Parliament.

The new Poor Law did not significantly reduce costs in many areas. Although the amount spent on outdoor relief may have decreased, the cost of building new workhouses added to the poor rates in many areas. In the south of England, depression in agriculture meant high unemployment in the late 1830s, and resultant high costs of relief, whether indoor or outdoor.

The Boards of Guardians consisted of magistrates and elected members. Those wishing to be elected had to occupy property, and were elected by the ratepayers with the number of votes based on a sliding scale; the richest property owners had six votes each, the poorer property owners had one vote, and the labourers had no votes. The boards were, as a result, invariably composed of men of property and substance. After 1875 women who owned property were allowed to vote for guardians and to stand for election to the boards. For many middle-class women it was their first real opportunity to be involved in politics, albeit at a local level only.

The Poor Law Amendment Act of 1834 was seen by most working people as the state's way of punishing those who, often through no fault of their own, were poor. The Act dealt with the **effects** of poverty by trying to 'care for' those who were poor when they were poor, but it did nothing significant to deal with the **causes** of poverty. The response of many working people to the imposition

158

WAS THE 1834 POOR LAW AMENDMENT ACT REALLY THE NEW STARVATION LAW?

of the 'starvation law', as they saw it, was to argue that the only way to improve their living conditions was through a Parliament that fully represented working people. In the years that followed 1834, partly as a result of reactions to the Poor Law Act, and partly due to economic problems which made life even harder for many working people, political groups that called for the extension of the franchise to all working men (and some even suggested to women, too) renewed their campaigns. In 1839 these became embodied in the Chartist movement, with universal male suffrage and the secret ballot among its demands.

Case study: an example of the problems of establishing a Poor Law union, Leeds 1834–58

Leeds already had a workhouse in 1834. One had been built as early as 1637, where the poor were provided with work in return for their food and lodging. By 1755 it housed 43 men, 60 women and 53 children. It was enlarged in the early 1800s, and by 1837 it could accommodate 250 people. By the early 1800s the cost of keeping a person in the workhouse was about 50 per cent higher than giving outdoor relief, so most ratepayers were anxious to keep the workhouse as small as possible. They also appreciated that a workhouse system such as the one laid down by the 1834 Act was not appropriate for a city such as Leeds with its frequent short-term unemployment problems. To build a workhouse to house the vast number affected by industrial depressions would have cost a great deal. It would be cheaper to give out a 'dole' (cash support). So in 1834 the parish vestries ignored the new Act and continued to give outdoor relief when necessary.

In 1843 an inspection found that the workhouse was overcrowded and the moral standards of the inmates were low. It was decided to set up a Board of Guardians to try to bypass the parish vestries, and build a new workhouse. In 1844 the board was elected, but no new workhouse was built. The guardians decided to 'make do' with the existing one, and possibly extend it. The conditions in this workhouse were bad, and the Poor Law inspector urged the guardians to 'render the workhouse tolerably creditable where the aged and infirm can be accommodated with decent comfort, the sick properly attended to, the helpless idiot sufficiently protected and the unruly and shiftless able-bodied male pauper kept apart from the vicious and abandoned of the other sex'.

Finally, in 1858 the foundation stone was laid for a new workhouse to provide accommodation for 810 paupers, at a cost of £31,000.

ACTIVITY

1 Why did the parish vestries in Leeds decide not to build a new workhouse in 1834?
2 Why do they appear to have changed their minds by 1843?
3 What do the inspector's words suggest about attitudes to the poor and the conditions they were subjected to?

SOURCE 9.46 The old Leeds workhouse, 1832

159

WAS THE 1834 POOR LAW AMENDMENT ACT REALLY THE NEW STARVATION LAW?

SOURCE 9.47 The new Leeds Union Workhouse

ACTIVITY

Write an essay in response to this question: To what extent did the Poor Law Amendment Act of 1834 achieve the aims of those who enacted it?

KEY POINTS FROM CHAPTER 9 **Was the 1834 Poor Law Amendment Act really the New Starvation Law?**

1 By 1830 the cost of poor relief, although lower than at its peak in 1818, was still 60 per cent higher than it was in 1802.
2 There was concern about outdoor relief and the policy of supplementing wages through allowance systems, and the effect this was having on labourers' wages and morals.
3 Utilitarianism was influential in the establishment of a parliamentary commission to inquire into the Poor Law and suggest ways to improve it.
4 The new Poor Law Act of 1834 aimed to reduce costs, cut poor rates and abolish outdoor relief.
5 Under the Act, union workhouses were set up, in which the regime and conditions were often harsh.
6 There was considerable opposition to the new workhouses, especially in the north of England.
7 Outdoor relief continued to be given, especially in the north of England.
8 Overall spending on poor relief fell initially, but began to rise again.
9 Reactions to the new law led many working men into campaigns for universal male suffrage.

10

The repeal of the Corn Laws: Peel's treachery or Peel's success?

CHAPTER OVERVIEW

17 June 1846

CORN LAWS REPEALED AT LAST!

PEEL'S GREAT ACHIEVEMENT

"PEELITE" CONSERVATIVES SURRENDER THEIR PRINCIPLES

CHEAPER BREAD ON ITS WAY!

TRAITOR PEEL!

HOPE FOR IRISH FAMINE VICTIMS!

NOW WE REALLY HAVE FREE TRADE

ANTI-CORN LAW LEAGUE GETS ITS DEMAND

30 June 1846

PEEL RESIGNS!

RIOTING IN IRELAND CONTINUES

'ROTTEN POTATOES PUT PEEL IN HIS DAMNED FRIGHT' – WELLINGTON

CONSERVATIVE PARTY SPLIT

PEEL FINISHED IN POLITICS

WELLINGTON CONDEMNS PEEL'S ACTION

Had there been mass press coverage at that time, these headlines might well have appeared in 1846. Peel, Prime Minister and leader of the Conservatives, was hailed as a hero by many but reviled as a traitor by many others, especially in his own party.

What action had Peel taken to cause such a reaction? He had repealed the Corn Laws. These laws had prevented the import of foreign wheat (corn) unless the price for British wheat was 80s (£4) a quarter (13kg) or more.

Many reasons have been put forward by historians for Peel's actions. You will need to evaluate the relative importance of these factors.

A What had happened to Peel and the Tory Party since 1829? (pp. 161–162)

B Why was there growing support for free trade and a decline in support for protectionism? (pp. 162–166)

C Was the Anti-Corn Law League a revolutionary group? (pp. 167–171)

D How did the Irish famine affect the campaign for repeal in 1845 and 1846? (pp. 171–176)

E Review: the repeal of the Corn Laws: Peel's treachery or Peel's success? (pp. 176–181)

A **What had happened to Peel and the Tory Party since 1829?**

161

THE REPEAL OF THE CORN LAWS: PEEL'S TREACHERY OR PEEL'S SUCCESS?

Sir Robert Peel's career from 1829 to 1850

In 1829 Peel was viewed by many Tories as a traitor to his party and his religion. He had forced through Catholic Emancipation against opposition from the Tories and with the support of the Whigs. In doing so he had split the Tory Party, which had led to Wellington's government being replaced by a new administration headed by Earl Grey. After the passing of the 1832 Reform Act, the Tories were heavily defeated in the general election but Peel won a seat at Tamworth. Despite his actions in 1829 he became the accepted leader of the Tories, but had only just over 100 MPs he could rely on to support him against Earl Grey's government. The rest of the Tories still regarded him as a traitor.

After 1833, the Tory Party began to revive under Peel's leadership. From December 1834 to April 1835 Peel and his party, by then known as Conservatives, were in government. His acceptance of the office of Prime Minister meant that he had to stand for re-election. In the Tamworth Manifesto, an election address to the voters of Tamworth, he set out what he later described as 'conservative principles'. The manifesto became the basis for the new Conservative Party, and it set out aims and policies that appealed especially to middle-class manufacturers and businessmen. The general election gave Peel about 100 additional seats but there were still more Whigs than Tories in the Commons. Peel tried to carry on, but was constantly defeated and on 8 April 1835 he resigned.

William IV died in 1837 and was succeeded by his niece, Victoria. As was usual, a general election was held on the accession of the new monarch. The Whig majority was reduced, and in May 1839 Melbourne, the Prime Minister, resigned after the government had a majority of only five at the end of a debate. Victoria, who relied heavily on Melbourne for advice and was at times openly sympathetic to the Whigs, was reluctant to accept Peel as Prime Minister. Peel, aware of the Queen's preference, asked that some of the ladies in the Queen's household, who were related to leading Whigs, should be replaced by Tory ladies as a sign of royal favour. Victoria refused, maintaining her right to choose her household. Peel responded by refusing to form a government, and Melbourne returned for another two years. In June 1841 Peel proposed a vote of no confidence in the government, which was carried by one vote. A general election was called and the Conservatives won a majority of over 70 seats. Peel became Prime Minister in August 1841.

CITY COLLEGE
LEARNING RESOURCE SERVICE

FOCUS ROUTE

1 Create a timeline to show the significant events for the Tory/Conservative Party between 1829 and 1841.
2 In your own words, explain Peel's attitude and approach towards the idea of reform as set out in the Tamworth Manifesto (Source 10.1). Give two examples from Peel's earlier political career at the Home Office in the 1820s to illustrate this attitude and approach.

SOURCE 10.1 Extracts from Peel's Tamworth Manifesto, 1834

I have the firmest convictions that ... confidence cannot be secured by any other course than that of a frank and explicit declaration of principle ...

I will never admit that I have been, either before or after the Reform Bill, the defender of abuses, or the enemy of judicious reforms ... I have not been disposed to acquiesce in acknowledged evils, either from the mere superstitious reverence for ancient usage, or from the dread of labour or responsibility in the application of a remedy ...

I consider the Reform Bill a final and irrevocable settlement of a great constitutional question ...

If by adopting the spirit of the Reform Bill, it be meant that we are to live in a perpetual vortex of agitation; that public men can only support themselves in public estimation by adopting every popular impression of the day – by promising the instant redress of anything which anybody may call an abuse ... I will not undertake to adopt it ... but if the spirit of the Reform Bill implies merely a careful review of institutions, civil and ecclesiastical, undertaken in a friendly temper, combining, with the firm maintenance of established rights, the correction of proved abuses and the redress of real grievances, – in that case, I can, for myself and colleagues, undertake to act in such a spirit and with such intention.

162

THE REPEAL OF THE CORN LAWS: PEEL'S TREACHERY OR PEEL'S SUCCESS?

SOURCE 10.2 Horace Twiss, Under Secretary of State for War and the Colonies (1828–30), writing after Peel's death in 1850. He worked with Peel when Peel was Home Secretary in Wellington's government

Peel was the best man of business and the best debater in England – but always thinking of his reputation and his outward character – never decided and courageous – thinking more of getting well through a business into which he had been led by circumstances, than bold and decided in his pursuit and assertion of great principles and worthy objects. With a great occasional show of affability and condescension, he was in reality selfish, cold and unconciliatory – and therefore never had, and never would have, a personal following.

ACTIVITY

1 What impression do you get from each of Sources 10.2–10.5 of Peel:
 a) as a person
 b) as a politician?
2 Why are there differences in these opinions of Peel?

TALKING POINT

Lord Shaftesbury described Peel as 'an iceberg with a slight thaw on the surface'. A fellow MP said that when Peel entered the Commons, he 'looks at no one, recognises no one, receives salutation from no one. He seems neither to know or be known by any member present.' Why might Peel's personality, as shown in these quotations and Sources 10.2–10.5, make objective assessment of him difficult?

FOCUS ROUTE

Sections B, C and D of this chapter deal with the factors that historians have identified as reasons why Peel repealed the Corn Laws. As you work through pages 162–176, compile your own list of factors. Make notes to explain how each factor contributed to repeal.

Some contemporary views of Peel

SOURCE 10.3 The political historian W. Bagehot, quoted in N. St John Stevas (ed.), *The Collected Works of Walter Bagehot, vol. 3,* 1968

[Peel had] the powers of a first-rate man and a creed of a second-rate man, changing his position to suit the political circumstances.

SOURCE 10.4 Charles Greville, *Journal,* February 1833. Greville was the grandson of the Duke of Portland. He was clerk to the Privy Council 1821–59, and would have known Peel well during Peel's time as minister and Prime Minister

Under that placid exterior he conceals, I believe, a boundless ambition, and hatred and jealousy lurk under his professions of esteem and political attachment. He is one of those contradictory characters, containing in it so much of mixed good and evil, that it is difficult to strike an accurate balance between the two, and the acts of his political life are of a corresponding description, of questionable utility and merit, though always marked by great ability: opposition to Reform in Parliament and to religious emancipation of every kind. His resistance to alterations with great ability, and for a long time with success; but he was endeavouring to uphold a system which was no longer supportable.

SOURCE 10.5 An obituary article on Peel in Chambers' *Papers for the People,* a cheap popular periodical aimed at mass circulation

He fell from official power into the arms of the people, whose enthusiastic plaudits accompanied him, on the evening of his resignation of office, to his residence in Whitehall Gardens. The spontaneous feeling of gratitude and respect which promoted those plaudits has since widened, strengthened and deepened, and will become more and more vivid and intense as the moral grandeur of his motives – the unselfish, self-sacrificing spirit which dictated his public conduct – pierce through and consume . . . the calumnious misrepresentations so unsparingly heaped upon him. By his humbler countrymen, that testimony to the moral worth of the departed statesmen was not waited for, nor needed. They felt instinctively that he must be pure and single minded, as he was intellectually vigorous and great; for what had he, raised aloft upon the bucklers of a powerful and wealthy party, to gain from stooping from that dazzling height, to raise up the humble and lowly from the mire into which ignorant and partial legislation had so long trampled them.

B Why was there growing support for free trade and a decline in support for protectionism?

The Corn Laws

In 1815 British farmers feared competition from food producers abroad as a consequence of the end of the Napoleonic Wars. They were especially worried about the possible impact of imported wheat. During the 1790s the price British farmers got for their wheat had increased dramatically and it had remained high throughout the war. They believed that an influx of cheap foreign wheat would inevitably lead to a fall in the price of British wheat and so ruin British farming.

ACTIVITY

1 What evidence is there in Sources 10.6 and 10.7 to show that the fears of British farmers might be genuine?
2 In 1815 the vast majority of MPs represented agricultural constituencies and many were themselves landowners. What reaction would you expect them to have towards farmers' demands for restrictions on the import of foreign wheat?

163

THE REPEAL OF THE CORN LAWS: PEEL'S TREACHERY OR PEEL'S SUCCESS?

SOURCE 10.6 Average wheat prices (per quarter), 1813–15

How can I pay my bills when I cannot get a good price for my wheat?

1813	1814	1815
109/9ᵈ	74/4ᵈ	65/7ᵈ

SOURCE 10.7 Average wheat prices (per quarter – approx. 13 kg), 1791–1810

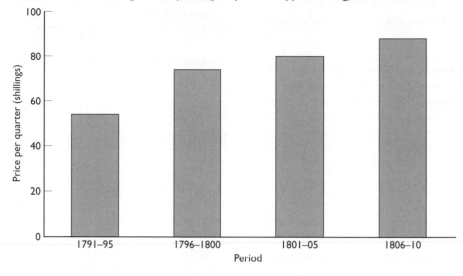

ACTIVITY

1 What was the aim of the restrictions outlined in Source 10.8?
2 For whose benefit were the restrictions imposed?
3 What impact would you expect the Corn Laws to have had on the price of bread?

SOURCE 10.8 The Corn Laws 1815

Be it enacted that such foreign corn, meal or flour, may be imported into the United Kingdom, for home consumption, without payment of any duty whatever, whenever the average prices of the several sorts of British corn, shall be at or above the prices hereinafter mentioned; that is to say,
whenever wheat shall be at or above the price of eighty shillings per quarter;
whenever rye, pease and beans shall be at or above the price of fifty-three shillings per quarter;
whenever barley shall be at or above the price of forty shillings per quarter;
whenever oats shall be at or above the price of twenty-seven shillings per quarter.
And be it further enacted, that whenever the average price of British corn shall be below the prices stated, no foreign corn, or meal, or flour, shall be allowed to be imported into the United Kingdom for the purpose of home consumption.

SOURCE 10.9 Two weekly budgets

ACTIVITY

1 Read Source 10.9. Calculate the percentage of their budget each family spent on bread and flour in a week.
2 How much meat per person per week did each family have?
3 What are the staple foods for the working man's family?
4 In what way is the diet of the gentleman's family:
   a) different
   b) better?
5 For which of these two families would the impact of the Corn Laws on the price of bread have the most significance and why?

A From Mrs Rundell, *A System of Practical Domestic Economy*, 1824

A 'model budget' for a gentleman, his wife, three children and a servant in 1824

	£	s	d
Bread and flour 1s each [person]		6	0
Butter, 3½ lb at average 1s a lb		3	6
Cheese, 1½ lb at 10d a lb		1	3
Milk		1	6
Tea, 5 oz at 8s a lb		2	6
Sugar 4½ lb at 8d a lb		3	0
Grocery, including spices/salt, etc.		3	0
Meat, 18 lb at 7d a lb		10	6
Fish		3	6
Vegetables and fruit		3	0
Beer and other liquors		7	0
Coals and wood		3	9
Candles, oil, etc.		1	2
Soap, starch, etc.		1	2
Sundries for cleaning, scouring, etc.			9
Total	£2	11s	7d

B From S. R. Bosanquet, *The Rights of the Poor and Christian Almsgiving Vindicated*, 1841

For a semi-skilled worker, his wife and three children in 1841

	£	s	d
5 4 lb loaves at 8½d		3	6½
5 lb meat at 5d a lb		2	1
4 lb potatoes		1	4
7 pints porter (beer) at 2d a pint		1	2
½ cwt coal			9½
3 oz tea, 1 lb sugar		1	6
1 lb butter			9
Soap and candles			6½
Rent		2	6
Schooling			4
Sundries			5½
Total		15s	0d

(12d = 1s; 20s = £1; 240d = £1)

TALKING POINT

Given the limited income of the working man's family in Source 10.9B, does spending 4d on schooling surprise you?

164

THE REPEAL OF THE CORN LAWS: PEEL'S TREACHERY OR PEEL'S SUCCESS?

■ Learning trouble spot

Nineteenth-century economic ideas

A problem when studying the Corn Laws is understanding some of the terms and names used for the various economic ideas and theories of the early nineteenth century that underpinned the arguments for and against repeal. Three of the principal ideas are explained here.

Mercantilism

This originated in the Tudor period, and developed over the succeeding 200 years. It was a collection of laws to protect home industry and boost the home economy. Its aims were to:

- ensure more goods were exported than were imported thus bringing more income to Britain
- control imports by putting tariffs (duties) on incoming goods to make them more expensive than home-produced ones. Some goods were banned altogether – for example, Indian cotton cloth
- ensure that home shipping was sufficiently strong to dominate trade.

Protectionism

This was a development of mercantilist ideas. The aim was to protect British home production by putting import duties (tariffs) on goods coming into Britain that might compete with home-produced goods, so making the imported goods more expensive than home-produced ones.

Free trade

This was the opposite of protectionism. Free trade meant that all countries' goods should move between countries without any restrictions or import duties. Free trade was popularised in *The Wealth of Nations* written by Adam Smith in 1776. He argued that countries should specialise in producing what they were best at, and trade freely for other goods with countries that were also producing what they were best at. He argued that there should be no government restrictions to hinder trade.

Was the repeal of the Corn Laws part of a wider trend towards free trade?

FOCUS ROUTE

1 Summarise in your own words the difference between protectionism and free trade.
2 List all the reasons put forward in the early nineteenth century for and against free trade.

■ 10A Hindrances to free trade

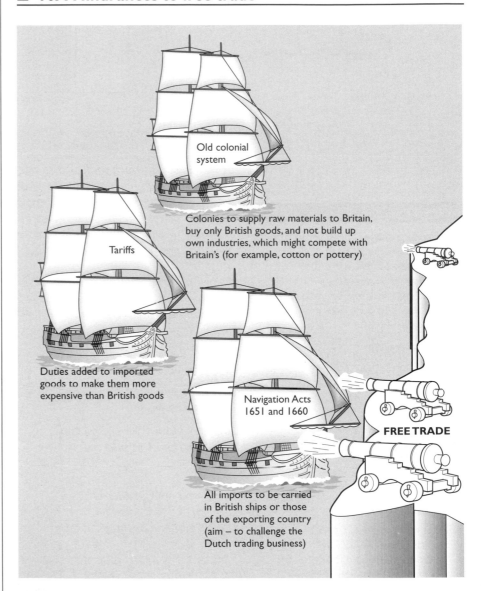

Old colonial system

Colonies to supply raw materials to Britain, buy only British goods, and not build up own industries, which might compete with Britain's (for example, cotton or pottery)

Tariffs

Duties added to imported goods to make them more expensive than British goods

Navigation Acts 1651 and 1660

All imports to be carried in British ships or those of the exporting country (aim – to challenge the Dutch trading business)

FREE TRADE

ACTIVITY

In the early nineteenth century, Britain was the only industrialised country in the world. Complete your own copy of this table to show why the perceived results of free trade would appeal to British businessmen.

Perceived results of free trade	Appeal to British manufacturers
Worldwide supply of raw materials	
Worldwide markets for finished goods	
Supplies of cheap food from abroad	
Greater variety of food from abroad	
Greater variety of goods from abroad	

'Freeing trade'

165

■ 10B From protectionism to free trade, 1780–1846

THE REPEAL OF THE CORN LAWS: PEEL'S TREACHERY OR PEEL'S SUCCESS?

PROTECTIONISM

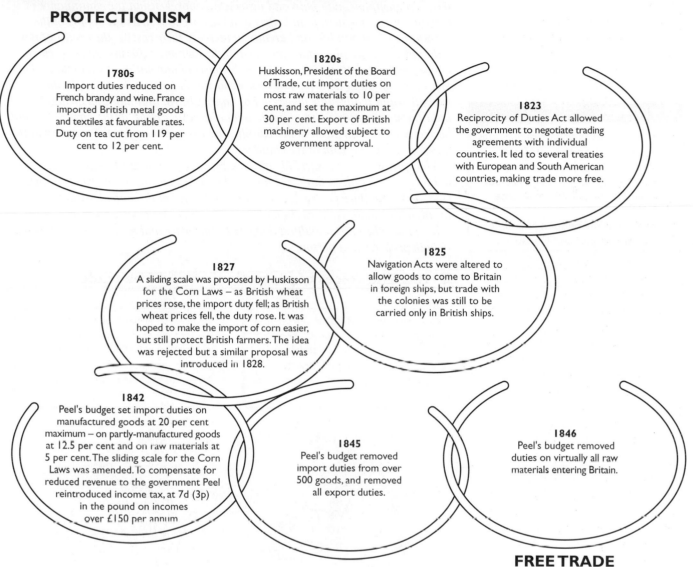

1780s
Import duties reduced on French brandy and wine. France imported British metal goods and textiles at favourable rates. Duty on tea cut from 119 per cent to 12 per cent.

1820s
Huskisson, President of the Board of Trade, cut import duties on most raw materials to 10 per cent, and set the maximum at 30 per cent. Export of British machinery allowed subject to government approval.

1823
Reciprocity of Duties Act allowed the government to negotiate trading agreements with individual countries. It led to several treaties with European and South American countries, making trade more free.

1827
A sliding scale was proposed by Huskisson for the Corn Laws – as British wheat prices rose, the import duty fell; as British wheat prices fell, the duty rose. It was hoped to make the import of corn easier, but still protect British farmers. The idea was rejected but a similar proposal was introduced in 1828.

1825
Navigation Acts were altered to allow goods to come to Britain in foreign ships, but trade with the colonies was still to be carried only in British ships.

1842
Peel's budget set import duties on manufactured goods at 20 per cent maximum – on partly-manufactured goods at 12.5 per cent and on raw materials at 5 per cent. The sliding scale for the Corn Laws was amended. To compensate for reduced revenue to the government Peel reintroduced income tax, at 7d (3p) in the pound on incomes over £150 per annum

1845
Peel's budget removed import duties from over 500 goods, and removed all export duties.

1846
Peel's budget removed duties on virtually all raw materials entering Britain.

FREE TRADE

For and against repeal

The general election of 1841 enabled feelings for and against free trade and protection to be aired as part of election campaigning. 'Free trade' and 'cheap bread' became popular election slogans. At the first meeting of the new Parliament, petitions from both sides were presented. Sources 10.10 and 10.11 are extracts from two of the petitions.

SOURCE 10.10 The humble petition of ... the inhabitants of North and South Cadbury, in the county of Somerset, 1841

The proposed alteration of the present Corn Law, will be, if carried into effect, attended with dangerous consequences to the Nation, deluding the people with the expectation that cheap bread could be obtained without a corresponding lowering of wages ... it is the first duty of the Legislature to ensure ... a certain, regular and sufficient supply of wheat for the consumption of the people, and that the present Corn Law effects that object as near as may be ... as experience has shown the uncertainty of commercial intercourse it will be most ruinous to all ranks of society to place dependence upon foreign countries for the supply of wheat, instead of mainly relying on our native resources, thereby throwing our labourers out of work, and risking the chance at a future day of famine in our now plenteous land.

166

THE REPEAL OF THE CORN LAWS: PEEL'S TREACHERY OR PEEL'S SUCCESS?

SOURCE 10.11 The humble petition of the undersigned Members and Friends of the Congregation of Protestant Dissenters, in the Old Gravel Pit Meeting House at Hackney, 1841

We ... contemplate with pain and distressing apprehension the continuance of certain laws ... the design and effect of which are to restrict the supply of the necessaries of human life, and greatly to increase their cost ... the results of those unhappy Laws are now made manifest in the extreme sufferings of those classes of our fellow subjects which constitute the basis of our national strength, in the depression of manufactures, and their exportation to rival countries, in the miserable and inadequate wages of both agricultural and manufacturing industry, in the entire want of work to an alarming extent, in the hazardous and pernicious direction given to mercantile pursuits, and in a fearful tendency to the impoverishing and ruin of the country ...

Your petitioners are especially affected by a rational and Christian conviction of the impiety involved in those Laws, as being in their nature a crime against God, and as in their practical operation productive of discontent, disloyalty, profligacy of conduct, a rejection of the authority of religion, and by necessary consequence the most appalling dangers to the peace and security of all classes as to both property and person.

ACTIVITY

1 What arguments against repeal does the petition in Source 10.10 put forward?
2 What arguments for repeal are put forward in the petition in Source 10.11?
3 Explain why the petition in Source 10.11 links repeal and Christianity.

■ 10C The voices of protectionism and free trade

We need free trade so we can buy raw materials cheaply, which will keep our production costs down, and allow us to produce goods more cheaply, creating more demand and therefore more jobs.

We need to protect our farmers against cheap, foreign imported food, which will ruin British agriculture and lead to unemployment in farming areas, and cut demand for British manufactured goods.

TALKING POINT

It is possible that all this talk about free trade, protectionism and corn is less than exciting to you as a student. Why was it so vital to ordinary people in the 1840s?

ACTIVITY

Chart 10C suggests that the argument over free trade was one of a simple division between town and country, between industry and agriculture. It was not so simple. Support for, or opposition to, free trade depended on more than just whether a person lived and worked in the country or in the town. Look at the arguments put forward in Chart 10C.

1 Write two speech bubbles, one for a worker in a Lancashire cotton mill explaining why free trade might not be a good idea, and one for a worker on a farm in south-east England explaining why he supports free trade.
2 Explain why the creation of the 40s freeholder voter in the counties in the 1832 Reform Act might have increased support for protection.

ACTIVITY

1 Choose a law you wish to change. Brainstorm all the ways in which you might:
   a) alert public opinion to your demands
   b) influence, and if necessary change, public opinion
   c) raise MPs' awareness of your demands
   d) persuade MPs to support your demands for a change in the law.
2 Go through your list and highlight the methods that would have been available to the Anti-Corn Law League in 1840.

FOCUS ROUTE

Make a list of the methods used by the League to raise awareness of their aim among:

a) MPs
b) businessmen
c) middle-class voters
d) the non-voting general public.

One way of altering the law is to persuade MPs that the law needs to be changed through a non-violent campaign. The Anti-Corn Law League used this kind of campaign against the Corn Laws. However, it is important to remember that this was not the only major issue of the 1840s. The League campaigned against a backdrop of the possibility of revolution, as widespread violence re-emerged in the late 1830s and early 1840s because of economic problems, a slump in industry (especially textiles), and rising unemployment. The emergence of the Chartist movement (see Chapter 11) led many to fear that violent revolution was not far away and that it might be the League's 'cheap bread' campaign that triggered revolution.

From the 1820s onwards, as trade became more free, pressure to remove the Corn Laws increased. From 1833 anti-Corn Law associations were set up in towns such as Birmingham and Nottingham. In September 1838 an association was formed in Manchester open to anyone willing to pay the annual subscription of 5s. Within two weeks there were 150 members. Among them were Joseph Parkes, experienced in political organisation, and Richard Cobden, a Manchester calico manufacturer. In January 1839 a dinner was held in Manchester to which came representatives of anti-Corn Law associations from across the country, and in March a national Anti-Corn Law League was formed in London.

The League's aims and motives

The League had one single, simple aim: the total and immediate repeal of the Corn Laws. However, the motives of the members of the Anti-Corn Law League were diverse. The most straightforward motive was the desire to help British industry. Many argued that as a result of protection, foreign countries had put import tariffs on British goods, which would eventually lead to the ruin of British industry, bankruptcies and mass unemployment. They also believed that foreign farming needed to be encouraged by free trade, otherwise foreign investors would put money into their home industry rather than home agriculture, creating unwanted competition for British manufacturers.

For some, repeal was the panacea for all social and economic ills. They believed that they were fighting to obtain justice by abolishing a tax on bread, which hit the poorest members of society hardest, or by attempting to expand industry and therefore create more jobs for working people. There were also those for whom repeal was another step in the great move towards freedom of trade, which they thought would inevitably lead to international understanding and peace. However, members of the Chartist movement believed that the main reason behind the campaign for repeal was that manufacturers would be able to cut wages if bread prices fell. This feeling led to a great deal of hostility between the Chartists and the League, at least initially. It also led to cheap bread being less heavily emphasised by the League's speakers. Many League spokesmen began to emphasise that wages would rise if markets for manufactured goods increased as a result of repeal, and labour was in demand.

For others, repeal was a way of changing the political and social balance of the country. In 1843 *The Times* suggested that the League's aim was 'not to open the ports, to facilitate commerce, to enrich England, but to ruin our aristocracy, whom Leaguers envy and detest'. *The Times* was not entirely wrong. There were those in the League for whom the ruin of British agriculture was the most effective way of removing wealth and power from the aristocracy who owned much of the land. This would leave a political vacuum into which the new wealthy middle class could step. Cobden himself said, 'Liverpool and Manchester will more and more assume their proper rank in commercial capitals and London must content itself with a gambling trade in the bills drawn by those places'.

ACTIVITY

In 1853, in his *History of the Anti-Corn Law League*, Archibald Prentice, a founder member of the Manchester Association, wrote 'happy it is when the interest of a class is the interest of a whole community'. What did he mean?

Leadership of the League

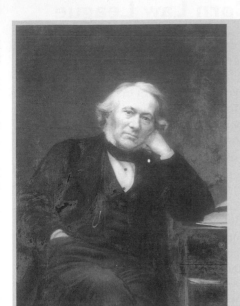

Richard Cobden (1804–65)

Cobden was born in Sussex, one of eleven children. His father was an unsuccessful farmer and Richard spent most of his childhood in poverty. Eventually he was sent to be looked after by an uncle in Yorkshire. He had little formal education, and at fourteen became a clerk in the textile industry. He next became a commercial traveller, developing a good knowledge of the cotton industry. In 1828 he started a company selling printed calico (a type of cotton cloth) in London. The business was a great success and Cobden became a wealthy man. During the 1830s Cobden travelled widely in Europe, America and Russia.

He wrote a pamphlet, *England, Ireland and America* in which he warned of the problems Britain would have in competing with the growing economic power of America. In 1838 Cobden became one of Manchester's first aldermen on its newly elected local council. In the same year he and others formed the Manchester Anti-Corn Law Association and played a leading role in establishing the national League. Elected as MP for Stockport in 1841, he continued his campaign for repeal of the Corn Laws from inside Parliament.

Following repeal of the Corn Laws, Cobden was a national hero, but his business had suffered and he was deep in debt. Supporters raised £8000 for him, with which he bought the farmhouse where he was born. Cobden refused a post in Russell's government after Peel's resignation in 1846, and began campaigning for further parliamentary reform and state-supported education. He joined Bright to campaign against Palmerston's foreign policy and British involvement in the Crimean War, which led to accusations of treason by some MPs and to both men losing their seats in 1857. He was elected MP for Rochdale in 1859.

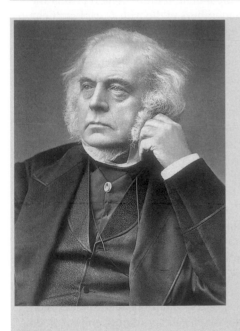

John Bright (1811–89)

Bright was born in Rochdale, son of a successful self-made cotton manufacturer. He attended Quaker schools in Yorkshire and Lancashire, developing a deep commitment to political and religious equality. He joined the family business and became involved in local politics. In 1839 he was recruited by Cobden to the Anti-Corn Law League. Bright was an outstanding public speaker, and drew large crowds whenever he spoke at meetings. He attacked the privileged position of the landed aristocracy and appealed to the middle and working classes to fight for free trade and cheaper food. In 1843 he was elected as MP for Durham. In the Commons he not only campaigned for the repeal of the Corn Laws, but also for universal male suffrage and the secret ballot. He was, however, opposed to any government regulation of factory working hours, which he feared would lower wages and threaten Britain's export trade.

Following the repeal of the Corn Laws, he was, like Cobden, a hero. As a Quaker he opposed Palmerston's aggressive foreign policy and involvement in the Crimean War. Like Cobden he lost his seat in the general election of 1857, but five months later won a by-election in Birmingham. He became a leading spokesman, actively supporting attempts by Russell and Gladstone in the 1860s to introduce parliamentary reform. In 1868 the Prime Minister, Gladstone, appointed Bright as President of the Board of Trade, and several reforms Bright had campaigned for were enacted, including the introduction of the secret ballot. In 1870 Bright retired from the Cabinet due to ill health, but he represented Birmingham as MP until his death in 1889.

The League's methods

- Funds were raised easily – for example, in 1842 £50,000 was raised, and in 1843 £100,000. In December 1845 £60,000 was pledged at one meeting in Manchester.
- League propaganda was disseminated – pamphlets and leaflets were distributed and the League made very effective use of the new Penny Post to ensure that their leaflets reached people. After 1840 the sender, not the recipient, paid for the mail.

Print inserted in the crown of the ' free trade hat'

- In 1842 every man on the electoral register received a package of pamphlets arguing for repeal.
  - Pottery and other souvenirs with League slogans and gentlemen's 'League waistcoats' were sold to supporters.
  - Two League Bazaars were held, one in Manchester in 1842, and one at Covent Garden in May 1845. The latter raised £25,000 for League funds.
  - For 1s it was possible to buy a set of eighteen small pieces of paper to stick down letters (in the days before gummed envelopes) produced by the League and carrying a short motto in favour of repeal.
  - The League published its own newspaper – *The Anti-Corn Law Circular* – at first fortnightly and then, from 1843, weekly.

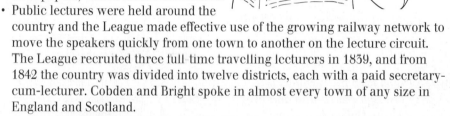

- The independent newspapers were targeted with free reports of League meetings, which editors were happy to use. The League bought up large numbers of the newspapers, which it then distributed.
- Public lectures were held around the country and the League made effective use of the growing railway network to move the speakers quickly from one town to another on the lecture circuit. The League recruited three full-time travelling lecturers in 1839, and from 1842 the country was divided into twelve districts, each with a paid secretary-cum-lecturer. Cobden and Bright spoke in almost every town of any size in England and Scotland.
- A special Free Trade Hall was built in Manchester (on the site of the Peterloo Massacre). It could accommodate nearly nine thousand people. In London in 1843–44 the League hired the Drury Lane Theatre and then Covent Garden for weekly meetings.

CITY COLLEGE
LEARNING RESOURCE SERVICE

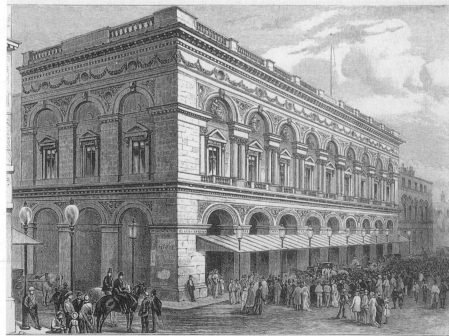

Free Trade Hall, Manchester

SOURCE 10.12 A description, January 1843, by Alexander Somerville, a journalist recruited by Cobden and secretly paid by the League. This, and other articles he wrote, appeared in *The Morning Chronicle*, under the pseudonym 'The Whistler at the Plough'

I was in Market Street, a principal thoroughfare in Manchester. A wide-open stairway, with shops on each side of its entrance, rises from the level of the pavement, and lands on the first floor of a very extensive house called 'Newall's Buildings'. The house consists of four floors, all of which are occupied by the League, save the basement. We must, therefore, ascend the stair, which is wide enough to admit four or five persons walking abreast.

On reaching a spacious landing . . . we turn to the left, and entering . . . see a counter somewhere between forty and fifty feet in length, behind which several men and boys are busily employed . . . this is the general office, and the number of persons here employed is, for the present, ten . . . behind this is the Council Room . . . upstairs . . . we have a large room . . . with a table in the centre . . . with seats around for a number of persons . . . called the Manchester Committee . . . during the day this room is occupied by those who keep the accounts of cards issued and returned to and from all parts of the United Kingdom . . . A professional accountant is retained for this department . . . We come to another [room] from which all the correspondence is issued. From this office letters to the amount of several thousand a day go forth to all parts of the kingdom . . . In this office copies of all the parliamentary registries [electoral registers] of the kingdom are kept . . . In another large room on this floor is the packing department. Here several men are at work making up bales of tracts each weighing upwards of a hundred weight, and despatching them to all parts of the kingdom for distribution among the electors. From sixty to seventy of these bales are sent off each week . . . Leaving this and going to the floor above, we find a great number of printers, presses, folders and stitchers, and others connected with printing . . . the League . . . have twelve master printers employed, one of whom, in Manchester, pays upwards of £100 a week in wages for League work alone.

- The League raised funds to pay the deposits of League candidates standing at elections. In 1841 Cobden was elected as MP for Stockport, and in 1843 Bright became MP for Durham. This raised the profile of the League within the Commons.
- MPs representing the League spoke forcefully in the Commons about the iniquities of the 'bread tax'.
- Whenever the Commons were discussing the Corn Laws, League delegates assembled in London to try to meet MPs. When in 1842 no MPs other than Cobden would agree to meet League members, 500 of them marched to Westminster, where they were refused entry, at which point they cheered for repeal loudly so that all those in the Commons chamber could hear them.
- Each year, usually in March, Charles Villiers MP introduced a bill into the Commons for repeal. He was not a League MP, but the League's leaders used the opportunity to hold a debate, which often lasted four or five days before a division and defeat for the motion. From 1841, when Cobden became an MP, he saw the need to convert ministers because their support was essential if repeal was to succeed.
- In 1844 the League began to purchase property for individuals who sent the League about £70, so that they qualified for a vote.

ACTIVITY

1 What impression does the article in Source 10.12 give about the size and nature of the League's organisation?
2 How does the writer convey this impression?
3 What do you think was the purpose of articles such as this one?
4 How useful is this description for historians, given the writer's links to the League?

Opposition to the League

The League faced vehement opposition from several sources. In the press *The Times*, which had long represented the farming 'lobby', was especially critical of the League, calling it 'a parcel of quacks and Cobden in particular'. It accused him of 'recklessly and unceasingly labouring to direct . . . odium personally . . . on [Peel]'. The majority of the Tory Party were landowners who opposed repeal. They claimed the only reason that industrialists wanted repeal was to reduce bread prices so that they could cut wages and make bigger profits. The leader of this opposition in the Tory Party was Benjamin Disraeli, a relatively new MP in the 1840s. Opposition from the landowners was brought together in the Central Agricultural Protection Society, formed in 1844 by the Duke of Richmond. The Society's aim was to maintain the Corn Laws.

SOURCE 10.13 Extracts from an article in the *Quarterly Review* about the activities of the League. The dossier on their activities was collected by the Home Office at Peel's request, and given to J. W. Croker to write up as an article, which appeared in December 1842. Croker used quotations from a speech by Cobden at a League conference in London. (J. W. Croker was Secretary of the Admiralty from 1809 to 1830)

Meanwhile the Conference continued its daily exercise of agitation; and ... Mr Cobden appeared there in person, and made a speech – which, coming from a man in his station, and conveyed, with the applauses of a hired press, to an excited populace, was well calculated to produce awful mischief ... he said, amongst a variety of similar ebullitions – 'Whatever they could do to embarrass the Government they were bound to do. They owed them no respect: they were entitled to none. They owed them no service which they could possibly avoid. The Government was based on corruption, and the offspring of *VICE, CORRUPTION, VIOLENCE, INTIMIDATION* and *BRIBERY.* The majority of the House of Commons was supported by the violation of morality and religion. He said for such a Government they should entertain no respect whatever ...'

We have shown that these societies [Anti-Corn Law Associations] set out ... to act 'by legal and constitutional means' but all their proceedings have been ... unconstitutional and ... illegal.

We have shown that ... the language of their speeches and their press has been not merely violent and indecent – but incendiary and seditious ... and finally we hope ... that no man of common sense of any party ... can hesitate to pronounce the existence of such associations – raising money – exciting mobs – organised and – to use a term of the same Jacobin origin as their own – affiliated – for the avowed purpose of coercing the government and legislature – can hesitate, we say, to pronounce the existence of such associations disgraceful to our national character, and wholly incompatible either with the internal peace and commercial prosperity of the country – or, in the highest meaning of the words – the SAFETY OF THE STATE.

ACTIVITY

1 In what ways does J. W. Croker suggest Cobden and the League were revolutionaries in Source 10.13?
2 Explain what opposition there was to the League and what arguments the opposition used.

D How did the Irish famine affect the campaign for repeal in 1845 and 1846?

economy

FOCUS ROUTE

1 Describe the problems caused by the failure of the Irish potato crop.
2 How did this cause a dilemma for Peel?
3 What impact did the Irish famine have on the debate about the repeal of the Corn Laws?

In the early nineteenth century Irish peasant farming families lived largely on a diet of potatoes. The climate and the poor soil in many areas, especially in the western counties such as Mayo, meant that it was difficult to grow good quality wheat for bread. Potatoes, however, grew in poor soil and a poor climate. Farms were very small, usually rented from an absentee English landlord and managed by a land agent on his behalf. Many of the farmers lived largely without cash, living on what they produced, or exchanging produce for goods such as pots and pans. On larger farms many labourers worked for starvation wages. Almost every year in the poorer parts of Ireland food was in short supply for about three months in the period after the previous year's potatoes had been used and before the new harvest was ready. In some years this amounted to a famine. There were famines in Galway and Mayo in 1831 and in Donegal in 1837. In 1835 an inquiry reported that over 1 million Irish peasants lived on less than 2s a week, and 2.2 million were unemployed or unable to buy the basic necessities of life for an average of 30 weeks a year.

The country as a whole, however, was not usually short of food. In parts of Ireland farms produced a surplus of meat and dairy products. The problem was that many of the Irish peasant farmers in the poor areas could not afford to buy this produce. Even during the famine years, Ireland continued to export meat and dairy produce. The rapid increase in the population of Ireland from around 5 million in 1800 to about 8 million at the census of 1841 exacerbated the problems.

In the spring of 1845 a virus, known as potato blight, attacked the potato crop in Ireland. When the potatoes were harvested they were rotten and inedible.

172

THE REPEAL OF THE CORN LAWS: PEEL'S TREACHERY OR PEEL'S SUCCESS?

The famine was reported in England, and images and descriptions of the distress of thousands of Irish men, women and children were published in the press. There was no television to thrust pictures of children dying from starvation in front of well-fed people, but the newspapers and periodicals did heighten awareness of what was happening in Ireland. They ensured that public and politicians alike could not ignore the problem.

SOURCE 10.14   Images showing the effects of the Irish potato famine – (**A**) a destitute family during the famine, 1846; (**B**) Father Matthew visits a farming family during the famine, 1846; (**C**) food riots in Dungarvon, County Waterford, 1846; (**D**) starving peasants at the gates of a workhouse

SOURCE 10.15   'Digging for potatoes' from *The Illustrated London News*, 1849

'Searching for Potatoes' is one of those occupations of those who cannot obtain outdoor relief. It is gleaning in a potato field, and how few are left after the potatoes are dug, must be known to everyone who has ever seen the field cleared. What the people were digging and hunting for, like dogs after truffles, I could not imagine, till I went into the field, and then I found them patiently turning over the whole ground, in the hopes of finding the few potatoes the owner might have overlooked. Gleaning in a potato field seems something like shearing hogs, but it is the only means by which the gleaners could hope to get a meal.

173

THE REPEAL OF THE CORN LAWS: PEEL'S TREACHERY OR PEEL'S SUCCESS?

SOURCE 10.16 Extracts from *The Times*, 16 December 1846

Under the imposing heads of 'Fearful Facts', and 'Hungers, Cold, Disease and Deaths', the Wexford Independent *gives a most alarming account of the state of part of that country. Here is an extract:*
'Our accounts from the northern parts of this country are most deplorable. What the poor people earn on the public works is barely sufficient to support them. All their earnings go for food; and the consequence is, that they have nothing left to procure clothing. Since the extreme cold set in, sickness and death have accordingly followed in its train. Inflammation of the lungs, fevers, and other maladies, resulting from excessive privation, have been bearing away their victims. Many have died in the course of last week; and the illness in every case was traceable to the want of clothing and firing, if not of sufficient food.'

TITHE
A tenth; also the tax paid to the Church (one-tenth of earnings).

ACTIVITY

1 What impression of conditions in Ireland do Sources 10.14–10.17 give?
2 How would they have been useful to the Anti-Corn Law League?
3 How reliable are the drawings as historical evidence?
4 Would photographs have been more reliable than drawings?

TALKING POINT

Explain the main features of this cartoon, for example, who are the dogs on the left of the fence?

SOURCE 10.18 'The Premier's Fix: Free trade and agriculture' – a cartoon from *Punch* magazine, 1845

SOURCE 10.17 Extracts from *The Times*, 10 February 1846

Ireland. (From Our Own Correspondent.) Dublin, Feb. 8
The distress
I regret to say that there is not the slightest mitigation in the accounts of the destitution received today. We are now in the midst of a second winter, the frost and snow of Christmas having apparently reset in with equal if not increased severity, so that any prospect of amelioration is just now as remote as ever. The progress of distress in the county of Cork may be learned from the Southern Reporter of Saturday: 'The duty of publishing reports of the inquests held on persons who have 'died by starvation' has now become so frequent, and such numbers are daily reaching us from every part of the county, that the limits of our space do not admit of their publication. Our reporter sends particulars of 15 of such cases from Bantry yesterday, and mentions that 20 more had occurred during the week, but inquests could not be held; and we received this morning from Mallow reports of 11 inquests held by Mr. Richard Jones on persons who had died from want of food. Communications pour in from every district, a TITHE *of which we could not find room for, stating similar appalling facts. Our reporters are daily occupied in attending meetings throughout the county, and there are as many applications to that effect as would require a corps equal to* The Times, *and a sheet of equal size, to present a daily record of.'*

THE PREMIER'S FIX.

FREE TRADE   AND   AGRICULTURE.

ACTIVITY

What is the significance of Peel's response to the debate in the Commons in March 1845 (see Chart 10D)?

BRIMSTONE
A foul-tasting medicine.

■ 10D A timeline of major events relating to repeal

1845	
March	• Following Cobden's attack on the Corn Laws in a debate in the Commons, Peel screwed up his notes for his reply and said to his Cabinet colleague Sidney Herbert who was sitting next to him: 'You must answer this, for I cannot.'
Summer	• The Irish potato harvest failed.
	• Peel arranged for £160,000 worth of maize to be imported from the USA to be sold at 1d a lb to the Irish. It was soon used up, and in any event made a strange-tasting bread. The maize was nicknamed 'Peel's BRIMSTONE' by the Irish because of the taste.
	• The English and Scottish potato crops failed.
	• The wheat harvest of 1845 was poor.
1–6 November	• At a series of meetings, Peel told the Cabinet that repeal of the Corn Laws was the only way to get cheap food into Ireland. He proposed to suspend the Corn Laws. Only Lord Aberdeen, Sidney Herbert and Sir James Graham supported Peel.
22 November	• Lord John Russell, leader of the Whigs, advised his constituents in Edinburgh to employ every lawful method of agitation to compel the government to repeal the Corn Laws.
23–24 November	• Two more Cabinet meetings were held without a decision being taken.
3 December	• At a Cabinet meeting Peel felt he had won over his colleagues. However, with Lord Stanley and the Duke of Buccleuch still opposed, Peel did not feel he could entirely rely on the support of all the rest.
4 December	• The Times announced that the government was planning to repeal the Corn Laws – a considerable journalistic 'scoop'.
6 December	• Peel offered his resignation to the Queen.
8 December	• Russell, in Edinburgh, received a summons from the Queen. He arrived at Osborne on the Isle of Wight, where she was living, on 10 December.
11 December	• Peel's resignation became public.
18 and 19 December	• Russell tried to form a Cabinet but failed. Without a majority in the Commons, the Whigs could not pass repeal without the support of large numbers of Tories, including Peel.
20 December	• Peel was recalled by the Queen and within three days had re-formed his Cabinet.
1846	
19 January	• Parliament met to hear the Queen's speech, which included a proposal for the repeal of the Corn Laws within a comprehensive set of measures for tariff reform. The proposal would phase out the Corn Laws over three years, alongside some other reforms, which would lighten the financial burden on landowners.
27 February	• The Commons passed the second reading of the Corn Bill by 337 to 240 votes.
15 May	• The bill passed its third reading in the Commons by 327 votes to 229.
28 May	• In the Lords, Wellington's support enabled the bill to be passed relatively easily by 211 votes to 164.
June	• The bill received royal assent and the Corn Laws were finally repealed.

FOCUS ROUTE

List the reasons put forward in the autumn and winter of 1845–46 for and against repeal.

ACTIVITY

Why does Peel advocate immediate and total repeal of the Corn Laws in the memorandum in Source 10.19?

During the autumn and winter of 1845–46, the repeal of the Corn Laws was in the forefront of the minds of politicians and public alike. Both sides needed to influence Peel, and persuade him which way to move on the issue. Sources 10.19, 10.21 and 10.22 are extracts from documents written during 1845 and 1846 as the debate in Parliament continued.

SOURCE 10.19 Extracts from Peel's memorandum to the Cabinet on 1 November 1845

I cannot disguise . . . that the calling of Parliament on account of apprehended scarcity . . . will constitute a great crisis and that it will be dangerous for the Government, having assembled Parliament, to resist with all its energies any material modification of the Corn Laws . . .

I greatly fear that partial and limited interference with the Corn Laws . . . will be no solution to our difficulties.

SOURCE 10.20 Two cartoonists' views of the proposed repeal of the Corn Laws in *Punch* magazine, 1846. **A** celebrates cheap bread while **B** shows Peel leaving his party behind

A

PEEL'S CHEAP BREAD SHOP,
OPENED JANUARY 22, 1846.

B

THE DEAF POSTILION.
A POLITICAL PARODY, AFTER GEORGE CRUIKSHANK.

SOURCE 10.21 Extracts from a letter from Henry Goulburn, Chancellor of the Exchequer, to Peel, dated 30 November 1845 and marked 'Private and Confidential'

The more I reflect on the observations which you made to me a few days since as to your difficulty in again defending a Corn Law in Parliament, the more do I feel alarmed at the consequences of your taking a different course from that which you have previously adopted. An abandonment of your former opinions now, would, I think, prejudice your and our characters as public men, and would be fraught with fatal results to the country's best interests ...

I fairly own that I do not see how the repeal of the Corn Law is to afford relief to the distress with which we are threatened ... I think it next to impossible to show that the abandonment of the law now could materially affect this year's supply, or give us any corn which will not equally reach us under the law as it stands ...

I view with greater alarm [the abandonment's] effects on public interests ... the party of which you are the head is the only barrier which remains against the revolutionary effects of the Reform Bill. So long as that party remains unbroken, whether in or out of power, it has the means of doing much good ... but if it be broken in pieces by a destruction of confidence in its leaders (and I cannot but think that an abandonment of the Corn Laws would produce that result) I see nothing before us but the exasperation of class animosities, a struggle for pre-eminence, and the ultimate triumph of unrestrained democracy.

ACTIVITY

1 Summarise in your own words Goulburn's views in paragraphs 1 and 2 of Source 10.21.
2 What is Goulburn's fear as expressed in paragraph 3?

176

THE REPEAL OF THE CORN LAWS: PEEL'S TREACHERY OR PEEL'S SUCCESS?

SOURCE 10.22 Extracts from a memorandum from Prince Albert to Queen Victoria, recounting a conversation he had had with Peel the previous day, after Peel had returned to office following Russell's failure to form a government in December 1845. The memorandum is dated 25 December 1845

He [Peel] said he meant at the end of the next Session to call the whole Conservative party together and to declare this to them, that he would not meet another Parliament pledged to the maintenance of the Corn Laws, which could be maintained no longer, and that he would make a public declaration to this effect before another general election came on. This had been defeated by events coming too suddenly upon him, and he had no alternative but to deal with the Corn Laws before a national calamity would force it on. The League had made immense progress, and had enormous means at their disposal. If he had resigned in November, Lord Stanley and the Protectionists would have been prepared to form a Government, and a Revolution might have been the consequence of it . . . Sir Robert . . . will adopt the principle of the League, that of removing all protection and abolishing monopoly, *but not in favour of one class and as a triumph over another, but to the benefit of the nation, farmers as well as manufacturers.*

ACTIVITY

1 What are the 'events' (line 6) to which Peel referred in Source 10.22?
2 What does this tell you about Peel's attitude towards the Corn Laws before the 'events'?
3 To which party did 'Lord Stanley and the Protectionists' belong?
4 What do the last four lines suggest about Peel's skill as a politician?

E Review: the repeal of the Corn Laws: Peel's treachery or Peel's success?

SOURCE 10.23 Peel responds to demands to repeal the Corn Laws, 1841

If I could bring myself to think – if I could believe that an alteration to the Corn Laws would preclude the risk of such distress – if I thought it would be an effectual remedy, in all cases, against such instances of lamentable suffering as that which have been described, I would say at once to the Agricultural interest, 'it is for your advantage rather to submit to any reduction of price, that if an alteration of the Corn Laws would really be the cure for these sufferings, to compel their continuance.' ... But it is because I cannot convince my mind that the Corn Laws are at the bottom of this distress, or that the repeal of them, or the alteration of their principle, would be its cure, that I am induced to continue my maintenance of them.

SOURCE 10.24 Peel asks the Commons to repeal the Corn Laws, 1845

I believe that scarcity left no alternative to us but to undertake the consideration of this question; and that consideration being necessary, I think that a permanent adjustment of the question is not only imperative, but the best policy for all concerned ... Now all of you admit that the real question at issue is the improvement of the social and moral condition of the masses of the population; we wish to elevate in the gradation of society that great class which gains its support by manual labour ... The mere interests of the landlord – the mere interests of the occupying tenants, important as they are, are subordinate to the great question – what is calculated to increase the comforts, to improve the condition, and elevate the social character of the millions who subsist by manual labour, whether they are engaged in manufacture or in agriculture?

SOURCE 10.25   Benjamin Disraeli, an up-and-coming member of the Conservatives, speaking about his leader in the Commons in May 1846

177

I am bound to say ... [Peel] may congratulate himself on his complete success in having entirely deceived his party ... the right hon. Gentleman has been accused of foregone treachery – of long meditated deception – of a desire entirely unworthy of a great statesman, even if an unprincipled one – of always having intended to abandon the opinions by professing which he rose to power ... when I examine the career of this Minister ... I find that for between thirty and forty years ... that right hon. Gentleman has traded on the ideas and intelligence of others. His life has been one great appropriation clause ... there is no statesman who has committed political petty larceny on so great a scale.

ACTIVITY

1 How and to what extent does the statement by Peel in 1841 (Source 10.23) reflect his attitude to reform as expressed in the Tamworth Manifesto (see page 161)?
2 What reasons for repeal of the Corn Laws does Peel put forward in the 1845 speech (Source 10.24)?

Why were the Corn Laws repealed? During the 1830s and early 1840s there was growing support for the idea of free trade, and Peel had himself continued the moves towards free trade begun by the Whigs earlier in the century in his budgets of 1842 and 1845. Following the Reform Act of 1832 the influence of the manufacturing and business interests in Parliament had grown, both directly through new MPs who were themselves businessmen, and indirectly through the increasing number of voters from the middle classes. The power of the agricultural interest, however, had not waned so much that it did not have a strong influence both in and out of Parliament between 1841 and 1845. The need for extra-parliamentary pressure pushing for repeal manifested itself in the campaign of the Anti-Corn Law League. The failure of the potato harvest in Ireland and the rest of the United Kingdom, together with a poor wheat harvest in a wet summer, led to an urgent need to import grain.

There is evidence to suggest that Peel had decided some time before 1846 that the Corn Laws had to be repealed. In 1845 in a debate in which Cobden delivered an especially effective attack on the Corn Laws, Peel, who was due to respond, screwed up his notes and whispered to Sidney Herbert sitting next to him, 'You must answer this, for I cannot' – a comment that suggests that he could no longer justify any argument for retaining the Corn Laws. Certainly in the budgets in 1842 and 1845 Peel had demonstrated that he was not an opponent of making trade more free in general. The obstacle that faced him was that his party was pledged to keep the Corn Laws. If he moved too quickly towards repeal he would inevitably split the party. He hoped to prepare the ground for repeal gradually, converting as many of the party as he could, and then when the next general election came, in 1848, to allow the country to decide.

ACTIVITY

1 Choose **one** of the following individuals: Sir Robert Peel, Duke of Wellington, Richard Cobden, John Bright, Daniel O'Connell, Lord Aberdeen, Lord John Russell.
2 Research the views of your chosen individual about repealing the Corn Laws in May 1846.
3 Prepare questions to ask the other individuals on the list about their views and why they hold them.
4 Hold a 'hot seat' session, in which each individual is asked firstly to explain their views and then is questioned about them by the rest of the class.

CITY COLLEGE
LEARNING RESOURCE CENTRE

THE REPEAL OF THE CORN LAWS: PEEL'S TREACHERY OR PEEL'S SUCCESS?

178

FOCUS ROUTE

Copy and complete this table by:

a) putting a tick in the appropriate columns to show whether the factor was important or not, and whether it was a long-term or a short-term influence. Space has been left at the bottom for you to add any other factors.

b) adding in the final column a letter a)–e) to show which of the areas in the 'Explaining motivation' list, below, the factor might belong to.

Factors influencing Peel to repeal the Corn Laws	Not very important	Important	Crucial	Long term	Short term	a) – e)
Peel's own views on reform						
Peel's family background						
The conversion of many of his Cabinet to repeal						
The support of the Whigs for repeal						
Increasing support for free trade						
Effects of the 1832 Reform Act on the make-up of the Commons						
Growth in the number of middle-class votes after 1832						
Increasing influence of industrialists and businessmen						
Campaign of the Anti-Corn Law League						
Cold spring and wet summer, 1845						
Failure of the potato harvest, 1845						
Poor wheat harvest, 1845						
Famine in Ireland						
Fear of revolts in Ireland						
Need for cheap bread to alleviate distress in England						

ACTIVITY

Using the table you have completed, choose the factor you think was *most* important in influencing Peel to repeal the Corn Laws in 1846, and justify your choice to others in the group.

ACTIVITY

Write an essay in response to this question: Why did Peel apparently betray his party and repeal the Corn Laws in 1846?

Explaining motivation

In explaining the motivation of an individual we must consider:

a) the attitudes and beliefs of the individual and the factors that over a long period of time influenced the individual
b) factors within the individual's control that may have led to a change of attitude and beliefs
c) events outside the individual's control that may have influenced and perhaps changed their attitudes and beliefs
d) actions that others took that may have influenced and perhaps changed the individual's attitudes and beliefs
e) changes in circumstances that may have necessitated a change in attitudes and beliefs.

FOCUS ROUTE

Using the information on pages 179–181, summarise the effects of the repeal of the Corn Laws.

COERCION BILL
A bill which gave the government military powers to control an area.

The results of repeal
For Peel

In June 1846 Peel resigned as Prime Minister, having been defeated by a coalition of the Whigs and many of his former Tory supporters over a COERCION BILL aimed at enforcing law and order in Ireland. Although it was not an issue many protectionists felt strongly about, they were determined to destroy the man who they believed had betrayed them. Although Peel never again held office as a minister he remained an MP until his death in 1850. In his resignation speech he paid tribute to Cobden, as the man whose name should really be associated with the successful repeal. He then went on to say how he expected to be remembered, but also how he hoped he might be remembered.

SOURCE 10.26 A statue of Sir Robert Peel, Bury, Lancashire

SOURCE 10.27 Extract from Peel's resignation speech, 29 June 1846

I shall leave a name, severely censured I fear by many, who, on public grounds, deeply regret the severance of party ties ... not from interested or personal motives, but from the firm conviction that fidelity to party engagements – the existence and maintenance of a great party – constitutes a powerful instrument of government: I shall surrender power severely censured also, by others who, from no interested motive, adhere to the principle of protection, considering the maintenance of it to be essential to the welfare and interests of the country: I shall leave a name execrated by every monopolist who, from less honourable motives, clamours for protection because it conduces to his individual benefit; but it may be that I shall leave a name sometimes remembered with expressions of good will in the abode of those whose lot it is to labour, and to earn their daily bread by the sweat of their brow, when they shall recruit their exhausted strength with abundant and untaxed food.

On 29 June 1850 while riding in London, Peel was thrown from his horse. He was badly hurt and died from his injuries on 2 July. Although he had split his party, his standing with the nation as a whole was barely challenged between 1846 and his death. One illustration of this popularity can still be seen in towns throughout the country in the large number of statues of Peel, many of which were funded by public subscriptions swollen by pennies given by working people, including Chartists.

Peel was described by Bagehot, writing in 1856, as a great administrator, but not a great statesman because he merely borrowed other people's ideas. Bagehot pointed out that Peel had begun by opposing the two measures which were later felt to be his greatest achievements – Catholic Emancipation and repeal of the Corn Laws. However, the historian Norman Gash saw Peel as, more than anyone, the architect of the early Victorian age. Peel as Prime Minister achieved financial stability, revived trade, all but defeated the Chartist movement, and restored good relations with France and the USA. Peel was not always popular with many of his contemporary colleagues (O'Connell said that when Peel smiled it was like the gleam of a silver plate on a coffin lid). However, there was a loyal band of 'Peelites' for whom he remained a 'leader'. Writing to Lady Peel after Peel's death, the Duke of Newcastle said that he never took a step in public life without reflecting how Peel would have thought of it. Lord Rosebery maintained that to be a 'Peelite' was a distinction in itself, since it denoted statesmanship, industry and conscience.

TALKING POINT

A-level students almost always identify Peel as the politician they most admire. Why? Is this view justified?

ACTIVITY

Either:
You are a member of the city council in Leeds. It is 1851 and there has been a suggestion that the council erect a statue to the memory of Sir Robert Peel. There has also been opposition from some of the 'old Tories' in Leeds. Write your speech to the council supporting the proposal.
Or:
As a group, debate in the council chamber in Leeds in 1851, with speakers for and against the motion 'that this council believes that the city should erect a statue to the memory of Sir Robert Peel'.

180

THE REPEAL OF THE CORN LAWS: PEEL'S TREACHERY OR PEEL'S SUCCESS?

For the Conservative Party

The repeal of the Corn Laws split the Conservative Party. Except for brief periods, in 1852 and 1858, the Conservatives were in opposition until 1866. However, the party had never been homogeneous. Following the split, Peel commented that he was more surprised that it had remained united for so long than that it had split. The leading figures in the Conservative Party after repeal were Lord Derby, Lord George Bentinck and Disraeli. The Peelites and others who supported free trade formed a separate group. They included Aberdeen, Gladstone, Sidney Herbert, Sir James Graham, the Duke of Newcastle, Dalhousie and Elgin. In 1852 they joined Lord Aberdeen's coalition government.

■ 10E The split in the Conservative Party after repeal

Conservatives   Peelites

SOURCE 10.28   *The Times*, 10 January 1847

Melancholy indeed are the latest accounts from all parts of this extensive country. From Bantry, Skibbereen, Crookhaven, Castletown, and Tracton, in Cork and in Dingle, in Kerry, the reports present the same gloomy features. The intelligence from these scenes of misery are summed up by the Cork Examiner *as follows. The details from Bantry were forwarded yesterday:*

'Skibbereen. In the parish of Kilmore 14 died on Sunday; 3 of these were buried in coffins, 11 were buried without other covering than the rags they wore when alive. And one gentleman, a good and charitable man, speaking of this case, says "The distress is so appalling, that we must throw away all feelings of delicacy", and another says, "I would rather give 1s. to a starving man than 4s.6d. for a coffin".'

'140 died in the Skibbereen Workhouse in one month; 8 have died in one day! And Mr. M'Carthy Downing states that "they came into the house merely and solely for the purpose of getting a coffin".'

'The Rev. Mr. Clancy visits a farm, and there, in one house, "he administered the last rites of religion to six persons". On a subsequent occasion, he "prepared for death a father and daughter lying in the same bed".'

'The Rev. Mr. Caulfield sees "13 members of one family lying down in fever".'

For Ireland

The repeal of the Corn Laws did not end the famine in Ireland. A system of providing manual work, such as building roads, was set up to provide some people with a little money to buy food. One of the problems in 1846 was that there was food in Ireland, but many of the peasant farmers did not have money to buy it. They had always been virtually subsistence farmers, and when their subsistence crop failed they had no cash with which to buy an alternative food source. In the spring of 1847, as food prices continued to rise and men could not earn enough to feed their families, the government stopped the system of providing manual work. In its place they set up soup kitchens in an unsuccessful attempt to feed the starving population. The soup kitchens were eventually closed the following autumn. What became known as the 'Great Hunger' grew worse.

By 1847, epidemics of typhus, cholera, dysentery, yellow fever and scurvy swept the country, claiming almost as many lives as hunger. The available medical resources were totally inadequate to deal with the problem. During the Great Hunger an estimated 1 million people died of starvation and disease, while a further 1.5 million emigrated to England, mainly to Liverpool, and to Canada, America and Australia. By 1851 the Irish population was reduced from a pre-famine total of 8.5 million to just over 6 million.

The effects of the famine and the government's response to it, despite Peel's repeal of the Corn Laws, had a significant effect on Irish, American and British politics for the rest of the nineteenth century and most of the twentieth century. The bitterness, anger and hatred of the British government that most of the Irish emigrants took to America led to much American support for the Irish republican movements in the second half of the nineteenth century. In Ireland anti-British feeling ran deep. As John Mitchell of the Young Ireland movement said, 'The Almighty indeed sent the potato blight, but the English created the famine'. The home rule for Ireland and republican movements had much support after 1846, both in Ireland and among the many Irish who had

181

THE REPEAL OF THE CORN LAWS: PEEL'S TREACHERY OR PEEL'S SUCCESS?

TALKING POINT

Do the descriptions of distress in Ireland and the effects of the famine on politics post-1850 mean that the repeal of the Corn Laws was in fact pointless?

emigrated to England. In 1857 the Fenian movement, pledged to the formation of an Irish republic separate from Britain, was set up in the USA, and in 1867 it began to operate in Britain, leading to several violent attacks by Fenians in Ireland and England.

For agriculture

The period from 1850 to around 1870 is frequently referred to as the 'Golden Age of British Agriculture'. In Britain the population continued to grow rapidly, and demand from cities for food increased. A prosperous middle class had money for a greater quantity and variety of food. The railway network in Britain gave farmers quick and easy access to these growing markets. At the same time there was little competition from abroad. The huge farming areas of the central USA that were to become the wheat-producing prairies were only just being settled in the 1850s and 1860s. The USA's economy was also badly affected by the American Civil War between 1861 and 1865. In Russia the potential to grow and export wheat was limited by the feudal system of farming and by the disruption caused by the Crimean War of 1854–56. Australia and New Zealand were still being colonised, and the meat-producing areas of countries such as Argentina were only just beginning to develop large-scale production. There was no regular and effective refrigerated steam shipping across the Atlantic, or railways across the USA and Canada, until the 1870s.

ACTIVITY

What does the description of the period 1850–70 as a 'golden age' imply about British farming after the repeal of the Corn Laws?

TALKING POINT

There have been suggestions that a middle-class revolution took place between 1841 and 1846. In his book *Victorian Years 1841–1895*, published in 1951, the French historian Elie Halévy called his chapter on the repeal of the Corn Laws, 'The Revolution of 1846'. What evidence would you put forward both to defend and oppose the argument that the repeal of the Corn Laws in 1846 was a middle-class revolution?

KEY POINTS FROM CHAPTER 10   **The repeal of the Corn Laws: Peel's treachery or Peel's success?**

1 The Corn Laws were introduced in 1815 to protect British farmers from potential ruin.
2 The idea that trade in all goods between countries should be free was growing during the late eighteenth and early nineteenth centuries.
3 Following the 1832 Reform Act, industrialists and businessmen had gained some power in Parliament and there were more voters from the business classes.
4 Between 1820 and 1845 there were several measures taken by both Whig and Tory governments to make trade more free.
5 The Anti-Corn Law League was set up with the sole aim of total repeal of the Corn Laws.
6 In 1845 the failure of the potato harvest led to famine in Ireland.
7 In 1846 Sir Robert Peel went against his party's policy of retaining the Corn Laws and pushed repeal through Parliament.
8 Repeal led to Peel resigning as Prime Minister, and to a split in the Conservative Party, which was effectively out of office until 1866.
9 Repeal did not end famine in Ireland. Anti-British feeling grew on both sides of the Atlantic.
10 Repeal did not lead to the ruin of British farming: 1850–70 was a 'golden age' for British farmers.

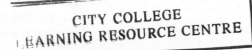

CITY COLLEGE
LEARNING RESOURCE CENTRE

Bread and cheese, or revolution: what did the Chartists want?

SOURCE 11.1   A verse that was part of the evidence used at the trial of four Chartists charged with conspiracy at Chester in August 1839 and sentenced to eighteen months in prison

In tyrant's blood baptize your sons,
And every villain slaughter,
By pike and sword your freedom try to gain
Or make one bloody Moscow of Old England's plain.

The six points demanded by the Chartists
1 A vote for all men over the age of 21
2 Voting to be secret
3 No property qualifications to become an MP
4 MPs to be paid
5 Constituencies to have an equal number of electors
6 Parliament to be elected once a year.

SOURCE 11.2   William Wynn MP commenting on Chartist activity, from *Hansard*, 15 May 1839

Mr William Wynn MP could not help expressing his surprise that so long an adjournment of the House should be proposed while the internal state of the country was so agitated. Six months had now elapsed since certain parties had recommended the people generally to procure arms. They knew that in different parts of the country those recommendations had been carried into effect, that firearms had been provided and that pikes had been made to a very great extent. Up to the present moment, they were being publicly sold, and no steps had been taken to put an end to it ... He was not afraid of the moderate excesses of the parties who were misleading the people. What he was afraid of was, that if this arming continued unchecked, it would lead to a lamentable degree of bloodshed.

If this was all the evidence you had about the Chartists what would you think of them? Like many people at the time, you would be confused. People living during the time of Chartist activity (1839–1848) and historians since have argued about what the Chartists wanted.

Some have seen them as working-class revolutionaries attempting to imitate their brothers and sisters in revolution in Europe. Other interpretations suggest they were more interested in jobs, wages and food than in political revolution. The aims of this chapter are therefore to investigate what the Chartists wanted to achieve; how they tried to achieve it; and how far they succeeded.

A What was happening in Europe between 1830 and 1849? (pp. 183–184)

B Which groups of people wanted more reforms in the period 1832–39 and why? (pp. 185–187)

C Why was it difficult for people to win reforms? (pp. 188–189)

D How did the Chartist movement begin? (pp. 189–191)

E Did the Chartists attempt to achieve their aims through revolution? (pp. 192–196)

F Why did the Chartists fail in the short term? (pp. 197–198)

G What did the Chartists achieve in the long term? (pp. 199–200)

H Review: bread and cheese, or revolution: what did the Chartists want? (pp. 200–201)

A What was happening in Europe between 1830 and 1849?

■ **Learning trouble spot**

Revolutionary activity in Europe 1830–49
Many students do not have enough knowledge and understanding of what was happening on the continent in the 1830s and 1840s, and/or do not make a link between those events and fear of the Chartists in England. To appreciate the fears of people in England, it is essential to be aware of events in Europe. Charts 11A and 11B give a brief summary of some of the major revolutionary events in Europe between 1830 and 1849. It will help your understanding of the attitudes towards Chartism in this period.

ACTIVITY

1 What two main aims of the revolutionaries in France, Italy, Poland and Germany can you identify from the information in Chart 11A?
2 Which of these aims would have inspired Chartists?

■ **11A   A map of revolutionary events in Europe 1830–31**

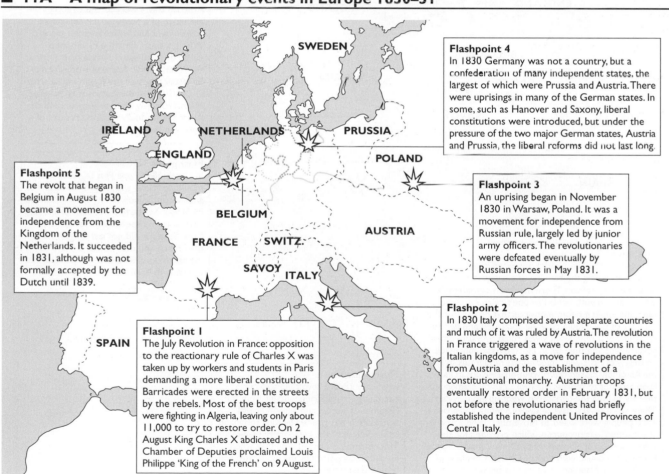

Flashpoint 4
In 1830 Germany was not a country, but a confederation of many independent states, the largest of which were Prussia and Austria. There were uprisings in many of the German states. In some, such as Hanover and Saxony, liberal constitutions were introduced, but under the pressure of the two major German states, Austria and Prussia, the liberal reforms did not last long.

Flashpoint 5
The revolt that began in Belgium in August 1830 became a movement for independence from the Kingdom of the Netherlands. It succeeded in 1831, although was not formally accepted by the Dutch until 1839.

Flashpoint 3
An uprising began in November 1830 in Warsaw, Poland. It was a movement for independence from Russian rule, largely led by junior army officers. The revolutionaries were defeated eventually by Russian forces in May 1831.

Flashpoint 2
In 1830 Italy comprised several separate countries and much of it was ruled by Austria. The revolution in France triggered a wave of revolutions in the Italian kingdoms, as a move for independence from Austria and the establishment of a constitutional monarchy. Austrian troops eventually restored order in February 1831, but not before the revolutionaries had briefly established the independent United Provinces of Central Italy.

Flashpoint 1
The July Revolution in France: opposition to the reactionary rule of Charles X was taken up by workers and students in Paris demanding a more liberal constitution. Barricades were erected in the streets by the rebels. Most of the best troops were fighting in Algeria, leaving only about 11,000 to try to restore order. On 2 August King Charles X abdicated and the Chamber of Deputies proclaimed Louis Philippe 'King of the French' on 9 August.

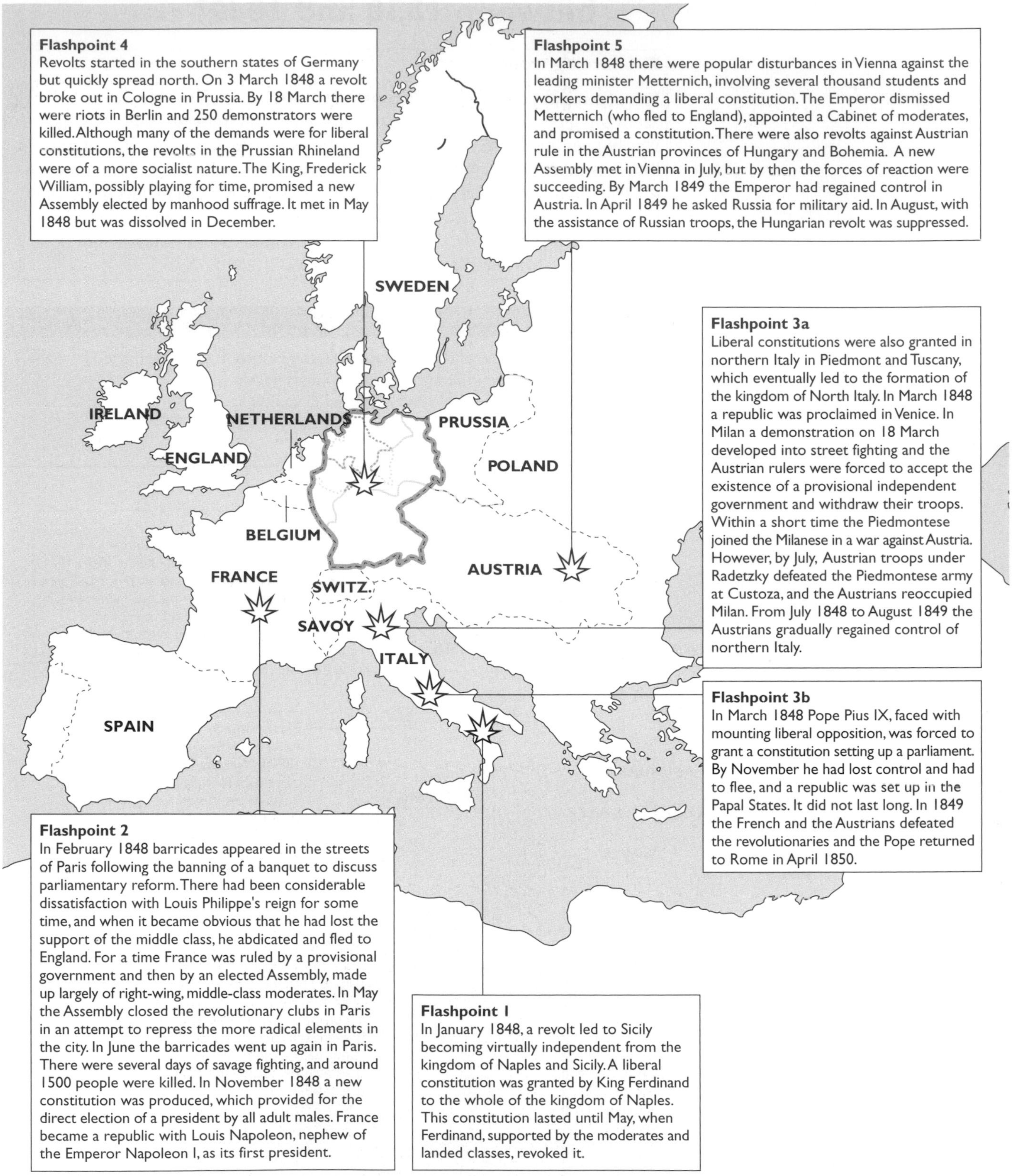

Flashpoint 4
Revolts started in the southern states of Germany but quickly spread north. On 3 March 1848 a revolt broke out in Cologne in Prussia. By 18 March there were riots in Berlin and 250 demonstrators were killed. Although many of the demands were for liberal constitutions, the revolts in the Prussian Rhineland were of a more socialist nature. The King, Frederick William, possibly playing for time, promised a new Assembly elected by manhood suffrage. It met in May 1848 but was dissolved in December.

Flashpoint 5
In March 1848 there were popular disturbances in Vienna against the leading minister Metternich, involving several thousand students and workers demanding a liberal constitution. The Emperor dismissed Metternich (who fled to England), appointed a Cabinet of moderates, and promised a constitution. There were also revolts against Austrian rule in the Austrian provinces of Hungary and Bohemia. A new Assembly met in Vienna in July, but by then the forces of reaction were succeeding. By March 1849 the Emperor had regained control in Austria. In April 1849 he asked Russia for military aid. In August, with the assistance of Russian troops, the Hungarian revolt was suppressed.

Flashpoint 3a
Liberal constitutions were also granted in northern Italy in Piedmont and Tuscany, which eventually led to the formation of the kingdom of North Italy. In March 1848 a republic was proclaimed in Venice. In Milan a demonstration on 18 March developed into street fighting and the Austrian rulers were forced to accept the existence of a provisional independent government and withdraw their troops. Within a short time the Piedmontese joined the Milanese in a war against Austria. However, by July, Austrian troops under Radetzky defeated the Piedmontese army at Custoza, and the Austrians reoccupied Milan. From July 1848 to August 1849 the Austrians gradually regained control of northern Italy.

Flashpoint 3b
In March 1848 Pope Pius IX, faced with mounting liberal opposition, was forced to grant a constitution setting up a parliament. By November he had lost control and had to flee, and a republic was set up in the Papal States. It did not last long. In 1849 the French and the Austrians defeated the revolutionaries and the Pope returned to Rome in April 1850.

Flashpoint 2
In February 1848 barricades appeared in the streets of Paris following the banning of a banquet to discuss parliamentary reform. There had been considerable dissatisfaction with Louis Philippe's reign for some time, and when it became obvious that he had lost the support of the middle class, he abdicated and fled to England. For a time France was ruled by a provisional government and then by an elected Assembly, made up largely of right-wing, middle-class moderates. In May the Assembly closed the revolutionary clubs in Paris in an attempt to repress the more radical elements in the city. In June the barricades went up again in Paris. There were several days of savage fighting, and around 1500 people were killed. In November 1848 a new constitution was produced, which provided for the direct election of a president by all adult males. France became a republic with Louis Napoleon, nephew of the Emperor Napoleon I, as its first president.

Flashpoint 1
In January 1848, a revolt led to Sicily becoming virtually independent from the kingdom of Naples and Sicily. A liberal constitution was granted by King Ferdinand to the whole of the kingdom of Naples. This constitution lasted until May, when Ferdinand, supported by the moderates and landed classes, revoked it.

Map labels: SWEDEN, IRELAND, ENGLAND, NETHERLANDS, PRUSSIA, POLAND, BELGIUM, FRANCE, SWITZ., SAVOY, AUSTRIA, ITALY, SPAIN

ACTIVITY

1 Study Chart 11B. Do the revolutionaries seem to have different aims from those of 1830 (Chart 11A) or are they similar?
2 What aspects of their aims would have seemed dangerous to the government facing Chartist activity in Britain?
3 How might the events of 1848 have inspired the Chartists?

B Which groups of people wanted more reforms in the period 1832–39 and why?

FOCUS ROUTE

Use Sources 11.3–11.12 to identify the reasons for discontent in England in the 1830s and 1840s.

ACTIVITY

It is 1847. You are a reporter on the *Leeds Mercury*. The editor has asked you to report on why there seems to be discontent among working people in Leeds and other northern industrial towns and cities. Write an article in which you outline the causes of people's distress. You must not write more than 500 words. You have the information in Sources 11.3–11.12 as your evidence.

SOURCE 11.3 Extracts from a report on the city of Newcastle, made by Dr D. B. Reid in 1845 and submitted to the Newcastle Corporation

The streets most densely populated by the humbler classes are a mass of filth where the direct rays of the sun never reach. In some of the courts I have noticed heaps of filth, amounting to 20 or 50 tons, which, when it rains, penetrate into some of the cellar dwellings. A few public necessaries [public toilets] have been built, but too few to serve the population ... a room was noticed with scarcely any furniture and in which there were two children of two and three years of age absolutely naked except for a little straw to protect them from the cold ... the absence of dustbins was everywhere a cause of great annoyance, and no such activity horrified me more than the attempt to keep the refuse of privies for the purpose of selling it to neighbouring farmers ... house drains, where they exist, have not been constructed properly and often become choked ... In numerous dwellings a whole family shares one room ... The lodging houses for the extreme poor present the most deplorable examples ... They are badly crowded, dirty, badly managed, ill-ventilated, where the sexes mix without control ... The most intolerable nuisance is certainly one resulting from a slaughter-house in the very centre just off the most fashionable part of town ... in the presence of great quantities of animal matter, the offal of beasts ... is left to rot until liquid streams run down High Friar Lane.

SOURCE 11.4 An engraving by Gustave Doré of a street in Whitechapel, London. Scenes like this could have been found in all the growing industrial towns of Britain

CITY COLLEGE
RNING RESOURCE CENTRE

BREAD AND CHEESE, OR REVOLUTION: WHAT DID THE CHARTISTS WANT?

186

Dissatisfaction with the 1832 Reform Act

Those who did not have the vote after 1832:

- most working men in the towns and cities
- most farm workers in the countryside
- all women.

Method of voting:

- openly, not by secret ballot.

TALKING POINT

Read through Section F of Chapter 8 (pages 133–135) on the results of the 1832 Reform Act. Make a list of any groups/types of people who might have been unhappy with the outcome of that Act and explain why they might have been unhappy.

SOURCE 11.5 Bronterre O'Brien writing about the effects of the Reform Act of 1832. O'Brien was a member of the Radical Reform Association and campaigned for universal male suffrage

What a farce the present system is! The present House of Commons does not represent the people ... Pawnbrokers are enfranchised, and two thousand brothel owners in London all have votes, but honest folk have none ... It is indeed disgusting to see how much of the honey is appropriated by the drones, and what a pittance is left to the bees of the hive; and how the parliamentary franchise is monopolised by one-tenth of the population – and that tenth the worst tenth.

SOURCE 11.6 Summary of the terms of the Poor Law Amendment Act, 1834

- *Outdoor relief will continue for the old and infirm.*
- *Outdoor relief will be abolished for the able-bodied. The only relief available to an able-bodied man (and his family) will be in a workhouse. (This was known as the 'workhouse test'.)*
- *Conditions in the workhouses are to be made 'less eligible' than those of the lowest paid labourers in work (the principle of 'less-eligibility').*
- *A central Poor Law Commission based at Somerset House in London will administer the new laws. Three commissioners will oversee the system and impose uniformity across the country.*
- *Parishes will be joined together to form Poor Law unions, each with a central workhouse. Each parish will contribute to the funds of the union from a poor rate.*
- *The workhouses will be run by an elected board of guardians, who will employ a full-time master and matron of the workhouse. Rate-payers will elect the guardians.*
- *There will be seven 'classes' of pauper, to be kept separate within the workhouse:*
  - *men infirm due to age or illness*
  - *able-bodied men and youths over fifteen*
  - *boys aged seven to fifteen*
  - *women infirm through age or illness*
  - *able-bodied women and girls over fifteen*
  - *girls aged seven to fifteen*
  - *children under seven.*

SOURCE 11.7 Evidence to the Factories Inquiries Commission of 1833 – a parliamentary investigation into factory working conditions -- given by Robert Blincoe who had worked in factories as a child. He was replying to a question as to whether he would send a child of his to work in a factory

No, I would rather have them transported [sent as a prisoner to Australia] ... there is heat and dust; then there are so many forms of cruelty used upon them; they are liable to have their fingers catched and to suffer other accidents from the machinery, then the hours are so long, that I have seen them tumble down asleep among the straps and machinery.

SOURCE 11.8 Extracts from the rules of a cotton factory published in W. Rashleigh MP, *Stubborn Facts from the Factories by a Manchester Operative,* 1844

Weavers absent at any other time when the engine is working will be charged three-pence per hour each loom for such absence, and workers leaving the room without the consent of the overlooker shall forfeit three pence ...

All shuttles, brushes, oil-cans, wheels, windows etc if broken shall be paid for by the weaver.

If any hand [worker] in the mill is seen talking to another, whistling or singing, he will be fined sixpence.

TALKING POINT

Read through Section E of Chapter 9 (pages 150–156) on reactions to the Poor Law Amendment Act. Make a list of people who would have been unhappy with the Act and explain why they would have been unhappy.

SOURCE 11.9 Summary of the main terms of the 1833 Factory Act, applicable to all textile factories except silk mills

- *No children under nine to work.*
- *Children aged nine to twelve to work no more than eight hours a day.*
- *Young people aged thirteen to eighteen to work no more than twelve hours a day.*
- *Working children to have two hours' schooling a day.*
- *Four government inspectors appointed to check the law is obeyed.*

Note: the law did not apply to adults' hours of work and was applicable only to textile factories. The four inspectors were supposed to inspect every mill in the country.

ACTIVITY

1 What is the artist saying in Source 11.11 about who creates wealth and who receives the benefits?
2 How do the sentiments expressed in Source 11.10 agree with those of O'Brien in Source 11.5 (page 186)?

SOURCE 11.10 Extract from the novel *Sybil* by Benjamin Disraeli, published in 1846

'This is a new reign,' said Egremont, 'perhaps it is a new era ... but say what you like, our Queen rules over the greatest nation that ever existed.'
'Which nation?' asked the young stranger, 'for she reigns over two ... between whom there is no intercourse and no sympathy.'
   'You speak of ... ?' said Egremont, hesitatingly,
   'THE RICH AND THE POOR ... The aristocracy of England form at this moment the most prosperous class that the history of the world can furnish ... it stands before Europe the most gorgeous of existing spectacles ... and it governs the most miserable people on the face of the globe.'

THE TREE OF TAXATION.

(FROM THE NORTHERN LIBERATOR OF AUGUST 13, 1838.)

THE above Engraving will give a visible representation of the MANNER in which the Taxing System works.
   The Community may be divided into FOUR classes. The pockets of the FIRST, or Highest Class, escape from the Roots of the Tax Tree altogether—they get back, in the shape of Windfalls, more than they pay. The pockets of the SECOND Class the Roots touch but lightly. The THIRD, or Labouring Class, is the source of the whole nourishment drawn up by the Tax Tree. The FOURTH Class, the very Poor, it touches but to destroy.

SOURCE 11.11 The Tree of Taxation, from the *Northern Liberator*, 1838. The cartoon shows a visual representation of the tax system

187

BREAD AND CHEESE, OR REVOLUTION: WHAT DID THE CHARTISTS WANT?

CITY COLLEGE
LEARNING RESOURCE CENTRE

C Why was it difficult for people to win reforms?

FOCUS ROUTE

1 Use Sources 11.12–11.15, and the text which follows, to explain why many people in the 1830s and 1840s found attempting to change or improve their way of life difficult.
2 Why might this situation lead to people joining a political protest movement such as Chartism?

ACTIVITY

1 Which phrase in Source 11.12 describes Burke's thoughts on the role of government?
2 In Source 11.13 what exactly is Macaulay saying the government should *not* do?

SOURCE 11.15 Estimated proportion of adult males entitled to vote (England and Wales), 1831 and 1833

1831   366,250   of   3,463,795
(11 per cent)
1833   652,777   of   3,577,538
(18 per cent)

SOURCE 11.12   Edmund Burke, *Thoughts on Security*, 1795

The State ought to confine itself to what regards the State ... namely its magistracy; its revenue; its military force by sea and land ... in a word ... to the public peace, to the public safety, to the public order.

SOURCE 11.13   Thomas Macaulay, *Edinburgh Review*, 1830

Jack-of-all-trades – architect, engineer, schoolmaster, merchant ... a Lady Bountiful in every parish, a Paul Pry in every house, spying, eavesdropping ... spending our money for us, and choosing our opinions for us.

SOURCE 11.14   Extract from the Combination Acts 1799–1800

Combinations of workmen ... for obtaining an advance of wages ... or altering their usual hours of ... working shall be illegal.

The Combination Acts were repealed in 1824, but a wave of strikes led to an amended version, which stated that combinations were legal 'for the sole purpose of consulting upon and determining the rate of wages ... or hours'. 'Molesting' or 'intimidating' or 'obstructing' fellow workers and/or masters would be an offence.

Many things made it difficult to form and express views and opinions. When men tried to form trade unions to make their views heard, these were soon suppressed. The Grand National Consolidated Trades Union (GNCTU) was formed in 1834 as an attempt to form a national trade union. From the start it was plagued with problems of communication in co-ordinating national action, and attempts to organise a general strike never got further than unco-ordinated local strikes. Many employers refused to employ workers unless they promised never to join the GNCTU, or 'locked-out' any who did join.

In February 1834 a group of farm workers from Tolpuddle in Dorset set up a branch of the GNCTU to resist a cut in wages. The men were arrested and charged with swearing an illegal oath (setting up the branch of the union was not against the law, but swearing oaths of allegiance to anyone but the monarch was illegal under an act against naval mutinies passed in 1797). The men were sentenced to transportation for seven years. They became known as the Tolpuddle Martyrs. The judge stated that the harsh sentence was passed to serve as 'an example and warning'. By August 1834 the GNCTU had folded. Trade unions did survive, though small in numbers, among some skilled trades.

Many people could not read or present their views in writing. Before 1870 there was no state or compulsory education. There was also no free education, except for a very small number of children who were able to attend a charity school. Although the fees were usually only a penny or two a week, most working-class people could not afford them. The children who did attend school, did not do so regularly, and often went only if there was no work available. In 1833 the government gave a grant of £20,000 to two church groups, the National Society, which ran Church of England Schools, and the British and Foreign Society, which ran schools for pupils of any Christian religion. The grant was to help the societies to set up more schools. The amount given was about the same as was spent on the royal stables in the same year. By 1839 the grant had increased considerably, but there was still no move towards national compulsory education. Most of those involved in politics, as well as many who were not, did not believe that it was the state's role to provide education.

Communications were poor, so information and ideas spread only slowly. Until 1840 letters were paid for by the person receiving them, not the sender. The cost of sending a letter about 300 miles was 1s. Not until 1840, when

Rowland Hill came up with the idea of a pre-paid 'stamp' to indicate payment, did the postal service become accessible at a cost of 1d regardless of distance.

There were few national newspapers, and even those there were had very small circulations. Even in 1850 *The Times* had a circulation of only about 60,000. In cities such as Leeds there were, however, thriving local papers. The *Leeds Mercury* and the *Leeds Intelligencer* had begun publication in the late eighteenth century and they were joined in 1833 by the *Leeds Times*. The *Intelligencer* had a wide circulation throughout Yorkshire. In 1837 Feargus O'Connor started the *Northern Star* in Leeds and by 1839 it had a circulation of 50,000 a week. Such numbers suggest it could not have been read only by the middle and upper classes.

TALKING POINT

In 1836 the stamp duty on newspapers was reduced from 4d to 1d, making newspapers considerably cheaper. How might this have helped the Chartists?

THE PEOPLE'S CHARTER

- *A vote for every man 21 years of age, of sound mind, and not undergoing punishment for crime*

- *The secret ballot*

- *No property qualification for Members of Parliament*

- *Payment for Members of Parliament*

- *Equal numbers of electors in all constituencies*

- *Annual Parliaments*

D How did the Chartist movement begin?

In 1836 the London Working Men's Association was formed by a group of London artisans and trade unionists as a response to their disappointment at the 1832 Reform Act. One of its aims was to promote the education of the working class through reading and debate. The association's secretary was William Lovett, a cabinet-maker by trade, and the treasurer was Henry Hetherington, a printer and publisher. During 1837 'missionaries' travelled throughout the country establishing over 100 working men's associations. In 1838, 150 more were formed. In Birmingham, the Birmingham Political Union was re-formed, led by Thomas Attwood.

In 1837 the London Working Men's Association presented a petition to Parliament calling for electoral reform. A small number of Radical MPs showed interest, and six MPs and six members of the association redrafted the petition as a parliamentary bill. In May 1838 the draft was published under the title The People's Charter, giving the Chartist movement its name. The aims of the Charter were by no means new. They existed in a plan for parliamentary reform issued by Major Cartwright in 1776, and all of the six points existed in the nine-point programme issued by the Westminster reform committee in 1780.

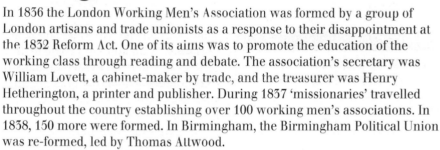

FOCUS ROUTE

1 How swiftly did the Chartist movement develop?
2 Explain the reasons behind each of the six aims (see page 182).
3 Many of the problems facing working people were economic and/or social, so why were the aims of this movement so clearly political?
4 How far does the 1832 Reform Act help you to explain your answer to question 3? (Read Chapter 8 again to help you.)

ACTIVITY

If television and radio had existed in 1839, William Lovett would certainly have been interviewed.

1 Write the script for an interviewer. He would expect to find out precisely what Lovett hopes to achieve from this Charter. He may be quite hostile towards Lovett, accusing the group of having revolutionary aims.
2 Write Lovett's answers to the interviewer's questions, justifying the aims of the Charter, and at the same time ensuring that listeners do not feel the movement is a revolutionary one.

An unemployed handloom weaver living in Bradford.

A worker in an iron foundry living in Birmingham.

A weaver living in Stroud in Gloucestershire.

A coal miner living in the north-east.

An unemployed farm labourer living in Suffolk.

A farm worker living in Kent.

A teacher in a church school living in a Cornish village.

A lawyer living in Manchester.

The owner of a publishing house living in London.

An MP for an industrial town in the Midlands.

ACTIVITY

For each of the people shown above, give reasons why they might have joined a Chartist group, explaining what they might have hoped to gain from the success of Chartism.

There was no one type of person who joined the Chartists. There were many reasons why all kinds of people in all areas of the country wished to improve their lives. Chartism existed in industrial towns in the north and Midlands, in coal-producing areas of Yorkshire and the north-east, in areas of 'old' industry such as the wool-producing areas of Wiltshire and the south-west, and among farm workers in Suffolk.

The skilled artisans in towns, such as the handloom weavers of the north and the nail-makers of the Midlands who had lost their relatively well-paid jobs to new machines, wanted jobs or support for their families, not the new Poor Law and its 'Bastilles'. Those who had worked in the declining industries, such as cloth production in Wiltshire and the south-west, wanted jobs. The workers who had jobs in the new mills and factories were unhappy with the working conditions and their inability to do anything about improving them. They wanted factory legislation that had some teeth and unions that could help them. The workers in the mines and other industries wanted action to prevent the periodic slumps that led to unemployment. Farm workers who had lost jobs through enclosure and the introduction of new machinery on farms wanted help and support without having to go into the workhouse. The farm workers who worked long hours for low wages wanted to be able to form unions without being transported for swearing an oath on joining. Many of the working class wanted the political power they had hoped for in 1832, and felt betrayed by the government.

Although the majority of Chartists were male, there was a substantial number of women involved in the movement. For some, their experience was to lead to more political activity after Chartism had folded. In most of the large towns in Britain, Chartist groups had a women's section. In Birmingham the Charter Association had over 2000 female members and the Hyde (Cheshire) Chartist Society had 200 women members, nearly as many as it had men. The women there were said to be more militant than the men. The National Female Charter Association argued that the 'order of nature is being inverted' with 'the female driven to the factory to labour for her offspring, and her husband unwillingly idle at home, dependent on female labour'. But it was not only the working class who became Chartists. Chartism's ranks included lawyers, landowners, businessmen and MPs, whose reasons for joining were less to do with their own lives than with the wish to improve the lives of others.

For most Chartists the main objective was to improve social and economic conditions for working people. It seemed that the only way to achieve this was through gaining political power, since experience showed that governments elected by the middle and upper classes were not prepared to do much to help the working classes. Recent experiences with the Poor Law Amendment Act of 1834 suggested that governments saw poverty as a crime to be punished, not as a problem to be solved. The treatment of the Tolpuddle Martyrs indicated that if working people were to have any power to change their lives it would have to be through exercising a vote and electing working men as MPs. For other Chartists the achievement of political power was always the aim.

The Chartist movement then was a widespread and diverse one, with groups in large industrial cities, in small market towns and in rural areas. Across the membership was a diversity of motivations. Historians have often identified this as one of the reasons for the failure of the movement.

ACTIVITY

1 From the files on the Chartists below, identify any factors about them that seem to be common to all or most.

Thomas Cooper

- Born in Leicester in 1805.
- His family was poor: he had little proper education.
- Became a shoemaker, and educated himself at home.
- Tried teaching for a time then became a journalist for a local paper.
- Became a Chartist in 1840.
- Produced a book of Chartist songs and hymns.
- Supported the physical force Chartists.
- Found guilty of organising the Plug Plot Riots and spent two years in Stafford Gaol.

Thomas Attwood

- Born in Halesowen in 1783.
- His father was a businessman and banker.
- Believed the Commons needed more people with business experience and knowledge of economics.
- Was one of the leaders of the Birmingham Political Union.
- Was a leading campaigner for parliamentary reform.
- Was elected as one of Birmingham's first two MPs in 1832.
- In 1837 the Birmingham Political Union's demands formed the basis of the People's Charter.
- Presented the first Chartist national petition to the Commons in 1839.

Feargus O'Connor

- Born in Ireland in 1796, a Protestant, and inherited a landed estate at the age of 24.
- Elected MP for Cork in 1832.
- Attempted to replace O'Connell as leader of the Irish radicals in the Commons: the two men became enemies.
- Lost his seat as an MP in 1835.
- Joined the London Working Men's Association in 1836.
- Moved to Leeds and started the newspaper the *Northern Star*, campaigning for parliamentary reform, in 1837.
- Supported violent action in the Chartist movement.
- Imprisoned for publishing seditious libels in 1839.
- Launched his Land Plan in 1845. Subscribers bought small plots of land on which it was intended they would practise self-sufficiency.

James Bronterre O'Brien

- Born in Ireland in 1805.
- Studied law at University of Dublin.
- Moved to London to become a lawyer.
- Joined the Radical Reform Association.
- Joined the London Working Men's Association in 1836.
- Published articles in several radical papers, including Henry Hetherington's *The Poor Man's Guardian* and O'Connor's *Northern Star*.
- Was arrested and imprisoned for making a seditious speech in Manchester, 1840.

Elizabeth Pease

- Born a member of an important Quaker family in 1807.
- Her father was an MP and she was niece of Elizabeth Fry, the prison reform campaigner.
- Led the Women's Abolition of Slavery Society in Darlington in the 1830s.
- Supported the campaign for the 1832 Reform Act.
- Was a supporter of the moral force Chartists.

Henry Hetherington

- Born in London in 1792.
- His father was a tailor.
- Began work as an apprentice printer.
- Set up his own printing press and published several radical newspapers including *The Poor Man's Guardian* (1831–35) which sold 22,000 copies a week by 1833.
- Was imprisoned twice for selling newspapers without paying stamp duty.
- Joined the London Working Men's Association in 1836 and became its treasurer.
- Helped draw up the Charter.

George Julian Harney

- Born in London in 1817.
- His father was a seaman.
- Attended the Boys' Naval School at Greenwich.
- Worked for Henry Hetherington.
- Joined the London Working Men's Association, but found it not radical enough.
- Became a founder of the republican East London Democratic Association in 1837.
- Persuaded the Chartist leaders to call a general strike in 1839.
- Became a journalist and later the editor of the *Northern Star*.

William Lovett

- Born in Penzance in 1800.
- His father was a captain of a fishing vessel.
- Trained as a rope-maker; later went to work in London as a cabinet maker.
- Met the radical publisher Henry Hetherington.
- Joined the National Union of the Working Classes to campaign for universal manhood suffrage.
- Helped form the London Working Men's Association in 1836.
- Arrested and imprisoned for making a speech in Birmingham in 1839, in which he described the Metropolitan Police as a 'bloodthirsty and unconstitutional force'.
- In prison wrote the book *Chartism: A New Organisation of the People*.
- Upset by criticisms from O'Brien, O'Connor and others, he retired from politics in 1842.

2 It is 1847. The Home Secretary, Sir George Grey, has been told of rumours that Chartist activity is about to begin again, following a trade depression and rising unemployment. As a civil servant, you have to prepare a report advising the Home Secretary about whether the Chartists pose a real threat of revolution. You have secret files on Chartists to work from. Prepare a report of not more than 500 words:

a) identifying some of the main Chartists who might be active

b) explaining whether you feel they are 'dangerous to national security', and giving your reasons.

192

BREAD AND CHEESE, OR REVOLUTION: WHAT DID THE CHARTISTS WANT?

 E ## Did the Chartists attempt to achieve their aims through revolution?

Chartist activity is identified as being concentrated in three periods. The first was from 1839–40, following the publication of the Charter and the first Chartist meetings, the second was during 1842, and the third was in 1848 and 1849. Historians have pointed to the often close coincidence between these periods of activity and slumps in trade and industry and times of rising or high unemployment.

Two 'types' of Chartist have often been identified: those who supported peaceful activities to achieve the six points – the so-called 'moral-force' Chartists, and those whose plans included violence to achieve their aims – the so-called 'physical force' Chartists. The activities of both can be seen in all three periods of Chartist activity. Many historians have maintained that this division over aims and tactics was one of the main reasons for the failure of the Chartist movement.

SOURCE 11.16 William Lovett, *Chartism: A New Organisation of the People*, 1840

The People's Charter is calculated to secure to all classes of society their just share of political power, and forming one of the most important steps to all social improvements, we are desirous of seeing the energies of all peacefully concentrated to cause that measure to be enacted as one of the laws of the country.

SOURCE 11.17 An article in the *Northern Star*, September 1838, reporting on the content of a speech made by the Rev Joseph Stephens, a Methodist preacher and radical, in Manchester

Chartism was no political movement, where the main question was getting the ballot . . . universal suffrage was a knife and fork question, after all . . . a bread and butter question . . . and if any man asked him what he meant by universal suffrage, he would answer, that every working man in the land had the right to have a good coat to his back, a comfortable abode . . . a good dinner . . . and as much wages . . . as would afford him the enjoyment of all the blessings of life.

SOURCE 11.18 Feargus O'Connor, speaking in 1838 about the situation if the Chartists remain unarmed

The National Convention will be about as powerful as forty-nine babes in their swaddling clothes.

SOURCE 11.19 George Harney

Universal suffrage there shall be – or our tyrants will find to their cost that we will have universal misery . . . Believe me, there is no argument like the sword, and the musket is unanswerable.

ACTIVITY

Read Sources 11.16–11.19. Into which category – moral force Chartist or physical force Chartist – would you place Lovett, Stephens, O'Connor and Harney?

FOCUS ROUTE

1 From the timeline opposite and Sources 11.20–11.25, identify any times when Chartist activity could be said to threaten revolution.
2 Explain whether the government's responses were a factor in preventing revolution breaking out, or whether there were any other factors at work.

	Chartist activity	Government/Parliament response
1838	Open-air meetings attended by mass crowds. Glasgow c.100,000, Manchester c.30,000, Leeds c.30,000.	
1839 Feb	National Chartist Convention met in London to organise a petition to Parliament. There were splits almost immediately between those who wanted a general strike and those wanting to keep within the law.	
June	The first petition, with 1.25 million signatures, was presented to Parliament by Attwood.	
July		The petition was rejected by 235 votes to 46.
Late summer/ early autumn	The 'physical force' supporters organised a 'sacred month' – a general strike along with protest meetings and demonstrations.	Army increased by 5000 and new police forces were set up in Birmingham, Manchester, Bolton and other centres. General Napier was put in charge. Many Chartist leaders were arrested.
Nov	Newport Rising – an attack on the town by 5000 miners led by John Frost, with the aim of releasing a Chartist leader from jail.	Troops met the Chartists with musket fire – about twenty were killed. Frost was first sentenced to death, but later transported.
1840		By June 1840 around 500 Chartists had been arrested, including virtually all the leaders.
July	The National Charter Association formed – to work through peaceful means for the Charter.	
1842	Many Chartist leaders released from jail. A fund of 1d per week started for a strike fund. National Charter Association had c.45,000 members. A second Convention met. A second petition, said to be over six miles long and with over 3 million signatures, was carried to Parliament in a procession of over 100,000 people.	
May	It was presented to the Commons by Thomas Duncombe and John Fielden.	Parliament rejected the petition by 287 votes to 49.
Summer	The Plug Plots: striking workers removed plugs from factory boilers to prevent the steam engines from working, thus forcing factories to close. The industrial areas of the north were virtually at a standstill. There was rioting in Preston, Stockport, Rochdale, Bolton and Bury, and food shops were looted in Manchester.	Peel's government acted promptly. Troops were rushed to trouble spots using the new railways. Hundreds of Chartist leaders were jailed. Within a week order was restored.
1843	Chartism all but disappeared – membership declined rapidly as trade revived.	
1845	O'Connor formed the Chartist Co-operative Land Society. Chartists bought shares for £1 6s and the money was used to buy plots of land. Four Chartist colonies were set up in Gloucestershire and Oxfordshire. Each family had a small plot of land – two to four acres – and a cottage, and paid £1 5s an acre in annual rent.	
1847	There was a trade depression and unemployment rose. By May 24,000 people were out of work in Manchester.	
July	O'Connor was elected as MP for Nottingham.	
1848 Feb April	Work began on a third petition. The Second National Convention received the finished petition (it only had five points – the demand for the secret ballot was dropped), supposedly signed by 6 million people. The Convention planned to hold a mass demonstration on Kennington Common and a procession to Westminster afterwards. Some speakers urged revolution and the Convention agreed that if the petition was rejected, a National Assembly would be formed to force Parliament to agree.	The march was banned: only ten people were allowed to present the petition.
10 April	The meeting went ahead but there were no massive crowds and no attempt to storm Parliament. O'Connor and supporters delivered the petition in three cabs. On examination the petition was found to contain fewer than 2 million signatures and included signatures from the Queen, Sir Robert Peel and the Duke of Wellington (apparently he had signed sixteen times)!	Troops were stationed at key points in London. Around 150,000 special constables were sworn in. Queen Victoria left London for her home on the Isle of Wight.
1849 June		The third petition was rejected – only fourteen MPs supported it.
1850	O'Connor's Land Plan was in difficulties – poor land, inexperienced farmers and poor organisation led to the failure of the scheme.	

CITY COLLEGE
LEARNING RESOURCE CENTRE

SOURCE 11.20 Extracts from Attwood's speech to the Commons in presenting the Charter, June 1839, reported in *Hansard*

The men who signed the petition were honest and industrious – of sober and unblemished character – men who had always obeyed the laws. Gentlemen enjoying the wealth handed down to them by hereditary descent, whose wants were provided for by the estates to which they succeeded from their forefathers, could have no idea as to the privations suffered by the working men of this country.

Yet at all the meetings which have been held, the persons attending them had confined themselves strictly to the legal pursuit of their constitutional rights, for the purpose of remedying the extreme sufferings which they had endured for so many years. They had seen no attempt to relieve their sufferings... They met with no sympathy or even support from the House... and therefore they felt themselves bound to exercise every legal and constitutional effort... to recover the whole of their constitutional rights... Therefore they had adopted the extreme course of entering upon that separate path, with the view of endeavouring to recover those privileges which they believed to form the original and constitutional right of the Commons of England... [the petition] stated, they only sought a fair day's wages for a fair day's work; and that if they could not give them that, and food and clothing for their families, they said they would put forward every means which the law allowed, to change the representation of that House...

He had never, in the course of his whole life, recommended any means, or inculcated any doctrine except peace, law, order, loyalty and union... He washed his hands of any idea, of any appeal to physical force... he wished for no arms but the will of the people, legally, fairly and constitutionally expressed.

ACTIVITY

1 Explain Attwood's frequent use of the word 'constitutional' in Source 11.20.
2 What impression of Chartists would a listener have got from hearing these extracts in 1839?
3 From the evidence of these extracts, would you label Attwood as a moral force or physical force Chartist?

SOURCE 11.21 Extracts from the *Bolton Chronicle*, 17 August 1839, about Chartism in Bolton

At the latter part of last week... about 1500 special constables were sworn in... The industrious operatives in this town took no share in the disturbances. A number of irritated ill-advised young men were the principal actors. Women with children in their arms, young girls and youths... were mingled amongst the insurgents... Mere boys constituted the chief part of the assemblage in many places...

Monday... at about five o'clock [a.m.]... the Chartists assembled on the New Market Place... and then paraded through the different streets... The town was in a state of greatest alarm; the major part of the shops in the Market Place were closed. To have witnessed the state of public feeling throughout the morning one would have considered a terrible attack to be at hand... No arms of any kind were displayed by the Chartists... An immense influx of persons poured into the town about this period... [at this point the magistrates decided to arrest the three leaders] the meeting then broke up... the suddenness of their dismissal surprised [the crowd] they... exhibited obvious disappointment... At ten o'clock a dead calm prevailed, not the calm of a peaceful borough but the boding stillness of a place preparing against an invader... The special constables patrolled the streets, but their services... were not demanded.

SOURCE 11.22 General Napier, writing in his journal, 1 December 1839

An anonymous letter came, with a Chartists' plan. Poor creatures, their threats of attack are miserable. With half a cartridge and half a pike, with no money, no discipline, no skilful leaders, they would attack men with leaders, money and discipline, well armed, and having sixty rounds a man. Poor men!

ACTIVITY

1 Does Source 11.21 suggest that the Chartists in Bolton were a real threat to law and order?
2 Why did the demonstrations there come to nothing?
3 Did Napier think the Chartist threat was serious (Source 11.22)?
4 Do you think Napier sympathised with the Chartists? Explain your answer.

SOURCE 11.23 The Chartists' attack on Newport, 4 November 1839

ACTIVITY

To what extent does the detail in Source 11.23 justify government fears of Chartists?

SOURCE 11.24 Plots of land bought by O'Connor's Chartist Co-operative Land Society and occupied by Chartists for an annual rent. **A** shows a Chartist cottage in Charterville near Oxford, in the mid-twentieth century, and **B** shows O'Connorville near Watford at the time it was built

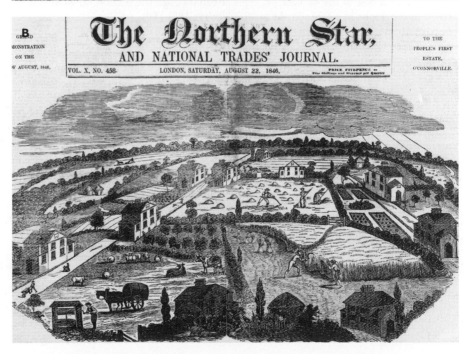

ACTIVITY

Does O'Connor's Land Plan as described in the timeline and seen here in the photographs suggest Chartism was revolutionary?

196

BREAD AND CHEESE, OR REVOLUTION: WHAT DID THE CHARTISTS WANT?

SOURCE 11.25 Thousands of people joined the Chartist demonstration on Kennington Common, London, 10 April 1848. This is one of the very earliest news photographs. In preparation for this meeting, the government called up 8000 soldiers and around 150,000 special constables, and placed cannon on some of London's main bridges

ACTIVITY

Source 11.25 is one of the earliest crowd photographs in existence. As a photograph, is it a more reliable and useful source for historians than a drawing?

ACTIVITY

Read through the section on what was happening in Europe between 1830 and 1849 (pages 183–184).

1 What similarities can you see between the situations in the European countries where there were revolutions in 1848–49, and in England in 1847–49?
2 What differences can you see?
3 How do these similarities and differences help to explain why there was no revolution in England?
4 To what extent does it help to explain why the government feared revolution from the Chartists?

F Why did the Chartists fail in the short term?

It is difficult to argue that Chartism had any short-term success. The failure of the movement to achieve its aims was due to a number of factors, including:

- the cycle of economic changes, which meant that economic conditions did not stay at their worst for too long
- the ways in which they tried to achieve their aims
- the variety of people involved in the movement and divisions amongst the leaders
- the response of the authorities when Chartist activity threatened to become a danger.

SOURCE 11.26 H. Fearn, 'Chartism in Suffolk', in A. Briggs (ed.), *Chartist Studies*, 1969

Taking Suffolk as a typical East Anglian county, the greatest failure of Chartism was its inability to capture the interest and continued allegiance of the agricultural worker ... the spadework in the rural area was done by the townsmen of Ipswich. The Chartist cause in the countryside was hindered by the isolation of the agricultural worker ... His horizon was a limited one, hence his resort to incendiarism in 1844 when angered by unemployment and the threat of the Poor Law 'Bastille' ... Suffolk Chartism can be likened to a boomerang, hurled from Ipswich in 1838, and returning to its place of origin in 1848 ... In Ipswich by 1850, improvements in trade and in the economic condition of the workers lessened the immediate need for the reforms which the Chartists advocated. As in other parts of the country, the intelligent workers looked elsewhere for their Utopia.

ACTIVITY

1 With a partner, brainstorm all the reasons you can think of for the failure of individual outbreaks of Chartism. Write each reason on a card.
2 Decide on a set of headings that describe major reasons for the failure of Chartism – for example, leadership.
   a) Group your cards under the headings.
   b) Feed back each pair's findings to the class. Discuss similarities and differences between headings and groupings.
   c) Using the same headings and groups, put your cards in order of importance as factors in the failure (for example, you may think government response is the most important).
   d) Feed back your priority list to the class. Discuss any differences and similarities.
3 Would some reasons for Chartism's failure be more important in some years than others – for example, more important in 1842 than in 1848?

The Chartist movement was active during the period that the Anti-Corn Law League campaigned for repeal of the Corn Laws. For some time there was rivalry between the two groups.

SOURCE 11.27 Extracts from a Chartist speech made in Leicester in 1840

When we get the Charter we will repeal the Corn Laws and all other bad laws. But if you give up your agitation for the Charter to help the Free Traders, they will not help you get the Charter. Don't be deceived by the middle classes again. You helped them get their votes. But where are the fine promises made to you? Gone to the winds. They said that when they got their votes they would help you get yours. But they and the rotten Whigs never remembered you. All the reforms of the Whigs have been for the middle classes ... 'Cheap bread!' they cry. But they mean 'low wages'. Do not listen to their cant and humbug. Stick to your Charter. You are slaves without your votes!

ACTIVITY

To what is the speaker in Source 11.27 referring when he says, 'Don't be deceived by the middle classes again. You helped them get their votes. But where are the fine promises made to you? Gone to the winds. They said that when they got their votes they would help you get yours.'?

CITY COLLEGE
LEARNING RESOURCE CENTRE

198

BREAD AND CHEESE, OR REVOLUTION: WHAT DID THE CHARTISTS WANT?

TALKING POINTS

1 On page 193 you read that the 1848 petition contained the signatures of Peel, Wellington and the Queen. How did this information affect your view of the Chartists and their organisation?
2 Many people who wanted to sign the petition could not read or write. They copied what somebody else had written. Does this information change your reaction?

ACTIVITY

In explaining the failure of Chartism, it may be helpful to consider the reasons for the success of the Anti-Corn Law League.

1 Copy and complete the following table with brief comments/bullet points. (You may need to consult Chapter 10 on the Anti-Corn Law League to help you.)

	Anti-Corn Law League	Chartists
Class origins of most supporters		
Reasons for joining the group		
Funding/financial organisation		
Number of leaders		
Homogeneity of leadership		
Number of aims		
Tactics used/activities		
Level of agreement on tactics/methods		
Support from MPs		
Tenacity of the campaign		
Reaction of the authorities to the group		

2 Having completed the table, explain the key factors that led to success for the Anti-Corn Law League.
3 If any of the points in the table are *not* among your set of cards from the Activity on page 197, add them now. Then sort the cards in order of priority in terms of reasons for the failure of the Chartists to achieve their aims in the short term.

ACTIVITY

Write an essay in response to one of the following questions.

a) Why did the Chartist movement fail, in the short term, to achieve any of the six points of the Charter?
b) Was it the strengths of the government's response, or the weaknesses of the movement, that led to the failure of Chartism to achieve its aims in the short term?

The six points of the Charter	Date achieved
1 A vote for every man over 21 years of age	1918
2 The secret ballot	1872
3 No property qualification for Members of Parliament	1858
4 Payment for Members of Parliament	1911
5 Equal numbers of electors in all constituencies	1885 redistribution led to more equality
6 Annual Parliaments	Not achieved but from 1911 the maximum time between elections was reduced to five years.

ACTIVITY

Does the list of changes on the right prove that the Chartists were successful in the long term?

In 1840 the writer Thomas Carlyle wrote that the Chartists had forced thinking men to consider the state of the country (see Source 11.28). During the 1840s a series of Acts of Parliament began to address some of the ills that led working people to become Chartists. However, many historians argue that these changes would have come about without the Chartists. They point out that some of the reforms were the result of investigations conducted before 1838. The impact the Chartists had in speeding up change is difficult to assess since few politicians of the 1840s would have publicly declared that they had been influenced, let alone pressured, by the Chartists into taking action. The historian Asa Briggs has even argued that Chartism delayed reform because it led to moderates siding with the government and feeling unable to put forward reform for fear of being seen as revolutionaries.

SOURCE 11.28 T. Carlyle, *Chartism*, 1840

The matter of Chartism is weighty, deep rooted, far extending; it did not begin yesterday; it will by no means end this day or tomorrow. Reform Ministry, constabulary rural police, new levy of soldiers, grants of money to Birmingham . . . all this will only put down the 'chimera' of Chartism . . . The melancholy fact remains, that this thing known at present by the name Chartism does exist, has existed; and, either put down, into secret treason, with rusty pistols, vitriol-bottle and match-box, or openly brandishing pike and torch . . . is like to exist till quite other methods have been tried with it . . . What will condemnation and banishment to BOTANY BAY do for it? . . . There are so many symptoms on the surface; you abolish the symptom to no purpose if the disease is left untouched . . . Delirious Chartism will not have raged entirely to no purpose . . . if it have forced all thinking men of the community to think of this vital matter, too apt to be overlooked otherwise.

SOURCE 11.29 E. Halévy, *Victorian Years 1841–95*, 1951

Nothing more was heard in England now of simultaneous meetings, conventions, national petitions, and general strikes. Chartism, as it receded into the past, became an heroic legend. The veteran Chartist no longer inspired loathing or terror as an agitator or accomplice of the revolutionaries of Paris and the Irish assassins. He was recognised as a genuine product of British civilisation, a man, brave, patient, and tenacious, who could suffer for an ideal, whose nobility was admitted when there was no prospect of its speedy realisation, a man who had been dismissed by his employer for his beliefs or gone to prison for them . . . But he played a distinctive part in the national life, preaching an extension of the franchise, running cooperative societies, working for the cause of popular education and contributing to the periodicals written for the instruction of the masses. Nor did he despair of seeing England one day reach the Chartist goal, though by other paths than those Chartism had foreseen.

ACTIVITY

1 Read Source 11.28. What does 'chimera' mean in this context?
2 Explain what Carlyle means in the phrase, 'There are so many symptoms on the surface; you abolish the symptom to no purpose if the disease is left untouched'.

BOTANY BAY
A penal colony in Australia to which convicts were transported.

ACTIVITY

What does Halévy see as the legacy of Chartism in Source 11.29?

200

BREAD AND CHEESE, OR REVOLUTION: WHAT DID THE CHARTISTS WANT?

Activities of some Chartists after 1848

Bronterre O'Brien

- Concentrated on writing for publications such as *Reynolds Weekly* and the *Glasgow Sentinel*.
- Gave public lectures.
- In 1851 he opened the Electric Institute in Denmark Street, Soho, London, where adult education classes were offered in English, French, science and mathematics.

George Harney

- In March 1848 he travelled to Paris to meet members of the Provisional Government following the revolution there.
- He formed his own newspaper, *The Red Republican*, to promote socialism and internationalism among working people.
- In 1850 he published the first English translation of *The Communist Manifesto*.
- He worked for several newspapers after *The Red Republican* was closed down in 1850.
- In 1863 he emigrated to the United States, but he returned to England after his retirement.

William Lovett

- After retiring from politics he decided to devote the rest of his life to the development of working-class education.
- He formed the National Association for Promoting the Political and Social Improvement of the People. The association provided circulating libraries and employed educational 'missionaries'.
- He continued to run his bookshop, wrote school textbooks and taught evening classes.

Anne Knight

- Formerly active in the Chartist movement, she became concerned about the way women campaigners were treated by some of the male leaders in both the Chartist and the anti-slavery organisations.
- In 1849 at a conference on world peace she met two of Britain's reformers, Henry Brougham and Richard Cobden. She was disappointed by their lack of enthusiasm for women's rights. For the next few months she sent them several letters arguing the case for women's suffrage. She attacked Chartist leaders who argued that the class struggle was more important than the struggle for women's rights.
- In 1850 she demanded that the Chartists should campaign for what she described as 'true universal suffrage'.
- In 1851 she established what is believed to have been the first association for women's suffrage. Its first meeting was held in Sheffield.

ACTIVITY

Does the information about the later careers of Chartists confirm what Halévy (Source 11.29) said about 'veteran' Chartists?

 Review: bread and cheese, or revolution: what did the Chartists want?

It has been said that there never has been any danger of revolution in Britain in the French style of 1830 and 1848 because British workers would spend so much time arguing over whose job it was to hammer the nails into the barricades that the authorities would regain control before the revolution even started. However, others think that the Chartists were capable of starting a revolution.

In studying the Chartist movement we have the inestimable benefit of hindsight. We can look back at the period 1838–50 and suggest that there never was any real threat of revolution. We can stand outside the events and see that the threats were perhaps more imagined than real. However, for the people who were living at the time, the threats may have seemed very real indeed.

201

BREAD AND CHEESE, OR REVOLUTION: WHAT DID THE CHARTISTS WANT?

They only had to look across the Channel to see revolutions happening. The Chartist meetings, the speeches by some of the leaders, the marches and events such as the attack at Newport must have seemed to echo very closely what was happening on the continent. We can look back and see that the actions taken by the government may well have been sufficient to defuse the situation, but at the time there was no guarantee that this was the case; the defusing may have only been temporary. Whether or not we, today, feel that there was a danger or not, many people living at the time of the Chartists did believe that a revolution might be imminent. Why else would Wellington have taken such careful military precautions in 1848?

SOURCE 11.30 E. Halévy, *The Triumph of Reform*, 1923, quoting an article written by a Frenchman in the late 1830s after a visit to England

Before I conclude, I must tell you of an episode which has given me no little amusement ... Feargus O'Connor, a little while ago, speaking at a mass meeting, propounded an infallible method of effecting a revolution ... [it] was to empower the Association to bring fifty republicans from Paris and pay them 5s to 10s a week ... so long as they remained in England ... I should advise you to settle in every large town where we wish to establish the movement ... and I promise you that once these good fellows are here, things will begin to look up.

KEY POINTS FROM CHAPTER 11

Bread and cheese, or revolution: what did the Chartists want?

1 In the 1830s and 1840s a number of social, economic and political issues made a great many people discontented with society and their place in it. Although the working class made up a large proportion of these people, the discontent was not confined only to working people.

2 The majority of people, especially the working class, had few ways of making their voice heard by government.

3 The Chartist movement emerged from the London Working Men's Association, which drew up the Charter with its six points – the aims of the movement.

4 The membership of the movement represented a diverse range of people with as diverse a range of reasons for being Chartists.

5 From the beginning there was division and disunity among both rank-and-file and leaders over how to go about achieving their aims, and whether physical force was an option if moral persuasion did not work.

6 Chartist activity fell into three periods, 1839–40, 1843 and 1848–49, often coinciding with trade depressions and high unemployment.

7 Chartism failed to achieve any of its aims in the short term due to a combination of factors, including a number of inherent weaknesses in the movement.

8 There was a genuine fear of revolution, even if in hindsight that possibility seems very unlikely.

9 The long-term impact of Chartism is difficult to assess in tangible ways. The political and organisational experience gained by some Chartists was used in their later life. Both at the time, and since, it has been argued that Chartism raised the awareness of many in power, perhaps for the first time, of the reasons for the discontent of the working classes.

10 All but one of the six points of the Charter were achieved within 70 years of the last Chartist petition in 1848.

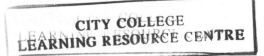
CITY COLLEGE
LEARNING RESOURCE CENTRE

Section 1 Review: How close did Britain come to revolution 1783–1851?

There were no guillotines in Britain. No kings or nobles were executed. The country was not taken over by an unelected government. Why, when continental Europe was riven by a series of revolutions during the period 1783–1851, was there no revolution in Britain?

ACTIVITY

1 Make a large copy of the table below and fill in the details in each column. Row 1815–32 has been started as an example. You will have more than one potential 'revolutionary group' in each period.
2 Compare the answers in the final column. When was Britain closest to revolution and how close did it come?
3 Why was there no revolution? Look at each of the issues shown in Chart A and brainstorm the main points you would make in answer to each question.

| | Which groups were demanding major changes? | What were their aims? | What support did they have from the: | | | What actions did they take? | What was the government response? | What did the group(s) achieve? | How revolutionary was this group? (Use the 'revolutionary Richter scale' on pages 10–11.) |
			working class	middle class	upper class				
1794–1815									
1815–32	1830 Swing rioters	Get rid of new machinery on farms and save jobs	Some from farm labourers in southern England	None	None	Wrote threatening letters, burnt hayricks, attacked landowners	Arrested leaders, transported many, hanged a few	No changes – new machines continued in use and jobs were lost	???
1832–51									

■ A Why was there no revolution in Britain?

Was there a situation in Britain that created the potential for revolution?

Were there sufficient leaders and rank-and-file revolutionaries?

Was the lack of revolution the result of actions taken by governments?

Were economic conditions sufficiently good for most of the time to prevent revolution?

SOURCE 1   J. W. Derry, *Reaction and Reform*, 1970

Was there a real danger of revolution after 1815? The upper classes undoubtedly thought so. Tales of machine breaking in the Midlands or dark rumours of workmen drilling para-military formations or supplying themselves with firearms or pikes, together with the extravagant language of many of the agitators, reminded the aristocrats and the prosperous bourgeoisie of the Jacobins. But the degree of organisation among the working men was exaggerated. Many of the more extreme 'revolutionaries' were ill-educated men, with only the vaguest notions of what the successful overthrow of established authority would mean. For many of the more desperate spirits in Nottingham it was associated with free beer and jolly trips down the Trent. The image in the minds of the organisers of the unrest was an unsophisticated return to the legendary good old days. There was no clear plan whereby the new republic was to be inaugurated. The spasmodic outbreak of disturbances, the ease with which they were suppressed and the pathetic futility which dogged their course indicates that though there was hardship, suffering, anger and frustration in abundance, there was little foresight and less genuine consciousness. Dreams of direct action, of dramatic deed which would restore vanished happiness, appealed to men to whom the more solemn arguments in favour of constitutional reform seemed cold and distant. Only as the more violent became discredited by the fury of their schemes and the naïve innocence which betrayed them into the traps laid by plausible agents provocateurs did parliamentary reform become the watchword of the working classes.

SOURCE 2   H. T. Dickinson, *British radicalism and the French revolution 1789–1815*, 1988

The radical movement in Britain had expanded in remarkable fashion in the early 1790s, but it had been subjected to enormous pressures which had at first stifled its growth and then severely suppressed its activities. Government repression and a wave of loyalist and patriotic sentiment, which gathered force as Britain engaged in a long and bitter armed struggle with revolutionary France, halted the rapid growth of radical societies. The militant radicals were driven underground into clandestine revolutionary conspiracies, but many of their groups were penetrated by government agents and their most serious plots were discovered. The activities of the revolutionaries never resulted in detailed plans, a co-ordinated strategy, mass support or an actual rising outside Ireland . . .

Political reform did not again become a subject for serious parliamentary debate, or a cause with widespread public support for at least a decade, but the desire for greater liberty never entirely disappeared as a topic of discussion. Small groups of reformers continued to operate in many towns, including London, Norwich, Leeds and Newcastle.

SOURCE 3   N. Gash, *Aristocracy and the People: Britain 1815–1865*, 1987

The question is sometimes asked whether Britain came close to revolution in these years – in 1817 for instance, or 1831–32, or 1842. To decide how near something came to happening that in the event did not is a difficult and perhaps unrewarding task. But there are certain general considerations which deserve to be taken into account. In an organised state such as Britain was during this period there are probably three preconditions for revolution. First, the existence of an active revolutionary group ready to take over power; second, a loss of nerves on the part of the traditional governing classes; and third, the weakness or failure of the instruments for enforcing order. Unless at least two of these preconditions are present, it is not easy for revolutions to take place. Of the first there is no real sign either among the radical reformers of 1816–22 or those of 1831–32 or the Chartist leaders of 1838–42. In each case they wanted reform, not revolution. Eccentric fanatics like the Spenceans or the Cato Street conspirators are irrelevant in this context. Of the second there is even less indication. Whatever faults the governing classes of Britain had in this period, cowardice was not one. It never

204

SECTION I REVIEW: HOW CLOSE DID BRITAIN COME TO REVOLUTION 1783–1851?

occurred to either their friends or opponents that their nerve would give way. The criticism has usually been that they reacted too energetically to disorder. This may be so. If there was one lesson they had learnt from the French Revolution it was that weakness by authority at the start of civil disturbance was the surest means of making it more dangerous.

The third condition raises the question of the discipline in the British army at this time. Up to 1829 the professional soldiers were the main and often the only protection against serious disorder both in the metropolis and in the provinces. Even in London as late as the Chartist demonstration of 1848, they acted as a reserve force at the government's disposal. Had the army not remained loyal and disciplined, their political rulers would have been in grave difficulty... There are no grounds for thinking that at any point the instruments in the hands of government for internal security purposes were other than reliable. That being so, the chance of any subversive movement succeeding by sheer force hardly existed...

At no time, it seems reasonable to conclude, was revolution physically possible in Britain between 1815 and 1848. It is doubtful whether it was even envisaged by a substantial part of the population. When the revolution occurred on the other side of the Channel in 1830 and 1848, the characteristic reaction of the complacent British public was to regard it as an attempt by benighted foreigners to catch up with British constitutional progress or as a horrid example of what happened in less fortunate countries. There was no parallel with the brittle authoritarian regimes abroad. British society was too interlocked, public opinion too influenced by moral and religious considerations, the governing classes too sensible and experienced, the government itself too resolute and efficient, for Britain to suffer the fate of the continental autocracies.

SOURCE 4 A. Briggs, *The Age of Improvement*, 1959

There was, in fact, little real sign that Britain was going the way of France twenty-five years earlier, although many frightened contemporaries thought so. While there was a highly distinctive mood of anger, alarm and strain, in many ways the general pattern of working-class agitation between 1815 and 1820 was typical of the whole pattern of subsequent agitation, at least until the rise of organised trade unions and political parties. The place of London in the strategy of agitation was changing. Although its COMMON COUNCIL was in the vanguard of reform in 1816, as in the eighteenth century, and carried an address to the Prince Regent designed 'to represent our national sufferings and grievances, and... to suggest the measures... indispensably necessary for the safety, the quiet and the prosperity of the Realm', the provinces supplied most of the energy behind the new campaigns. The main spur to political activity was unemployment; in times of full employment, such as 1818, there was a marked decline in political pressure and a keener concentration on industrial action – strikes for higher wages, battles not with 'government' or 'authority' but with employers.

COMMON COUNCIL
A group which formed part of the local government in London.

ACTIVITY

1 Summarise briefly the view of each historian quoted in Sources 1–4 on whether Britain was close to revolution between 1783 and 1851, and if so when.
2 What are the main differences in opinion?
3 Which historian do you agree with most closely, and why?

TALKING POINTS

1 You may well feel that there had been a revolution in Britain during this period, even if it was not a violent, political revolution. Revolutions come in more than one size and shape. It cannot be denied that there had been an industrial revolution during this period. Had there been any other sort also? In what ways, and why, was Britain different in 1851 from 1783?
2 If you had been born in 1780 and lived to visit the Great Exhibition, how would you look back on your lifetime? Would you be likely to think there had been a revolution in British life?

How successful was British foreign policy 1783–1851?

This section deals with British foreign policy between 1783 and 1851. During that period Britain was involved in a long war with France, and went on to play a central role in the reorganisation of Europe. This section deals with the foreign policies of the three principal foreign secretaries of the period: Castlereagh, Canning and Palmerston. You will look at the problems of foreign policy that they each had to face, the solutions that they each arrived at, and the extent to which they all followed a basic set of principles for foreign policy.

■ **A   The principles of British foreign policy passed on by William Pitt to his successors until 1914**

1 Protect British colonial interests

2 Defend British trade and commercial interests

3 Preserve the balance of power in Europe

4 Defend Britain and its interests by deploying its naval strength

5 Keep the war 'over there' — that is, in continental Europe. If war breaks out, Britain should try to fight by supporting its allies with its navy, and its financial and industrial wealth

BALANCE OF POWER

Preserving the balance of power was a diplomatic device to ensure that one country did not become so powerful as to endanger others. This was practised after 1815 when Britain particularly used it to protect its economic and political interests.

ACTIVITY

Before studying a topic in detail, it is important to have an outline understanding of the events and issues involved – a sense of the 'big picture'. The Diplomacy Game will help you to build up this outline.

You are William Castlington, Britain's Foreign Secretary. Britain's greatness is in your hands! Your task is to work through the decisions on page 206, making the choices that you think will do most to achieve Britain's objectives – you can see these objectives in Chart A. You can find out what choices were really made on page 261.

ACTIVITY

1 It is 1793. The King of France has been executed in the midst of the French Revolution. Will you:

   A declare war on France because it is important to defend monarchy from attacks

   B delay making a decision on war until you learn more about the new government's plans and attitudes towards Britain

   C rule out war against France because Britain needs to maintain its trading links with France?

2 It is 1808. Napoleon has invaded Spain and Portugal to prevent them trading with Britain. Will you:

   A wait to see how successful the Spanish guerrilla warfare is against Napoleon

   B send troops to drive Napoleon out of Spain and Portugal

   C allow Napoleon to waste his money – there are plenty of other countries that Britain can trade with?

3 It is 1815. The Duke of Wellington and Marshal Blücher have beaten Napoleon at the Battle of Waterloo. Will you:

   A withdraw from all negotiations about the future of Europe now that the danger from France is over

   B lead the demand for France to be punished severely. Britain is the most powerful country so you can dictate terms to the rest of Europe

   C join the negotiations but argue that the treaty should be moderate and France should not be punished too harshly?

4 It is 1825. Spain's colonies in South America have declared themselves independent. Will you:

   A recognise them as independent because they will be good trading partners

   B ignore the issue as beneath the dignity of the world's strongest country

   C support Spain in retaking control of its colonies – you need to support other monarchies or revolution will spread?

5 It is 1826. The Greeks have rebelled against the Turkish empire. They want to set up their own country but this will weaken Turkey, which is an important buffer against Russian expansion, especially in the direction of India. Will you:

   A send help to the Greeks – public opinion is in favour of the Greeks after news of Turkish atrocities

   B negotiate a settlement in order to stop Russia intervening and winning control over the area

   C ignore these events – intervention will be very expensive and it may antagonise Russia?

6 It is 1839. The Emperor of China has pleaded with Britain to stop selling opium to his people and has seized British-owned opium in Canton. Will you:

   A send an apology to China and help put a stop to this immoral trade

   B send a gunboat (or more) to threaten the Emperor – British trade must be protected and the merchants are complaining to the government that their trading rights have been violated

   C send a gunboat, win back the opium (as B) but also use the opportunity to gain territory in the region that will make trading easier?

7 It is 1850. There has been a revolt in Hungary against the Austrian Empire. You condemned Austrian brutality but sent no help to the Hungarians because British interests were not affected. Now the Austrian general who suppressed the revolt has been 'roughed up' while visiting a London brewery. Will you:

   A send an apology to Austria and punish those who attacked the general

   B send an apology but comment that the general was lucky to get off so lightly

   C hold a meeting with the Hungarian rebel leader to show your support for the rebels?

8 It is 1850. The house of a British citizen has been burned down during a riot in Athens. He has made a ludicrously high claim for compensation, which the Greek government has turned down. Will you:

   A send a gunboat to threaten the Greeks – all British people should be defended

   B tell the man to make a more reasonable claim and then you will negotiate on his behalf

   C tell the man he's on his own – after all, he was born in Gibraltar, is of Portuguese-Jewish descent and has not lived in Britain?

Conclusion

The Diplomacy Game will have been successful if you can suggest answers to the following questions:

1 What were the main kinds of issues that faced British Foreign Secretaries?

2 What have you learned about Britain's priorities?

3 What questions do you now want to ask about foreign affairs in this period?

1783	Loss of American colonies
1789	French Revolution
1793	France declares war on Britain
1797	Naval mutinies
1798	Irish Rebellion
1801	Act of Union
	Pitt's resignation
1802	Peace of Amiens
1803	Napoleon plans invasion of England
1804	Pitt returns as Prime Minister
1805	Battles of Trafalgar and Austerlitz
1812	Britain at war with United States
	Napoleon's Russian campaign
1815	Battle of Waterloo
	Vienna Settlement ends Napoleonic War
	Quadruple Alliance
	Holy Alliance
1818	Congress of Aix-la-Chapelle
1820	Revolutions in Spain, Portugal, Naples and Piedmont
	Congress of Troppau
1821	Congress of Laibach
	Greek Revolt
1822	Congress of Verona
	Castlereagh's suicide
	George Canning returns as Foreign Secretary
1830	Greek independence recognised
	Revolutions in France, Poland, Belgium, Germany, Italy, Portugal
	Louis Philippe becomes King of France
1833	Treaty of Unkiar Skelessi
	British intervention in Portugal
1834	British–French intervention in Spain
1839	Belgian independence
	Opium War
1841	Straits Convention
1846	Spanish marriage crisis
1848	Revolutions in France, Austria, Germany and Italy
	Louis Napoleon Bonaparte becomes President of French Republic
1850	Don Pacifico Affair
1851	Louis Napoleon Bonaparte becomes Emperor Napoleon III

■ C   Some British Foreign Secretaries, 1783–1852

Duke of Leeds	1783–1791
Lord Grenville	1791–1801
Robert Jenkinson (later Lord Hawkesbury and then Earl of Liverpool)	1801–1804
George Canning	1807–1809
Marquess Wellesley	1809–1812
Viscount Castlereagh	1812–1822
George Canning	1822–1827
Earl of Aberdeen	1828–1830
Viscount Palmerston	1830–1834
Duke of Wellington	1834–1835
Viscount Palmerston	1835–1841
Earl of Aberdeen	1841–1846
Viscount Palmerston	1846–1852

12

Why was Britain successful in the French Wars 1793–1815?

CHAPTER OVERVIEW

FOCUS ROUTE

As you work through this and later sections summarise the impact of the major factors for Britain's success, using a table like the one below. Collating your findings on a spreadsheet or in a word processing program is an efficient way of approaching this exercise.

Factor	Impact of this factor
Naval power	
Industrial and economic strength	
Alliances	
Individual leadership	
Weaknesses and mistakes of opponents	
Others?	

Wherever we travel, there are reminders of the long wars with France. Street names, pubs, statues, and historic monuments remind us of these events. In literature, the adventures of Bernard Cornwell's Sharpe, who fought in the British army during the French Wars, and C. S. Forester's Hornblower of the British navy excite popular interest. War game societies claim that the Napoleonic era grips the imagination more than any other. However, what is interesting today was truly frightening at the time. During the 22 years of the war there were numerous occasions when well-informed, intelligent people expected Britain to be invaded and defeated. In 1803, for example, instructions were issued on how to evacuate people from towns, and local defence groups were set up to harry the invading army.

In the end, after the Battle of Waterloo, itself a 'close-run thing', Britain was successful. This chapter investigates the reasons for that success. Your task will be to identify the part each factor played and how they came together to defeat France.

A Why did Britain go to war with France in 1793? (pp. 209–211)

B What were Britain's war strategies? (pp. 212–214)

C Why did Ireland pose a problem during the Revolutionary War? (p. 215)

D What was Britain's contribution to the defeat of Napoleon? (pp. 216–222)

E Review: why was Britain successful in the French Wars 1793–1815? (pp. 223–225)

ACTIVITY

The diagram on the right shows you the major reasons for Britain's success in the French Wars. Although you have not yet studied this topic, see how much you can work out or know already. This will help to provide a framework for the detail you are about to study.

1 How would each of these factors contribute to defeating France?
2 What do you already know about each of the topics in relation to the French Wars?
3 Which of these factors do you think was likely to be the most important in Britain's success?
4 If you were asked to write an essay answering the question at the centre of the diagram, how would you structure the essay? Think about what each paragraph might discuss and what kind of conclusion you would reach.

A Why did Britain go to war with France in 1793?

'Unquestionably there never was a time in the history of this country when, from the situation in Europe, we might more reasonably expect fifteen years of peace than at the present moment.' So said the Prime Minister, William Pitt, in February 1792. One year later Britain was at war with France. This was not a case of a politician making a hopeless misjudgement. Between 1792 and 1793 events moved rapidly and attitudes changed. In 1792 there was guarded support for the French Revolution among many people in Britain. Amongst radicals and reformers there was great enthusiasm. However, attitudes began to change when *émigré* nobles sought asylum in Britain. This led to the French government accusing Britain of 'counter-revolutionary' activity. The Terror also produced shock waves in Britain. By 1792 patriotic 'Church and King' demonstrations had broken out as anti-French feeling increased. Then came the execution of Louis XVI in January 1793, followed by the Edict of Fraternity in which the French government encouraged the peoples of Europe to rise up against their governments.

However, it was not the revolution or the execution of the King that led the British government into war. Diplomatic negotiations went on to avoid war but then in November 1792 the French occupied the River Scheldt, gaining control of the Low Countries (Belgium). This was a violation of British trading interests because much of Britain's continental trade passed through this area. It was also a threat to Britain's security because it gave France control over the lengthy coastline facing Britain. Britain had hitherto avoided war (even though Prussia and Austria had been fighting France for several months), but now the French Ambassador was dismissed from London. On 1 February 1793 France declared war on Britain.

Britain was not prepared for war. Only a year before Pitt had made defence cuts. The army and even the navy, the linchpin of British defence, were undermanned. There was no Commander-in-Chief of the army until the Duke of York (of nursery rhyme fame) was appointed in 1795. Nevertheless, Pitt thought the war would be short, and in the meantime he relied on other powers to 'keep the war in Europe' whilst deploying the British navy elsewhere defending British interests.

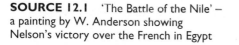

SOURCE 12.1 'The Battle of the Nile' – a painting by W. Anderson showing Nelson's victory over the French in Egypt

CITY COLLEGE
LEARNING RESOURCE SERVICE

LEARNING RESOURCE CENTRE

WHY WAS BRITAIN SUCCESSFUL IN THE FRENCH WARS 1793–1815?

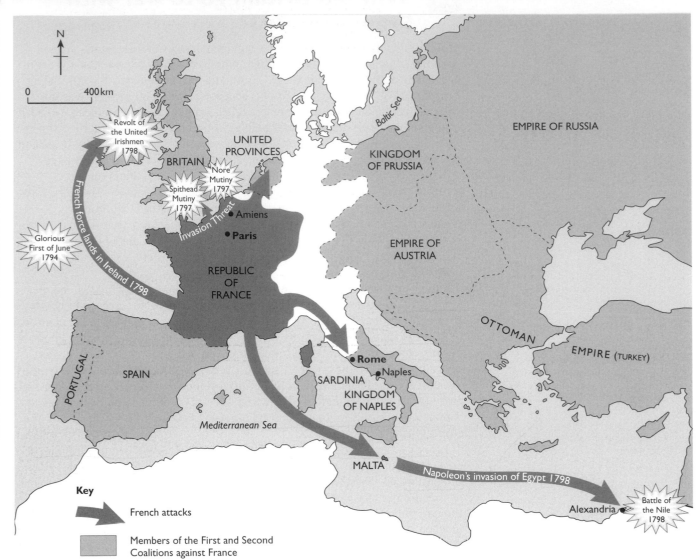

Key

French attacks

Members of the First and Second Coalitions against France

Map labels:

N

0   400km

Revolt of the United Irishmen 1798

BRITAIN

UNITED PROVINCES

Nore Mutiny 1797

Spithead Mutiny 1797

French force lands in Ireland 1798

Glorious First of June 1794

Invasion Threat

Amiens

Paris

REPUBLIC OF FRANCE

Baltic Sea

EMPIRE OF RUSSIA

KINGDOM OF PRUSSIA

EMPIRE OF AUSTRIA

PORTUGAL

SPAIN

Mediterranean Sea

SARDINIA

Rome

Naples

KINGDOM OF NAPLES

OTTOMAN EMPIRE (TURKEY)

MALTA

Napoleon's invasion of Egypt 1798

Alexandria

Battle of the Nile 1798

ACTIVITY

1 Draw a timeline to identify:
   a) British successes (mark these in red)
   b) British failures (mark these in blue)
   c) crisis points (mark these in black).
2 Look at Chart 12A and the text on page 209. Which of Britain's interests were most relevant to the outbreak of war in 1793?
3 Why do you think Britain did not go to war over the execution of Louis XVI?

■ 12B   The Revolutionary War (1793–1802) at a glance

1793	The First Coalition (Britain, Holland, Prussia, Spain, Austria, Sardinia)
	Duke of York invades Netherlands, only to be driven back to England
	British force sent to Toulon, but fails
1794	'The Glorious First of June' – Lord Howe sent to intercept French grain ships coming from America, in mid-Atlantic. French routed but grain ships escape
	Naval clashes in West Indies
	French armies advance into the Rhine
1795	United Provinces, Spain and Prussia break from Coalition
	Attacks on French sugar islands in West Indies
	Britain captures Cape of Good Hope, part of Dutch Empire, as a valuable port for British ships trading with India
1796	Sardinia defeated
1797	Austria defeated. Britain stands alone
	British navy defeats Spain at Cape St Vincent
	Naval mutinies at Spithead and the Nore
	British defeats Dutch at Camperdown
1798	France seizes Malta
	Egyptian Campaign: French threaten trade with India
	Battle of Aboukir Bay: French fleet sunk. Napoleon stranded in Egypt
	Revolt of the United Irishmen
1799	The Second Coalition (Britain, Russia, Austria, Naples, Turkey)
	Bonaparte's Syrian Campaign: defeated at Acre. Napoleon retreats (May), and returns to Europe (October)
1800	Austrians defeated
	Tsar Paul forms league of Armed Neutrality (Russia, Prussia, Sweden, Denmark) to prevent Britain's use of the Baltic
1801	Pitt resigns (January) over George III's refusal to grant Catholic Emancipation
	Nelson defeats Danes at Battle of Copenhagen
1802	Peace: Treaty of Amiens

SOURCE 12.2   'The Battle of Marengo', 1800 – a painting by Lejeune showing Napoleon defeating the Austrian army in northern Italy

FOCUS ROUTE

Add evidence to your copy of the table on page 208.

ACTIVITY

Make notes to answer the following questions:

1 What strategies did Pitt adopt at the outbreak of war?
2 What role did the navy play in the war?
3 Why was 1797 a year of crisis?
4 Why was Britain's status as the 'first industrial power' so important in the war effort?

B What were Britain's war strategies?

Pitt is not regarded universally as a good war-time Prime Minister. He went to war unprepared; he failed to see that European allies had strategies different from how he perceived them; he believed the war would not last long; he failed to adapt to the changing war situation; he underestimated France's military capability and the depth of French patriotism; he was indecisive and often dithered when confronted by conflicting advice. However, despite that long list of criticisms, Pitt did deploy certain strategies from the start that he thought would bring the war to an early conclusion.

Pitt wished to avoid sending a huge army over to the Continent, so he subsidised Britain's allies to the tune of £9 million between 1793 and 1802. This sum bought arms and mercenaries and was used to support anti-revolutionary groups in France. A fleet and troops were sent to the important naval base of Toulon where there was a royalist rebellion. However, the young Napoleon Bonaparte drove the British off in 1795.

■ 12C The role of the navy

- Most importantly, it defended Britain from French invasion.
- It transported British troops and supplies to the Continent.

- It blockaded the French coast so that it was difficult for France to import necessary goods.
- It attacked the French coast (e.g. Toulon, an important French port in an area populated by counter-revolutionaries).

- It maintained British trade and colonial interests (e.g. the West Indies and India).
- It won valuable victories in the West Indies, at Cape St Vincent, Camperdown, and Copenhagen, which enabled Britain to gain commercial or strategic territory. Victory at Aboukir Bay (the Battle of the Nile) was important as Egypt was regarded as the gateway to India; the capture of Malta in 1800 had strategic value.

NAVAL MUTINIES, 1797

1797 was a year of crisis. The First Coalition was shattered and Britain stood alone. There was the threat of rebellion in Ireland on which France could capitalise. In Britain there was mounting discontent due to Pitt's repressive policies and the prospect of a poor harvest. The government had financial problems due to the cost of the war. Pitt was feeling the strain, made worse by an unhappy love affair and his own debts. Only naval supremacy stood between Britain and the enemy. Then the navy mutinied.

In April the Channel Fleet was ordered out of Spithead, but it refused. The sailors had many grievances. Food was atrocious: salt meat was old and as hard as leather; cheese and ship's biscuits were often crawling with worms. Water was slimy and undrinkable. Many sailors were serving because they had been press-ganged. Pay was often in arrears. Medical attention was very bad, sometimes at the hands of drunken surgeons; badly wounded men were sometimes thrown overboard alive. Flogging was carried out for minor offences such as coming down the rigging too slowly; crew men died when a hundred lashes instead of the normal twelve were administered by sadistic officers. The mutineers demanded: better pay, provisions and medical services; payment for the wounded; opportunities for leave; the dismissal of brutal officers.

Faced with the mutiny spreading, Pitt agreed to some of their demands. However, the fleet at the Nore refused to end their mutiny because they were not guaranteed a King's Pardon, and because unpopular officers had not been removed. The Admiralty made a stand. Twenty-nine ringleaders were hanged. Many mutineers were imprisoned or flogged. The main leader, Richard Parker, was hanged from the yardarm of his ship. Throughout the mutiny the men had professed their loyalty to the Crown, though they had used an effigy of Pitt for shooting practice. Three months later, with Admiral Duncan in command, they routed the Dutch fleet at Camperdown, and Britain was safe from invasion.

SOURCE 12.3   'A Sailor's Yarn' – a cartoon by George Cruikshank

The Sailor's description of a Chase & Capture.

ACTIVITY

What do you think the cartoonist in Source 12.3 is telling us about life in the navy?

ACTIVITY

Divide into two groups.

- Group A. You are ringleaders of the mutiny at Spithead. You are deeply concerned about conditions on board ship, but you are also aware of the consequences of your actions. Write a speech to be delivered to your fellow mutineers and perform it in front of the class who will act as the other mutineers. At the end they can shout out questions and express their feelings, for or against.
- Group B. Prepare a government reply in Parliament condemning the mutiny and its possible consequences.

LEARNING RESOURCE CENTRE

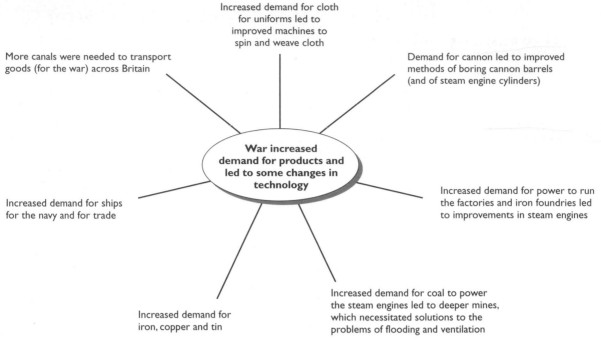

Increased demand for cloth for uniforms led to improved machines to spin and weave cloth

More canals were needed to transport goods (for the war) across Britain

Demand for cannon led to improved methods of boring cannon barrels (and of steam engine cylinders)

War increased demand for products and led to some changes in technology

Increased demand for ships for the navy and for trade

Increased demand for power to run the factories and iron foundries led to improvements in steam engines

Increased demand for iron, copper and tin

Increased demand for coal to power the steam engines led to deeper mines, which necessitated solutions to the problems of flooding and ventilation

Sunderland
Ship building
Coal mining

Textiles – wool
Leeds
Coal mining
Coal mining
Hull
Ship building

Ship building
Liverpool ● Manchester
Textiles – cotton
● Sheffield

Coal mining
Iron ● Birmingham

Coal mining
Cardiff
Ship building
Iron
● Bristol
Textiles – wool

London
Ship building

Ship building
Southampton

Tin, copper, China clay
Plymouth
Ship building

0   100 km

SOURCE 12.4   Areas of industrial development that benefited from the French Wars

C Why did Ireland pose a problem during the Revolutionary War?

FOCUS ROUTE

Add evidence to your copy of the table on page 208.

ACTIVITY

1 What were the objectives of Wolfe Tone and the Society of United Irishmen?
2 How successful was the Irish rebellion of 1798?
3 Why did Pitt resign?

SOURCE 12.5 Wolfe Tone

SOURCE 12.6 The Battle of Vinegar Hill

There had been rumblings of rebellion in Ireland for some time. The vast majority of the population was Catholic, but they were under the subjugation of the minority Protestants, backed by military force. Catholics couldn't run schools, hold commissions in the army or navy, vote or sit in Parliament. Inspired by the French Revolution, a Belfast lawyer, Wolfe Tone, founded the Society of United Irishmen in 1791, made up of Catholics and Protestants. Its objective was to free Ireland from Britain, to bring about religious equality and to establish democratic government. Help was sought from the French who sent an invasion force of 35 ships and thousands of men to Bantry Bay in December 1796. Wolfe Tone arrived in a French uniform and remarked that the shore seemed so close he could toss a biscuit onto it. But not for the first time the weather came to Britain's aid. Violent storms made it impossible for them to land, and the invasion was abandoned.

This incident proved to the British government how serious a threat there could be from an Irish–French alliance. In 1797 another French expedition was fitted out in Holland but was frustrated by Duncan's blockade and the eventual defeat of the Dutch. In the meantime the army used brute force to track down rebels. An eyewitness described how people were 'stripped naked, tied to a triangle and their flesh cut without mercy. And though some stood the torture to the last gasp sooner than become informers, others did not, and one single informer in the town was enough to destroy all the United Irishmen in it'.

Brutal tortures were successful in extracting information. Thousands of arrests were made and stashes of arms discovered. Whilst they weakened the United Irishmen's cause, they also inflamed anger and resentment. In 1798 another rebellion broke out in Wexford, but was crushed at Vinegar Hill. It spread to other parts of the country such as Dublin and Ulster, but they too were defeated. A small French force did land in County Mayo, but it was too late and surrendered. Wolfe Tone eventually arrived off the northern Irish coast with a French invasion fleet, but was beaten by the superior British navy. Tone was brought to Dublin for trial but committed suicide in his cell.

Pitt was now even more conscious of the danger from Ireland. His solution was the Act of Union (1800), which joined the Irish and British Parliaments together in London. As part of the deal, Pitt agreed concessions to Catholics, including Catholic Emancipation, which would allow Catholics to sit in Parliament. However, George III was vehemently opposed to Catholic Emancipation and so the plan had to be abandoned, leaving many Irish people even more resentful. As a result of the King's refusal to accept his plans, Pitt resigned at the height of the war.

FOCUS ROUTE

Add evidence to your copy of the table on page 208.

■ 12E The wars against Napoleon

1802	Peace of Amiens
1803	Britain declares war on France (May)
1804	Pitt returned as Prime Minister (May)
	Third Coalition (Britain, Austria, Russia)
1805	British naval victory at Trafalgar
	Napoleon defeats Russians and Austrians at Austerlitz
1806	Pitt dies (January)
	Berlin Decree
	Break-up of Third Coalition
	Napoleon's victory at Jena
1807	Milan Decree
	Orders in Council to combat Continental System
	Napoleon's victory at Friedland
1808	Wellesley sent to help Portuguese (June)
	Peninsular War
	French defeated at Rolica and Vimeiro
	Convention of Sintra (defeated French army allowed to leave Portugal)
	Napoleon captures Madrid and puts his brother Joseph back on throne
1809	Battle of Corunna
	Wellington British Commander in Peninsular War
	Defeats Soult at Oporto (Portugal) and Talavera (Spain)
	Torres Vedras
1810–13	Wellington drives Massena from Portugal, Spain and over Pyrenees into France
1811	Wellington's victories at Fuentes de Onoro, Almeida and Albuera
1812	Wellington's victories at Badajoz and Ciudad Rodrigo. He captures Madrid
	Napoleon's Russian Campaign defeats Russians at Borodino, but is defeated in Moscow
	Britain at war with USA (until 1814)
1813	Decisive Fourth Coalition
	France defeated at Leipzig
1814	Wellington wins battle of Toulouse
	Fall of Paris
	Napoleon gives up French throne and is exiled to Elba
	War with USA ended
1815	Napoleon escapes
	Waterloo
	Defeated Napoleon sent to St Helena
	Congress of Vienna

D What was Britain's contribution to the defeat of Napoleon?

Pitt was replaced as Prime Minister by Henry Addington (later and better known as Viscount Sidmouth). In the autumn of 1801, peace negotiations began, with Britain in a position of strength after Nelson defeated the Danish fleet at Copenhagen. This finished off the alliance known as the League of Armed Neutrality. Negotiations culminated in the Treaty of Amiens (March 1802). Crowds gathered in London and Paris to cheer at the news. The British public thanked Pitt for seeing the country through those stormy years and 'Pitt Clubs' were established in his honour. But this was to be a 'phoney peace'. The treaty had not dealt with the real causes of the war – the French threat to the security of its neighbours, and to trade through the seizure of Holland and lands up to the Rhine. It was only a matter of time before war began again. For now the participants could rest, regroup and re-arm.

THE ARMED NEUTRALITY 1800–01

This was a league involving Russia, Sweden, Denmark and Prussia to prevent Britain using the Baltic. It collapsed after Tsar Paul's death and the British fleet's destruction of the Danish fleet at Copenhagen.

Napoleon Bonaparte (1769–1821)
Born in Corsica, Napoleon became an artillery officer in 1785. After victories against the Austrians in northern Italy in 1796, he was acknowledged as a great general. In 1799 he overthrew the revolutionary government and became the First Consul of France. He was made Consul for life in 1802 and crowned himself Emperor in 1804. A series of remarkable victories gave him control of much of Europe by 1809 but he suffered a major defeat in the Russian campaign (1812), which virtually destroyed his army. He was forced to abdicate in 1814 and was exiled to Elba. In February 1815 he escaped and ruled France for the 'Hundred Days' before his final defeat at Waterloo on 18 June 1815. He was exiled to St Helena where he died in 1821.

Horatio Nelson (1758–1805)
Horatio Nelson was the son of a Norfolk clergyman. He joined the navy at the age of twelve and served in the Arctic and the West Indies before taking part in the American War of Independence. In 1793 he sailed with Admiral Hood to the Mediterranean, where he lost his right eye in the fighting off Corsica. He was involved in the victory at Cape St Vincent (1797). He lost his right arm in the unsuccessful attack on Santa Cruz, Tenerife, but he became a hero after defeating the French at the Battle of the Nile (1798). He was promoted to Rear-Admiral in 1801, and won the Battle of Copenhagen. He used the tactic of breaking the line (see Chart 12F) to good effect in winning the Battle of Trafalgar (1805). He was killed during the battle on his flagship *Victory*.

The main terms of the treaty

The Peace of Amiens was only a temporary truce. Both sides prepared for another period of conflict. Napoleon planned the invasion of Britain, his Grand Design, commenting, 'In the existing situation every treaty of peace means no more to me than a brief armistice'.

Napoleon restarted the wars by conquering northern Italy and invading Switzerland and the Netherlands. In May 1803 Britain declared war, with Pitt returning as Prime Minister in May 1804. Pitt organised the Third Coalition with Austria and Russia. Preparations for the expected invasion attempt got underway. Volunteer Corps were set up and Martello towers were constructed along the coast.

The threat to Britain was real. Napoleon planned to bring over an army of around 150,000 men from Boulogne in hundreds of flat-bottomed boats. The thousands of white tents in the French camp could be seen from the south coast of England. There is no doubt that this could have been Britain's 'darkest hour' but the navy, as before, played a vital role in combating these plans. It controlled the Channel even though Napoleon could now rely on the Spanish navy to help him; British attacks on Spanish treasure ships had led to a Franco-Spanish agreement. The crucial event came when the French Admiral, Villeneuve, linked up with the Spaniards at Cadiz and tried to lure Nelson out to the West Indies. However, the superiority of the British navy and the genius of Nelson resulted in a British victory at the Battle of Trafalgar off the coast of Spain.

TREATY OF AMIENS

- *Britain returned all her colonial conquests except Trinidad (from Spain) and Ceylon (from Holland).*

- *The French withdrew from Rome, Naples, Portugal and Egypt.*

- *Britain promised to hand back Malta (after twelve months) to the previous rulers, the Knights of St John.*

SOURCE 12.7 Martello towers were built in the south-east and East Anglia to give warning of an invasion and to protect the coastline

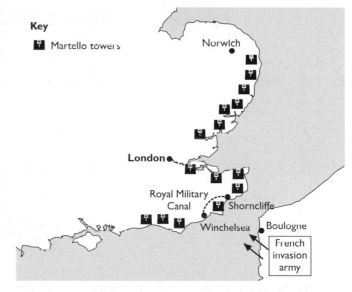

Key
- ■ Martello towers

Norwich
London
Royal Military Canal
Shorncliffe
Winchelsea
Boulogne
French invasion army

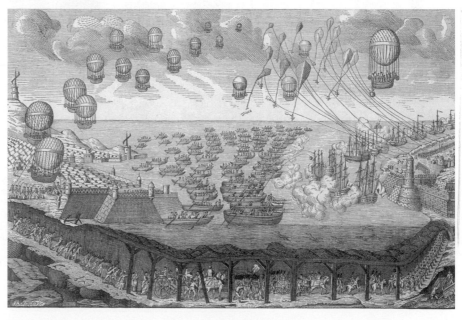

SOURCE 12.8 A satirical view of Napoleon's invasion plans, an engraving by E. Morieu, 1803. Despite the tone of this illustration the threat to England was real

SOURCE 12.9 Sailors and Royal Marines aim their guns on board *HMS Victory* at the height of the Battle of Trafalgar, 21 October 1805

■ 12F Nelson's plan of battle at Trafalgar: breaking the line

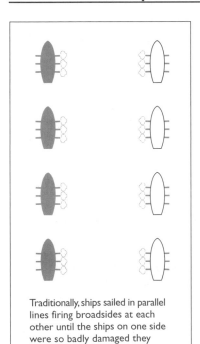

Traditionally, ships sailed in parallel lines firing broadsides at each other until the ships on one side were so badly damaged they could be boarded.

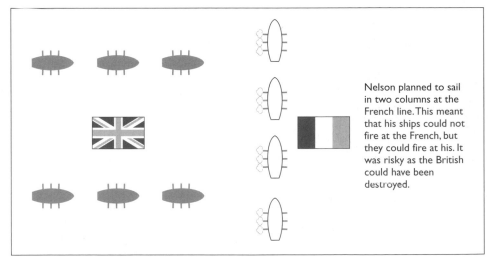

Nelson planned to sail in two columns at the French line. This meant that his ships could not fire at the French, but they could fire at his. It was risky as the British could have been destroyed.

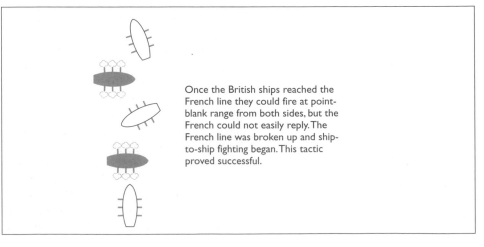

Once the British ships reached the French line they could fire at point-blank range from both sides, but the French could not easily reply. The French line was broken up and ship-to-ship fighting began. This tactic proved successful.

THE DEATH OF PITT

On 23 January 1806 William Pitt died, aged 46. He had been racked with gout due to his fondness for port wine, but he was also worn out by his dedicated service to his country. It is often claimed that he was more successful in peacetime than in war. He was criticised for tactical failure (disastrous expeditions to the Continent, giving too much emphasis to the West Indies, underestimating France in the early stages, and so on), and for subsidising inefficient allies. But could anyone have done better against such a formidable foe as Napoleon?

SOURCE 12.10 E. Evans, *William Pitt the Younger*, 1999

The acid test was that Britain was not defeated in the two darkest years of the wars – 1797 and 1805; in both years Pitt was in command. As friend and foe alike recognised at the end of January 1806, Pitt had bestridden a confusing and rapidly changing world with authority. He was not much loved but he was enormously respected.

Arthur Wellesley, Duke of Wellington (1769–1852)
The son of an Irish peer, Wellesley entered the army in 1785. His great military qualities were first recognised in India (1796–1805). His outstanding achievement was in the Peninsular War in Spain and Portugal when he drove the French out of the Iberian Peninsula. For this he was made a duke. He ended Napoleon's reign at Waterloo. He was popularly known as the 'Iron Duke'. After the war he became a politician and was a Tory Prime Minister (1828–30).

Trafalgar confirmed Britain's superiority at sea and its ability to defend its coastline from invasion. However, Napoleon's armies were still rampaging over Europe and within weeks of Trafalgar they crushed the Austrians and Prussians at Austerlitz, in December 1805. Frustrated by Britain's naval dominance, Napoleon developed a different tactic. He decided to use 'economic warfare' to bring Britain to its knees. In November 1806 he issued the Berlin Decree, which declared that the European coastline was closed to British trade. This meant that the rest of Europe could not buy British goods. This tactic became known as the Continental System.

Britain reacted to the Berlin Decree with the Orders in Council (November 1807), which meant that neutral vessels had to pay a duty to trade with the continent of Europe, and that European ports could be blockaded by the British navy. This led to war with the USA in 1812–14 when British sailors boarded American ships, a violation of rights in the eyes of the American government.

There is no doubt that Britain suffered from Napoleon's Continental System. In 1807 around 42 per cent of its exports went to Europe. British exports dropped from £48.8 million in 1810 to £32.4 million in 1811. By 1811 Britain's economy was being affected and there was concern in manufacturing districts from Birmingham to Leeds. In Leeds there was widespread unemployment, workers were on short time, and food prices were high. There were serious disturbances, not least among Luddites. The local militia, which had been set up to repel the French, was now directing its energies against insurrection at home.

However, France and its allies suffered at least as much as Britain. They required goods that only Britain could supply. West Riding mills were producing cloth for French uniforms, whilst in 1811 French corn was coming into Britain. Smuggling by the French and the British was common in an attempt to circumvent trade restrictions. In the end there was much unrest in Europe as unemployment increased and economic restrictions caused resentment. Spain, Portugal and Russia showed dissent at Napoleon's domination and turned against him. In the meantime Britain developed new markets in South America, the Near East and the Baltic. The Continental System could never succeed in cutting off Britain from the whole of Europe.

The Peninsular War

In trying to extend the Continental System over Europe, Napoleon gave Britain a military opportunity. The focus was Portugal because there was extensive trade between Britain and Portugal and its colony, Brazil. Napoleon wished to eradicate this trade and persuaded Spain to allow him to send troops across the peninsula to conquer Lisbon. But what followed turned out to be a fatal error. Napoleon decided to replace the Spanish royal family with his brother, Joseph, and then sent more troops into Spain. This led to a revolt by the Spanish people, which allowed the British to capitalise on the deep resentment in Spain and Portugal by supporting their struggle.

A small expeditionary force under Sir Arthur Wellesley (later the Duke of Wellington) landed in Portugal in June 1808. The Spaniards drove Joseph Bonaparte out of Madrid, but this only drew Napoleon personally into the Peninsular War. Only a rearguard action by Sir John Moore at Corunna saved southern Spain, although Moore was killed in the process. With 10,000 British troops remaining in Lisbon, more soldiers were sent in under Wellesley. Within a few weeks the French were forced out of Portugal, and Joseph Bonaparte was defeated at Talavera in Spain in 1809. For this Wellesley was made the Duke of Wellington. For the first time in the war, the British army was enjoying success.

French troops now poured into Spain. However, Spanish rebels, with British encouragement and financial support, were able to hold up two-thirds of the force. North of Lisbon, Wellington dug in with the construction of the defensive network known as the lines of Torres Vedras, which the French found impossible to penetrate. The disastrous winter of 1810, in which many French soldiers died from disease and starvation, forced the French retreat into Spain. Throughout 1811 Wellington was able to secure his position, while much needed French forces were being bogged down in Spain causing Napoleon to

CITY COLLEGE LEARNING RESOURCE CENTRE

SOURCE 12.11 The Peninsular War Memorial in Torres Vedras, Portugal, commemorates soldiers who fought in the campaign

■ 12G   A map of the Peninsular War

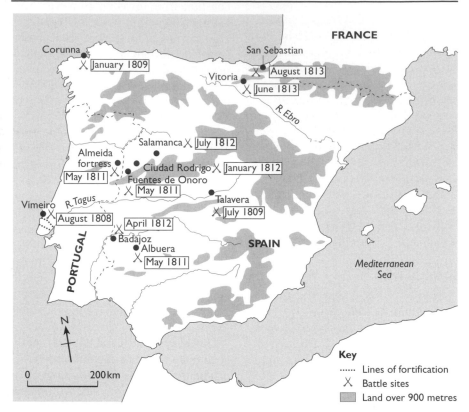

Key
...... Lines of fortification
✕ Battle sites
▨ Land over 900 metres

TALKING POINT

Was Napoleon right to refer to the Peninsular War as his 'Spanish ulcer'?

suffer irritation from his 'Spanish ulcer'. The British army negated the French use of artillery, and their rate of fire in a line against a French column was faster and superior. In 1812 Wellington was victorious at Salamanca but it was not until the summer of 1813, with French soldiers being withdrawn for the Moscow campaign, that he made the final breakthrough at Vitoria. The British army had inflicted a crucial defeat on Napoleon; Wellington had called his own soldiers 'the scum of the earth' who had 'enlisted for drink', but they had been turned into a disciplined fighting force under his efficient leadership.

The Russian Campaign

Napoleon had lost the Peninsular War. It proved that Napoleon, who paid the penalty for ignoring nationalistic feelings within his empire, was not invincible and it gave heart to others who wished to throw off the Napoleonic yoke. It inspired the setting up of the Fourth Coalition (Britain, Russia and Prussia, followed by Austria and Sweden) in the spring of 1813.

During his Spanish campaign, Napoleon had split his forces to launch an attack on Russia which would not co-operate with the Continental System. A French army of approximately 500,000 men invaded Russia in June 1812. Here Napoleon met stoical resistance as Russians fought bloody running battles and pursued a 'scorched earth policy', destroying crops, animals and buildings as they retreated. Napoleon believed that his army should travel lightly and feed off the land. This proved to be fatal, as the French began to starve and, as the winter set in, even victory at Borodino could not halt the collapse of French morale. By December 1812 only 30,000 of the Grand Army remained, and Napoleon was in retreat from Moscow.

SOURCE 12.12 Napoleon's explanation in the *Memoirs of General de Caulaincourt, Duke of Vicenza*, 1812–13

It is the winter that has been our undoing. We are the victims of the climate. The fine weather tricked me. Everything turned out badly because I stayed too long in Moscow. If I had left four days after I had occupied it, as I thought of doing when I saw it in flames, the Russians would have lost. The Tsar would gladly have accepted my peace terms.

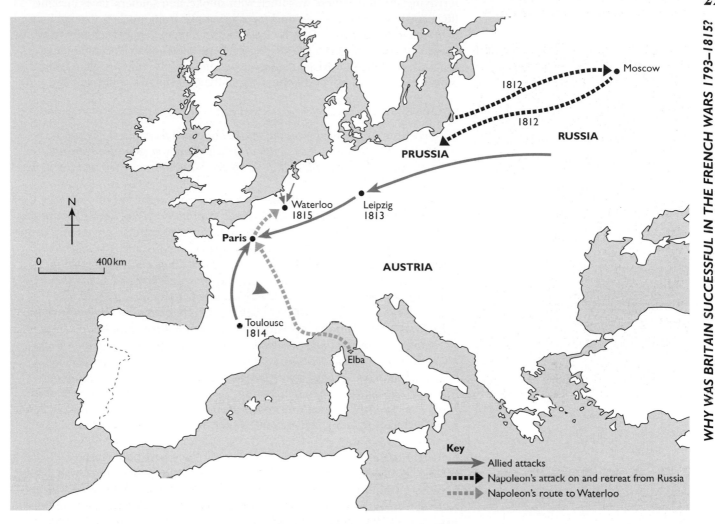

SOURCE 12.13   C. Barnett, *Bonaparte*, 1978

In fact the army lost more than 350,000 men on the way to Moscow: only some 80,000 during the retreat. It lost 35,000 men in fair weather in one week: 15,000 to 20,000 during the week of snowfall mentioned by Napoleon as the beginning of the disaster. Very many of the horses died of hunger and overwork before the cold struck. The sorry story of Napoleon's military incompetence was changed into the epic story of an army's courage.

The end of the wars

In October 1813 the combined forces of Russia, Prussia, Sweden and Austria defeated Napoleon at Leipzig. France was now on the defensive, both on the Pyrenees and along the Rhine. Napoleon put up a spirited resistance on French soil, but in the spring of 1814 the Allies captured Paris. Napoleon abdicated. He was sent into exile on the island of Elba and the Allies met to sort out a peace treaty. However, whilst they were wrangling over the spoils of victory, Napoleon made a dramatic escape and took back the throne from the restored Louis XVIII.

As Napoleon rapidly recruited another army, Wellington was put in charge of what he called 'an infamous army', comprising many raw recruits (the most experienced had been sent to fight in America) and allied troops largely made up of Dutch and Hanoverians. They were to be joined by the Prussians under the command of Blücher. On 18 June 1815 Wellington's 67,000 men faced Napoleon's army of 74,000 near the village of Waterloo in Belgium. Napoleon planned to defeat Wellington before Blücher could arrive with his force.

ACTIVITY

Read Sources 12.12 and 12.13.

1 How do the two extracts differ in their explanation of Napoleon's defeat?
2 Do they reveal any defects in Napoleon's military qualities?
3 Which explanation do you find more convincing?

CITY COLLEGE
LEARNING RESOURCE CENTRE

The battle lasted from midday to late evening. The noise and confusion were terrifying, the atmosphere was thick with smoke, and soldiers' faces became blackened by gunpowder. So thick was the smoke from muskets that soldiers heard charging horses before they saw them, suddenly appearing only two strides away. As the day wore on, they became deafened by the cannon and muskets, clashing swords, pounding hooves and a sound like 'a violent hailstorm on panes of glass' – bullets hammering on the breastplates of the cavalry.

SOURCE 12.14   One of Wellington's foot guards describes the Battle of Waterloo

We were nearly suffocated from the smoke and smell from burnt cartridges. It was impossible to move a yard without treading upon a wounded comrade, or upon the bodies of the dead; and the loud groans of the wounded and dying was most appalling.

At four o'clock our square [Wellington's army was organised into squares] was a perfect hospital, being full of dead, dying, and mutilated soldiers. The charges of cavalry were in appearance very formidable, but in reality a great relief, as the artillery could no longer fire on us; the very earth shook under the enormous mass of men and horses. I shall never forget the strange noise our bullets made against the breastplates of the cuirassiers, six or seven thousand in number who attacked us with great fury ... One might suppose that nothing could have resisted the shock of this terrible moving mass ... in an almost incredibly short period they were within twenty yards of us shouting 'Vive l'Empereur!' The words of command, 'Prepare to receive cavalry', had been given. Every man in front ranks knelt, and a wall bristling with steel presented itself to the enemy.

I should observe that just before the charge the Duke entered by one of the angles of the square, accompanied by one aide-de-camp; all the rest of the staff being either killed or wounded. Our Commander in Chief, as far as I could judge, appeared perfectly composed but looked very thoughtful and pale.

For much of the day a French victory seemed likely but at last General Blücher's Prussian army arrived. When Napoleon's Imperial Guard was forced to retreat, Wellington knew the battle was won. Wellington claimed it was 'the nearest run thing you ever saw in your life'. When he was given news of the casualties (15,000 of his own soldiers; 47,000 in all) he wept. He said, 'I don't know what it is to lose a battle, but certainly nothing can be more painful than to gain one with a loss of so many of one's friends.'

SOURCE 12.15   A view of the Battle of Waterloo

E Review: why was Britain successful in the French Wars 1793–1815?

ACTIVITY

During this chapter you have been collecting arguments that help to explain why Britain was successful in the wars against France. Now is the time to complete the table you began on page 208. Look at Charts 12I and 12J and add any new information to your table.

■ 12I Why was Napoleon beaten?

- Napoleon eventually bit off more than he could chew, and he didn't know when to halt his ambitions, which is typical of a megalomaniac. He wanted to be accepted as royalty, and with his marriage to Marie-Louise of Austria he even married into royalty. He installed his brothers on European thrones, such as Holland, Spain and Naples, in order to establish a Napoleonic dynasty.
- Napoleon denied nationalism in other countries, creating resentment and revolt in Austria, Spain, Russia and Prussia.
- The most consistent resistance to Napoleon came from Britain whose industrial and economic strength was superior to that of any other country.
- Britain's navy was supreme and could maintain trade and commercial links with the continent, whilst landing and supplying forces, such as in the Iberian Peninsula. Trafalgar was a turning point. By 1813 Napoleon only had 71 ships of the line (ships in the navy) and most of these were blockaded in port, whereas the British had 235.
- The Continental System backfired on him. Even when Britain was experiencing economic difficulties in 1811, Napoleon allowed French grain to enter Britain, probably to placate French traders and farmers.
- After 1808 he made a series of military blunders in Spain and Russia. He had been successful at first because his opponents were either ill-equipped, unprepared or had no answer to his tactics – for example, the Italian campaigns (1796–97; 1800); Austria (1805); Prussia (1806). As time went on his strategies were exploited, and Wellington was clever enough to match him – for example at Vitoria and Waterloo.
- In a desperate attempt to increase the size of his armies, Napoleon conscripted foreigners. By 1814 only 40 per cent of Napoleon's army consisted of Frenchmen, which led to disunity. In the meantime, his enemies were increasing the size of their armies.
- Napoleon would not delegate authority. He expected his marshals to obey every order and gave them no opportunity to use their initiative. For example, by the time his instructions arrived in Spain from the other side of Europe circumstances had changed. He was also running the domestic policies of France while planning military campaigns, and this was too much for one man to handle.
- The Fourth Coalition, which remained intact when others did not, proved to be decisive.

■ 12J Napoleon's health report

The effect of long campaigns, rushed meals, and rough conditions brought about a decline in Napoleon's health and ultimately his efficiency. He suffered from colic and a peptic ulcer, which affected his temper. His quickness of thought began to slow down.

At Borodino (1812) he had a bladder complaint, which made it difficult for him to ride. At Dresden (1813) he was exhausted and suffered from a severe stomach condition. At Leipzig (1813) he was doubled up with stomach pains and he had an overwhelming need for sleep. He suffered from pituitary dysplasia, which grew progressively worse as he grew older. He had prolapsed piles, which made it painful for him to mount his horse at Waterloo (1815).

I'm afraid it's not looking good.

EGYPT. | SPAIN. | ITALY. | CHINA. | GERMANY. | PRUSSIA | FRANCE. | TURKEY.

RUSSIA | SWEEDEN. | HOLLAND | PORTUGAL | AMERICA | ASIA | ENGLAND

NATIONAL OPINIONS on Bonaparte.

SOURCE 12.16 'National Opinions on Bonaparte' – an English cartoon of 1808 showing different countries' views towards Napoleon

■ 12K Factors in Britain's success in the French Wars

Naval power

Industrial and economic strength

Others?

Why was Britain successful in the French Wars?

Weaknesses and mistakes of opponents

Alliances

Individual leadership

ACTIVITY

1 Draw a set of diagrams to show the various alliances that were formed against France between 1793 and 1815.
2 Plan an essay entitled 'Why was Britain successful in the French Wars 1793–1815?'

TALKING POINT

Was there one key turning point in the French Wars?

1 From 1792 there was a build-up to war, but Britain thought it might be able to avoid being involved. However, the French occupation of the River Scheldt led to war, largely for economic reasons.
2 The role of the navy was crucial to the defeat of France. The Battle of Trafalgar was a turning point and ended any chance of a French invasion of Britain.
3 Britain's economic and technological strength was essential to British success in the war.
4 The Continental System backfired on Napoleon.
5 The Peninsular War saw the first effective involvement of the British army under Wellington. Victory in Spain proved to be a turning point.
6 Britain did not defeat Napoleon on its own as the Russian and Waterloo campaigns showed.
7 Further explanations for Napoleon's defeat can be found in his own personality and strategies. He is an example of how leadership qualities, and the course of history, can be affected by personal physical and psychological factors.

CITY COLLEGE
LEARNING RESOURCE CENTRE

13

Was Castlereagh a great Foreign Secretary or the 'pawn of Metternich'?

CHAPTER OVERVIEW

On 12 August 1822 Lord Castlereagh, the British Foreign Secretary, slit his throat. Castlereagh was worn out by overwork and stress brought on by the pressures of dealing with difficult allies and criticism from within the Cabinet. To make matters worse, rumours were circulating, fired by his enemies, that he was involved in a homosexual scandal. For several days before his suicide, he had exhibited irrational behaviour which was of great concern to his wife and close friends. He had confided in a member of his staff on 8 August, 'I am quite worn out; and this fresh responsibility is more than I can bear'. He was also extremely unpopular among sections of society because, as Leader of the House of Commons, he was seen as the representative of Lord Liverpool's repression at home and in Ireland. This all became too much for him and he descended into deep depression. Despite efforts to keep a watchful eye on him, and to keep guns and sharp implements out of his grasp, he took his own life by cutting his throat with a penknife. At his funeral Castlereagh was vilified by the crowd. Some hurled abuse and spat at his coffin as it was taken into Westminster Abbey.

FOCUS ROUTE

As you work through this chapter collect evidence that supports each of these two views of Castlereagh in a table like the one below.

The 'pawn of Metternich'	A brilliant Foreign Secretary	Other interpre-tations?

Lord Castlereagh was a great Foreign Secretary, a man to whom the whole country owes a debt of gratitude.

The pawn of Metternich more like!

Put Europe before his own country.

Repression and tyranny – that's what Castlereagh stood for.

Not surprisingly, there have been very different views of Castlereagh. One is that he was a brilliant and distinguished Foreign Secretary. The other is that not only did he support repression at home but he also did so abroad by supporting absolutist monarchs and, perhaps more importantly, that he pandered to European leaders and put Europe before Britain. This was what led to the view that he was 'the pawn of Metternich', the Foreign Secretary and Chancellor of Austria.

But which of these views is the fairest? Decide for yourself by studying:

A Why was Castlereagh so unpopular at home? (pp. 227–228)

B What did Castlereagh achieve at the Vienna Settlement? (pp. 229–232)

C How successful was Castlereagh's involvement in the Congress System? (pp. 233–235)

D Review: was Castlereagh a great Foreign Secretary or the 'pawn of Metternich'? (pp. 235–237)

A Why was Castlereagh so unpopular at home?

Robert Stewart, Viscount Castlereagh, 2nd Marquess of Londonderry (1769–1822)

Castlereagh was involved in Irish affairs and in promoting the Union of the English and Irish Parliaments under Pitt the Younger. He was in favour of Catholic Emancipation and the abolition of slavery but was haunted by the impact of the French Revolution and saw liberalism and nationalism as evils. As Foreign Secretary (1812–22) he played a major role in consolidating the Fourth Coalition, which brought about the defeat of Napoleon, and in finalising the peace settlement at Vienna in 1815. Here he prevented the imposition of a vindictive peace settlement on France, and curtailed Prussian and Russian ambitions in order to establish a balance of power. He developed 'personal diplomacy' by forging a close relationship with Metternich of Austria and Tsar Alexander of Russia. He was a skilful mediator who saw Britain as part of Europe and wished to achieve lasting peace.

KEY EVENTS DURING CASTLEREAGH'S TIME AT THE FOREIGN OFFICE 1812–22

1814–15 Congresses:	Vienna Settlement 1818 – Aix-la-Chapelle 1820 – Troppau 1821 – Laibach 1822 – Verona
1820	Castlereagh's State Paper Trouble in Spain, Naples and Greece
1822	Greek War of Independence

Prince Metternich (1773–1859)

Metternich was Foreign Secretary and Chancellor of Austria. He played a leading role in the Vienna Settlement, reconstructing Europe on conservative lines. The 'Metternich System' governed European affairs from 1815 to 1848. It tried to restore and preserve the old power of the monarchies against the new forces of liberalism and nationalism. It ultimately failed and Metternich fled to England in the revolution of 1848. The English historian A. J. P. Taylor called him 'the most boring man in European history'.

SOURCE 13.1   P. B. Shelley, 'The Mask of Anarchy'. Although not published until 1832, ten years after his death, Shelley originally wrote this in reaction to the Peterloo Massacre in August 1819

I met murder on the way –
He had a mask like Castlereagh
Very smooth he looked, yet grim;
Seven bloodhounds followed him:
All were fat and well they might
Be in admirable plight,
For one by one, and two by two,
He tossed them human hearts to chew
Which from his wide cloak he drew.

TALKING POINT

The lines of poetry in Source 13.1 come from 'The Mask of Anarchy' by Percy Bysshe Shelley (1792–1822). Shelley, the son of an MP, was an atheist, radical, political pamphleteer and poet. Poetry and politics for him went together in poems such as 'The Mask of Anarchy', which was written after the Peterloo Massacre when Castlereagh supported the actions of the Manchester magistrates. How valuable are the lines of poetry for a historian studying Castlereagh?

Before going on to evaluate Castlereagh's success or failure as Foreign Secretary, it is important to separate his unpopularity at home from his work as Foreign Secretary. Castlereagh was not just Foreign Secretary from 1812 until 1822 but also Leader of the House of Commons. In this post it was his job to defend and justify government policies on all issues because other senior members of the government, notably the Prime Minister, Liverpool, were members of the House of Lords. Castlereagh was a nobleman but his Irish peerage did not qualify him for a place in the House of Lords. It was his role as the government's spokesman in the Commons that led to him taking much of the blame for the government's policies and actions at home. He was seen as a reactionary on domestic issues and therefore it was easy to assume he was reactionary on foreign issues too.

SOURCE 13.2   J. W. Derry, *Castlereagh*, 1976

So dominant was Castlereagh's personality in the Commons that many Radical critics regarded Liverpool's administration as in many ways Castlereagh's government. This did scant justice to the skill and intelligence of Lord Liverpool, but it helps to explain why Castlereagh became so hated. He had to defend measures such as the suspension of Habeas Corpus and the Six Acts.

SOURCE 13.3   C. K. Webster, *The Foreign Policy of Castlereagh*, 1925

He had, in fact, no trust in public opinion. He preferred to keep Parliament in ignorance rather than appeal to it boldly. It is the great defect in his career, and in one sense it made the rest of his policy of no avail, since he could not obtain for his plans the support of an enlightened body of opinion amongst his countrymen.

ACTIVITY

1 Why was Castlereagh criticised for the government's domestic policies when he was Foreign Secretary?
2 Explain in your own words the assessment of Castlereagh in Source 13.3.

B What did Castlereagh achieve at the Vienna Settlement?

FOCUS ROUTE

1 What were Castlereagh's aims at Vienna?
2 In what ways did his aims differ from those of other statesmen?
3 What were the key elements of the settlement?
4 How effectively did the settlement achieve British foreign policy objectives (see page 205)?

TALKING POINT

Can knowledge and discussion of historical events help us to decide on the extent to which Britain should be integrated with the rest of Europe?

FOCUS ROUTE

Use the evidence in this section to complete your table from page 226.

To understand what Castlereagh was trying to achieve at the Congress of Vienna, we must go back to the French Wars. In 1805 Pitt was pondering the principles of peace, which he believed should involve 'a general agreement and guarantee for mutual security and protection of the different Powers, and for re-establishing a general system of Public Law in Europe'. As a protégé of Pitt, Castlereagh supported this principle. It formed the basis of his thinking at the peace conferences, and resulted in the Congress System, which he masterminded. From 1812, as Foreign Secretary, he had been very much involved in keeping the Allies together in the Fourth Coalition, which ultimately defeated Napoleon. His 'personal diplomacy' with European leaders brought him praise and respect from the Allies. He thought that if European powers could work together in war, they should be able to do this in peacetime too. The germination of this idea led to the Congress System.

What were the aims of the European statesmen at Vienna?

- To make France pay for involving Europe in war from 1793 to 1815.
- To ensure that the victors were suitably compensated for their efforts.
- To prevent France from making war and disrupting European peace and security in the future.
- To restore rulers overthrown by Napoleon.

However, this list of aims hides the differences that existed amongst the countries represented at Vienna. Castlereagh wanted to make sure that the French were not punished so severely that they would soon want revenge. Other European representatives were eager to 'collect trophies' and Castlereagh, acting as a conciliator, had to try to curb these demands. There was friction, which led to suspicion and distrust. In addition, Talleyrand for the French wished to pursue a policy of damage limitation and protect French interests. His task was made more difficult when, in the midst of the peace negotiations, Napoleon escaped from Elba. After Waterloo there was the temptation to punish France even more severely. Yet, though the Vienna Settlement became more severe, it was still relatively lenient.

SOURCE 13.4 The Congress of Vienna, 1815. Wellington stands to the extreme left, Metternich points to Castlereagh and Talleyrand is seated second from the right

CITY COLLEGE LEARNING RESOURCE CENTRE

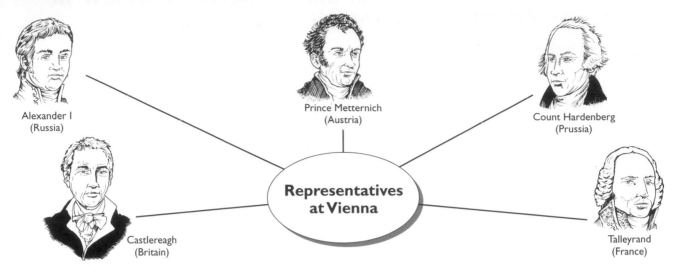

Alexander I
(Russia)

Prince Metternich
(Austria)

Count Hardenberg
(Prussia)

**Representatives
at Vienna**

Castlereagh
(Britain)

Talleyrand
(France)

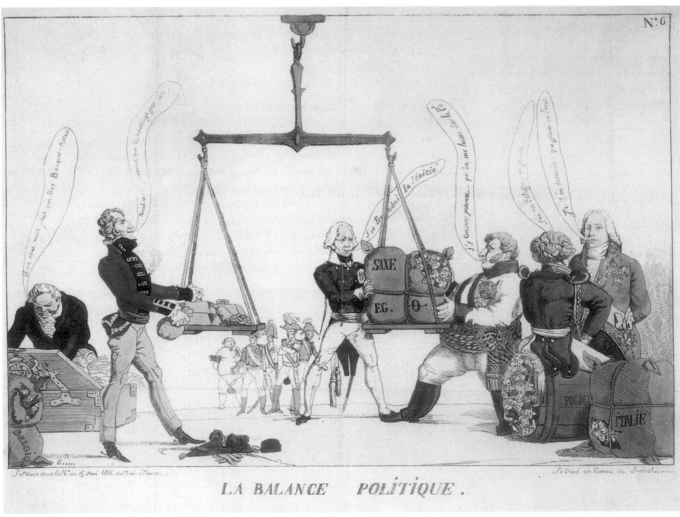

LA BALANCE POLITIQUE.

SOURCE 13.5 *La Balance Politique*, 1815. Wellington places money on the scales opposite the King of Prussia and Metternich, who speaks as sovereign of Austria. On the right the Tsar is in conference with Talleyrand

The Vienna Settlement

■ 13B   The terms of the Vienna Settlement, 1815

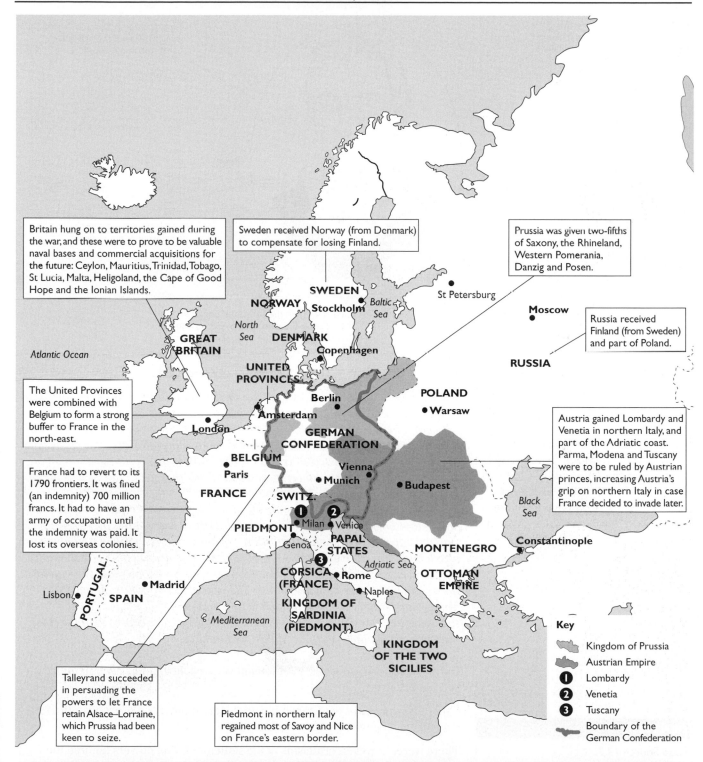

Britain hung on to territories gained during the war, and these were to prove to be valuable naval bases and commercial acquisitions for the future: Ceylon, Mauritius, Trinidad, Tobago, St Lucia, Malta, Heligoland, the Cape of Good Hope and the Ionian Islands.

Sweden received Norway (from Denmark) to compensate for losing Finland.

Prussia was given two-fifths of Saxony, the Rhineland, Western Pomerania, Danzig and Posen.

Russia received Finland (from Sweden) and part of Poland.

The United Provinces were combined with Belgium to form a strong buffer to France in the north-east.

Austria gained Lombardy and Venetia in northern Italy, and part of the Adriatic coast. Parma, Modena and Tuscany were to be ruled by Austrian princes, increasing Austria's grip on northern Italy in case France decided to invade later.

France had to revert to its 1790 frontiers. It was fined (an indemnity) 700 million francs. It had to have an army of occupation until the indemnity was paid. It lost its overseas colonies.

Talleyrand succeeded in persuading the powers to let France retain Alsace–Lorraine, which Prussia had been keen to seize.

Piedmont in northern Italy regained most of Savoy and Nice on France's eastern border.

Key

- Kingdom of Prussia
- Austrian Empire
- ❶ Lombardy
- ❷ Venetia
- ❸ Tuscany
- Boundary of the German Confederation

ACTIVITY

Complete a table like the one below showing how the terms of the settlement met the various aims of the negotiators.

To make France pay for involving Europe in war from 1793 to 1815	To ensure that the victors were suitably compensated for their efforts	To prevent France disrupting European peace and security in the future	To restore rulers overthrown by Napoleon

232

WAS CASTLEREAGH A GREAT FOREIGN SECRETARY OR THE 'PAWN OF METTERNICH'?

■ 13C   What did Castlereagh achieve at Vienna?

He persuaded Prussia to tone down its demands for territory so that France was not treated too harshly.

He was hostile to the view that great powers had the right to interfere in the internal affairs of other countries.

He prevented Russia and Prussia gaining too much territory and hence too much power.

He tried to maintain peace by co-operation through the Congress System whereby the powers would meet to discuss international problems and find solutions without reverting to war (the Concert of Europe). He worked closely with Metternich in setting up the Quadruple Alliance in November 1815 (Britain, Austria, Prussia and Russia).

He ensured that France gained a lenient peace so there would be no grounds for revenge.

Britain's territorial gains emphasised its naval supremacy by providing valuable bases; they were important sources of raw materials and markets, which were vital to future imperial and commercial expansion.

He preserved the balance of power in Europe, in order to ensure that no one country became too powerful, as had happened with France under Napoleon.

SOURCE 13.6   Castlereagh, December 1815

It is the province of Great Britain to encourage peace by exercising a conciliatory influence between the Powers, rather than put herself at the head of any combinations of Courts to keep others in check … It is not my wish to encourage on the part of this country an unnecessary interference in the ordinary affairs of the Continent.

SOURCE 13.7   C. K. Webster, *The Congress of Vienna*, 1934

The work of the Congress of Vienna was dealt with faithfully by the publicists of its own time, and has been severely handled by historians in the century that followed. The spectacle of a dozen statesmen transferring 'souls' by the 100,000 from one sovereign to another has inspired many mordant pens; and in the light of the history of the nineteenth century the validity of these criticisms cannot be disputed. Such criticisms, however, neglect the fact that the Congress was the close of one epoch as well as the beginning of another. The main object of the statesmen of the day was the overthrow of the Napoleonic Empire completely; and in that object they succeeded to a much greater degree than they expected … Had any attempt been made to substitute for the contracts, written and unwritten, which had united Europe against Napoleon, the vague principles of nationality and democracy, so imperfectly understood alike by the peoples and the statesmen, the result would have been disastrous. The primary need of Europe, once the Napoleonic tyranny was overthrown, was a period of peace; and this the statesmen at Vienna undoubtedly secured in a far greater degree than the most sanguine of the publicists of the time dared to hope.

Despite conflicting motives, a settlement was reached. It has been heralded a success because:

- there was no major war involving all the great powers of Europe until 1914
- a balance of power had been achieved.

There were, however, criticisms of the settlement. The powers ignored the forces of 'nationalism' and 'liberalism', primarily because they viewed them as dangerous, and a product of the French Revolution. However, in 1815 they were not the forces they were to become later in the nineteenth century. Nevertheless, liberals criticised the restoration of autocratic rulers such as Ferdinand IV, the Bourbon King of Naples, who was guilty of misgovernment and repression as Ferdinand I, King of the Two Sicilies. In the reconstruction of Europe, seeds of discontent were also sown: the Belgians under Dutch rule; Italians under Austria; Finns under Russia; Norwegians under Sweden; Poles under Russia; the creation of a German Confederation of 38 states instead of a united Germany. Rebellions were to follow.

ACTIVITY

Read Source 13.7.

1 Summarise in your own words what Webster's verdict was on the Congress of Vienna.
2 Webster helped with the preparation of the Peace Conference of 1919 and was a British army officer in the First World War. How do you think these factors might have affected his view of the Vienna Settlement?

How successful was Castlereagh's involvement in the Congress System?

THE HOLY ALLIANCE

In 1815 Tsar Alexander, an erratic religious fanatic, suggested the formation of a Holy Alliance through which 'the kings of Europe should agree to treat each other as Christian brothers and to rule their peoples on principles of Christian benevolence'. What this meant in practice was open to interpretation, but at the time it was seen as a right-wing reaction, with Alexander claiming it gave rulers the right to interfere in the internal affairs of other countries. Metternich thought the Tsar was crazy: 'The Tsar's mind was quite clearly affected'. Castlereagh's response is contained in a letter he wrote to Lord Liverpool in which he called it a 'piece of sublime mysticism and nonsense'. Nevertheless, it was signed by the Emperors of Russia, Prussia and Austria. Castlereagh had an ideal excuse for the British monarchy not signing it: George III was insane and the Prince Regent was not allowed to sign such a treaty under the British constitution.

Metternich was converted to the view that it could be a useful alliance, but Castlereagh was distrustful and it marked Britain's alienation from the other major powers. Ironically, many people in Britain believed Castlereagh sympathised with the Holy Alliance – this was largely due to his inability or unwillingness to explain his aims and policies to the public.

FOCUS ROUTE

Use the evidence in this section to complete your table from page 226.

At Vienna it was agreed that Britain, Austria, Russia and Prussia, as the Quadruple Alliance, would meet at fixed periods. This was to be known as the Congress System.

SOURCE 13.8 Article VI of the Quadruple Alliance, November 1815

To facilitate and to secure the execution of the present Treaty, and to consolidate the connections which at the present moment so closely unite the four Sovereigns for the happiness of the World ... [and] for the purpose of consulting upon their common interests, and for the consideration of the measures which at each of these periods shall be considered the most salutary for the repose and prosperity of Nations, and for the maintenance of the peace of Europe.

It was felt that since the Vienna Congress had worked well, others could be held to develop international relations and to discuss problem issues. There is a tendency to equate this proposal with organisations like the League of Nations, United Nations and the European Union, but there was no formal structure nor organisation as seen in these twentieth-century organisations. The powers were not certain as to whether they should meet regularly or only when there was a crisis that threatened peace. Castlereagh's flexibility is seen in his statement: 'Nothing in our system is absolutely unchangeable'. But whereas he believed that congresses should be convened only to deal with major crises, he soon realised that 'congress diplomacy' meant different things to different countries. For example, whilst Britain wished to prevent conflict by international co-operation, Austria wished to use the system to crush nationalism and revolution. The other powers wanted to interfere in the affairs of other states, largely through the Holy Alliance.

SOURCE 13.9 N. Gash, *Aristocracy and the People: Britain 1815–1865*, 1979

The objects of Britain's diplomacy in 1815 were to obtain security in Europe, to safeguard its possessions overseas, and to promote freedom of commerce everywhere ... The guiding principles followed by British policy were containment and order, not conquest and expansion.

The Congresses 1818–22

The Congress of Aix-la-Chapelle, 1818

The Congress of Aix-la-Chapelle was called to settle French affairs. Castlereagh believed the time was right to re-admit France to European politics. The Allied Powers agreed to take their armies of occupation out of France, which had now paid its indemnity and seemed stable under Louis XVIII. France was re-admitted to the European fold. The Quadruple Alliance now became the Quintuple Alliance.

The Congress of Troppau, 1820

In 1820 a secret society called the Carbonari led a revolution in Naples to overthrow the repressive Bourbons and establish a republic. As most of northern Italy was part of the Austrian Empire, Metternich claimed the right to interfere in Naples and put down the revolution. Castlereagh agreed that the Austrians should put down the rising in Naples because it was a 'domestic affair'. (In so doing he was condemned by radicals and liberals for having no sympathy with revolutionary movements and for supporting reactionary regimes.)

CITY COLLEGE
LEARNING RESOURCE CENTRE

Austrian action over Naples led to Metternich persuading Russia and Prussia to sign the Troppau Protocol by which they agreed to intervene whenever there was a rising against a legitimate ruler. As a result, the British delegate to Troppau was withdrawn and Castlereagh issued his State Paper on 5 May 1820. In it he denounced the principle of intervention generally, but also explained British policy towards Spain.

Problems had been bubbling up in Spain when the reactionary Ferdinand VII was forced to accept a new constitution. Ferdinand appealed for help from other European powers, but Castlereagh believed this was a Spanish matter needing no intervention. As Ferdinand assembled an army in January 1820 in Cadiz to recapture Spain's South American colonies, the soldiers revolted and Ferdinand was forced to accept a liberal constitution. Tsar Alexander was in favour of collective intervention and was eager to send Russian troops across Europe to crush the revolution. France also viewed the situation with concern as it did not like the idea of one of its own (a Bourbon) being ousted.

Castlereagh, however, was opposed to intervention for several reasons. He had no sympathy for popular movements but believed suppression should be the responsibility of the power whose interests were being threatened. Whilst the Austrians might have the right to put down a rising in Naples, it was not a signal for other major powers under the guise of the Holy Alliance to interfere in the internal affairs of other states. He also knew that the Opposition in Parliament was against Britain supporting intervention. He had written in his State Paper that events in Spain did not appear to 'menace other states with that imminent danger which had always been regarded, at least in this country, as alone constituting the case which would justify external interference'. In addition, interference by countries such as Russia and France would threaten British interests and the balance of power in Europe. Castlereagh was opposed to a Franco-Russian alliance and any increase in Russian power in Western Europe. Metternich held the same view so Castlereagh was able to work with him in opposing Russian policy. He followed this up by strong protests against any interference, but would not support this with military action.

The Congress of Laibach, 1821

Metternich ignored Castlereagh's objection to the principle of intervention. At Laibach, Austria, Russia and Prussia agreed to send in troops to Piedmont to put down a liberal rising. Castlereagh protested, but was criticised for not taking stronger action. The Congress System was collapsing. It was obvious that most of the powers were more interested in interfering in the domestic policies of other countries than in settling disputes between states.

The Congress of Verona, 1822

This congress was held to discuss the matter of rebellion against the absolute monarchy in Spain and its South American colonies, and in Greece against the Turks. Castlereagh and Metternich were concerned that the Russians would intervene in Greece. They negotiated with the Russians and the Turks and were able to initiate some concessions. Castlereagh had little sympathy with Greek aims but he did not wish to see the revolt crushed by external interference. It was because of the Greek revolt that Castlereagh believed Britain needed to participate at the Congress of Verona. Alas, he never saw the outcome because he took his own life, and thus left Metternich without an ally in handling the revolts in Spain and Greece.

SOURCE 13.10 The Troppau Protocol, presented by Metternich at the Troppau Congress, 15 November 1820

States which have undergone a change of Government due to revolution, the results of which threaten other states, ipso facto cease to be members of the European Alliance, and remain excluded from it until their situation gives guarantees for legal order and stability. If, owing to such alterations, immediate danger threatens other states, the Powers bind themselves, by peaceful means, or if need be by arms, to bring back the guilty state into the bosom of the Great Alliance.

ACTIVITY

Read Sources 13.10 and 13.11. How do they differ in their attitudes to intervention in the affairs of other states?

SOURCE 13.11   Castlereagh's State Paper, 5 May 1820

The principle of one state interfering by force in the internal affairs of another is always a question of the greatest possible moral as well as political delicacy. To generalise such a principle and to think of reducing it to a System is utterly impracticable and objectionable. We shall be found in our place when actual danger menaces the System of Europe but this Country cannot, and will not, act upon abstract and speculative Principles of Precaution: the Alliance which exists had no such purpose in view in its original formation.

WHAT OTHER ISSUES DID CASTLEREAGH HAVE TO DEAL WITH AFTER 1815?

South America

During the French Wars, trade had increased between Britain and the Spanish South American colonies of Argentina, Bolivia, Colombia and Mexico. Castlereagh saw the possibility of recognising their independence in 1808 before they broke away from Spain. He detested the Spanish Bourbons but, more importantly, felt that support for the South American republics was in Britain's interests as it would stimulate trade and commerce. He managed to prevent any European intervention (which he knew the British naval power could prevent) whilst restraining the United States' interest in the region. Canning was later associated with supporting the independence of the South American states but he was merely building on Castlereagh's policies, and like Castlereagh he saw British trading interests as paramount.

The United States of America

Castlereagh recognised the importance of establishing good relations with the United States. The loss of the American colonies had left bitter resentment among some politicians, but Castlereagh believed it was time to put the past behind them. The war against the United States (1812–14) brought about by British blockades and the searching of neutral ships was inconclusive. Castlereagh wished to settle this messy war as quickly as possible through the Treaty of Ghent (1814). His policy towards the USA was conciliatory. Over the vexed question of the United States–Canadian border, he favoured the forty-ninth parallel, which was eventually agreed in 1844.

D Review: was Castlereagh a great Foreign Secretary or the 'pawn of Metternich'?

ACTIVITY

Read Sources 13.12–13.19

1 Briefly summarise what each historian says about Castlereagh as Foreign Secretary.
2 Explain why the historians' views differ in some respects.

Contemporary opinion of Castlereagh's policies was distorted by the fact that Castlereagh represented and defended Liverpool's repressive policies in the House of Commons. He was also criticised by some for becoming involved in discussions with other European countries. These critics believed Britain, given its power, should have stayed aloof from its European neighbours. From this criticism it was a short step to believing that Castlereagh was dominated by European leaders, and that he was the 'pawn of Metternich', powerless in the face of the conniving Holy Alliance. However, more recent historians' opinions emphasise the positive contribution Castlereagh made to foreign affairs.

SOURCE 13.12   M. E. Chamberlain, *Pax Britannica? British Foreign Policy 1789–1914*, 1988

Castlereagh stayed at the Foreign Office for ten years until his suicide in August 1822. During his lifetime he was the subject of an extraordinary smear campaign and he remained out of public favour during most of the nineteenth century . . .

The serious rehabilitation began during the flowering of diplomatic studies between the two World Wars. Sir Charles Webster's two massive volumes The Foreign Policy of Castlereagh, 1812–1815 *(1931) and* The Foreign Policy of Castlereagh, 1815–1822 *(1925) revealed Castlereagh's sheer technical skill and also showed that the tag of 'ultra-conservative' was misconceived. But the very detail of Webster's work meant that it remained inaccessible to all but those with a quasi-professional interest in diplomacy. In more recent years Castlereagh has been the subject of two fair and balanced biographies by C. J. Bartlett (1966) and Wendy Hinde (1981) and a penetrating biographical study by John Derry (1976). It has become more and more apparent that the virulent public opposition to Castlereagh owed more to his role in Irish politics and to his supposed role in English domestic policies after 1815 than to any considered criticism of his foreign policy . . .*

236

WAS CASTLEREAGH A GREAT FOREIGN SECRETARY OR THE 'PAWN OF METTERNICH?'

Up to a point Castlereagh was his own worst enemy. He could not project himself to the public, and, only to a limited extent, to the House of Commons. He was a competent but not an eloquent speaker. He radiated no warmth or geniality. His immediate associates respected him, but even they sometimes distrusted him. Castlereagh felt no obligation to try to explain his policy to a wider public. International diplomacy he saw as a highly skilled, very technical, entirely confidential profession. In this, as in much else, Castlereagh was a man of the eighteenth century. He paid the price in reputation but public lack of approbation is a poor measure of Castlereagh's real success. Only a detailed analysis of the diplomatic transactions of 1812 to 1815 can reveal how Castlereagh, starting with very few cards in his hands, held the fragile coalition together, safeguarded Britain's vital interests and secured a settlement which, although he did not regard it as ideal in all aspects, achieved its main purpose of establishing a stable and lasting peace after twenty-five years of war.

SOURCE 13.13   J. W. Derry, *Castlereagh*, 1976

The image of the icy apostle of universal reaction is nowhere more false, more shamelessly inaccurate or more wilfully misleading than when applied to Castlereagh's sophisticated and judicious attitude towards American questions ... He was not trying to unify Europe. He was attempting to minimise the inevitable tensions between the Powers.

SOURCE 13.14   M. E. Chamberlain, 'New Light on British Foreign Policy' in *History Today*, July 1985

It was the measure of Castlereagh's personal triumph that, with hardly a diplomatic or military card in his hand, he negotiated a peace settlement with the other allies which would protect all Britain's vital interests.

SOURCE 13.15   A. Wood, *Nineteenth-Century Britain*, 1960

Castlereagh was one of the greatest British Foreign Secretaries. The settlement at Vienna and the uneasy years that followed are a tribute to his shrewd sense of restraint. He was concerned with what was possible and immediately relevant, but he never lost sight of the goal of lasting peace and security. His judgement was never unbalanced by the disputes of the moment, or more important, by the intoxication of military victory ...

SOURCE 13.16   D. R. Ward, *Foreign Affairs, 1815–1865*, 1984

His policies are not so incomprehensible and although he was distant and unapproachable to many of those he encountered, Castlereagh's personality and character emerge as distinctive and powerful ...

Castlereagh certainly preferred monarchy to republicanism, and conservatism to liberalism, but he was not prepared to commit Britain to polices of combating liberalism and nationalism unless they threatened British interests directly, as his policy over Spain, the Spanish Colonies and Naples show ...

His powers of work, his seriousness of purpose and his judgement combined to give Castlereagh stature as a politician ...

Many contemporaries saw him as aloof and impenetrable. He might appear glacial; certainly he was shy, especially on social occasions. He did have charm and grace and was strikingly handsome ...

He was one of the greatest of British Foreign Secretaries.

SOURCE 13.17   N. Lowe, *Mastering Modern British History*, 1984

Though his career was tragically cut short, Castlereagh's achievements after Vienna must be remembered: he must take the credit for the introduction of the Congress System; this was a new departure in international co-operation and personal contact between the statesmen of Europe, a policy he pursued with commonsense and restraint.

SOURCE 13.18   R. J. Evans, *The Victorian Age*, 1968

Few Englishmen realised what had happened ... Henceforth the prosperity of industrial Britain reflects the ups and downs of European history. Every war, or threat of war, meant an interruption or dislocation of trade, and Britain's advocacy of peace and sweet reasonableness in international affairs was to some extent enlightened self-interest. It was this ignorance or insularity which put Castlereagh in such an unfavourable light. Obviously the strong man of the Government, he was invariably held responsible for the miseries of the people, when in fact he was wearing himself out with the colossal tasks involved in the remaking of Europe ... Castlereagh was brilliant, and his cold, clear, reasoning intellect unequalled in dealing with political problems on their own merits, among men at his own level ... in essence an eighteenth-century figure.

237

WAS CASTLEREAGH A GREAT FOREIGN SECRETARY OR THE 'PAWN OF METTERNICH'?

SOURCE 13.19 N. Gash, *Aristocracy and the People*, 1979

The most creative and imaginative of nineteenth-century British Foreign Secretaries, he had an aristocratic scorn of popular movements, was indifferent to public opinion, and was unmoved by abstract theories. His civilised outlook and serene intelligence . . . made him value peace, order and freedom above everything else in international life.

There is no doubt that historical opinion of Castlereagh has changed since the nineteenth century. Experiences of two world wars have led historians to better understand Castlereagh's thinking. The First World War was to be the war to end all wars, but in 1939 war broke out again. Millions died and the financial cost was astronomical. The League of Nations and then the United Nations were to be the instruments for maintaining peace and stability. In 1815 Castlereagh was aiming, through the Congress System, to sort out international conflict by talking around the table instead of resorting to war. He was the architect of the peace settlement at Vienna.

His policies were personal, based on relationships with other foreign statesmen and rulers. Sometimes this approach was misconstrued as the result of Castlereagh's domination by others. This was not the case and he was certainly not the pawn of Metternich. Metternich admired and respected Castlereagh. Whilst Castlereagh was at the helm, Metternich trusted Britain.

There was a popular feeling in Britain after 1815 that other countries should look up to Britain as it had saved Europe from Napoleon. It was thought that these countries should be coming cap in hand to Britain. Castlereagh's 'personal diplomacy' seemed to give out opposite signals. The fact that he did not appear to communicate his actions effectively only confirmed this. Because Canning, his successor as Foreign Secretary, did not have these personal contacts, he adopted a different approach, which was popular at home. As a result Castlereagh, who was a brilliant Foreign Secretary, was much maligned long after his death.

ACTIVITY

Answer the following essay question: Was Castlereagh a great Foreign Secretary or the 'pawn of Metternich'?

KEY POINTS FROM CHAPTER 13

Was Castlereagh a great Foreign Secretary or the 'pawn of Metternich'?

1 Castlereagh was a distinguished Foreign Secretary, who was acclaimed by some, but severely criticised by others. He was criticised for being 'a good European' and 'the pawn of Metternich'.

2 He played a major role in consolidating the Fourth Coalition, which defeated Napoleon in 1815. He made a leading contribution to the peace settlement in Vienna.

3 He persuaded the other powers at Vienna that France should be punished relatively leniently so it would not have grounds for revenge.

4 Britain's territorial gains at Vienna were to provide valuable naval bases and commercial acquisitions.

5 He tried to maintain peace through the Congress System. He wished to maintain the balance of power, and work in concert with leading European countries. He established links with other European leaders through his 'personal diplomacy'.

6 He opposed the Holy Alliance and supported a policy of non-intervention, which was explained in his State Paper of 1820.

7 Historians have not always agreed about Castlereagh's achievements and merits.

8 By the time of his suicide in 1822, the Congress System was on the verge of collapse.

14

How liberal was Canning's foreign policy?

CHAPTER OVERVIEW

With the death of Castlereagh in 1822, Lord Liverpool had no doubts about his successor, George Canning. He had been Foreign Secretary from 1807 to 1809, and was appointed the President of the Board of Control in 1816. A very able politician, he also made enemies because of his wit and arrogance. Some of his colleagues thought he was 'too clever by half', and others looked down on him because he did not have an aristocratic background. His mother had been an actress and involved in various scandals.

There had been particular rivalry between Castlereagh and Canning, which culminated in a duel in 1809. Canning had wanted Castlereagh removed from the War Office because he did not agree with his policies. As Foreign Secretary he carried on a hate campaign behind Castlereagh's back. When Castlereagh found out, he accused Canning of damaging his honour and reputation. On 15 September 1809 he challenged Canning to a duel. Canning had never fired a pistol in his life. Canning spent that evening making his will and writing a letter to his wife, Joan. '... how dearly I have loved you. I hope I have made you sensible of this, dearest, dearest Joan. I hope I have been kind and good and affectionate towards you. I hope I have made you happy. If you have been a happy wife – and if I leave you a happy mother and a proud widow, I am content. Adieu, Adieu.'

FOCUS ROUTE

As you read through this chapter, draw up a table to summarise areas in which Canning's approach was similar to and different from Castlereagh's. Also note any evidence for and against his liberalism.

Canning and Castlereagh		Was Canning a liberal?	
Similarities	Differences	Evidence for liberalism	Evidence against liberalism

---

The duel took place at 6 o'clock in the morning. From twelve paces both men shot – and missed. Despite the suggestion from their seconds that they should call it a draw, the opponents insisted on another shot. Canning missed again, but Castlereagh's bullet went through Canning's left thigh. Canning's second and Castlereagh helped him walk away to where a surgeon was waiting to give medical assistance. George III was displeased at this 'dereliction of duty', and the two Secretaries of State were criticised by members of the Cabinet, though most of the sympathy was with Castlereagh.

The two major debates surrounding Canning are whether Canning changed Britain's foreign policy after Castlereagh's death or whether he essentially pursued the same policies, and whether Canning's reputation as a liberal is justified.

A How did Canning handle the international problems of Spain and Portugal? (pp. 239–240)

B How successful was Canning in dealing with the question of Spain's South American colonies? (pp. 240–241)

C Did Canning succeed in answering the Eastern Question? (pp. 242–243)

D Review: how liberal was Canning's foreign policy? (pp. 244–247)

A How did Canning handle the international problems of Spain and Portugal?

George Canning (1770–1827)
Canning was an able, brilliant politician. After his father died, his mother became an actress and a linen-draper to support herself, since her husband had been disinherited when he had married her. His uncle, Stratford Canning, took George into his own family and sent him to Eton and Oxford. Through the system of patronage, he entered Parliament in 1794. He was influenced by Pitt and occupied several posts such as Paymaster General in 1800 and Foreign Secretary under Portland (1807–09). He was a flamboyant, controversial figure, who often made enemies within the Tory Party, which blighted his political ambitions.

He identified with liberal policies at home and abroad, and he opposed the European autocracies who wished to use the Congress System to suppress liberal and revolutionary movements. He was Foreign Secretary (1822–27) after Castlereagh. He supported the independence of Spain's South American colonies, mainly because they had become important to British trading interests. He welcomed the Monroe Doctrine in the USA. He supported Greek independence and checked Russian influence. He was a supporter of Catholic Emancipation, but opposed parliamentary reform. He was briefly Tory Prime Minister (April–August 1827) but died on 8 August 1827.

Canning's aims differed little from Castlereagh's, though his method and style were often different. He was not enthusiastic about liberalism and revolution abroad, but he did believe that if governments were bad they should be changed. His overriding aim was to protect British interests and he had little concern for preserving the Alliance. Wendy Hinde has argued that his policies were based on careful and even opportunist calculations of what would best preserve peace whilst, at the same time, promote the prestige and prosperity of Britain. He did not know European rulers and politicians, as Castlereagh had done, so he couldn't enter into 'personal diplomacy'. He withdrew from the Alliance, but when necessary he would enter into talks.

Spain

Spain had set up a constitutional government but in 1823 the French invaded to restore the autocratic monarchy of Ferdinand VII. Like Castlereagh, Canning was concerned about other powers interfering in affairs in which they were not directly concerned. Wellington was sent to the Congress at Verona where it was agreed that Alexander I should not send in Russian troops to suppress the Spanish revolution. However, without consulting Wellington, the French then intervened to restore autocratic government under Ferdinand VII in April 1823.

This was a humiliation for Britain and Canning, who was powerless and isolated in the wake of the French action. What was particularly humiliating was that Wellington had driven the French out of Spain in 1813, and now they were back. The British public was angry and Canning was able to capitalise on this by haranguing the French through vitriolic speeches. Canning was an opportunist who was skilful in turning failure into success and thus deflecting any personal criticism. The French were seen as the aggressors and Canning bided his time until he could regain the advantage over the French. Out of the jaws of a diplomatic defeat, he was able to increase his popularity amongst the public and enhance his reputation for being a liberal.

Portugal

After the restoration of autocratic government in Spain, Canning was concerned that the new constitutional monarchy established in Portugal in 1822 might also be under threat. Dom Miguel, the son of King John VI, who was appointed Regent for his niece Maria in 1826, wished to turn Portugal into an absolute monarchy. He had French support and Canning was concerned that France might intervene as it had done in Spain. This time he was prepared to take direct action, a gamble which paid off.

Over the question of Portugal, Canning was determined to restore British prestige. In a speech in the Commons he stressed: 'We go to Portugal to defend and preserve the independence of an ally.' Britain had had a 'special relationship' with Portugal for hundreds of years. Since the seventeenth century Britain had supported Portugal against foreign attacks. After a request from Portugal, Canning sent a naval force to Lisbon in July 1823. In 1826 he despatched 5000 British troops to defend the young Queen Maria's government. This was a triumph for Canning. He was popular at home and amongst liberals because he had prevented intervention and had successfully defied the reactionaries, such as Metternich, in the Alliance.

It would be easy to conclude that Canning was a supporter of liberal causes, but liberalism was something he exploited rather than followed. P. J. Rolo claimed that he fostered 'the legend of his own liberalism'. He had referred to Portugal's constitutional party as 'the scum of the earth ... fierce, rascally, thieving, ignorant ragamuffins'. He also remarked that 'as a matter of taste, I should much prefer to do without them'.

B How successful was Canning in dealing with the question of Spain's South American colonies?

■ 14A   The South American colonies

Spain's South American colonies had taken advantage of the turmoil of a European war, and had become more independent. Though revolts had been crushed, the ending of the Napoleonic Wars brought a series of conflicts between 1816 and 1825 in countries such as Chile and Peru. To the powers of Europe the overthrow of monarchy and the establishment of republics was an anathema to the ideology of the Vienna Settlement. With French intervention in Spain in 1823, the basic concern to Britain was whether France and other European countries might next try to smash the South American republics.

Castlereagh had supported a move to recognise the republics' independence and now Canning was determined that this should be a fact. Smarting from defeat over French intervention in Spain, he resolved 'that if France had Spain, it should not be Spain with the Indies'. His desire for the future independence of Colombia, Mexico, Argentina and Chile might be interpreted as Canning's pursuit of a liberal cause. He had to battle against George IV and Wellington who were opposed to recognising republics that had been established through rebellion. There was also the question of intervention by other powers. Through the Polignac Memorandum of October 1823, he was able to obtain an assurance that France would not intervene to restore the colonies to Spain.

Canning's major interest was that Britain had increased trade in South America. Commercial rather than liberal motives were his driving force. To safeguard these interests, he entered into an agreement with the United States known as the Monroe Doctrine of December 1823. Canning followed this up with his 'New World Speech'. In it he claimed that 'I called a new world into existence to redress the balance of the old'. But it was not as simple as that. President Monroe had declared that the whole American continent was closed to further European colonisation (including colonisation by Britain). Russia had claims in Alaska and Britain in Canada.

Nevertheless, Canning was able to take the opportunity to convince the Houses of Parliament and the British public that he had chalked up a victory by defending the republics and preventing intervention by European powers, especially France. In 1825 he recognised Mexico, Colombia and Argentina as independent republics. Britain's defeat in Spain had been avenged, and the balance of power restored. The Alliance had been thwarted and the Congress System was just about destroyed. Canning could claim he had defended British interests as further trade agreements were signed with the new republics. Though he might have preferred these republics to have become monarchies, he had shown that success could be achieved by flair and positive action. Into the bargain, he had fostered the legend of his own liberalism.

CITY COLLEGE
LEARNING RESOURCE SERVICE

TALKING POINT

What do you think Canning meant by 'I called a new world into existence to redress the balance of the old'?

C Did Canning succeed in answering the Eastern Question?

14B The Eastern Question

The Big Picture
After 1815 the Turkish Empire was in decline. As Turkey fell apart Russia was hoping to gain land and access through the Black Sea into the Mediterranean. Britain feared that if this happened Russia would be able to threaten British trade and naval dominance in that area and also its trade routes to India.

The Flashpoint
Greece declared its independence from the Turkish Empire in 1822. This threatened to lead to the collapse of the whole Empire, and gave Russia an excuse to become involved to defend the Greeks as fellow Christians.

The Response
Canning did not have any sympathy for the Greeks. His objective was to prevent a Russo-Turkish war, in order to preserve British interests. Therefore he acted as mediator between Turkey and Greece to bring the problem to an end before Russia attacked Turkey. Canning's method differed from Castlereagh's. Castlereagh had wanted the Congress of Verona to address the question of Russian designs after the Greek revolt against the Turks in 1821. He had worked closely with Metternich, but Canning's style was to bypass the Congress System and work more independently.

"You must stop this slaughter!"

"Save the Greeks!"

"I need a quick victory to show that I will be a great Tsar."

The Crisis

Turkey needed help to fight the Greek revolt and turned to Mehmet Ali, ruler of Egypt. The Egyptian army, led by Ibrahim Pasha, committed atrocities in putting down the revolt. This aroused British sympathy for the Greeks. Those with a classical public school education saw Greece as the cradle of civilisation, democracy and learning. Volunteers went out to join the Greek struggle, most famously Lord Byron, who died there. Canning was now under pressure to support the Greeks, especially as, by late 1825, Russia was about to intervene on the side of the Greeks. Metternich managed to stall the Russians on the grounds that to intervene would be to encourage revolution.

The Crisis Deepens

In December 1825, Alexander I of Russia died and was succeeded by Nicholas I who wished to establish himself quickly in the eyes of his people and Europe. He was desperate to intervene to avenge atrocities against Greek Christians and to weaken the Turkish Empire, which would bring advantages to Russia. Canning now had to act positively to preserve the position of Turkey as a buffer against Russian expansionism. His task was to make sure that the Russians did not gain too much advantage.

The Treaty

Canning tried to prevent war by siding with the Russians in negotiating the Treaty of London (July 1827) with the Turks, which would lead to Greek independence. Britain, Russia and France guaranteed Greek self-government, by force if necessary. However, Canning, as Prime Minister, was under great pressure because the Austrians and Prussians objected, and the Turks were refusing to sign the treaty. In August 1827 Canning died, his health destroyed by overwork as he struggled with the crisis.

The Battle

British and French fleets, already in the Mediterranean, ordered the Turkish and Egyptian fleets to Navarino Bay, from where they would return to Egypt under escort. The Egyptians refused to comply. Despite being ordered to avoid hostilities, an allied fleet under Admiral Codrington entered the bay and destroyed the Turkish–Egyptian fleet in four hours. The Greeks could now be guaranteed their independence, but Wellington, now Prime Minister, apologised to the Turks and removed Codrington from his post.

The Balance Sheet

Canning's death threw British policy into confusion. With Wellington as Prime Minister, Britain distanced itself from the Eastern Question. This allowed Russia to declare war on Turkey, leading to the Treaty of Adrianople in 1829, by which the Russians gained territory around the Danube delta. Canning had not intended that Russia expand her influence in the Balkans, nor that the Turks suffer a military defeat. Therefore Canning's aims had not been achieved entirely, but some historians have argued that the Eastern Question was Canning's greatest success. Webster claimed that he used it to divide Austria and Russia. By working with Russia and restraining her through co-operation, he had, according to Rolo, created 'the Anglo-Russian alignment which established a diplomatic revolution'. Finally, Greece had gained her independence, which was recognised in 1832.

ACTIVITY

Work in groups of four. Each person in the group takes the part of one of the following nations: Britain, Russia, Turkey, Egypt. Explain to each other:

a) what you wished to achieve by your involvement in the issue of Greek independence
b) to what extent you achieved those objectives.

Review: how liberal was Canning's foreign policy?

■ 14C   Key events during Canning's time at the Foreign Office

1822	Canning becomes Foreign Secretary
	Portugal becomes a constitutional monarchy
	Eastern Question: Greece declares independence from Turkey
1823	French troops invade Spain and restore the autocratic Ferdinand VII to the throne
	Monroe Doctrine
	Canning's 'New World' speech
1825	Britain recognises the republics of Mexico, Colombia and Argentina
1826	Dom Miguel attempts to overthrow constitutional monarchy in Portugal
	Greek War of Independence: St Petersburg Protocol results in Russia and Britain mediating between Greece and Turkey
1827	British navy successfully prevents France intervening in Portugal
	Turkish fleet destroyed at Navarino
	Death of Canning: foreign affairs in the hands of the Duke of Wellington

Though Metternich rejoiced on hearing of the death of Canning, the reaction in Britain was that it was a national tragedy.

SOURCE 14.1   W. Hinde, *George Canning*, 1973

The funeral was intended to be private, but the immense popular interest turned it into a public, even a national, event. There were nearly 800 people inside the Abbey and the road to it from Canning's house in Downing Street, where his body had been taken, was made almost impassable by the dense throng. The crowd was quiet and respectful – which was not always the case in those days at the funerals of the great. The Times *commented the next day: 'The loss of such a man at such a time was well calculated to draw forth the strongest expressions of deep regret among all classes of his fellow subjects. That regret was exhibited in the conduct of the assembled multitude of yesterday more strongly and intensely than, we believe, was witnessed at the death of any subject within the memory of the oldest person now living.'*

. . . But to many it also seemed little short of a national tragedy. Canning's name had become so firmly associated in the public mind with progressive policies at home and the maintenance of peace abroad that his death aroused widespread feelings of depression and even dismay, especially among the commercial and manufacturing classes.

TALKING POINT

Compare the funerals of Castlereagh and Canning. Why do you think the public reaction was so different?

Canning had fostered a reputation for supporting liberalism abroad. His standing among European liberals was high. He was regarded as a 'liberal Tory' but, though he was in favour of Catholic Emancipation, he was opposed to parliamentary reform, which was the major liberal issue in Britain at the time. Canning was an opportunist who exploited liberalism but had no genuine desire to extend it in Europe. However, in comparison with other European leaders such as Metternich, he appeared liberal, especially when he supported constitutional monarchies in Spain and Portugal, independence for Greece, and recognised republics in South America. Furthermore, his style of facing up to the more autocratic European leaders made him popular amongst the British public because it seemed to enhance Britain's position as a strong European power. Anything that put foreign governments in their place was popular, and Canning was always eager to exploit this in his public speeches. The country felt that as he was more open than Castlereagh, they understood what he was trying to do, and he became the popular hero. But how has he been viewed by historians?

Views on Canning

HOW LIBERAL WAS CANNING'S FOREIGN POLICY?

ACTIVITY

1 Read Sources 14.2–14.6 and complete your own copy of the table below.
2 Are there any other qualities and skills mentioned in this chapter or from your background reading that should be added?

Historian	Historians' views on Canning's:		
	Achievements	Weaknesses	Qualities
Webb			
Hayes			

SOURCE 14.2 R. K. Webb, *Modern England*, 1980

By his policy of disengagement from the Continent and by his skilful actions in Portugal, Latin America and Greece, Canning had become a hero to all Englishmen of liberal inclinations. He should have been more puzzling to them than he was. He had little sympathy with revolutionary movements, unless supporting them might forward British interests, and except for Catholic Emancipation, he remained a bitter opponent of all reform at home ... But perhaps the liberals were indulgent because Canning had turned his victories in foreign policy to such good effect. He played skilfully on public opinion; he cultivated the press; his speeches in the House were intended to have their chief effect outside. In all this he was employing a changed style and a novel technique in politics.

SOURCE 14.3 P. Hayes, *Modern British Foreign Policy: the Nineteenth Century, 1814–80*, 1975

His major achievements in Spain, Portugal and the Americas marked him out even during his lifetime as a great statesman. His most important achievement was the destruction of the system of the neo-Holy Alliance which, if unchallenged, must have dominated Europe. Canning realised that it was not enough for Britain to boycott conferences and congresses; it was essential to persuade the Powers that their interests would not be advanced by a system of intervention based upon principles of legitimacy, anti-nationalism and hostility to revolution. Metternich rightly recognised Canning as a dangerous enemy to his system.

SOURCE 14.4 W. Hinde, 'George Canning 1770–1827: A Career Blighted by Ambition?' in *Britain 1815–67*, 1994

Canning was not a comfortable colleague because of his restless energy, his impatience, his occasionally sharp tongue, his general tendency to stir things up. On the other hand they knew he was a great asset. The very qualities that made him a difficult colleague around the Cabinet table, his brilliance and his domineering personality, made him invaluable in the House of Commons. He was a splendid speaker and debater, capable on occasion of electrifying and completely dominating the House ...

Canning's aim, first, foremost and always, was to do whatever seemed necessary to maintain and increase Britain's prestige and prosperity. His second aim was to preserve European peace and stability by maintaining a balance between the European powers. He refused to intervene against liberal revolts not because he necessarily sympathised with them but because he could see no benefits to Britain, and perhaps considerable dangers, in helping autocratic rulers to interfere in the domestic affairs of other states ... He only broke his rule of non-intervention once, when in 1824 he intervened diplomatically to install a pro-British government in Lisbon, because he felt that the alternative, a government subservient to the French, would be against British interests.

SOURCE 14.5 E. J. Evans, *Britain Before the Reform Act: Politics and Society 1815–1832*, 1989

Canning took great pride in his Latin American policy, yet it is doubtful if it brought quite the benefits he anticipated ... Yet visionary though his policy was, Canning grossly exaggerated the extent of immediate commercial benefit Britain would derive. Paradoxically, the great growth of Latin American trade was in the last decade before the spate of independence declarations, not in the first decade after. British exports to Latin America stood at £2.5 million in 1815 and £5 million in 1825. By 1835, they had hardly increased at all and had fallen back from 13 per cent of British exports to 11 per cent.

SOURCE 14.6 M. E. Chamberlain, *British Foreign Policy in the Age of Palmerston*, 1980

The real contrast between Castlereagh and Canning was in personality and the public image they presented. Canning, unlike the formal and expressionless Castlereagh, was witty, brilliant (his enemies said flashy) and a good public speaker in the rhetorical tradition of the times ... Ironically, it is the attitude of European conservatives which established Canning's reputation as a crusader for liberalism and nationalism. Metternich called Canning's death 'an immense event, for the man was a revolution in himself'.

Castlereagh vs Canning

A good deal of historical writing has focused on the rivalry between Castlereagh and Canning and traditionally it was assumed that there was a contrast between their foreign policies. However, it is now agreed that there was much continuity, and that difference was due more to style than substance.

D. Southgate (*The Most English Minister: the Policies and Politics of Palmerston*, 1966) has argued the differences were of personality rather than ideology. C. K. Webster (*The Foreign Policy of Castlereagh*, 1925) believed there was more continuity in their policies. J. W. Derry (*Castlereagh*, 1976) sees the flamboyant Canning as being more concerned about how he would be judged by history, and that is why he attached so much value to his popularity and public image.

WHAT WERE THE SIMILARITIES AND DIFFERENCES BETWEEN CASTLEREAGH AND CANNING?

Similarities

1. Opposed intervention by states in the affairs of other countries. Canning followed the views set out in Castlereagh's State Paper of 1820.
2. Did not trust the Russians.
3. Were opposed to French intervention in Spain.
4. Defended Portuguese independence.
5. Wished to restrain the Greek Revolt in order to maintain the balance of power in Europe.
6. Believed Turkey's independence was necessary to avert Russian expansionism.
7. Recognised the necessity for the Spanish colonies in South America to be independent, especially as it would benefit British trade and industry.
8. Were opposed to the slave trade.
9. Believed in the balance of power.
10. Were prepared to co-operate with European powers when it was necessary – for example, over Greece.
11. Followed the principles of British foreign policy established by Pitt.
12. Protected British interests.

Differences

1. Castlereagh believed in the Congress System and was saddened by its limitations. Canning was happy to see the system destroyed.
2. Castlereagh believed foreign policy was too complex to explain to the public. Canning courted public opinion.
3. Castlereagh cultivated his 'personal diplomacy' through the international contacts he had made. He was prepared to work with Metternich. Canning despised Metternich, and believed in 'every nation for itself and God for us all'.
4. Castlereagh had tried to foster good relations with the USA. Canning was scathing about America and was not trusted by President Monroe.
5. They differed in personality. Castlereagh was shy and reserved; Canning was more extrovert, flamboyant and opportunist.

ACTIVITY

Copy and complete the table below.

	Canning's aims	Action	Similar to or different from Castlereagh
Spain			
Portugal			
France			
Russia			
South American colonies			
Turkey			
Greece			

ACTIVITY

1 List the qualities that you think both Castlereagh and Canning displayed to become outstanding Foreign Secretaries.
2 Complete one of the following essays:
   a) How far do you agree that 'the real contrast between Castlereagh and Canning was in personality and the public image they presented'?
   b) How liberal was Canning's foreign policy?

KEY POINTS FROM CHAPTER 14

How liberal was Canning's foreign policy?

1 There was more continuity in Castlereagh and Canning's foreign policies than contrast.
2 Overall, Canning achieved his objective of defending British interests.
3 He succeeded in Portugal and was able to prevent intervention by the other powers.
4 He was able to ensure independence for South American states, though the Monroe Doctrine applied as much to Britain as any other European country.
5 His handling of the Eastern Question proved he was 'a genius in the international game of chess' (Hinde).
6 Though his policy in Spain failed, he did salvage some personal success out of it.
7 Although popular with supporters of liberalism, his reputation as a liberal has probably been exaggerated.

Did Palmerston deserve his high reputation as Foreign Secretary 1830–51?

CHAPTER OVERVIEW

What links Palmerston to the outbreak of the First World War?

Who accused Britain of putting profits from the drug trade before morality and the lives of its people?

Why was an Austrian general roughed up in a London brewery?

How did a house fire in Athens lead to a debate in the House of Commons?

■ 15A Palmerston's key aims as Foreign Secretary

Identified in M. Chamberlain, *Lord Palmerston*, 1987

1 A desire for peace and stability in Europe through the balance of power.

2 To befriend stable constitutional states because they make good trading partners.

3 Non-involvement with Europe unless British interests are involved.

4 To have sympathy for liberal movements against despotic regimes, which might justify British intervention.

5 To engage in dramatic gestures if there was no risk to Britain.

The answers to all these questions can be found in the career of one man, Henry Temple, Viscount Palmerston, who was at the heart of British politics from the 1820s until his death, aged 80, in 1865. He was Foreign Secretary for fifteen years and Prime Minister for nine years. For most of this time he was enormously popular with the British public and was often portrayed as John Bull, the symbol of Britain's strength and common sense. When well over 70 he still 'bounded [rather] than walked', worked at his papers from early morning and attended Parliament from four in the afternoon until well after midnight, much to his wife's dislike. However, Lady Palmerston had much to complain about. Not for nothing was Palmerston known as 'Lord Cupid'.

Despite Palmerston's popularity in his lifetime, historians have been less convinced about his qualities. The historian Temperley (1964) said that Palmerston was 'not a man of principle or system, yet he was a superb opportunist. He excelled in calling "bluffs" and in making them'. This chapter will therefore assess to what extent Palmerston achieved real success or whether he was simply a master of 'political spin'.

A How successful was Palmerston's first period as Foreign Secretary 1830–41? (pp. 249–252)

B How successful was Palmerston's second period as Foreign Secretary 1846–51? (pp. 252–254)

C Review: did Palmerston deserve his high reputation as Foreign Secretary 1830–51? (pp. 255–256)

A How successful was Palmerston's first period as Foreign Secretary 1830–41?

Palmerston was a Canningite who defected from the Tory Party after resigning from Wellington's government in 1828. With the Whig victory in 1830 he became Foreign Secretary. His aims were no different from those of Castlereagh and Canning.

FOCUS ROUTE

As you work through this section, copy and complete this 'Palmerston score card'. For each issue decide whether to give Palmerston:

- 3 points – for completely achieving the aims of British policy (see Chart 15A)
- 2 points – for mostly achieving the aims of British policy
- 1 point – for achieving some minor success
- 0 points – for failing to achieve the aims of British policy.

	Summary of the problem	Palmerston's solution	Palmerston's score and your justification
Belgium Question			
Portugal			
Spain			
The Polish Revolt, 1830			
Eastern Question			
Opium War			

The Belgium Question, 1830

1 The problem
Belgium had been placed under the control of the Dutch at Vienna. The principal aim had been to create a buffer against France but this arrangement was clearly not working because the Belgians, who felt like second-class citizens, were restless for independence. It was possible that the Belgians might turn to the French for support, but this would violate British interests because France would gain greater influence along the Belgian coast. Furthermore, French expansion could lead to war as the other European powers grew increasingly suspicious of France's intentions.
Therefore Palmerston had to:
– secure Belgian independence from the Dutch
– avoid war
– keep Belgium free from French influence.

2 The conference
A conference was arranged in London in 1831 to decide who would rule an independent Belgium and what would be its boundaries. The Belgians wanted the son of Louis Philippe of France as king. This was unacceptable to Britain. The British wanted Leopold of Saxe-Coburg as king. He was the favourite uncle of the future Queen Victoria. Eventually, the French agreed.

3 The events
– The Dutch, reluctant to release their hold over Belgium, refused to accept Leopold as king and marched into Belgium. This created an even greater problem for Palmerston. How could he stop France taking advantage of this situation? Belgium was bound to ask France for help.
– Palmerston decided to conspire with the French and agree to them sending in a military force. However, he also had to find a way of preventing French troops staying in Belgium permanently.
– He persuaded Prussia and Russia to put pressure on France. The result was that the French withdrew. After long diplomatic negotiations, the Dutch backed down.

4 The result
By the Treaty of London (1839) the Dutch recognised Belgian independence so long as Luxembourg became a Duchy under Dutch control. The other European powers guaranteed Belgian independence and neutrality. This treaty was the 'scrap of paper' that Germany ignored in 1914 when it invaded Belgium, plunging Europe into war.

LEARNING RESOURCE CENTRE

250

DID PALMERSTON DESERVE HIS HIGH REPUTATION AS FOREIGN SECRETARY 1830-51?

Henry John Temple (1784–1865)
Henry John Temple, Viscount
Palmerston, was involved in British
politics from 1807 to his death in 1865
aged 80. He sat in the Commons
because his family's title was an Irish
peerage, and Irish peers could not sit
in the Lords. Thus Palmerston could
become an MP in the Commons (as
could Castlereagh for the same
reason). He was appointed Secretary at
War in 1809, aged 25, and remained in
that post until 1828. He resigned from
Wellington's government in 1828
because he supported the liberal
Tories rather than Wellington. He was
Foreign Secretary in Grey's and
Melbourne's Whig governments from
1830 to 1841 and under Russell
between 1846 and 1851. He later
became Home Secretary before
becoming Prime Minister in 1855 and
again in 1859.

ACTIVITY

For the Eastern Question, produce a
flow chart similar to the one used on
page 249 to summarise the Belgium
Question.

TALKING POINT

The Turkish Foreign Minister remarked,
'A drowning man will clutch at a
serpent'. What did he mean?

What had Palmerston achieved?

- He had averted war successfully.
- He had secured Belgian independence.
- He had prevented the French from capitalising on the situation.
- He had deployed skilful diplomacy and preserved British interests.
- The balance of power had been preserved in Europe. Palmerston was assisted
  by the fact that Russia was concerned with the Polish revolt in 1830, and the
  Austrians were preoccupied with affairs in Italy. However, he could take
  satisfaction in that he had been successful.

Spain and Portugal

In the 1820s the rulers of Spain and Portugal were both young girls. Maria was
Queen of Portugal and Isabella Queen of Spain. Both were opposed by an uncle
– Maria by Miguel and Isabella by Carlos – who were both autocratic and
wanted to overthrow the girls and their liberal supporters. In the early 1820s
Canning sent troops to support Maria, but Wellington later withdrew them, and
Miguel seized the throne. In 1832 supporters of Maria began a civil war against
Miguel. Palmerston planned to support the two queens. To this end he worked
with the French, but hoped to prevent France taking advantage of the situation
to gain influence for itself. Palmerston sent a fleet to the coast of Portugal and
financed a naval expedition, which defeated Miguel in 1833.

The Quadruple Alliance, signed in 1834 between Britain, France, Spain and
Portugal, was intended to lead to joint action to prevent Miguel and Carlos from
gaining power. In Portugal this worked as Miguel never returned, but Carlos
returned to Spain and resumed the civil war, until he was finally defeated in
1839. By then, France had withdrawn from the Alliance, but France's influence
in Spain and Portugal had been kept to a minimum, as Palmerston had hoped.
He had also prevented possible interference from the Holy Alliance powers.

The Polish Revolt of 1830

When the Poles revolted in 1830, Palmerston was content to let the Russians deal
with it as this was within their sphere of influence. The revolt was quickly put
down and though Palmerston did express publicly his sympathies for the Poles,
the attempt to throw off Russian domination had no effect on British interests.

The Eastern Question

Mehmet Ali, the ruler of Egypt, was bitter because he believed he had not been
suitably rewarded by the Sultan of Turkey for providing aid during the Greek
War of Independence (see page 243). Therefore, in 1831, he sent his son
Ibrahim Pasha, with an army, into Palestine and Syria. Before long Egyptian
forces were threatening the very heart of Turkey. Turkey turned to Russia,
which had been its enemy in the Greek War. This had two consequences.
Firstly, Russian forces stood in the way of Ibrahim's march on Constantinople,
although they did nothing to prevent the occupation of Syria and Arabia.
Secondly, Russia and Turkey entered into a secret deal (the Treaty of Unkiar
Skelessi) in 1833 by which the Turks agreed to close the Bosphorus and the
Dardanelles to foreign warships whenever Russia requested it.

This 'secret' treaty was leaked to Britain. It affected British trading interests as
Russia could now control the sea routes between the Black Sea and the
Mediterranean. However, Palmerston could do nothing and had to bide his time
before he could begin to take any initiative. His opportunity came when France
gave support to Mehmet Ali. Louis Philippe of France felt that Mehmet Ali could
be successful with French support. In 1840, eager as ever to destroy French
influence, Palmerston agreed with Austria, Prussia and Russia to expel Mehmet
Ali from Syria. After the Greek War, the Sultan of Turkey had promised to
confer the title of Pashalik of Syria on Mehmet Ali, but he went back on his
word. Mehmet Ali therefore decided to take it by force. Palmerston's tactics
worked, for a strong British naval presence in the Mediterranean was too much
for Mehmet Ali. Britain bombarded the Syrian coast and captured Acre. The
Egyptians were forced out of Syria, and the French, who were no match for the
combined forces of Britain, Austria, Prussia and Russia, backed down.

Palmerston had again proved successful. He was rewarded by Turkey through the Straits Convention (a treaty signed in 1841 between Turkey and Britain, Russia, Prussia, Austria and France), which overturned the Treaty of Unkiar Skelessi. The Bosphorus and the Dardanelles would be closed to all warships of any nation when Turkey was at peace. This also meant that the Turks' allies could use the Bosphorus and Dardanelles in wartime. Russia's exclusive rights under the Treaty of Unkiar Skelessi were terminated. Turkey, the 'sick man of Europe', had been revived, and France and Russia's ambitions had been thwarted. As a bonus, Britain acquired Aden (a useful strategic acquisition) as a 'protectorate' because it feared future encroachments by the Egyptians. The Eastern Question, however, was to rumble on. The 'sick man of Europe' had not been cured. He had merely made a temporary improvement.

The Opium War 1840–42

In the 1830s British merchants were engaged in a lucrative trade in opium, which they were selling in large quantities in China. The Emperor of China, Tao Kwang, wanted to stop this trade, which was having serious effects on the welfare of the Chinese population whilst also draining the economy. China sent a letter to Queen Victoria saying, 'So long as you tempt the people of China to buy [opium] you will be showing yourselves careful of your own lives but careless in your greed for gain of the harm you do to others'.

In 1839 the Chinese authorities seized British-owned opium in Canton and prohibited trade with Britain. Britain saw this as a violation of her trading rights. British merchants claimed they should be protected by the government. Palmerston immediately sent a despatch to Peking, demanding compensation and a guarantee that British trade would not be disrupted.

The Chinese refused. Palmerston, using gunboat diplomacy, backed up his demands by sending a naval force to bombard Canton. The Chinese surrendered. At the height of these events, the Whig government collapsed and it was left to Peel's Tory government to complete matters. Under the Treaty of Nanking the Chinese had to compensate British merchants, Hong Kong was ceded to Britain, and Chinese ports were opened to foreign trade.

The Opium War was profitable for Britain and, though it created hostility with China for many years, this was of no concern to Palmerston. China was a small fish in international affairs and could be overwhelmed by Britain's navy. Gladstone led a tide of alternative opinion, which attacked Palmerston's foreign policy on the moral ground that it was wrong to sell opium to the Chinese. Historians such as Professor Kenneth Bourne (*Palmerston: the Early Years 1784–41*, 1982) have also criticised Palmerston for his overall handling of the issue, arguing that during this time he had the technical mastery but 'lacked qualities of moral leadership' and tended 'to go with the tide of public opinion'.

TALKING POINT

Is it worth discussing whether you would have supported Palmerston or Gladstone, or has morality changed so much since 1840 that such a discussion would be anachronistic?

252

DID PALMERSTON DESERVE HIS HIGH REPUTATION AS FOREIGN SECRETARY 1830–51?

ACTIVITY

Review your Focus Route table from page 249.

1 How successful had Palmerston been in defending British interests?
2 Is there any justification for seeing his work in this period as 'a triumph of style over substance'?

PALMERSTON OUT, ABERDEEN IN

With the Tories, under Peel, coming back into power in 1841, Palmerston was succeeded by Lord Aberdeen, who had previously occupied the post of Foreign Secretary under Wellington. Aberdeen, like Castlereagh, had more of a European perspective. He was liked and respected by European leaders because of his quiet diplomacy, which contrasted with that of Palmerston. Relations improved between France and Britain and an entente cordiale was established. Queen Victoria and Prince Albert went to France with Aberdeen in 1843 to cement the friendship. It was the first time that an English reigning monarch had been to France since Henry VIII.

A major crisis facing Aberdeen was deciding on the official border between Canada and the USA. Canada was part of the British Empire and ever since the USA came into being after the end of the American War of Independence in 1783, there had been disputes over the American–Canadian border. In 1819 Castlereagh had made an arrangement that this should be the forty-ninth parallel but this did not include the Oregon territory, which was hardly populated. Rapid settlement of the area, however, changed the situation. When President Polk was elected in 1844, he resisted British suggestions that Canadian territory should extend to the Pacific coast, demanding that the USA should have all the west coastline as far north as Alaska, which was, at the time, owned by Russia. This would have cut Canada off from the Pacific. Some US extremists demanded war to settle the dispute. Eventually Polk gave way and the forty-ninth parallel (latitude 49N) became the boundary, with a detour so that Vancouver Island remained wholly British as part of Canada.

B How successful was Palmerston's second period as Foreign Secretary 1846–51?

FOCUS ROUTE

Repeat the Focus Route on page 249 for the events shown in the table below.

	Summary of the problem	Palmerston's solution	Palmerston's score and your justification
Spanish marriages			
The European revolutions			
General Haynau affair			
Don Pacifico affair			
Louis Napoleon's coup			

The Spanish marriages, 1846

In his second period as Foreign Secretary, Palmerston had to deal with the recurring problem of French attempts to gain influence in Spain. Palmerston had objected to the marriage of the Spanish queen's sister to the son of King Louis Philippe of France. This created the possibility of a French king inheriting the Spanish throne. However, the threat came to an end when Queen Isabella produced heirs herself. The issue led to a breakdown of the entente established by Aberdeen. When demonstrations broke out in Paris in February 1848, Palmerston did nothing to help Louis Philippe. In fact, he gained some satisfaction in seeing him overthrown, and pleading for exile in England.

Louis Napoleon (Napoleon III) (1808–73)

Louis Napoleon was the nephew of Napoleon Bonaparte. With the overthrow of Louis Philippe in 1848, he was elected President of the new French republic. He made himself Emperor in 1851. During the Second Empire, France prospered and there was major building work in Paris. Disasters in foreign policy, ending with defeat by the Prussians in 1870, led to his downfall. He went into exile in England.

ACTIVITY

How might Palmerston's reactions to risings across Europe have been influenced by events in Britain in 1848?

The European Revolutions of 1848

Before you read any further, look again at the map of 1848–49 on page 184 and re-read the flashpoints 1–5. The year 1848 saw a series of liberal or nationalist uprisings in Italy, France, Austria, Prussia and other German states. Throughout 1848 Palmerston's main concern was that British interests should not be harmed. Once these were assured, he tended to support liberal movements and those wishing to throw off the yoke of oppression by foreign powers. For example, Palmerston gave support to the new French republic, but only after he was convinced that it would not lead to war in Europe. For Palmerston it was Britain first and liberalism second, yet he achieved popularity with liberals in Britain and across Europe, becoming known as 'the disciple of Canning'.

Despite his public popularity, Palmerston's style was seen as scandalous in royal and political circles. He was accused of adopting dangerous tactics and of high-handedness. His recognition of Louis Napoleon led to friction with Queen Victoria who was indignant because she had not been briefed about his intentions. Palmerston believed he had no time for such niceties as consulting the Queen. He wanted quick action and could not wait for the Queen to mull over the paperwork. He added further to her anger and that of his colleagues when guns were sent from Woolwich to assist Sicilian rebels with whom he sympathised. His advice to Spain that it should set up a more liberal government led to another diplomatic crisis.

The General Haynau affair, 1850

Liberal movements tended to receive only diplomatic support from Palmerston, despite requests for military assistance. When the Hungarians asked for help in their revolt against Austria, Palmerston condemned Austrian brutality in putting down the revolt, but did not send military aid. However much he disapproved of Hapsburg absolutism, he regarded the Austrian Empire as a useful buffer against Russia.

In 1850 General Haynau, who had been instrumental in suppressing the Hungarian revolt, visited England. Whilst being taken round the Barclay and Parkins' brewery in London he was given a hostile reception from the brewery workers who knew of his atrocities and the floggings inflicted on Italian and Hungarian women. Austria issued an official complaint, only for Palmerston to make matters worse by claiming that Haynau was lucky to get away with just his clothes torn and whiskers pulled. Palmerston suggested that Haynau should have been 'tossed in a blanket, rolled in a kennel, and then sent home in a cab'. The Austrians were angry. Queen Victoria was angry at the way her Foreign Secretary had treated a foreign guest. Even his apology only inflamed the incident by suggesting that if Haynau had stayed at home the incident would not have occurred. Characteristically, Palmerston drafted and sent the apology without referring it to the Queen. Such behaviour enhanced Palmerston's reputation with the public but it was seen as increasingly irritating and rude by the royal family. To add insult to injury, in 1851 Palmerston invited the escaped Hungarian rebel leader, Kossuth, to tea. This was a blatant indiscretion, which prompted observers to question how long even Palmerston could remain in office.

The Don Pacifico affair, 1850

The pressure on Palmerston increased even further when he faced a vote of censure in Parliament over a bizarre incident known as the Don Pacifico affair. Pacifico was a Portuguese Jew who qualified for British nationality because he had been born in Gibraltar. When his house in Athens was burnt down in a riot, he claimed compensation from the Greek government. The claim was extortionate and included the loss of documents valued at £26,000. Palmerston knew the claim was grossly exaggerated but he believed in the principle that a British citizen had a right to be protected by his government. Palmerston promptly dispatched a gunboat, enforced a blockade and seized Greek shipping assets to the value of the claim.

CITY COLLEGE LEARNING RESOURCE CENTRE

LEARNING RESOURCE CENTRE

254

DID PALMERSTON DESERVE HIS HIGH REPUTATION AS FOREIGN SECRETARY 1830–51?

ACTIVITY

Review your Focus Route chart from page 252.

1 How successful had Palmerston been in defending British interests?
2 Is there any justification for seeing his work in this period as 'a triumph of style over substance'?

This action aroused deep Greek resentment. France offered to mediate but it, too, was given the cold shoulder, even though the Cabinet had agreed to its offer. Critics complained that this was typical of Palmerston's high-handedness, and some questioned whether he was fit for the job. The House of Lords, at the instigation of Aberdeen, passed a vote of censure against Palmerston. When the motion was debated in the House of Commons his critics included some of the most eminent of nineteenth-century politicians. The debate saw Peel's last speech and Gladstone's first on foreign affairs. Cobden and Bright provided a moral perspective on foreign policy and expressed concern that Palmerston's reckless diplomacy and brinkmanship could lead to war. All attacked Palmerston.

Some would say that this was Palmerston's 'finest hour'. He dominated the proceedings with a speech which lasted for four and a half hours, reviewing his conduct of foreign policy since 1830, based on 2000 volumes of Foreign Office papers. He concluded with the words: 'As the Roman in days of old held himself free from indignity when he could say "*Civis Romanus sum*" [I am a Roman citizen], so also a British subject, in whatever land he may be, shall feel confident that the watchful eye and the strong arm of England will protect him against injustice and wrong.'

Palmerston won the day and the hearts of the British public, even though it was through defending an unscrupulous wretch such as Don Pacifico. Perhaps by now he felt untouchable.

Louis Napoleon's coup, 1851

In 1851 Louis Napoleon carried out a coup that led to him becoming Emperor Napoleon III. Palmerston sent his congratulations, yet again without submitting the despatch to the Queen. The Queen's sympathy had been with the Orleanists (supporters of the House of Orleans). The last Orleanist ruler of France was Louis Philippe, the Citizen King, from 1830 to 1848. Palmerston regarded Louis Napoleon as less dangerous than the extreme Republicans or the Orleanists. The Queen was correct in complaining that she should have been consulted and that Palmerston's behaviour was leading to diplomatic embarrassments. Palmerston defended his actions by claiming that Victoria was too young (she was 32 at the time) to understand the complexities of foreign affairs, and that she was being given a German view from her husband Albert, whom he did not trust. Palmerston was irritated by the inconvenience of having to consult with the Queen about every issue. In 1848 alone he had sent 2900 despatches and was often working late into the night in the Foreign Office. He believed that he understood foreign issues better than anyone. He simply could not be bothered to consult the Queen.

However, this was the last straw. Victoria and the Cabinet were worried that his behaviour would lead to war if he went on upsetting too many governments. 'Lord Pumicestone', as they called him, had to go. Royal pressure mounted and Russell, the Prime Minister, who generally agreed with Palmerston's policies though not always his methods, finally agreed with the Queen and the Cabinet that Palmerston had gone too far. Within three weeks Palmerston gained his revenge, his 'tit for tat' with Russell, by helping defeat the Whigs over the militia bill. The Conservatives were back with Aberdeen in charge of foreign affairs.

C   Review: did Palmerston deserve his high reputation as Foreign Secretary 1830–51?

■ 15C   Key issues in foreign policy

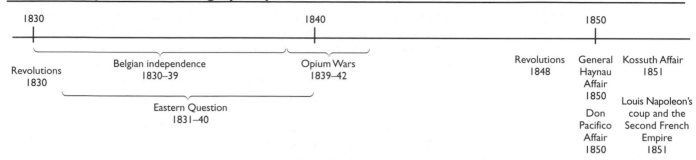

SOURCE 15.1   M. Chamberlain, *Pax Britannica? British Foreign Policy 1789–1914*, 1989

From 1815 to 1871 Britain's role in the settlement of European affairs was often peripheral. Only occasionally, as over Belgium or Portugal, when immediate British interests were considered to be at risk, did Britain become deeply involved. Her voice was not decisive in the settlement of Greece, or of Italy, or of Germany. Equally she played little real part in the great revolutionary upheavals of 1848–49. This was not the image that Englishmen cherished of their role in the world. They believed, as they had in 1815, that Britain could give the law to the world both materially and morally. The man who told them so repeatedly and frequently was Henry John Temple, third Viscount Palmerston. As a young man, Palmerston was an indifferent speaker and publicist but in the 1840s he seems to have stumbled on the secret of how to rouse his countrymen to patriotic fervour and, incidentally, win public support for himself. Sometimes, of course, he paid the price of his success, as when he lost office in 1858 because he was judged to have been too subservient in agreeing to Napoleon III's demands that he should change British law to prevent what would today be called terrorists from finding asylum in Britain.

The heirs of the Palmerston tradition were, in their different ways, Benjamin Disraeli and Joseph Chamberlain. Palmerstonian bluster passed easily into imperialist fervour in the late nineteenth century. The idea that British policy dominated Europe began to look a little unconvincing even to the most patriotic after the unification of Italy and Germany and the rise of Otto von Bismarck. The transition of attitude was easily made. British power was now turned outwards towards her empire and her chosen stance in Europe was that of 'splendid isolation'. Scholars today would not accept that isolation was ever Britain's preferred position ... If it had been, there could be no greater irony than the fact that Britain's decline can realistically be dated – although this is more apparent with hindsight than it was at the time – from the First World War which, despite its name, was essentially a great war about the balance of power in Europe.

ACTIVITY

The information you have collected and the conclusions reached in answering the Focus Routes on pages 249 and 252 should have built up a good overview of Palmerston's policies. Now use those conclusions and Sources 15.1–15.8 to plan one or more of these essays.

a) What did Palmerston achieve in his handling of foreign affairs between 1830 and 1851?

b) 'Palmerston was the natural heir of Castlereagh, not Canning.' To what extent do you agree with this judgement?

c) 'A triumph of style over substance'. Did Palmerston deserve his high reputation as Foreign Secretary 1830–51?

SOURCE 15.2   H. C. F. Bell, *Lord Palmerston*, 1936

In his desire that England should stand upon her own feet, his appreciation of the great force of public sentiment, and his taste for constitutional government as the proper medium between autocracy and democracy, he was a natural Canningite.

SOURCE 15.3   S. J. Lee, *Agents of British Political History 1815–1914*, 1994

It could certainly be argued that Palmerston was closer to Castlereagh than to Canning in his emphasis on the balance of power in Europe, in his belief in maintaining the integrity of Austria and in his use of multilateral diplomacy. Above all, he did everything possible to contain France and to prevent a possible Franco–Prussian alliance, both of which had been priorities of Castlereagh ... It is most likely that he ... adapted their ideas in a way which was considered appropriate to the changing conditions of international diplomacy after 1830.

256

DID PALMERSTON DESERVE HIS HIGH REPUTATION AS FOREIGN SECRETARY 1830–51?

SOURCE 15.4 M. Chamberlain, *British Foreign Policy in the Age of Palmerston*, 1980, on the Belgian issue

An example of Palmerstonian policy at its best, when he showed not only firmness and decisiveness but also the tact and patience which he so often lacked.

SOURCE 15.5 D. Judd, *Palmerston*, 1975, on the Eastern Question

Palmerston had won a tricky game hands down.

SOURCE 15.6 H. M. V. Temperley, *England and the Near East: The Crimea*, 1964

[Palmerston] was a man of great courage and of boundless energy and vivacity … He was indeed not a man of principle or system, yet he was a superb opportunist. He excelled in calling bluffs and in making them. It was not the highest statesmanship but it often served.

SOURCE 15.7 C. K. Webster, *The Foreign Policy of Palmerston 1830–41*, 1951, on the Eastern Question

The triumph of Palmerston in 1840 was perhaps the greatest which he ever won in his long connection with foreign affairs.

SOURCE 15.8 M. Chamberlain, *British Foreign Policy in the Age of Palmerston*, 1980

Palmerston believed that bluff was an essential part of diplomacy, and perhaps he bluffed his countrymen as well as foreigners into believing that his successes were greater than they were. His achievements in Europe were really very modest and some of them were the result of well calculated inaction.

ACTIVITY

1 Palmerston's style is known as 'gunboat diplomacy'. His critics argued that he was belligerent and that Britain was, as a result, poised on the edge of war. Do you agree?
2 Why do you think Palmerston is regarded as a 'natural Canningite'?

KEY POINTS FROM CHAPTER 15

Did Palmerston deserve his high reputation as Foreign Secretary 1830–51?

1 Palmerston was a dominant figure in nineteenth-century foreign affairs. His style made him popular with the British public. He was a master of improvisation and often identified with 'gunboat diplomacy'.
2 He had sympathy for liberal causes, but British interests always came first.
3 He was successful in bringing about Belgian independence in 1839.
4 He had a setback over the Eastern Question, when the Russians secretly negotiated the Treaty of Unkiar Skelessi with the Turks, but this was successfully overturned by the Straits Convention.
5 He came under attack for his gunboat diplomacy during the Opium War, though he defended Britain's commercial interests. Peel's Conservative government had to complete negotiations with the Chinese, which ended with Britain acquiring Hong Kong (which was returned to China in 1999).
6 1848 was 'the year of revolutions' in Europe. Palmerston was popular with liberals in Europe but he offered them more sympathy than direct help because Britain's interests had to come first. 'We have no eternal allies, and we have no perpetual enemies. Our interests are eternal and perpetual, and those interests it is our duty to follow.' (Palmerston, 1848)
7 He was unpopular with Queen Victoria and members of the Cabinet for his high-handed tactics and his refusal to consult the Queen. His tactics led to diplomatic crises – for example, over Hungary and Austria (General Haynau and the Kossuth affair).
8 He successfully pursued the case of Don Pacifico though he faced a censure motion, which he cleverly defeated by way of the 'Civis Romanus sum' speech.
9 By congratulating Louis Napoleon on his coup in 1851, again without consulting the Queen, he found himself in deep trouble, and this led to his dismissal.

Section 2 Review: How successful was British foreign policy 1783–1851?

Britain played a very significant role in international affairs during the nineteenth century. However, to some extent, a myth has built up around its role. This tends to portray Britain as the John Bull character at the centre of everything, mediating, sorting out problems, supporting liberal and national movements and opposing autocratic regimes. It tends to play down the involvement of other countries. However, the Russian part in the defeat of Napoleon must not be underestimated. And while Britain was obviously involved in the question of Greek independence from Turkey, France played an important part, as it did in the unification of Italy. In Spain and Portugal, France was just as influential. Britain did nothing to help the Poles, and German unification was achieved without any assistance from Britain.

The handling of foreign affairs was the most demanding of political offices. This is epitomised by Palmerston who often worked twelve to sixteen hours a day. Colleagues leaving their clubs after midnight could often see lights flickering in the Foreign Office as Palmerston burnt the midnight oil. He even had a specially made table, which allowed him to work standing up in case he fell asleep.

Today we are used to international news coming directly into our homes as the result of television, satellite links and shuttle diplomacy. It is perhaps surprising that Foreign Secretaries in the first half of the nineteenth century rarely left Britain. Castlereagh was an exception. As part of his 'personal diplomacy' or 'new diplomacy' as Bartlett described it, he would travel throughout Europe establishing personal contacts. Canning and Palmerston tended to remain in London, preferring to send representatives abroad.

Foreign policy was a major priority for any government, but the pressure and stress it put on individuals was immense. It contributed to the death of Castlereagh. It also placed British representatives in a position of great responsibility, as they had to make on-the-spot decisions. Despatches could take days, weeks or even months to arrive, so Foreign Secretaries had to use their initiative. They also had to contend with interfering monarchs, although royal influence tended to wane after 1832. Nevertheless, the monarch still had the constitutional right to read despatches, and in some cases they even altered them. It was on this issue that Queen Victoria fell out with Palmerston. Monarchs tried to put pressure on Prime Ministers to remove Foreign Secretaries they disliked. George IV hated Canning, and criticisms from Victoria and Prince Albert led to the dismissal of Palmerston after his support for Louis Napoleon's coup in 1851.

British foreign policy protected trade and commercial interests. This might range from defending ports in the Netherlands, to the protection of British trade routes in India. Defending Britain's global interests inevitably meant Britain needed a strong navy. This was effective during the Revolutionary and Napoleonic Wars, and was a powerful weapon in Palmerston's 'gunboat diplomacy'.

Although the principles of British foreign policy basically remained the same, whatever the political party in power right up to 1914, methods were flexible. Britain's main concern was for peace and stability because this benefited British

CITY COLLEGE
LEARNING RESOURCE SERVICE

trade and commerce. To be tangled up in a war was also a costly business. The maintenance of stability could come through alliances or co-operating with other countries, or, as a last resort, the threat of war.

Britain was fortunate in that it could rely on Foreign Secretaries of outstanding ability. Castlereagh and Canning were both disciples of Pitt and they followed the principles established by him during the French Wars. Palmerston was labelled the disciple of Canning. All this suggests continuity. Major differences were not in policies, but in style and personality. Castlereagh tended to handle foreign affairs privately, using personal diplomacy to good effect, whereas Canning and Palmerston were more public in their style and attempted to popularise foreign policy.

Britain's industrial strength and naval power facilitated its leading role in foreign affairs. It also led to a national pride. In later Victorian times, a child living in extreme poverty in London, Leeds or Manchester, could at least look at the world map on the board school wall and know that the sun never set on the British Empire. Whatever the social, economic and political problems at home, there was a knowledge that Britain counted for something in the world. Unity at home could be enforced by a successful foreign policy. During the French Wars (1793–1815) the British nation rallied behind Pitt, and other important issues such as parliamentary reform were set aside. The jingoism adopted by Palmerston was popular among the lower classes who saw him putting the foreigner in his place. On a sour note it is perhaps this nineteenth-century notion of Britannia ruling the waves, and the myth of British dominance, which is responsible for the behaviour of 'Brits abroad' on holiday, or English hooligans following their national football team in international tournaments.

Conclusion

ACTIVITY

The Introduction to this book (on pages 2–3) gave you one simple interpretation of Britain's history in this period; a stark contrast between **disaster** in 1783 exemplified by the loss of the American colonies, and **triumph** in 1851 encapsulated by the Great Exhibition. Now that you have studied the period 1783–1851 it is time to reflect upon that simple interpretation by answering the major question posed in the Introduction. Which of these interpretations do you most agree with?

Was Britain's story from the 1780s to the 1850s one of ...

a steady, calm progression to world dominance ...

... or was it

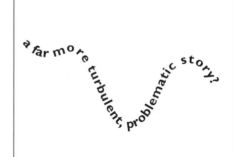

a far more turbulent, problematic story?

To help you think about this, imagine it is 1851 and you are a seventy-five-year-old looking back on your life.

Complete a diagram like this, firstly listing as many of the triumphs or improvements you have lived through as possible.

Then repeat the activity for disasters – anything in Britain that has gone badly for individuals or the country as a whole. Use the Topic Box on page 260 to help you with both diagrams.

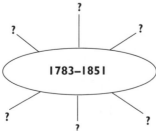

1783–1851

continued

ACTIVITY (continued)

Was 1783–1851 a significant period in British history?

How do we decide whether a period is significant? Here are two criteria:
* the people and events of the time had a long-lasting influence on later periods
* the events of the time had an impact on the wider world, then and later.

Use these criteria and the Topic Box to discuss the questions below.

1 Who were the three most significant people you have studied during this course?

2 What are the three most significant events you have studied during this course?

Was 1783–1851 a significant period in British history?

3 Which events and people from this period should it be compulsory for everyone to learn about in history lessons at school?

4 What have you learned from studying this period that has helped you to better understand events in the world today or has made you think more deeply about life today?

Topic Box

urbanisation	technology	culture
role of government	laws and reforms	
leisure	warfare	empire
ideas and attitudes	communication	public order and safety
employment	standards of living	
life expectancy	medicine	others?

Answers to Activities

p. 93

A	John Fielden	Whig
B	Francis Burdett	Independent
C	William Gladstone	Tory
D	Henry Brougham	Whig
E	George Hudson	Conservative
F	Lord Palmerston	Tory
G	Benjamin Disraeli	Tory
H	Lord John Russell	Whig
I	Michael Sadler	Tory
J	Joseph Hume	Tory, later a Whig
K	Thomas Duncombe	Whig
L	William Joliffe	Tory
M	George Howard	Whig
N	Earl Grey	Whig

p. 95

Tory reforms

1823	C	Penal Code
1828	I	Repeal of Test and Corporation Acts
1829	E	Metropolitan Police
1829	F	Catholic Emancipation

Whig reforms

1832	B	Reform Act
1833	X	Abolition of slavery
1833	L	Factory Act: no children under nine to work
1833	O	Government grant to education
1834	M	Poor Law Amendment Act
1835	J	Municipal Corporations Act
1835	K	Prisons Act
1836	H	Registration Act (of births, marriages and deaths)
1836	N	Marriage Act
1836	D	Tithe Commutation Act
1839	Q	Custody of Infants Act
1840	A	Penny Post

Tory/Conservative reforms

1840	R	Grammar Schools Act
1842	Y	Mines Act
1844	T	Bank Charter Act
1844	V	Companies Act
1844	W	Railway Act
1846	S	Railway Gauge Act
1846	U	Repeal of Corn Laws
1847	P	Factory Act
1848	G	Public Health Act

p. 205

1	B
2	B
3	C
4	A
5	B
6	C
7	B
8	A

CITY COLLEGE
LEARNING RESOURCE CENTRE

Bibliography and Selected Reading

Dates in brackets are dates of first publication.

Adelman, P. and Pearce, R., *Great Britain and the Irish Question*, Hodder and Stoughton, 2001

Aspinall, A. and Smith, E. A. (eds), *English Historical Documents*, Eyre and Spottiswood, 1959

Barnett, C., *Bonaparte*, Allen and Unwin, 1978

Bartlett, C. J., *Castlereagh*, Macmillan, 1966

Beales, D., *From Castlereagh to Gladstone*, Nelson and Sons, 1969

Beales, D., *Peel, Russell and Reform*, Cambridge Historical Journal, 1974

Behagg, C., *Labour and Reform: Working-Class Movements 1815–1914*, Hodder and Stoughton, 1994

Behagg, C., *Politics and Production in the Early Nineteenth Century*, Routledge, 1990

Belehem, J., *'Orator Hunt': Henry Hunt and English Working-Class Radicalism*, Oxford University Press, 1985

Blake, R., *The Conservative Party from Peel to Churchill*, Fontana, 1970

Brady, A., *William Huskisson and Liberal Reform*, Oxford University Press, 1928

Brasher, N. H., *Arguments in History – Britain in the Nineteenth Century*, Macmillan, 1968

Briggs, A. (ed.), *Chartist Studies*, Macmillan, 1969

Briggs, A., *The Age of Improvement 1783–1867*, Longman, 1960

Brock, M., *The Great Reform Act*, Hutchinson, 1973

Brock, W. R., *Lord Liverpool and Liberal Toryism 1820–27*, Cambridge, 1972 (1941)

Brown, R. and Daniels, C., *Documents and Debates: Nineteenth-Century Britain*, Macmillan, 1980

Brown, R., *Economic Revolutions in Britain 1750–1850*, Cambridge University Press, 1992

Brundage, A., *The Making of the New Poor Law 1832–39*, Hutchinson, 1978

Cannon, J., *Parliamentary Reform 1640–1832*, Cambridge University Press, 1973

Chamberlain, M. E., *British Foreign Policy in the Age of Palmerston*, Longman, 1980

Chamberlain, M. E., *Lord Palmerston*, University of Wales Press, 1987

Chamberlain, M. E., *'New Light on British Foreign Policy'*, History Today, July 1985

Chamberlain, M. E., *Pax Britannica? British Foreign Policy 1789–1914*, Longman, 1988

Cole, G. D. H., *Chartist Portraits*, Macmillan, 1965

Cookson, J., *Lord Liverpool's Administration 1815–1822*, Scottish Academic Books, 1983

Darvall, F. O., *Popular Disturbances and Public Order in Regency England*, Oxford University Press, 1934

Derry, J. W., *Castlereagh*, Allen Lane, 1976

Derry, J. W., *Politics in the Age of Fox, Pitt and Liverpool*, Macmillan, 1990

Derry, J. W., *Reaction and Reform*, Blanford, 1970

Dickinson, H. T., *British Radicalism and the French Revolution 1789–1815*, Blackwell, 1988

Digby, A., *The Poor Law in Nineteenth-Century England and Wales*, Historical Association, 1982

Dinwiddy, J. R., *From Luddism to the First Reform Bill*, Blackwell, 1986

Emsley, C., *British Society and the French Wars, 1793–1815*, Macmillan, 1979

Engels, F., *The Condition of the Working Class in England*, Penguin, 1987 (1845)

Epstein, J. and Thompson, D. (eds), *The Chartist Experience*, Macmillan, 1982

Esdaile, C. J., *The French Wars 1792–1815*, Routledge, 2001

Evans, E., *The Great Reform Act of 1832*, Methuen, 1983

Evans, E., *Political Parties in Britain 1783–1867*, Methuen, 1985

Evans, E. J., *Britain Before the Reform Act: Politics and Society 1815–1832*, Longman, 1989

Evans, E. J., *The Forging of the Modern State: Early Industrial Britain 1783–1870*, Longman, 1983

Evans, E. J., *William Pitt the Younger*, Routledge, 1999

Evans, R. J., *The Victorian Age*, Edward Arnold, 1968 (1950)

Finlayson, G., *England in the Eighteen Thirties: Decade of Reform*, Edward Arnold, 1969

Firth, G., *A History of Bradford*, Phillimore, 1997

Foster, R. F., *Modern Ireland 1600–1972*, Viking, 1993

Gammage, R. C., *History of the Chartist Movement 1837–54*, Merlin Press, 1969

Garfield, S., *The Last Journey of William Huskisson*, Faber and Faber, 2002

Gash, N., *The Age of Peel*, Edward Arnold, 1968

Gash, N., *Aristocracy and People: Britain 1815–65*, Edward Arnold, 1983

Gash, N., *Lord Liverpool*, Weidenfeld, 1984

Gash, N., *Mr Secretary Peel*, Longman, 1961

Gash, N., *Politics in the Age of Peel*, Longman, 1953

Gash, N., *Sir Robert Peel*, Longman, 1976

Gregg, P., *Modern Britain: a Social and Economic History Since 1970*, Pegasus, 1965

Grove, E. (ed.), *The Great Battles of the Royal Navy*, Colour Library Direct, 1998

Halévy, E., *The Triumph of Reform 1830–41*, E Benn Ltd, 1951

Halévy, E., *Victorian Years 1841–95*, E Benn Ltd, 1950

Hammond, J. L. and Hammond, B., *The Skilled Labourer 1760–1832*, Longman, 1919

Hayes, P., *Modern British Foreign Policy: the Nineteenth Century 1814–1880*, A & C Black, 1975

Hinde, W., *Castlereagh*, London, 1981

Hinde, W., *George Canning*, Collins, 1973

Hobsbawm, E., *Uncommon People: Resistance, Rebellion and Jazz*, Weidenfeld and Nicolson, 1998

Hobsbawm, E. J. and Rude, G., *Captain Swing*, Lawrence and Wishart, 1969

Hollis, P., *The Pauper Press: a Study of Working-Class Radicalism in the 1830s*, Oxford University Press, 1970

Hopkins, E., *A Social History of the English Working Classes, 1815–1914*, Edward Arnold, 1979

Hovell, M., *The Chartist Movement*, Manchester University Press, 1918

Huggett, F., *Cartoonists at War*, Guild Publishing, 1981

Hunt, E. H., *British Labour History 1815–1914*, Weidenfeld and Nicolson, 1981

Hunt, J. W., *Reaction and Reform*, Collins, 1977 (1972)

Jones, D., *Chartism and the Chartists*, Allen Lane, 1975

Jones, M. W., *Cruikshank: His Life and London*, Macmillan, 1978

Jones, R. B., *Napoleon: Man and Myth*, Hodder and Stoughton, 1977

Keane, J., *Tom Paine: a Political Life*, Little, 1995

Kee, R., *The Green Flag: a History of Irish Nationalism*, Weidenfeld and Nicolson, 1972

King, D., *Everyman Will Do His Duty: an Anthology of First-Hand Accounts from the Age of Nelson*, Conway Maritime Press, 1997

Kitson Clark, G., *The Making of Victorian England*, Methuen, 1962

Kitson Clark, G., *Peel and the Conservative Party*, Frank Cass, 1964

Lee, S. J., *Aspects of British Political History 1815–1914*, Routledge, 1994

Litton, H., *Irish Rebellions 1798–1916*, Wolfhound Press, 1998

Longford, E., *Wellington: Pillar of State*, Weidenfeld and Nicolson, 1972

Longmate, N., *The Workhouse*, Temple Smith, 1974

Mather, F. C., *Chartism*, Historical Association, 1965

Mathias, R., *The First Industrial Nation*, Routledge, 1983

McCord, N., *The Anti-Corn Law League*, Allen and Unwin, 1958

Mingay, G. E., *Rural Life in Victorian England*, Heinemann, 1976

Mitchell, A., *The Whigs in Opposition 1815–30*, Oxford University Press, 1967

Morris, R. J., *Class and Class Consciousness in the Industrial Revolution 1780–1850*, Methuen, 1979

O'Ferrall, F., *Daniel O'Connell*, Gill and Macmillan, 1998

O'Gorman, F., *The Whig Party and the French Revolution*, Macmillan, 1967

Pakenham, T., *The Years of Liberty: the Great Irish Rebellion of 1798*, Weidenfeld and Nicolson, 1998

Parker, C. S., *Robert Peel*, John Murray, 1891

Pearce, R. and Stearn, S., *Government and Reform, 1815–1918*, Hodder and Stoughton, 1994

Plowright, J., 'Lord Liverpool and the Alternatives to Repression in Regency England', *History Review*, September 1997

Plowright, J., *Regency England: the Age of Lord Liverpool*, Lancaster Pamphlet, 1996

Read, D., *Cobden and Bright*, Edward Arnold, 1967

Read, D., *Peterloo: the Massacre and its Background*, Manchester University Press, 1958

Read, D. and Glasgow, E. L., *Feargus O'Connor*, Edward Arnold, 1961

Rendall, J., *Women in an Industrialising Society: England 1750–1880*, Blackwell, 1990

Ridley, J., *Lord Palmerston*, Constable, 1970

Royle, E., *Modern Britain: a Social History 1750–1985*, Edward Arnold, 1990

Royle, E., *Radical Politics 1790–1900: Religion and Unbelief*, Longman, 1984

Royle, E. and Walvin, J., *English Radicals and Reformers 1760–1848*, Harvester Press, 1982

Royston-Pike, E., *Human Documents of the Industrial Revolution in Britain*, George Allen and Unwin, 1966

Scott-Baumann, M. (ed.), *Years of Expansion: Britain 1815–1914*, Hodder and Stoughton, 1995

Southgate, D., *The Most English Minister: the Policies and Politics of Palmerston*, London, 1966

Steer, C., *Radicals and Protest 1815–1850*, Macmillan, 1986

Stevenson, J., *Popular Disturbances in England 1700–1870*, Longman, 1979

Stiles, A., *Religion, Society and Reform 1800–1914*, Hodder and Stoughton, 1995

Styles, S., *The Poor Law Society*, Macmillan, 1985

Thomis, M. and Holt, P., *Threats of Revolution in Britain 1789–1848*, Macmillan, 1977

Thompson, E. P., *The Making of the English Working Class*, Pelican, 1968

Ward, D. R., *Foreign Affairs 1815–1865*, Collins, 1984

Ward, J. T., *Chartism*, Batsford, 1973

Ward, J.T. (ed.), *Popular Movements 1830–1850*, Macmillan, 1970

Watson, R., *Edwin Chadwick: Poor Law and Public Health*, Longman, 1974

Watts, D., *Tories, Conservatives and Unionists 1815–1914*, Hodder and Stoughton, 1994

Webb, R. K., *Modern England*, George Allen and Unwin, 1980

Webster, C. K., *The Congress of Vienna*, Thames and Hudson, 1963 (1934)

Webster, C. K., *The Foreign Policy of Castlereagh*, Bell and Son, 1925

White, R. J., *From Waterloo to Peterloo*, Mercury, 1963

Wood, A., *Nineteenth-Century Britain*, Longman, 1960

Woodham Smith, C., *The Great Hunger: Ireland 1845–49*, Hamish Hamilton, 1962

Woodward, L., *The Age of Reform 1815–70*, Oxford University Press, 1962

Wright, D. G., *The Chartist Risings in Bradford*, Bradford Libraries, 1987

Wright, D. G., *Democracy and Reform 1815–1885*, Longman, 1970

Young, G. M., *Victorian England: Portrait of an Age*, Oxford University Press, 1936

Index

CITY COLL...
LEARNING RESOURCE CENTRE